Selecting Materials for Instruction

Selecting Materials for Instruction

—Three Handbooks for Educators—

Issues and Policies

Media and the Curriculum

Subject Areas and Implementation

Selecting Materials for Instruction

Subject Areas and Implementation

Marda Woodbury

Libraries Unlimited, Inc., Littleton, Colorado — 1980

LIBRARIES UNLIMITED, INC.
P.O. Box 263
Littleton, Colorado 80160

Library of Congress Cataloging in Publication Data

Woodbury, Marda.
    Selecting materials for instruction.

    Includes bibliographies and indexes.
    CONTENTS: [1] Issues and policies.--[2] Media and the curriculum.--[3] Subject areas and implementation.
    1. Audio-visual materials. 2. Teaching--Aids and devices. I. Title.
LB1043.W66   371.33   79-18400
ISBN 0-87287-197-5 (v.1)
ISBN 0-87287-212-2 (v.2)
ISBN 0-87287-213-0 (v.3)

This book is bound with James River (Scott) Graphitek® — C Type II nonwoven material. Graphitek — C meets and exceeds National Association of State Textbook Administrators' Type II nonwoven material specifications Class A through E.

PREFACE

"So much has already been written about everything that you cannot find out anything about it."

— James Thurber

□ □ □

I began *Selecting Materials for Instruction* with one very full file drawer left over from a Phi Delta Kappa *Fastback, Selecting Instructional Materials*, a research-writing project which in itself took far more time and effort than I had expected.

Reluctant to discard documents and first drafts of two months' research, I decided to whip up the definitive book on selecting instructional materials. I had hoped to simplify and rationalize this multi-faceted topic, using as assets a good knowledge of educational sources, an acquaintance with educational theories, much experience in selecting instructional materials in school situations, and selection principles largely derived from a book selection course taken long ago at Columbia University School of Library Service.

In the intervening months, the research has taken over one entire room of my apartment and threatened to engulf my whole life and my whole apartment. The single volume has grown into three companion texts, and I have had to abandon my smug if naive belief that one book would suffice to simplify and rationalize the complex process of selection.

The result is this series on *Selecting Materials for Instruction*, which comprises *Issues and Policies, Media and the Curriculum* and *Subject Areas and Implementation*. These volumes can, I believe, be used separately by individuals involved at any level in the process of selecting and using instructional materials. *Issues and Policies* is a handbook for the establishing of an effective and efficient selection process. *Media and the Curriculum* approaches the acquisition and evaluation of materials in various print and nonprint media. And *Subject Areas and Implementation* will aid the selector in choosing materials for particular areas of study.

Since educational selection occurs in so many areas for so many purposes at so many levels, it is difficult to see the process as a whole, but these books, so far as I know, are the first to bring together the perspectives, insights, approaches and contributions of that medley or muddle of groups who participate some way, somehow, some time in selecting instructional materials. The groups and individuals who engage in this process include theorists and practitioners; among them educational theorists, curriculum designers and developers, educational evaluators, publishers, producers, distributors, market experts, library educators and librarians, media advocates and practitioners, school board members, administrators, legislators at all levels, citizen groups, advocacy groups, parents and community groups, individual and organized teachers, consultants, and even students, who may sometimes be the victims rather than the beneficiaries of the aggregated procedures. I have actively solicited and gathered information from all sorts of groups and individuals: government agencies, professional associations, publishers, teachers, teacher-librarians, teacher centers, parents, students, curricular theorists, educational researchers, media specialists, bibliographers, and, of course, librarians. Undoubtedly I have overlooked some organizations and some individuals who should have been consulted.

In organizing this vast amount of data as compactly and practically as I could, I have considered both the ends and the practices of education and the nature of my materials. In *Subject Areas and Implementation* I have examined the process of determining the best instructional material for presenting particular areas of the school curriculum or specific topics within these areas. The selection and evaluation tools included in each chapter emphasize the qualities essential to any effective source of information and of interest in a given subject. These qualities vary widely. The discussions in this volume — and the books, articles, and organizations listed here — are designed to single them out. If materials in math should challenge the student's problem-solving capabilities by emphasizing the integrity of logical systems, language arts materials should challenge the child by presenting some of the complexities of contemporary issues. If nutrition education materials should examine the cultural sources of eating practices, health education materials should treat the environmental sources of many health trends. The selection of materials for their instructional emphases is as important as being certain they lack all forms of bias.

Part II of this volume treats the experience of putting an appreciation of selection processes into action. An integral selection policy must begin with an awareness of the available resources and of the level of controversy likely to be involved in broadening the range of those resources. The final chapter provides suggestions and models for training selectors to meet that experience.

A variety of individuals and agencies have been kind enough to let me reprint their charts, criteria, checklists and the like for low costs or no costs. I greatly appreciate permissions given for these reprints. Such items as are copyrighted should not be reproduced in any way without the written permission of the original issuing agencies (whose addresses are included).

Other forms included in this book were developed at taxpayers' expense, and must remain in the public domain. These forms may be re-used or adapted freely but may not be copyrighted by another.

In the course of preparing *Selecting Materials for Instruction* I have imposed widely on the time, patience and facilities of a variety of individuals — most particularly of colleagues in Bay Area Education Librarians (BAEL) and the Education Division of the Special Libraries Association. The following in particular have gone even beyond their well-honed professional responsibilities in assisting my research.

Special thanks to Lenore Clemens, just retired from the San Mateo County Education Resources Center; Priscilla Watson at Lawrence Hall of Science; Jennifer Futernick and Jean Lee of Far West Laboratory; Joan Thornton from the Education Library at California State University at Hayward; Barbara Nozik and Urania Gluesing of San Francisco State University; and all the patient folks at the reference desk of the Ed-Psych Library at the University of California, Berkeley.

Sue Klein of the National Institute for Education has been extremely helpful in forwarding documents on evaluation. The Multicultural Resources at California State University, Hayward, and its librarians, Margaret Nichols and Peggy O'Neill, have been similarly helpful in providing materials relating to ethnic bias, while the Women's Educational Equity Information Network has been a substantial source for materials on sex. Bob Muller of Bay Area Media Evaluation Guild (BAMEG), Faith Hektoen of the American Library

Association and David Elliott of Educational Products Information Exchange (EPIE) have all simplified the task of research considerably. Thanks also to Alice Wittig of Mendocino for taking time from her busy personal and professional life to read and critique this manuscript, and to Joan Rankin who has an outstanding ability to transcribe scrawls and to correct typographic errors.

In the course of researching this final volume, I have taken advantage of some fine federally funded clearinghouses. I would like especially to acknowledge my gratitude for the quality of responsiveness demonstrated by the Consumer Education Resource Network (CERN) and the Resource and Referral Service (RRS) of the National Center for Research in Vocational Education.

TABLE OF CONTENTS

Preface 5

PART I — SUBJECT AREAS

SELECTING MATERIALS FOR SCIENCE 13
Piaget and Process Skills 16
Direct Experiences 16
Models, Equipment and Supplies 16
Kits and Programs 18
Recycled Science Materials 19
Media Materials 20
Printed Materials 20
Textbooks 21
Scientific Vocabulary 22
Trade Books 22
Cutting Costs 25
Interdisciplinary Materials 26
Science and Social Issues 26
Key Organizations 27
Key Publications 31
For Further Reading 35

SELECTING MATHEMATICS MATERIALS 37
Overview 37
Types of Materials 41
Interdisciplinary Mathematics 42
Thinking and Process Factors 44
Textbooks: Use and Selection 44
Parental Role in Selection 45
Key Organizations 48
Key Publications 53
For Further Reading 57

**INTERDEPENDENT SELECTION FOR
ENVIRONMENTAL EDUCATION** 60
Overview 60
Recommended Learning Approaches 63
Materials Criteria 64
State Criteria 65
Interdisciplinary Survey 66
The Local Environment 66
Types of Materials 69
Key Organizations 74
Key Publications 80
For Further Reading 82

**THE FEELING DOMAIN: Materials for Affective Education,
Bibliotherapy, Mental Health, and Psychology** 85
Rationale and Premises for Affective Education 86
Rationale and Premises for Psychology 87
Rationale for Mental Health and Bibliotherapy 88
Appropriateness 89
Types of Materials 93

The Feeling Domain (cont'd)
Content Criteria..94
Key Organizations..95
Key Publications..99
For Further Reading..107

SELECTING MATERIALS FOR HEALTH EDUCATION....................109
Key Organizations..112
Key Publications..114
For Further Reading..115

SELECTING MATERIALS FOR NARCOTICS EDUCATION...................117
Key Organizations..118
Key Publications..121
For Further Reading..123

THOUGHT FOR FOOD: Selecting Materials for Nutrition Education.............124
Key Organizations..135
Key Publications..138
For Further Reading..138

SELECTING MATERIALS FOR SEX AND FAMILY LIFE EDUCATION........140
Overview..140
Criteria for Selection...141
Key Organizations..143
Key Publications..145
For Further Reading..146

SELECTING MATERIALS FOR SOCIAL STUDIES AND SOCIAL SCIENCES....149
Concept Teaching..149
Appropriate Materials...152
Specific Criteria...154
Key Organizations..162
Key Publications..164
For Further Reading..169

SELECTING MATERIALS FOR LEGAL EDUCATION.......................172
Key Organizations..173
Key Publications..175
For Further Reading..175

SELECTING MATERIALS FOR MULTICULTURAL EDUCATION.............176
Overview..176
Instruments and Criteria...178
Key Organizations..185
Key Publications..189
For Further Reading..194

SELECTING FOREIGN LANGUAGE AND BILINGUAL MATERIALS..........197
Key Organizations..203
Key Publications..208
For Further Reading..213

SELECTING MATERIALS FOR THE LANGUAGE ARTS....................215
Overview..215
Student Selection and Individualization.......................218
Using Frameworks for Selection Criteria......................220

Selecting Materials for the Language Arts (cont'd)
Materials for "Reluctant Readers"......................................222
Cognition 223
Roles and Needs...225
Quantitative Standards..226
Censorship 226
Criteria for Selection..227
Key Organizations...229
Key Publications..233
For Further Reading...242

SELECTING MATERIALS ON THE WORLD OF WORK.....................245
Key Organizations...255
Key Publications..258
For Further Reading...266

THE COMPLETE CONSUMER..268
Key Organizations...272
Key Publications..275
For Further Reading...276

PART II – IMPLEMENTATION

EVALUATING MEDIA PROGRAMS.......................................279
Introduction..279
Standards 281
Key Organizations...290
Key Publications..291
For Further Reading...293

HANDLING CONTROVERSY..294
Key Organizations...298
Key Publications..299
For Further Reading...300

TEACHING SELECTION..301
Key Organizations...309
Key Publications..312
For Further Reading...313

Acronym Index...315

Author/Title/Subject Index...319

"To enrich the quality of life, education must generate curiosity, creativity, competence, and compassion."

— Dr. Albert V. Baez

PART I

SUBJECT AREAS

SELECTING MATERIALS FOR SCIENCE

"Despite the rapidity with which science has advanced, its achievements have engulfed our lives so gradually that millions of people are almost totally unaware of the new world—the new culture—in which we live, a culture based on science."
    —Ellsworth Osbourn, *Science as a Way of Life* (1967)

" ... the reason why public understanding of science is important ... is that science, or any intellectual activity for that matter, can continue to flourish only in a social environment in which the nature of the enterprise is reasonably understood and supported for its own sake, rather than out of fear ... "
    —Morris Shamos, *The Price of Scientific Literacy* (1963)

"In this day and age, it is more important for the public to appreciate and understand the place of science in society than it is to devote all instruction to the few who will practice it."
    —William R. Ogden, *Scientific Literacy: A Recommitment* (1974)

□ □ □

Though there are many excellent materials for teaching science and a great deal of (scattered) guidance in choosing and using these, the selection of science materials—like current science teaching—is apt to be stereotyped or haphazard—particularly at elementary levels.

One basic consideration is cost. With the decline in National Science Foundation (NSF) funds for materials and teacher training, student achievement scores in science—as measured by the National Assessment of Educational Progress and the College Entrance Examination Board—have been declining at elementary and secondary levels—though the rate of decline appears to be tapering off.

While the decline in training and materials undoubtedly influenced these lower scores, an increase in funds for materials may not be either necessary or sufficient to increase them. With the current attention to back-to-basics, most school districts are not apt to receive substantial funds for science. For schools with funds, the choice is largely between textbooks, laboratory kits, and free-form, go-your-own-way selection. Some schools and school districts have almost no funds for science.

Whatever the virtues of the laboratory-sponsored kits and programs—formerly funded by NSF—they are overly expensive for many school budgets and time-consuming to maintain. Textbooks—often strongly influenced by these programs—are sometimes transformed to similarly expensive kits; others are deadening; most are apt to be obsolete, at least in part, by the second year of a five-year adoption cycle. Ad hoc selection is probably the best way to get the most for each dollar of the science materials budget; still, teachers, especially at the elementary level, often lack background in science as well as in science selection principles. Since this shortage of funds is a real problem that affects science materials, I have placed some emphasis on tools that provide assistance in selecting inexpensive materials.

Fortunately for would-be selectors in science, there is substantial concensus among writers and reviewers of science books and many experienced science teachers on what to look for in selecting materials for science.

Some major desiderata are:

- Materials that build on or relate to other science courses or experiences without excessive repetition
- Materials that stimulate interest and active participation
- Materials that emphasize experience, problem solving, and cognition
- Individualized and open-ended materials, some suitable for science projects
- Materials with advanced concepts or procedures for students who are interested in or talented in science
- Career information for such students
- Authentic portrayal of the scientific method for everyone
- Materials that deal with the interrelationships between science and other fields
- Materials that lead to wider or deeper explorations

In terms of Dale's Cone of Experience (*see* page 19, *Issues and Policies*, a companion to this work), science should offer direct experience in first-hand observation and investigation, as well as a chance to abstract and analyze. It is important to have a range of materials which include both.

Types of materials considered most important are:

- Community resources and materials providing direct experiences
- Equipment and supplies for demonstrations and hands-on investigations
- Models for concepts, demonstration, and manipulation
- Printed materials for current and background information, reference and research, concept development, relations to other fields, recording and display
- Media materials for concepts and accurate representation
- Kits, if convenient and inexpensive (often include all of the above)

Since science is based on observation, science curricula and materials should be selected to involve or extend all senses:

- hearing
- sight
- taste
- touch
- smell
- kinesthetics

The categories printed below are science processes and experiences that the developers of *Science—A Process Approach* (National Science Foundation, 1973) considered essential for the learning of science. Process and experiential categories such as these can be considered simultaneously with factual content in evaluating and selecting materials and can easily be transformed into a checklist. Do materials, for example, allow and/or encourage students to classify, observe, etc? Such questions, of course, are closely related to cognitive criteria and are appropriate for all science materials, not merely those called "process."

SCIENCE PROCESS CRITERIA

Materials

Processes	omit	permit	encourage
Observing: Identifying objects and object properties, noting changes in physical systems, controlled observations, ordering of a series of observations.			
Classifying: Classifications of physical and biological systems, multi-stage classifications, coding, tabulation.			
Using Numbers: Identifying sets and their members, ordering, counting, adding, multiplying, dividing, finding averages, using decimals, and powers of ten.			
Measuring: Identification and ordering of lengths, demonstration of rules for measurement of length, area, volume, weight, temperature, force and speed.			
Using Space/Time Relationships: Identification of shapes, movement and direction, rules for straight and curved paths, changes in position, and finding of linear and angular speeds.			
Communicating: Bar graph descriptions of simple events, describing physical objects and systems, construction of graphs and diagrams for observed results of tests.			
Predicting: Interpolation and extrapolation in graphic data, formulation of ways of testing predictions.			
Inferring: Making inferences from observations of physical and biological phenomena, construction of situations to test inferences drawn from hypotheses.			
Defining Operationally: Distinguishing between operational and non-operational definitions, constructing operational definitions in new problems.			
Formulating Hypotheses: Distinguishing hypotheses from inferences, observations, and predictions, constructing and testing hypotheses.			
Interpreting Data: Describing graphic data and inferences based upon them, constructing equations to represent data, relating data to hypotheses, generalizing from experimental findings.			
Controlling Variables: Identifying manipulated and responding (independent and dependent) variables in a description or demonstration of an experiment, conducting an experiment, identifying the variables, and describing how variables are controlled.			
Experimenting: Reiterating the sequence for controlling variables, interpreting accounts of scientific experiments, stating problems, constructing hypotheses, and carrying out experimental procedures.			

A clear exposition of the process approach and the concepts on which it is based (largely those of J. S. Bruner and Robert Gagné) is Arthur H. Livermore's "The Process Approach of the AAAS Commission on Science Education," in *Journal of Research in Science Teaching*, v. 2, no. 4 (1964), pp. 271-82.

PIAGET AND PROCESS SKILLS

The process approach in the teaching of science is partly based on the theories of Jean Piaget, which, simply stated, are that children progress through cumulative stages of readiness and that it is essential to introduce intellectual concepts at appropriate times.

Science 5/13, published by MacDonald Educational, is an English-developed Schools Council program for children between 5 and 13. It takes as its starting premise that student goals for science are 1) developing an inquiring mind and 2) introducing a scientific approach to problems. Within this overall context subgoals include:

- Developing interests, attitudes and esthetic appreciation
- Observing, exploring and ordering observations
- Developing basic concepts and logical thinking
- Posing questions and developing experiences to answer them
- Acquiring knowledge and learning skills
- Communicating
- Appreciating patterns and relationships
- Interpreting findings critically

For each of these goals, *Science 5/13* bases particular objectives on the supposed capabilities of students at different intellectual levels or Piagetian operational stages (defined in the chapter on cognitive criteria in *Issues and Policies*). Other process curricula tend to bow, at least in their introductions, in the direction of Piaget.

DIRECT EXPERIENCES

Science teaching should involve not only a community's people and places, but its other resources as well — snow in Minnesota, sand at ocean beaches, raindrops or small animals in country and city, and alarm clocks and hinges for everyone. Students should have opportunities for first-hand investigations and background research, as well as for field trips, visiting exhibits, or meeting local experts. For example, in forested areas, studies should include the characteristics of, say, leaves, wood and sawdust, as well as visits to sawmills and discussions with loggers and conservationists, and library research on all of these. Kits, discussed on page 18, are a middle ground between supplies and direct experience.

MODELS, EQUIPMENT AND SUPPLIES

Science teachers — and possibly students — should have access to a variety of catalogs for selecting equipment, supplies and services. These should be selected for classroom demonstrations and for student experiments; they should include, if possible, student-made projects and/or models that teach principles.

Especially at the elementary level, models, supplies and equipment need not be expensive or, for that matter, commercially purchased. There are many books suggesting ways to use such commonplaces as kitchen utensils, food, dandelions, soil, recycled junk, or even garbage in worthwhile science projects. In their excellent chapter on "Science Materials" [from *The Teaching of Science in the Elementary School*, 2nd ed. (Englewood Cliffs, NJ: Prentice-Hall, 1970), pp. 53-62], June E. Lewis and Irene C. Potter suggest that materials be:

- appropriate to the learning situation
- a stimulus to the attitude of inquiry
- safe and easy to manipulate
- appropriately sized and chosen for the method of use (e.g., large scale or noisy for demonstration, smaller or quieter for individual use)
- accurate
- durable
- helpful in expanding interests
- helpful in working toward specific goals

To add to this list, if made by kids, they should be easily constructed, and finally they should clearly demonstrate the target principle.

Lewis and Potter's chapter also includes many helpful suggestions for selecting and maintaining science materials in the elementary classroom. Some of their principles, rearranged in list form, are:

- Select the simplest materials you can find for the intended purpose
- Order equipment that can be dismantled whenever possible (so the students can discover how things are put together), *or*
- Order duplicates to take apart
- Check local stores (which may be cheaper or more convenient) before placing orders with scientific supply houses
- Buy only what you will use, and then use what you have bought
- Buy at least one piece of permanent equipment each year
- Include funds for upkeep in an annual cooperative budget, with some discretionary funds available during the year
- Have one person responsible for inventory, for checking equipment in and out, for keeping items in repair, and for replacing and replenishing supplies (a simple checklist record of use can be maintained without difficulty, to help evaluate quantity of use)
- Display new materials to maximize use and familiarization

They suggest, before purchasing materials, working out a master list based on needs and interests expressed by individual teachers. These lists can be coordinated by either an administrator or a small committee, preferably with the assistance of a science consultant or a high school science teacher who knows prices, sources, and equipment.

Before budget time each year, all equipment should be called back into the equipment or supply room for one day to be checked against this inventory. The next year's list should then begin with items that need to be replaced or replenished. The bulk of the annual budget should be spent on one major order since better prices are available on composite orders. Some money should be left for emergencies or opportunities that occur during the year.

Some valuable approaches for handling supplies and materials are given in Daniel Donovan's article, "Supplying a Science Center," in *Science and Children*,

v. 13, no. 1 (Sept. 1976), pp. 34-35. His concrete suggestions include sample purchase order forms for local merchants, recommended as an alternative to the difficulties inherent in petty cash funds.

The principles and practices suggested in these two sources rationalize procedures and cut down the inordinate amount of time that is sometimes devoted to maintaining and inventorying science supplies.

KITS AND PROGRAMS

The laboratory-sponsored, materials-centered kits which flourished with National Science Foundation funding in the 1960s are probably as far as one can go with direct experiences of science. These are still popular with the scientific community who recognize their congruence with the scientific process, their value in problem-solving and thinking skills and in training scientists. These materials—especially in the hands of a knowledgeable teacher—are popular with children who prefer working with their hands rather than with books and are salutary, if more difficult, for good students who learn most easily with books.

Their defects are closely related to their virtues. They are, according to critics, overly constrained by their emphasis upon direct experience, with few opportunities, for instance, to move backward in time to the lives of famous scientists or even further to the lives of dinosaurs or the origin of the universe. Despite, or because of, the direct experience, students are limited to those concepts discoverable through student facilities and materials.

A rather different line of criticism stems from administrative concerns, largely costs and flexibility. These programs are extraordinarily expensive and can present major administrative headaches. Some questions to ask are: 1) How well do its materials fit in with materials already available or in use? 2) Are there problems in replacing or replenishing kits? 3) Can this program be adopted a year or a unit at a time? 4) Will the program be tied forever to expensive, no-substitute materials? 5) Do teachers require expensive and frequently-maintained training to handle this program? The Science Framework of the State of California has developed the following series of questions for examining performance requirements and constraints for innovative programs. The lists are reprinted with permission from the *Science Framework for California Public Schools: Kindergarten-Grades One Through Twelve* by the California State Advisory Committee on Science Education (Sacramento, California State Department of Education, 1970), which includes among other desiderata eight performance requirements and constraints to be considered in adopting science curriculum components and seven reasons for local tryouts before adoption.

PRACTICAL PERFORMANCE REQUIREMENTS AND CONSTRAINTS

1) What personnel additions and/or changes will be required?
2) What competencies and attitudes should teachers and other personnel have in order to implement the innovation in an effective manner?
3) Are the teaching strategies and techniques advocated in the innovative program compatible with the existing school organization and facilities?
4) Can the proposed innovation be readily coordinated with other components now in the science curriculum or contemplated in the revised curriculum?
5) How much teacher preparation time and classroom time will be required to implement the proposed innovation?
6) What additional equipment and instructional materials will be needed?
7) Is the initial and long-term cost per pupil feasible in terms of currently available or obtainable funds?

IMPORTANCE OF LOCAL TRYOUT

Among the reasons for local tryout of promising innovations prior to their selection for adoption and installation are the following:

1) Teachers will have better attitudes toward an innovation if they are involved in an experimental tryout program.

2) Administrators, supervisors, and teachers are persuaded to consider and eventually adopt innovations primarily through seeing them succeed in their schools.

3) Although innovative programs may produce excellent results in field tests supervised by the program producers, they may not produce the same results when they are used in situations not connected with the developing agency.

4) Some basically sound programs must be modified because of unique local conditions that were not present in the field testing schools.

5) Local pilot testing provides data relative to teacher competencies, time, materials, and other factors that must be considered prior to adoption and installation of the innovation.

6) Opportunity is provided for teachers and supervisory personnel to develop competencies and experience needed for training other personnel who will be using the innovation.

7) Evaluation of local tryout can provide a variety of information for decision making; e.g., attitudes of local personnel toward the innovation, effectiveness of the program in attaining the desired objectives for the intended learners, and durability of instructional materials when subjected to local classroom conditions.

The composite criteria (pages 23-24) and the process criteria (page 15) are also important for kits.

RECYCLED SCIENCE MATERIALS

One satisfying way around the cost barrier is to use recycled and inexpensive materials for teaching science. Creative teachers, natural pack-rats, and teachers in war-devastated countries have often managed activity-centered courses without funds by using commonly-available materials, such as olive and peanut-butter jars, swizzle sticks, sand, and water.

This particular approach was promoted by Unesco after World War II and is still a necessity for many teachers in underdeveloped countries. It is also advocated by conscientious recyclers who seek productive uses for the by-products of our throw-away society.

Pre-service courses for teachers often include some creative scrounging aspects. I have taken one course in Science for Substitute Teachers which leaned heavily on balloons, rubber bands and yardsticks. Harold Jaus, a visiting professor of education at Purdue, suggested a curriculum of pre-service courses for science teachers in pack-ratting.

Another, possibly more likely approach, is that of Fairfax County, Virginia, where the Elementary Science Study project set up an Instructional Materials Processing Center in a low-income area in the county. This IMP Center, which employed mostly local housewives (part time) and neighborhood youth workers, managed to produce science kits for amazingly low costs, using scrap or easily-available materials. Microscopes, for instance, required only $0.26 worth of materials in 1973—thread spools, steel strap, wooden dowels and squares, mirrors, screws and penlight bulbs were assembled into 100x microscopes, and the employees made thousands of them. According to an article by Marie Benford in *Science Activities* (Oct. 1973), the Center saved the district more than $57,000 in its first six months of operation, and yet was able to maintain and refurbish these kits—services not supplied by most commercial suppliers.

Marshalltown, Iowa, uses volunteers and paid workers to supply and maintain its science program. Volunteers range from a Girl Scout troop at one end of the age spectrum to a Science Cadre of elderly citizens with members in their eighties. The Girl Scouts, backed by preliminary telephone calls, specialize in locating, collecting and organizing "junk." The Science Cadre marks, labels and organizes the materials. The paid workers—paraprofessionals and laboratory assistants—provide technical expertise, help in storage and inventory, and work on materials development, often in their spare time.

Other recycling programs—such as SCRAP in San Francisco—tend to recycle largely for art, but have the potential of providing an ongoing supply of science materials.

MEDIA MATERIALS

Media materials occupy a middle range in science education. They are less direct than hands-on approaches, and not as good as printed materials in presenting concepts, current information or organizing principles, but they are crucial for visualization of concepts. Their chief value is immediacy. They bring actual sounds and sights into classrooms; they motivate students by presenting the wonders of science; and they are vehicles for interdisciplinary presentations. As representational art, they should be accurate and authentic, and, if biased, they should clearly indicate the bias. Many industrial companies—with their own axes to grind—offer free films and filmstrips. These need to be carefully assessed for propaganda content.

It is particularly important to check the copyright date for media materials, especially materials in sets. Old films and filmstrip sequences have a way of reappearing in new multimedia packages. These packages, too, are sometimes peculiar composites of uneven quality tied together for sales purposes. It is well to preview before buying and best to avoid tie-in sales in which you pay for records you do not want in order to get usable filmstrips.

PRINTED MATERIALS

There is a vast range of printed materials appropriate for science; each type has its particular strengths and capabilities.

Trade books can lead in many directions, foster interests, promote thinking and experimentation, explore issues, develop ideas and concepts, move over space and time. Reference books provide authoritative information and illustrations, and help students learn library research processes. Periodicals are good for current information and research. Pamphlets are valuable for current data and viewpoints. Charts and graphs are good for developing communication skills as well as visual and mathematical literacy, and for interpreting data. Posters and photographs are good for verisimilitude and concept presentation. Textbooks offer an organized presentation of a subject, and, in some cases, are quasi-reference books.

Schools and classrooms need a good variety of these materials, including at least three or four science periodicals and an estimated science reference budget of at least $100.00 per class.

TEXTBOOKS

Though teachers without science backgrounds find textbooks—and their teachers' guides—helpful in presenting some sort of organized science program, science textbooks have few advocates among either professional science reviewers or scientists. Reviewers tend to prefer trade books because of their superior content; scientists tend to prefer first-hand science.

Major criticisms of science textbooks as a genre are that they are often:

- stereotyped
- inadequate for interdisciplinary concerns
- inadequate for research or concepts
- out of date when adopted
- inadequate for students interested in or gifted in science
- inadequate for teachers who wish to teach for excellence

Administrators like Eldon Grom as well as reviewers like Howie and Pollendorf have seriously advocated replacing science textbooks with trade books—particularly for elementary science teaching and for good science students. Some experienced science teachers such as Lewis advocate setting up a sort of textbook library with five or six copies each of five or six sets of texts for each classroom—buying limited numbers of each new text when issued. This does keep science information more up to date, and provides a relatively inexpensive quasi-reference library collection. Although, dollar for dollar, there is less scope and content in such a textbook library than in a well-selected collection of science trade books based on children's interests, such a collection does provide opportunities for grouping and alternative approaches for students with different learning styles, and may be a good starting place for teachers who are afraid to get too far away from textbooks.

While most of the criticisms are justified, some good science textbooks are available. Most of the post-1960s texts have—in self-defense—incorporated the inquiry-centered process approaches popularized by the laboratory-sponsored programs of the 1960s. In some cases these seem pasted on; sometimes, as in *Science 5/13*, this approach is integral. At their best, texts, such as the *Examining Your Environment Series* now issued by Holt, Rinehart & Winston, can present inquiry far more cheaply and probably more usably than many laboratory kits. At a minimum, textbooks provide teachers and students with a comprehensive overview of their fields.

Odvard Egil Dyrli, one of the few advocates of texts, presents a mixed appraisal in a recent article in *Learning Magazine* (Jan. 1976), "Is There Anything New about the New Science Textbooks?" and suggests certain means and criteria for fast appraisal of science texts.

He notes, first, that authorship means little, and that supposed scope-and-sequence charts bear little resemblance to their texts. In the days of composite authorship, whatever the name or the expertise of the purported author, the bulk of the writing is apt to be delegated to graduate students, assigned to teachers, or left to the publishers' secretaries. Teachers' editions, in particular, are often farmed out to new teams of writers.

Consequently it is important to check writing style throughout: Does the book sound like a textbook? Is the writing lively? Are the examples concrete? Do teachers' editions provide specific, usable information, or vague generalities? Are questions and answers fuzzy and repetitive?

Since scope and sequence charts themselves may be quite unrelated to the actual text, Dyrli suggests that evaluators,

- Check unit titles for intentional sequence
- Ascertain whether process skills and their sequences make sense
- Look for evidence of sequential—rather than arbitrary—development through the grades
- Note whether inquiry activities
    - include measurement and record keeping
    - are the same old demonstrations in new guise
    - are so predictable that students do not have to do the work to know the answers
- Note whether questions require thought or can be answered yes or no
- Note whether illustrations are consciously related to the text

SCIENTIFIC VOCABULARY

Dyrli also suggests that texts be checked for scientific vocabulary, and cautions that not too many scientific terms should be introduced at one time. This contravenes somewhat the recommendations of most scientific writers and reviewers (and some prestigious scientist-educators like Maria Montessori) who emphasize the importance of accurate scientific vocabulary and strongly deny the relevance of publishers' vocabulary lists to children's science books. These lists are constructed by reading experts using outmoded research which omitted scientific words from consideration. Once established, such lists—rather than children's interests or abilities—determine content, limit concepts, and infuse early elementary textbook writing with a ritualistic, sing-song quality. My personal belief is that readability formulae based on vocabulary lists should not be used to restrict vocabulary in children's science books. If materials are logically organized and clearly written, if glossaries themselves are clearly worded (possibly illustrated), and if new words are skillfully introduced in context and/or explained through illustration, children are not apt to have any problems with scientific vocabulary. Certainly children who are interested in what they are reading can handle far more than the educators' standards of two new words per page. Children's librarians suggest five unknown words per page as a (literally) handy guideline.

In the Further Reading section at the end of this chapter, I have cited two articles, by Mallinson and Smith, in *Reading in the Content Areas*, that provide admirably thorough discussions of scientific vocabulary and other aspects of readability in science.

TRADE BOOKS

An impressive number of thoughtful articles and books deal with criteria for writing and reviewing children's science materials; all are worth reading. Quite a few are summarized in the April 1974 issue of *Library Trends* (v. 22, no. 4) edited by George Brown. The following checklist is derived from the content criteria presented in several of these publications:

COMPOSITE CRITERIA FOR SELECTING CHILDREN'S SCIENCE BOOKS

Topic Choice

- Should meet a need
      and/or
- Deal with topics interesting to children
      and/or
- Present accurate understanding of science

Content should provide:

- authenticity — general scientific theories should be correctly stated (avoiding over-simplification, over-generalization, over-writing, and false analogies)
- accuracy — specific facts should be represented accurately, historically as well as scientifically (including information on failures)
- observation based on all senses
- opportunities for safe experimenting, illustrating, recording, and/or reporting
- thorough coverage
- currentness — materials should be up to date or timeless
- interest — materials should provide children with something to think about

Style and Vocabulary should be:

- clear, readable and interesting
- scrupulously accurate
- skillful in introducing concepts and/or vocabulary
- sensitive to children's vocabulary and thought processes with operational rather than dictionary definitions
- inspiring — conveying excitement of discovery

Organization

- should be logical
- should be sequential
- should include: table of contents
                    well-developed index
                    bibliographies and mediagraphies
                    glossary if needed

Illustrations

- should be simple but accurate
- should be well integrated with text
- should be logically placed not to interrupt thought processes
- should do what words cannot
- should extend text
- should use scientific symbols

Things to Avoid

- patronizing attitudes
- incompleteness and over-generalization
- ignorance of process
- stereotypes (white male scientists, boy chemists)
- sexist vocabulary (for humans or animals)
- anthropomorphism

(List continues on page 24)

- teleology (ascribed purpose)
- confusion of meaning of experiments
- series or sets of books (evaluate each title individually)
- gee-whiz books
- mixed genres except in case of genius (where it is almost impossible to separate fantasy or fiction from facts)

These criteria agree rather well with a list of 150 criteria for selecting supplementary secondary science books which was compiled by Barnes and colleagues from responses to a questionnaire submitted to 150 members of the Association for Research in Science Teaching in 1958. Two important categories were "qualities of the book" and "effect on the reader." The "qualities of the book" which the Association considered most significant were:

- accuracy and authoritativeness
- fairness and sincerity in presentation of controversial subject matter
- enrichment materials beyond that of secondary textbooks
- good literary standards
- lasting value

The "effects on the reader" considered most important were identified as follows:

- provoking thinking and discussion
- developing interest in science
- stimulating further reading
- articulating and elucidating scientific concepts and principles
- suggesting further problems
- providing insights into social implications and contributions of science

While these criteria were originally intended to be used for selection of materials for gifted students, the study indicated that these standards were applicable to all students.

In *Matters of Fact* (New York: Crowell, 1972), Margery Fisher discusses factual books as a genre. While it is almost impossible to summarize her interesting demonstration of selection principles, her comments that are relevant to science books can and should be presented here. According to Fisher, the writer's obligations are to be accurate, to explain matters clearly, to be stimulating and to arrange materials logically. Children's writers need to consider the ages and aptitudes of their readers and their probable vocabulary, and to see that a book is designed and illustrated in a way that is appealing to children. Beyond the technological aspects, a book is not a mere collection of facts. At a minimum, it needs to include facts, concepts and attitudes, and to be written with an end in view, a generalization toward which the facts are arranged. The business of a natural history book, for instance, is to relate facts to a pattern of life. The evaluator must assess the writer's attitude as well as his or her factual accuracy. Is the writer, for example, partisan, patronizing, or enthusiastic? The writer's enthusiasm or boredom are both contagious. Fisher feels it is important that writers respect the readers, use scientific vocabulary and proper categories and terms, and not oversimplify.

A somewhat less extensive criteria list is that of the Book Review Committee appointed by the National Science Teachers Association in cooperation with the Children's Book Council. The criteria they use in their annual *Outstanding Science Trade Books for Children* are discussed in Key Publications.

Children's science books, of course, are reviewed in media which review children's books and in science journals for teachers and children. Special review journals for science are discussed as Key Publications or under Key Organizations.

CUTTING COSTS

On any particular topic it is wise to consider what kinds of materials can be scrounged, which are available locally, and which might be free or inexpensive, in all kinds of media, from all kinds of sources. A satisfactory unit on weather, for example, could be developed from free or minimal-cost items like the following:

Direct Experience
- actual weather—to be observed, charted, experienced (day and night), described, researched
- data from local sources—newspaper, weather bureau, postal delivery, weather newscaster, hobbyist, farmer, local historian (for greatest local storm, most unusual weather year, etc.), truckers
- field trips and consultation with local experts, as above, and visits to weather station
- weather signs observed locally, like the slant of trees and signs of erosion (this could be tied in with local folklore)
- beliefs on weather—from science, folklore, local pundits, nudists, roofing experts (these apt to be affected by weather)
- instruments and equipment for measuring weather—could be made from home and dimestore supplies like balloons, tin cans, rulers (metric or otherwise), string
- clothing and housing (as protection against weather)

Media Materials
- films, filmstrips, weather sounds and sights, especially for unusual weather or weather not experienced locally (some might be available from weather bureau, libraries, and media centers; some could be locally- or children-produced)

Printed Materials
- outline maps—to be filled in (local copies)
- weather maps
- government documents—Weather Bureau publication teaching aids
- posters on climate
- magazine pictures which indicate weather
- from the library:
  - magazine indexes for articles on changing climates and theory of weather
  - fiction with the word "storm" in the title
  - weather proverbs from book of quotations

Other topics may require more expensive materials. Topics like the solar system or the circulatory system, which can best be understood through visualization, ideally need models, supplemented by slide projections, filmstrips which can be stopped, color motion pictures and transparencies or expensively-illustrated books. While such models and motion pictures are expensive, they often can be located with a little ingenuity. If they are not available in the school system or easily borrowed from another, they may be available at local museums, planetariums, or travelling medical exhibits, or be lent and demonstrated by volunteers from local medical schools, universities, hospitals, heart or lung associations or other community groups.

INTERDISCIPLINARY MATERIALS

One easy, inexpensive way to expand resources in science instruction is to extend scientific topics into other curriculum areas, looking for connections and materials. Libraries, museums, and lists of free materials are the logical primary sources for inexpensive resources and documentation.

The weather unit developed on the preceding page could possibly be expanded by student research projects into other curriculum areas. Some possible topics for each of these are:

EXPANSION OF THE WEATHER UNIT

Art

    Pictorial representations of weather
    Clouds (first presented by an artist)
    Art representing the sun (research project)
    Architecture as related to weather and climate

Shop

    Homemade weather instruments

Music

    Songs and musical compositions about weather
    Sounds of weather

Math

    Weather statistics and weather record maintenance

Social Studies

    International weather agreements and conventions (relief efforts)
    History of the Weather Bureau
    Weather and agriculture—crop failures and successes—such as the Irish potato famine and American history
    Social effects of blizzards, drought

English/Language Studies

    Folklore of weather
    Weather reporting
    Descriptions of weather and climate in novels and poetry
    Origins of weather vocabulary
    Student mood pieces on weather

Science

    Weather satellites
    Weather and health
    Water supply and weather
    Air pollution and weather

SCIENCE AND SOCIAL ISSUES

The most important interdisciplinary area for science is probably the science-social studies interface, since most issues that affect our lives and futures occur in the intersection of public issues with current scientific technology. The entire February 1975 issue of *Social Education* (v. 139, no. 2) deals with the necessity of "Integrating Social Studies and Science." Some areas considered vital are:

- environmental education
- population
- energy
- medicine and health
- food production
- wars and technology interactions
- metrification
- data processing
- science fiction
- history of science and technology

Other possible areas are:
- politics of pollution
- our chemical cuisine
- small technology
- futurology
- the ethics and values of science
- the unspoken assumptions of science

An emphasis upon the social and ethical implications of science is one important way of making the field of science interesting and accessible to students who are not particularly interested in science for its own sake. Materials for this approach can be found in trade books, current magazines, and newspapers and their indexes, in pamphlets issued by advocacy organizations and in media documentaries. Government documents are often helpful for factual documentation and statistics.

Until a joint curriculum is developed for these vital areas, teachers and librarians will have to select materials on their own from trade sources. Fortunately, such materials are available at all levels. *Science and Society*, by the American Association for the Advancement of Science, now in its sixth edition, is an excellent resource guide.

Problem areas for science materials selection also occur in the areas where science overlaps with values and/or with social studies. Free materials supplied by industry, for example, are apt to be scientifically accurate—at least technically—but have been criticized for presenting partial or distorted information in such areas as agriculture, nutrition, medicine, policy, and pollution.

Science educators—or some of them—get more excited about the area of evolution. About ten state legislatures and many major school districts have taken action to include the "creationist" viewpoint in courses on biology and evolution. The organizations that are attempting to influence policy range from fundamentalist religious groups at one end to the American Humanist Association at the other (the latter is also recognized as a tax-exempt religious group by the Internal Revenue Service). Since this process of revision includes input from a spectrum of viewpoints, it seems less dangerous to me than the oversupply of (usually unquestioned) materials from industry. But both situations can be used to develop in students the scientifically desirable practice of critical thinking.

KEY ORGANIZATIONS

American Association for the Advancement of Science (AAAS)
1776 Massachusetts Ave., NW
Washington, DC 20036   (202) 467-4400

The AAAS has a science education department concerned witĥ science education through the college years. Its publications include the following:

AAAS Science Books and Films, quarterly, $17.50/year.

This magazine contains reviews of trade books, textbooks, reference books, and 16mm films in the pure and applied sciences for all ages, with grade levels and recommendations. One whole section of each issue is devoted to reviews of children's science books. This particular periodical updates three other publications from AAAS: *AAAS Science Book List for Children, AAAS Science Book List* (for adults), and *AAAS Science Film Catalog*. New editions of each of these books are published every few years.

Science and Society: A Bibliography, by Joseph M. Dasback. 6th ed., 1976. 104p. $3.00.

This bibliography, now in its sixth edition, focuses on the relationships between humans, the environment, science, and technology. It is a thesaurus of ideas, largely collated from recent books and periodicals, to make the interrelationships of science and society more accessible. It is designed to supplement course work at the secondary and college levels, for a variety of users with different backgrounds and library resources. It is an excellent source of ideas for mini courses, learning modules of independent study. Areas covered in this edition include aging and death, conflict, energy, environmental manipulation, ethics and values, health care, natural resources, pollution, population, technology, and transportation. Each of these 11 areas has been organized into a framework. The bibliography does include some materials other than print, primarily phonograph records, tape recordings, and periodicals in braille or large type.

Association of Science-Technology Centers (ASTC)

Traveling Exhibits Service (TES)

1016 16th St., NW

Washington, DC 20036   (202) 452-0655

ASTC, a membership organization, is also a clearinghouse for science museum information. In 1974, the Association initiated a Traveling Exhibits Service—basically for member museums and science-technology programs. It then began to develop its own exhibits, including the very popular "Think Metric" produced cooperatively with the National Bureau of Standards. With the help of the National Science Foundation, TES is now expanding its traveling exhibits service and administering small grants for educational programs.

While its major clients are still science-technology centers and museums, TES does lend exhibits to schools that meet requirements for space, size, and security. It now sponsors approximately 20 traveling exhibits on science, technology, architecture, science/art centers, and topics such as energy, birds of prey, holography and medicine. Some exhibits come with educational program suggestions and/or posters, films, slides, and brochures or catalogs. A few films may be ordered separately. Prices for exhibits range from $50.00 (for a *Children's Science Book Fair*) to substantially more. Most exhibits are booked from five to six weeks in advance.

The parent organization, ASTC, has a publication department whose purpose is to facilitate the exchange of information about science-technology centers and their exhibits. Their publications include a bimonthly *ASTC Newsletter* with information on programs and exhibits of member institutions. The *ASTC*

Traveling Exhibitions Service Catalog outlines current exhibits, films, and services. Single copies of each of these publications are free.

Other publications that may be purchased include *Starting a Science Center?* (1977), an illustrated booklet covering all facets of science center planning ($5.00 for non-members), and *Traveling Exhibitions*, by Victor Danilov (1977) ($3.50 for non-members). The latter is an illustrated profile of the traveling exhibitions services of 14 agencies. *Survey of Education Programs at Science-Technology Centers* (at $3.50) covers teacher-training programs, field trips, and similar educational programs at some member institutions.

Biological Science Curriculum Study (BSCS)
8383 South Boulder Road
P.O. Box 930
Boulder, CO 80306   (303) 666-6558

The BSCS is interested in the improvement of biological education at all levels, though chiefly at the secondary levels. The project itself has created a wide variety of materials, including laboratory materials and textbooks, motion pictures, teacher aids, and research reports.

Its free *BSCS Newsletter* provides rather interesting summaries (reports of field tests and the like) for the BSCS materials and programs, as well as broad discussions of controversial issues in science curriculum and materials. It is an easy and literate tool for keeping upwith the thinking and attitudes of science curriculum developers.

ERIC Clearinghouse for Science, Mathematics, and Environmental Education (ERIC/SMEAC)
Ohio State University
1200 Chambers Road, Third Floor
Columbus, OH 43210   (614) 422-6717

This ERIC Clearinghouse deals with science education, mathematics education, and environmental education. Like other ERIC Clearinghouses, it collects, processes and disseminates reports on research, the learning-teaching process, and cognitive concepts related to these three fields, such as the impact of interest, intelligence, values, and concept development upon learning science and related subjects. The Clearinghouse also collects information on teaching materials and activities in these fields and even produces its own. Its library houses more than 100,000 items in these areas of interest, and is open to the public.

In addition to processing documents and articles for inclusion in *Resources in Education* (RIE) and *Current Index to Journals in Education*, this clearinghouse has an extensive publication program. Publications include special bibliographies, summaries of research and trends, and guides to the literature. Available materials are listed in a free catalog, *ERIC/SMEAC Publications*. Some publications particularly relevant to science education are listed below. Others are listed in the chapters on mathematics and environmental education. Publications are distributed by the SMEAC Information Reference Center which also answers queries and provides custom services in reference and literature searching.

The publications below are available directly from the Information Reference Center, at prices somewhat lower than those of central ERIC's Educational Document Center.

A Review of British Science Curriculum Projects: Implications for Curriculum Developers, by A. M. Lucas and D. G. Chisman, 1973. 149p. $4.50 (ED 076 427).
Includes discussion of content, teaching materials, and techniques and implications for the United States.

Handbook of Unpublished Evaluation Instruments in Science Education, by Victor J. Mayer, 1974. 322p. $4.50 offset (ED 095 015).
Several instruments are included in the appendix.

Logical Reasoning in Science Education, by F. Michael Connelly and Richard W. Binns, 1974. 48p. $1.50 offset (ED 097 198).
Includes an extensive annotated bibliography.

Guide to FUSE Modules Abstracted in RIE—1976, by Victor Showalter, 1977. 115p. $3.30 offset (ED 148 603).

Science Education, Abstracts and Index from Resources in Education, 1976-1977, 1978. Looseleaf with three-hole notebook. $255.25.
Abstracts, with subject and other indexes to science materials in RIE in 1976 and 1977. Similar abstract volumes for earlier years are also available.

International Clearinghouse on Science and Mathematics Curriculum Developments
Science Teaching Center
University of Maryland
College Park, MD 20742   (301) 454-4028

The International Clearinghouse is an ongoing operation that collects "software" and exemplary examples of "hardware" of worldwide science and curriculum development projects and issues detailed reports on these projects. The work began at the University of Maryland in October 1962 and has continued thereafter, sometimes with the cooperation of Unesco and/or the American Association for the Advancement of Science.

The Clearinghouse began to issue reports on American science projects in 1963, and started issuing *International Clearinghouse Reports* on international projects in 1966. These reports were issued in 1967, 1968, 1970, 1972, 1975, and 1977. *Twenty Years of Science and Mathematics Curriculum Development: The Tenth Report of the International Clearinghouse on Science and Mathematics Curriculum Developments*, edited by J. David Lockard (1977. 540p. $10.00), provides a good summary of curricular developments in science and mathematics for the preceding 20 years.

This tenth report includes detailed information on new science and mathematics curriculum projects throughout the world, with summary information on project titles, background, headquarters, staff, materials, availability, language(s), teacher training requirements, and future plans, as well as keys for locating projects by country, grade levels, and/or subject. In addition to this information (which is included in all reports) the tenth report includes a 20-year directory summary of projects that appeared in the previous nine editions of *International Clearinghouse Reports*.

Back issues of these *Reports* which contain more detailed information on their contemporary projects are available for $5.00 for the ninth (1975) *Report*, and $2.00 each for earlier reports.

The center is open by appointment to visitors to Washington in summer and winter.

National Science Teachers Association (NSTA)
1742 Connecticut Ave., NW
Washington, DC 20009   (202) 265-4150

This organization of science teachers, founded in 1944, attempts to improve science knowledge among its members and their students and to improve science teaching through conventions, special projects, and publications.

Membership ($15.00 for elementary teachers, $20.00 for secondary or college teachers) includes appropriate journals (*Science and Children* for elementary teachers, *Science Teacher* for secondary teachers) and an *NSTA News-Bulletin* as well as discounts on supplementary publications. It is also a good source of information on safety.

NSTA has an extensive and growing publication program, with a "how-to-do-it" series at prices from $0.60 to $1.00 which includes *How to Present Audible Multi-Imagery in Environmental-Ecological Education* ($0.60), *How to Ask the Right Questions* ($0.60), *How to Use Behavioral Objectives in Science Education* ($1.00) and many more.

The *Careers* series includes *Keys to Careers in Science and Technology* (1973. 74p. $1.00), which lists sources of career materials as well as sources of loans and awards.

The *Elementary Science Packets*, at $3.00 each, all include more or less extensive listings of resources. These deal with *Environment and Energy, Career Awareness, Measurement and Metric System*, and other topics. Items from industry in some packets may overbalance other points of view. Its *Resource* series (from $2.85 to $27.50) includes compilations of articles, biographies of black scientists, metric exercises, a perpetual science calendar, and tapes of women scientists. Finally, its *Bibliography of Science Courses of Study and Textbooks K-12* (1973. 99p. $2.50) is still useful.

KEY PUBLICATIONS

The section on Science in Mary Sive's *Selecting Instructional Media* (Littleton, CO: Libraries Unlimited, 1978) includes many additional sources. United States government agencies are good sources of informational documents, maps, and illustrative materials, particularly for the earth sciences. Some sources and subject lists are provided in the section on government documents in *Media and the Curriculum*.

Activities for Lower Primaries, developed by African Primary Science Program.
Newton, MA: Educational Development Center, 1973. 11 booklets. $6.00. (From Publications Office, 55 Chapel St., Newton, MA 02160).

These interesting elementary science activities developed for African schools use free local (African) and universal materials. The set includes attractive informative photographs of African children, schools, and environments.

Separate booklets are entitled *Introduction, Arts and Crafts, Construction, Cooking, Dry Sand, Exploring the Local Community, Plants in the Classroom, Water, Wet Sand, Wheels,* and *Woodwork.*

Appraisal: Children's Science Books, by Children's Science Book Review Committee, Cambridge, MA, 1968. 3 issues/year. $6.00/year. (From Appraisal, Children's Science Book Review Committee, 13 Appian Way, Cambridge, MA 02138).

This unusual evaluation source combines in one attractive format, evaluative annotations and ratings by science specialists and children's librarians. An inexpensive tool for locating high-quality, relevant books for all grade levels.

Bibliography of Science Courses of Study and Textbooks—K-12, compiled by National Science Teachers Association, Washington, DC, 1973. 99p. $2.50pa.

A convenient listing of major curriculum projects, courses of study available through state and local school departments of education, and science textbooks—kindergarten to grade 12.

Course and Curriculum Improvement Materials, by the National Science Foundation. Washington, DC: GPO, 1976. 53p. $2.15.

This bibliography of instructional materials for elementary, intermediate and secondary school science courses lists books and films as well as some instructional equipment for mathematics, astronomy, biology, chemistry, oceanography, meteorology, physics, and the social sciences.

Elementary Science Information Unit, compiled by Far West Laboratory for Educational Research and Development, San Francisco, 1971. 6 reports, 7 color filmstrips, 7 audiotapes, 1 review booklet, 1 instruction booklet. $75.00. (Booklets now available without cost, while supply lasts, from 1855 Folsom St., San Francisco, CA 94103).

This multimedia package still constitutes a model of how to examine and choose materials, though many new products have been developed in the years since 1971. Its dual purposes were to train individuals in selection and to present information on science curricula. It uses a parallel format to examine and compare six elementary science curricula. Characteristics examined include subject areas, grade levels, suggested use(s), teacher and student materials, goals, sample topics, student evaluation, unit sequencing, instructional strategy, teacher preparation, cost, and availability.

The Elementary Science Study—A History, compiled by Emily Romney and Mary Jane Neuendorffer. Newton, MA: Education Development Center, 1973. 263p. $6.00. (From Publications Office, 55 Chapel St., Newton, MA 02160).

"This account has ... been intended both as a documentary record and a celebration of The Elementary Science Study," derived from written sources, direct quotations, personal interviews, and (occasionally) from conflicting accounts.

The ESS Reader, compiled by Educational Development Center, Newton, MA, 1970. 236p. $2.50pa. (From Publications Office, 55 Chapel St., Newton, MA 02160).

This anthology "represents some of the published and persistent expressions of the developing ESS point of view over the decade of the project's existence ... under a single cover." Many deal with open education.

Games for the Science Classroom: An Annotated Bibliography, by Paul B. Hounshell and Ira R. Trollinger. Washington, DC: National Science Teachers Association, 1977. 24p. $3.75pa. (Also available as ED 141 071).

This guide, designed to enhance the learning environment through instructional games, includes information on how to choose, order, or prepare more than 100 science games, along with brief summaries of their rules. Many deal with life science, ecology, population, and pollution. Commentary for educators includes purpose of each game and assessment of its usability for classroom purposes.

Guidebook to Constructing Inexpensive Science Teaching Equipment, edited by J. David Lockard. College Park, MD: Science Teaching Center, University of Maryland, 1977. Volume I—*Biology*, 288p.; Volume II—*Chemistry*, 287p.; Volume III—*Physics*, 318p. $10.00 per set. (Available from Dr. J. David Lockard, Inexpensive Science Teaching Equipment Project, Science Teaching Center, University of Maryland, College Park, MD 20742).

These three guidebooks are an outgrowth of the Inexpensive Science Teaching Equipment Project, the purpose of which was to identify laboratory equipment needed for introductory science courses in developing countries and to design inexpensive science teaching equipment for biology, chemistry, and physics. The completed guidebooks—not limited to developing countries—include detailed drawings and comprehensive instructions on ways of constructing such equipment from easily-obtained and inexpensive materials.

Living Things in Field and Classroom: A Minnemast Handbook for Teachers of Elementary Grades, by Zachariah Subarsky and others. Minneapolis, MN: Minnesota Mathematics and Science Teaching Project. 134p. $3.00pa. (From 720 Washington Ave., SE, Minneapolis, MN 55414).

This separable section of the Minnemast project is filled with practical, helpful, and thoughtful suggestions for maintaining and learning from classroom plants, gardens, zoos, and museums. It covers what to do when children bring things in, what to do at the end of the school year, suggestions for field trips and calendar activities around the year, and includes valuable reading suggestions on animals, ecology, fossils, plants, rocks and minerals, and shells. It provides interesting activities, good illustrations, and appropriate questions to guide observations.

A Materials Book for the Elementary Science Study, by Elementary Science Study (ESS). Newton, MA: Educational Development Center, 1972. 68p. $3.75pa. (From Publications Office, 55 Chapel St., Newton, MA 02160).

Discusses alternative ways of collecting and maintaining science materials—especially those for ESS, though it is helpful for elementary science in general.

Outstanding Science Trade Books for Children in 1977, by the National Science Teachers' Association in cooperation with the Children's Book Council. New York: Children's Book Council, annual listing. Single copy free for stamped ($0.24) self-addressed large envelope. (From CBC, 67 Irving Place, New York, NY 10005).

Lists and annotates around 80 outstanding children's science trade books. The 1977 list had 77 titles evaluated by a book review committee appointed by the NSTA in cooperation with the CBC. Books were selected 1) for accuracy, readability, and pleasing format, 2) for encouraging independent work, 3) for feasible, safe experiments, leading to understanding of basic principles, 4) for inclusion of significant facts, 5) for clear distinctions between facts and theories, 6) for factual support of generalizations, 7) for fair presentation of controversial issues, and 8) for avoidance of sexism, racism, violence, and anthropomorphism. Annotations are very clear and useful for teachers. This inexpensive guide is a valuable browsing list for educators and librarians and a good selection tool—especially for schools with modest budgets. It also appears in *Science and Children*.

Science Equipment in the Elementary School, by R. W. Wolton with J. Richt-myer. Rev. ed. Boulder, CO: Mountain View Center for Environmental Education, 1975. 51p. $3.00pa. (From Mountain View Center for Environmental Education, University of Colorado, Boulder, CO 80302).

An illustrated guide to inexpensive materials for preschool and elementary school science arranged by topic, with comments and approximate prices. Covers materials and equipment for studying electricity and magnetism, force and motion, heat, light and color, liquids, living things in the classroom, mathematics equipment, measurement, outdoor activities, sorting and sieving, sound, tools, miscellaneous apparatus, safety, and junk.

Science in the Open Classroom, edited by Ruth Dropkin. New York, Workshop Center for Open Education, 1973. 49p. $2.00. (From 6 Shepard Hall, City College of New York, 140th St. and Convent Ave., New York, NY 10031).

Includes theoretical articles on elementary science by educators from the U.S., Canada, and England, examples of actual classroom investigations by Workshop Center staff and participants, and a list of resources: programs, books, magazines, and miscellaneous.

Science Materials for Children and Young People, edited by George S. Bonn. *Library Trends*, v. 22, no. 4 (April 1974).

This issue of *Library Trends* is a series of commissioned articles by distinguished authors, editors, reviewers, librarians, and science teachers intended to assist parents, librarians, and teachers in selecting and evaluating all types of science materials. It contains excellent lists of science periodicals, science reference books, and science media materials, as well as explicit criteria for selection.

Sciences. Washington, DC: National Audiovisual Center, 1978. 50p. Free(pa.). (From National Audiovisual Center, Washington, DC 20409).

This free NAC Catalog lists about 600 available, government-produced, rent and sale media items (mostly films, but also slides and other items) on topics like aerospace, biology, energy, environmental studies, oceanography, and weather. Many are appropriate for the secondary level. Sales and rental prices are both apt to be lower than those of commercial producers.

Topics-Aids: Biology: A Catalog of Instructional Media for College Biology, edited by Robert S. Egan. College Station, Texas A&M University, College of Science Instructional Resources Committee; distr., College Station, Texas A&M University Press, 1977. 286p. (Topics-Aids Series). $5.00pa.

This is a very useful, well-arranged listing of educational media selected for college-level biology classes, which includes many items appropriate for high school or even for younger children. It is the first of a prospective series of Topic-Aids planned by the Instructional Resources Committee of the College of Science of Texas A&M University under the general editorship of Rod O'Connor, and serves, in a sense, as a topical index to biology items in media producers' catalogs.

The catalog covers films (16mm, 8mm, and Super 8), filmloops, filmstrips, color slides, audio formats, charts, models, and miscellaneous media materials. Each entry includes the title, type of medium, a code for the producers, and more or less lengthy descriptions of the contents. Entries generally do not include release date, length, number of frames, and the like; prices, intended audiences, and catalog numbers are excluded as a policy. The subject arrangement is logical, clear, and concise, with items arranged alphabetically by title under subdivisions of thirteen major biology topics. The table of contents functions well as a topic outline. Address lists of media producers and biological supply companies are included at the end of the book.

FOR FURTHER READING

*Items marked with an asterisk include other criteria checklists.
+ Items marked with a plus include substantial lists of references.

*Barnes, C. V., and others. "Criteria for Selecting Supplementary Reading Science Books for Intellectually Gifted High School Students," *Science Education*, v. 42 (April 1958), pp. 215-18.

Benford, Marie Delores. "The Materials Processing Center," *Science Activities*, v. 10, no. 2 (Oct. 1973), pp. 23-26.

Donovan, Daniel B. "Supplying a Science Center," *Science and Children*, v. 13, no. 1 (Sept. 1976), pp. 34-35.

*Dyrli, Odvard Egil. "Is There Anything New about the New Science Textbooks?," *Learning*, v. 4, no. 5 (Jan. 1976), pp. 30-35.

Eagle, David L. "Helpers—Nine to Ninety," *Science and Children*, v. 11, no. 5 (Jan.-Feb. 1976), p. 22.

Jaus, Harold H. "Let's Train Teachers to Be Pack Rats," *Science and Children*, v. 11, no. 7 (April 1974), pp. 14-15.

Lapp, Douglas M., and Leslie J. Benton. "Supporting an Elementary Science Program through Community Industry," *Science and Children*, v. 11, no. 6 (March 1974), pp. 11-13.

* + Lewis, June E., and Irene C. Potter. *The Teaching of Science in the Elementary School*. 2nd ed. Englewood Cliffs, NJ: Prentice-Hall, 1970. (Especially Chapter 5, "Science Materials").

Livermore, Arthur H. "The Process Approach of the AAAS Commission on Science Education," *Journal of Research in Science Teaching*, v. 2, no. 4 (1964), pp. 271-82.

*+Mallinson, George G. "Reading in the Sciences: A Review of the Research," in James L. Laffey's *Reading in the Content Areas*. Newark, DE: International Reading Association, 1972, pp. 127-52.

+Nelkin, D. *Science Textbook Controversies and the Politics of Equal Time*. Cambridge, MA: M.I.T. Press, 1977.

Newport, John. "The Readability of Science Textbooks for Elementary Schools," *Elementary School Journal*, v. 66, no. 1 (Oct. 1965), pp. 40-43.

Ogden, William B. "Scientific Literacy: A Recommitment," *High School Teacher*, v. 58, no. 8 (May 1974), pp. 351-55.

*+Smith, Carl Bernard. "Reading in the Sciences: Classroom Implications," in James L. Laffey's *Reading in the Content Areas*. Newark, DE: International Reading Association, 1972, pp. 153-76.

+Unesco. *The New UNESCO Source Book for Science Teaching*. Paris: Unesco, 1973. (Also available from Unipub, P.O. Box 433, New York, NY 10016).

+Waters, Barbara S. *Science Can Be Elementary*. New York, Citation Press, 1973.
Appendixes provide excellent source lists (as of 1973) for science materials, curriculum programs, professional organizations, and federal programs.

SELECTING MATHEMATICS MATERIALS

"Mathematics is not just applied to the real world. It comes from the real world."
— Morris Kline

"Once we have a curriculum that respects children's interests and intuition, in which every idea and skill makes sense to young students, mathematical skills will finally become available to everyone."
— Mitchell Lazarus, "Elementary Math and Common Sense"

"(Mathematics) is a system expressed by numerals and explained in a verbal language ... often far less precise and sometimes far more complex than the quantitative system which the student is expected to master. These words and the concepts they embody pose a distinct problem of interpretation for the student, particularly if he is not a good reader or if he is not 'mathematically inclined.' "
— Myron L. Coulter, "Reading in Mathematics ... Classroom Applications"

□ □ □

OVERVIEW

There are two strands coexisting in mathematics education today. One, based on the logical structure of mathematics, is the discovery method (exemplified by MINNEMAST and Nuffield mathematics), where at least some of the teaching is based on on-site investigations and measurements or manipulations of concrete objects and the like. The other, more "traditional," back-to-basics math, is now oriented toward "survival" math and other applications such as consumer math and career math. Its teaching methods are rooted in computation, exercises, repetition, formula learning, and, largely, textbook teaching.

The "new math" in a sense has its roots in the old faculty psychology, where the study of mathematics was supposed to increase the power of reasoning, as well as in the theories of Maria Montessori, whose inventions are still excellent teaching tools for mathematical concepts. The direction of the revisions, however, was shaped to a large degree in the curriculum reform movement of the sixties, by the need for better college preparatory curricula. The new basic math greatly resembles the "socially useful arithmetic" advocated by Guy M. Wilson back in the years of progressive education and the Depression.

New curriculum areas — metrication, statistics, interdisciplinary math, computer math and calculator math — are pushing for inclusion in both these strands. These are eminently practical fields, which require logical thinking for effective use. They may provide means and curricula for integrating the two approaches.

Neither the old math nor the new is popular with sizable groups of children, though the old math ranks higher with traditionally-oriented parents. While math scores have shown a rather steady decline on the Scholastic Achievement Test, this probably represents a general educational decline rather than a just criticism of the new math. A study of what actually happens in math classes as reported in "Overview and Analysis of School Mathematics" [*Mathematics Teacher*, v. 76, no. 6 (Oct. 1976), pp. 440-68] indicates that, in practice, new math or no, math in-class time is dominated by seat work and computations. A survey of adults by the National Assessment of Educational Programs as reported by Thomas P. Carpenter, et al. [*Arithmetic Teacher*, v. 22, no. 6 (Oct. 1975), pp. 438-50] indicates that the math that preceded the new math was equally unsuccessful in teaching the ability to solve simple consumer math problems.

According to the first NAEP mathematics assessment, 13-year-old students perform computational skills about as well as adults. Elementary students are reasonably strong or up to curriculum level for whole-number computation, knowledge of numeration concepts, analysis of one-step word problems, intuitive and practical measurement concepts, and recognition of geometric figures and relationships. They are weak in complex word problems, percentage, fraction concepts, measurement tasks and understanding of geometry concepts. To a degree these may be the fault of materials, as well as of a curriculum that fails to connect either with common sense or current realities.

Mitchell Lazarus notes that today in the elementary grades most children work with numbers that mean nothing at all and, "in the never-never land of math books," attempt to solve contrived word problems that are unreasonable to begin with.

Many students (more frequently girls than boys) suffer—like many adults—from mathophobia, a widespread anxiety about mathematics that starts in school and results in widespread quantitative illiteracy. While a basic understanding of some aspects of math seems essential for our technological, computerized society, neither the coursework nor the teaching tools as taught today seem relevant to many. Geometry, for example, which occupies two to four hours a night in my daughter's life, and reduces her to tears an average of two nights a week, is only used subsequently by about 2.5 percent of the students who take it. (Some consider even that estimate high.) We are not Egyptian farmers or indeed predominantly agriculturists who need geometry to assay our fields, but largely urban citizens in a technological society, who should aspire to computer literacy, calculator literacy and statistical literacy as part of our basic education. While geometry has for me a certain intrinsic charm and appeal, it is not usually taught with materials or methods to charm the disaffected with, say, demonstrations of geometry's functions in art, architecture or history.

Both the old math and the new math are, unfortunately, unsuccessful as well as unpopular with a large number of children. Problems in the old math are the boredom and repetition, the failure to teach concepts, the lack of appeal and reference points, and often the lack of application to daily life. They are, too often, a disjointed conglomerate of specific techniques. Major problems in new math are the rigor, the formalism and, especially at higher (more gifted) levels, the pace. Some experts consider the new math suitable for only the top one-third of the student body, where it does allow teaching for excellence.

Since the two approaches are difficult and unpopular for many children, even though successful with others, we obviously need alternative programs and materials for teaching math that use current tools and are appropriate for individual learning styles and interests.

One approach is that of Education Development Center's *Project One* television series which attempts to integrate basic literacy with problem-solving methods at the elementary level. Some of its elementary goals are outlined below. Obviously, combined criteria such as these could be used for materials selection as well as for curriculum development.

1) Counting and ordering, including
   number system
   decimal notation
   powers of 10
   very large and very small numbers (e.g., 6×10^6 or 6×10^{-6})
   arithmetic with small integers
   approximate arithmetic
2) Concepts and units of measurement, using real objects and real situations
3) Estimation (of size, place, time, and quantity)
4) Concept of size-scale and mapping, and underlying concept of ratio
5) Graphs in one dimension (number lines)
   Graphs in two dimensions (crossed number lines)

Following a massive survey of 30 million elementary children, 9 million high school students, 750,000 elementary and 75,000 high school math teachers, the National Advisory Committee on Mathematics in Education (NACOME) recommended the creation of certain new, improved instructional materials as a first priority. According to their final report, the "Overview and Analysis of School Mathematics, K-12," new instructional materials at all levels are urgently needed for the following areas:

- use of calculators
- applications and modeling
- statistics *and* the general ability to collect, organize, interpret and understand qualitative information
- combinatorial mathematics
- metric system measurement

Slightly lower priorities were given to:

- materials for supporting and developing abilities in problem solving, reasoning and critical thinking
- effective materials and techniques for remedial instruction
- short-test scales (as contrasted with broad achievement tests) directed at specific objectives
- sensitive measures for the affective components in math education

They also suggest that:

- all curricula be revised for metric instruction
- statistical ideas be inserted into courses in natural, physical, and social sciences and the humanities
- interdisciplinary courses be created for statistics

Other courses recommended were a variety of courses in computers and calculators.

Mitchell Lazarus also strongly recommends using calculators to reduce the need for computation with pointless and difficult procedures and allowing students to work with problems that interest them. (How much does King Kong need to spend on groceries?)

Parents, of course, have strong feelings about calculators in education. While some parents or groups of parents donate calculators to their children's schools, other parents make impassioned addresses at school board meetings opposing taking time from computations to work with calculators.

A great deal of information and evidence on selecting and using calculators is being assembled by the Calculator Information Center headed by Dr. Marilyn Suydam and housed at the ERIC Clearinghouse on Science, Mathematics and Environmental Education (listed on page 49).

Computers, despite their high expense, are now actually more available to high school students than to college students, and are used in some elementary schools, which seems to many their most appropriate setting. The argument is that computers play so large a role in our late twentieth century world that "computer literacy," or at least exposure to the capabilities, limitations, and effects of computers, should be part of every child's general education.

One advantage is motivational; children are fascinated by computers and often are more ready to use and understand computers than adults. Most advocates mention the general air of excitement in computer classrooms and rapt attention at the computer. Many students seem to learn more thoroughly and remember better with computers; some studies show improved attendance records. While one major thrust of computer programs is merely familiarization and awareness, for many children computers are a useful introduction to logical rigor and exactness, to flow charts, to breaking activities and processes into logical sequences, to precise habits, and to learning other languages like BASIC. For others it is a pleasurable introduction to algebra and complex mathematical operations. Computers, of course, are a good interdisciplinary bridge between math and the social sciences where they are used to process all those data.

Computer-based learning systems tend to generate their own computer-based learning materials (CBLM) which may include the whole gamut: textbooks, lab manuals, data bases, animated films, prepared programs, program systems and packages, and simulation packages. These may appear in such physical forms as reel tapes, magnetic tapes, card decks, and keyboards, etc.

An excellent information source on these is Robert Seidel's *Learning Alternatives in U.S. Education: Where Student and Computer Meet* (Englewood Cliffs, NJ: Educational Technology, 1975), prepared under the auspices of Human Resources Research Organization (HUMRRO) which conferred the acronym CBLM on these materials.

Another excellent free-lance, free-wheeling source on educational computing is the People's Computer Company, P.O. Box 310, Menlo Park, CA, which has originated many computer games and activities for elementary school children, and serves as a mail order source for books and games on computers. It has published issues on evaluating computers. Other sources are listed as further readings.

Computer companies are rather good as idea sources on educational activities, though each company, understandably, believes its own computers the best for educational purposes. Educators shopping for computers should prepare a detailed want list first, then find out which computers meet their specifications at what costs.

Other inexpensive but highly effective mathematics materials are manipulatives, puzzles, math games of all sorts, and directed experiences that involve measurement and calculation, such as cooking, carpentry, and construction. These have been successful with all groups from remedial to gifted students. They are good ways to introduce metric measures.

Math can be taught to a large extent without purchased commercial materials. Counting devices include fingers and environmental items like pebbles; string, straight edges and shadows can be used for geometry and measurement; cardboard and milk cartons can be used to construct three-dimensional materials. I have included a few books on *Cheap Math Lab Equipment, Teacher-Made Materials* and the like in Key Publications for those who would like to explore these possibilities further.

All of these materials—computers, calculators, games, manipulatives, and free items—have one thing in common: they succeed in relating math to the real world. So do books like Marilyn Burns' *The I Hate Mathematics! Book* (Boston: Little, Brown and Co., 1975) and the comic-book-style calculus primers which are best-sellers on college campuses.

Another way of tying materials to the real world is to select at least some materials from outside educational sources. Grocery store bottles and liquor bottles, for example, often have metric contents, as does some cooking equipment purchased from gourmet shops, or science equipment purchased from science supply houses. The agencies of the federal government that have the responsibility for our transition to the metric system are good sources for charts and other metric information to support the tangible units that are the first choice for teaching metrics. Other "free or inexpensive" lists can be consulted for materials from outside sources.

TYPES OF MATERIALS

Like science, math is both abstract (inferential) and concrete (specific). On Dale's Cone of Experience, the most suitable teaching materials—by research and common sense—are direct experiences and pictorial materials; flat and, especially, three-dimensional visual materials are vitally important for math concepts, but printed materials are the usual teaching mode. Some (by no means all) appropriate materials are listed below.

MATERIALS NEEDED IN MATH

Direct experiences (for concrete manifestations of concepts)

Materials for construction of models and other aids (e.g., string, cardboard, egg and milk cartons, paper, wood, pebbles, ping-pong balls, etc.)

Materials for measurement (e.g., weights, volumes, rulers, strings, scales, containers, pendulums—for time, clocks, metric measures, calipers)

Outdoor math materials (e.g., compasses, sextants, transits, trundle wheels, other measuring devices, binoculars, topographic maps, cameras, notebooks)

Geometric models, of prisms, pyramids, cones, spheres, polyhedrons (and paper and patterns for creating more)

Tiles, cubes, pegboards, geo-boards, tangrams, etc., Cuisinaire rods, attribute blocks, stacking metric weights

Demonstration slide rules and practice rules

Calculators, computers

Demonstration models

Manipulatives

Tops, blocks, balls and other math toys (*see* chapter on toys in *Media and the Curriculum*)

Math games and simulations (e.g., card games, dominoes, number cubes, simulation exercises, math games from other cultures, three-dimensional tic-tac-toe)

Math puzzles

Pictorial materials
Charts, graphs, visual models, diagrams (materials for charting and graphing)

Posters, photographs

Math art materials

Media materials (mostly visual and symbolic modes)
Possibly television, films, filmstrips, slides, transparencies

Printed materials (visual, symbolic, and verbal for exposition of concepts and for exercises)
Textbooks

Supplementary texts and workbooks

Reference books (including dictionaries, histories, tables)

Pamphlets on math careers (including computer careers)

Pamphlets on applications (water meters, etc.)

Periodicals

Curriculum guides and idea books

Trade books, including math puzzles, fun math, math comic books

Printed realia (e.g., checkbooks, income tax forms, credit applications, newspaper ads, car insurance calculations, batting averages, stock market quotations).

Criteria (and references) for manipulatives, games and pictorial media are highly relevant in selecting materials.

INTERDISCIPLINARY MATHEMATICS

To broaden selection and increase interest, look for materials (in all media) in areas where mathematics overlaps with other curriculum areas. Trade books, posters, and other pictorial sources are probably the most easily located. Some possibilities for each area of mathematics are:

Mathematics (overall) — music, science, decorative art

Graphs and Charts — all subjects

Measurement — carpentry, metal shop, home economics, cooking, outdoor education, environmental studies, drama (set construction), science, history (navigation, exploration, travel)

Geometry — art, architecture, engineering, history, environmental studies

Trigonometry — science, history (navigation, earth size, etc.), logic, games

Number Systems — history (Arabs, French Revolution, metrics, etc.), logic, games

Statistics—all subjects, especially sciences, social studies, environmental education, sports, humanities

Applied Math—daily life experiences, driver education, sports, computer math, consumer math, and others

Calculators and Computers—all subjects, including applied math, business, social studies, science, games

Chronology—history, futurology, biology, geology, time charts

Games and Puzzles—play, art, music, chess, cross-cultural math games and puzzles, weaving, sports.

As mathematics has—potentially, at least—many roles and appeals, math materials (in all media) should reflect major aspects of mathematics. Before looking for and selecting new materials, it might be advisable to survey existing materials (at all locations) in your school or school district to see if materials are available that, collectively, address all the concerns below, as well as others deemed significant in your location. The selection criteria printed below can be used for scanning new materials as well.

CONSIDERATIONS IN SELECTING MATH MATERIALS IN ALL MEDIA

	Estimation of materials			
	none	poor	fair	good
Supportive of required math curriculum				
Related to other course materials				
Addresses student needs and interests				
Appropriate for student background and readiness in math processes				
Relevant to real life problems (preferably those that interest students)				
Significant for math's role in culture and/or history (e.g., computers in today's technology)				
Emphasizes math's logical structure				
Potentially valuable in fostering or inspiring desirable skills and/or attitudes, e.g.,				
creativity				
imagination				
open-mindedness				
problem solving				
accuracy				
order				
logical thinking				
deduction				
_____				
_____				

One rather interesting local set of mathematics selection criteria is that of New York City, which suggests that materials for grades one through six should be evaluated in terms of the following criteria in addition to the course of study:

- developing topics in a meaningful way
- providing a variety of well-illustrated experiences reflecting the daily lives of children in a large city
- providing materials to supplement the experiences developed in the classroom
- challenging pupils' thinking in problem solving
- providing for practice through experiences rather than through isolated drill on number facts

Additionally, materials should be as non-sexist as possible. Every survey so far of math textbooks and problems indicates that the illustrations and specific problems are overwhelmingly biased toward males. These may or may not contribute to girls' lesser achievements in math after the age of nine.

THINKING AND PROCESS FACTORS

The process skills listed on page 15 in the chapter on science are generally relevant for math also. Process skills considered most specific for math are: analysis, explication, divergent thinking, reformulation (generalization and implication), use of axiomatic systems, and redefinition and extension of systems. The inquiry approach in math emphasizes the intellectual skills of observing, describing, classifying, comparing, ordering, measuring, symbolizing, representing, graphing, and communicating. The materials chosen should provide opportunities for developing and using these skills. Hands-on and pictorial materials are most appropriate for inquiry.

Though process skills are not always easy to convert into behavioral objectives, several other skill-retrieval classification systems, such as those listed in the chapters on special education and on commercial retrieval systems in *Issues and Policies*, do retrieve math materials and exercises and translate math skills into objectives.

Piaget is the psychologist most influential in math curricula (see the references to Piaget in the chapter on cognitive criteria in *Issues and Policies*); Copeland's article in this chapter's further reading specifically applies Piaget to math. The Guilford Structure of Intellect model is also relevant for math; in fact, one of Mary Meeker's SOI *Workbooks* discussed in the same chapter is on *Mathematics*. Some followers of Thurstone used mental math or rapid math exercises (which need not require materials) to raise intelligence quotients.

TEXTBOOKS: USE AND SELECTION

The NACOME survey, unlike many, actually surveyed the means of instruction as well as the classroom time spent on mathematics per day (43 minutes per day on a weighted average time). It confirmed that the major means of teaching was the textbook. Fifty-six percent of the teacher-respondents used a single text; 26 percent used one predominantly among two or more. Only 7 percent used none. The use of multiple texts increased with the grade. About 70 percent of teachers found their texts relatively new and fairly satisfactory; 42 percent preferred texts that emphasized skills over contents; 48 percent preferred equal emphasis; while a meager 2 percent preferred texts emphasizing concepts over skills.

Though 53 percent of teachers followed their texts closely, most teachers reported that students actually read less than one page, or at most one or two pages, out of five. To students, texts are primarily a source of problems and abstract exercises. For most students in most classes, math textbooks do not provide opportunities for concrete instructional activities, independent learning, discovery learning, individualized instruction, problem-solving exercises, or anything of much interest. They are simply — for many students — extremely hard to use.

As a reference librarian and parent, I would rate the average indexing of definitions and glossaries as confusing and unhelpful. At a minimum, definitions should be locatable through an index, while terms in glossaries should be keyed to examples in the text. The glossary itself should be easily located through an index and through the table of contents.

Myron L. Coulter's "Reading in Mathematics" [in *Reading in the Content Areas* (Newark, DE: International Reading Association, 1972)] analyzed arithmetic texts and commented on some other problem areas common to many texts. Aside from their organization, their unique and difficult vocabularies and the need to acquire new systems of symbols, the language itself provides many difficulties. According to Coulter:

> The language of the elementary school arithmetic materials may present a greater challenge to many students than the quantitative expressions, concepts and operations which are to be mastered.... Another factor which affects readability is the improperly written verbal problem. Many poorly phrased problems have been written into widely used materials with the unfortunate result that students are forced to either ignore the imprecision or "fill in" the unintentionally missing language. Critical reading ability can be a handicap in this instance.

Some recent texts, attempting to bypass reading difficulties, are considerably better organized and are very easy to read, but are low in concepts and rely heavily on drill and repetition. Though they are more comprehensible, they attempt to teach very little; however, while they are boring, they are apt to be more successful with these limited ends.

PARENTAL ROLE IN SELECTION

As a parent I have had to listen over the years to three children complaining bitterly — and for the most part justifiably — about their mathematics texts. As a consequence I am now a strong advocate of formalized parental and student input as well as input by other non-mathematicians (possibly English teachers and reading consultants) into the selection of these texts. Far better liaison is needed between school and parents vis-a-vis math materials. Math teachers, after all, have their experience and their teachers' editions. Parents, like their children, are facing the bare texts.

When I followed up my children's complaints by looking at their texts, I found these illogically arranged, racing from one topic to another; explanations and definitions tended to be unclear, misplaced, hard to understand, and often redundant, even while omitting key points. They were usually under-indexed or even mis-indexed. Graphics were underused, misplaced, and misused. Some explanations—of simple topics like ratio—were utterly incomprehensible to me, even though I had gone through college calculus with A's. Examples and problems were often confusing and usually far removed from experience, though better ones could have been devised easily. Ratio, for example, was not correlated in my son's text with either fractions or decimals, and the text overlooked sure bets like batting averages and gambling.

All three of my children—like millions of others—have had to put far too many hours of work into math homework. Teachers' editions of math workbooks and homework assignments need to incorporate realistic appraisals of the ranges of time needed for assignments so that teachers will not discount student complaints as exaggerations.

Parents have other complaints ranging from the exclusion of important topics to the parent-instigated crusade against the promotion of real-life junk foods in math texts. Some of the problems would be resolved if alternate texts and materials were available for different children and if testing instruments for math placement were more discerning or more widely used.

My children, for instance, though certainly intelligent, were not particularly gifted in math, but were placed in advanced math because of general intelligence scores. My daughter, who handles theory better than computations, would probably benefit greatly from using concrete materials.

Project TORQUE has a unique method of validating its new tests for mathematics by comparing student performance on tests with student performance on games and hands-on activities that approximate real-life uses of math. Their tests were designed to:

- assess the skills teachers, parents, and researchers think important
- motivate children's best efforts
- identify specific strengths and weaknesses of individual children
- allow school systems to monitor overall progress
- treat children as individuals instead of comparing them to one another
- respect children's diverse cultural and linguistic backgrounds
- inform parents about their child's learning

These criteria seem appropriate for math materials as well.

Craig Pearson's article in *Learning* [v. 5, no. 8 (April 1977), pp. 30-37] discusses these tests further. Additional information is available from Educational Development Center (EDC), 55 Chapel St., Newton, MA 02160.

According to studies, students using manipulative materials and pictorial aids enjoy math more and learn better, in less time. For example, some studies showed that students who worked with math manipulatives and/or in mathematical laboratories scored as well on achievement tests as students who had 20 percent more time with traditional instruction. Marilyn Suydam's *Activity-Based Learning in Elementary School Mathematics: Recommendations from Research*, annotated under the ERIC Clearinghouse for Science, Mathematics, and Environmental Education, provides a most thorough review of research on this topic.

In "Considerations for Teaching Using Manipulative Materials," a chapter in *Teacher-Made Aids for Elementary School Mathematics* (Reston, VA: National Council of Teachers of Mathematics), Robert Reys listed some common reasons for using math manipulatives. The list below is adapted from his:

- to vary instructional materials
- to provide experiences in actual problem-solving situations
- to provide concrete representations of abstract ideas
- to provide a basis for analyzing sensory data (an essential in concept formation)
- to provide an opportunity to discern relationships and formulate generalizations
- to provide active participation by pupils
- to provide for individual differences
- to increase motivation for learning in general (not for a single mathematics topic)

These materials may be particularly important for children — such as most children in remedial math classes — whose modes of learning are not abstract and verbal. Appropriately, special education catalogs often include well-designed, interesting and relatively inexpensive math manipulatives. The brightly-colored tactile manipulatives intended for visually-handicapped and blind children particularly seem to provide a great deal of concept reinforcement. These can be located through catalogs of such organizations as the American Printing House for the Blind.

The pedagogical and physical criteria for manipulatives below are slightly shortened and adapted from Robert Reys's article, "Considerations for Teachers Using Manipulative Materials," in *Teacher-Made Aids for Elementary School Mathematics*, and are printed here with the kind permission of the National Council of Mathematics and the author. They would seem to be appropriate for pictorial media and metric tangibles as well.

CRITERIA FOR MATH MANIPULATIVES

Pedagogical Considerations:

1) Materials should provide a true embodiment of the mathematical concept or ideas being explored (they should be mathematically appropriate)
2) Materials should represent the mathematical concept clearly (without extraneous distractors)
3) Materials should be motivating (with favorable physical characteristics such as attractiveness and simplicity)
4) Materials should be multipurpose, *if possible* (e.g., logic or attribute blocks)
   - for different grade levels, and/or different levels of concept formation
   - for more than one concept
5) Materials should provide a basis for abstraction (the level of abstraction should be commensurate with the student's ability to abstract)
6) Materials should provide for individual manipulation (preferably using several senses, e.g., visual, aural, tactile and kinesthetic)

Physical Considerations

1) Durability
   - strong enough to withstand normal use
   - maintenance should be readily available and reasonable if needed

2) Attractiveness
   - aesthetically pleasing design
   - precise construction
   - durable, smooth (colorful) finish
3) Simplicity of operation (should not require time-consuming inventories or maintenance)
4) Size
   - designed for children's physical competencies
   - easy to manipulate
   - proportioned to scale or to avoid distorted mental images or misconceptions
5) Cost factors
   - should cover initial expenditure, life expectancy, maintenance, and replacement factors, plus time teachers need to learn how to use materials effectively

In deciding whether to make or buy materials, Reys says:

> Many manipulative materials are relatively easy to make and can often be produced by the teacher and/or pupils. There are many priceless, intangible by-products, such as additional mathematical insight and increased motivation, that result directly from classroom projects. Nevertheless, one should weigh production costs for homemade materials, including labor, materials, and so on, against the cost of similar commercial products. Quality, of course, is another consideration. Frequently there is a marked difference in quality between homemade and commercially produced materials.

KEY ORGANIZATIONS

Some Key Organizations listed under science cover mathematics as well. Some organizations that serve as math information sources or provide free materials on mathematics are listed in the National Council of Teachers of Mathematics' publication, *Free Materials for the Teaching of Mathematics*. Some teachers' centers, listed in the *Teachers' Centers' Exchange Directory*, specialize in mathematics workshops and materials. Organizations listed under "Commercial Retrieval Systems" in *Issues and Policies* usually have means of retrieving math materials for specific purposes, as do some listed in the chapter on special education in that book.

Activity Resources Company, Inc.
P.O. Box 4875
Hayward, CA 94540   (415) 782-1300
This is a publisher, developer and distribution center for inexpensive, activity-oriented, classroom materials, mostly in mathematics. Some were originally developed and published by Activity Resources; others were first published elsewhere. A free catalog is available.

American National Metric Council
1625 Massachusetts Ave., NW
Washington, DC 20036   (202) 232-4545

This national professional organization for planning and coordinating voluntary metrication, publishes a biweekly newsletter, the *Metric Reporter*, which covers all aspects of metrication including education. It is a membership organization, with special rates for educators and guidelines for metric materials. Some publications particularly relevant for education are its *Metric Guide for Educational Materials* and *The Metric System from Day to Day* (quantity discounts available). Write for their free publications brochure.

ERIC Clearinghouse for Science, Mathematics, and Environmental Education (ERIC/SMEAC)

Ohio State University
1200 Chambers Road, Room 310
Columbus, OH 43212   (614) 422-6717

Dr. Marilyn Suydam heads the Mathematics Education division of ERIC/SMEAC, described more fully under science. The staff of this division, in addition to answering questions, processing documents and editing manuscripts, is actively involved in PRISM, Priorities in School Mathematics, an ongoing project of the National Council of Teachers of Mathematics, which surveys mathematics education to obtain reactions about what is and what should be in math education.

Dr. Suydam is also the director of the NIE Calculator Information Center, founded in 1978 and housed at the same address. The CIC is collecting information on calculator use and preparing and disseminating various reference and information bulletins and other publications on calculators.

Some available publications of the Calculator Information Center include:

Reference Bulletins:

Instruction K-12 (annotated, No. 19)

Books K-12 (No. 20)

Research K-12 (annotated, No. 21)

Information Bulletins:

Types of Calculators, by Jon Higgins (No. 1)

Suggestions for Calculator Selection, by Marilyn Suydam (No. 3)

Calculators and Instruction: An Information Bulletin for Administrators, by Mary Harley Jones and R. C. Bosley

Leading a Calculator Workshop, by Jane D. Gawronski (No. 5)

Calculations in Grade K-3: Why? What? How?, by Therese Denman (No. 6)

Investigations with Calculators, edited by Marilyn Suydam, 1979

State-of-Art Review on Calculators, by Marilyn Suydam, 1978

Some current ERIC publications in math, not priced as of date of writing, are:

Bilingual Materials for Mathematics, by James Lovett and Ted Snyder

Problem-Solving Modes, edited by Gerald Goldine and Edwin McClintock

Compilation of References on Calculators, edited by Marilyn Suydam

Models for Mathematics Learning, edited by William Geeslin

Some older relevant priced publications are listed below.

Teaching Resources for Low-Achieving Mathematics Classes, by Kenneth J. Travers and others. July 1971. 66p. $1.80. offset. (ED 053 980).
Reviews teaching approaches and general resource materials for low achievers in elementary and secondary classes, with two bibliographies of references and resource materials.

Use of Computers in Mathematics Education Resource Series: Computer Innovations in Education, by Andrew R. Molnar. Feb. 1973. 87p. $2.35 offset. (ED 077 731).
Discusses computer impact, systems and languages, instructional applications, the design of computer-oriented curriculum, and cost-effectiveness.

Ability and Creativity in Mathematics, by Lewis R. Aiken, Jr. April 1973. 50p. $1.80 offset. (ED 077 730).
Reviews correlations between intelligence, achievement, age, sex, heredity, psychosocial factors and math creativity.

Recent Research in Cognition Applied to Mathematics Learning, by M. C. Wittrock. April 1973. 37p. $1.80 offset. (ED 077 773).

Evaluation in the Mathematics Classroom: From What and Why to How and Where, by Marilyn N. Suydam. Jan. 1974. 70p. $2.35 offset. (ED 086 517).
Many helpful suggestions for classroom teachers, with annotated source lists of mathematics evaluations and tests.

Cognitive Psychology and the Mathematics Laboratory, edited by Richard Lesh. 1974. 149p. $3.55 offset. (ED 108 893).
Deals with issues and problems on concrete embodiments of mathematics ideas, applications of such ideas, computer activities, and diagnosing student errors.

Mathematics Laboratories: Implementation, Research and Evaluation, by William M. Fitzgerald and Jon L. Higgins. Nov. 1974. 81p. $2.35 offset. (ED 102 021).

Mathematics Laboratories: 150 Activities and Games for Elementary Schools, by Jon L. Higgins and Larry A. Sachs. Dec. 1974. 207p. $4.50 offset. (ED 104 720).
150 activities and games grouped into eight sections dealing with number concepts, addition and subtraction, multiplication and division, number skills review, measurement, fractions, graphs and functions, geometric concepts.

Materials for Metric Instruction, by Gary R. Bitter and Charles Geer. Aug. 1975. 85p. $2.20 offset. (ED 115 488).
Compilation of metric kits, task cards, filmstrips, films, slides and assorted metric materials intended as a quick reference. Includes for each item the source, cost, learning level, and a brief description.

Activity-Based Learning in Elementary School Mathematics: Recommendations from Research, by Marilyn N. Suydam and Jon L. Higgins. Sept. 1977. 178p. $3.85 offset. (ED 144 840).

Competent summary of activities-based teaching approaches, including the use of manipulative materials. It concludes that lessons using manipulatives are more likely to produce greater mathematical achievement; manipulatives and pictorial representations are highly effective; symbolic treatments are less effective. This holds true with children from all ability levels, age levels and socioeconomic levels.

Recent Research Concerning the Development of Spatial and Geometric Concepts, by Richard Lesh and Diane Mierkiewicz. 1978. 352p. $6.60 offset.

Fourteen papers reporting recent research on the development of geometric ideas in children and adults, arranged according to Piagetian stages.

National Bureau of Standards
Office of Weights and Measures
Washington, DC 20234   (301) 921-2401
    Actual location: Quince Orchard and Cloppers (Rte 124) Rds.
                     Gaithersburg, MD

This governmental organization is responsible for maintaining the technical correctness of metric informational and educational materials. As such, it has a library on metric teaching materials, publishes a variety of materials on the metric system, and answers inquiries about the metric system and the teaching of metrics.

Its publication holdings include textbooks and other teaching materials on metrics, as well as publications of other governments undergoing metrication, such as the British Metrication Board, the Canadian Metric Commission, and the Australian Metric Conversion Board.

Its publications — generally available free in single copies to educators — include: *Some References on Metric Information, Brief History of Measurement Systems*, and *All You Will Need to Know about Metric*, as well as metric charts, assorted pamphlets and others.

Its free information services include reviewing drafts of educational materials on metrics, reference services, and advisory services.

National Council of Teachers of Mathematics (NCTM)
1906 Association Drive
Reston, VA 22091   (703) 620-9840

The NCTM, an affiliate of the NEA, may be the best single source of information on instructional materials in mathematics. It is a professional membership organization for teachers ($15.00/year) dedicated to improving classroom instruction at all levels.

Through its services and publications, it functions as a forum for discussing, sharing, and evaluating experiences, materials, approaches and trends in mathematics instruction.

Its headquarters offices in Reston, Virginia — open 8:15 a.m. to 4:45 p.m. Mondays through Fridays — include a mathematics library with comprehensive catalogs and displays of mathematical teaching aids.

The official journals of the NCTM, the *Arithmetic Teacher* (elementary) and the *Mathematics Teacher* (secondary), are probably the best sources of information on all facets of mathematics education. Published monthly during the school year, they include articles, advertising lists and reviews of textbooks and other educational materials, which collectively are rather comprehensive indicators of currently-available materials. The review columns in *Arithmetic Teacher* include one for "Metric Materials" and a miscellaneous "Etcetera." *Mathematics Teacher* has a "New Products" column in addition to reviews. Both journals (the appropriate one is included in each NCTM membership) have annual indexes, while cumulative indexes can be obtained from NCTM.

NCTM also provides separate guides or information sheets to resource materials on topics like metrication, microcalculators, mathematics careers, free materials, and similar topics. These change from time to time, but currently include: *Minicalculator Information Resources* (8p., regularly updated), *Free Materials for the Teaching of Mathematics* (5p.), and *NCTM Metrication Update and Guide to Suppliers of Metric Materials.*

Its publications include an outstanding yearbook series dealing comprehensively with major topics in mathematics of current or permanent importance. For example, its current (1978) yearbook, *Developing Computation Skills*, covers teaching of computation including chapters on diagnosis and assessment, estimation, mental arithmetic, and the use of calculators in teaching computation. Other publications (a complete list is available on request) deal with topics ranging from teaching and studying techniques to do-it-yourself computation, to bibliographies, compilations, math classics, and puzzles.

Some publications dealing with particular types of mathematics materials include:

Bulletin Board Ideas for Elementary and Middle School Mathematics. 1977. 82 photos. 56p. $3.60.

The Overhead Projector in the Mathematics Classroom, by George Lencher 1974. 32p. $1.80.

A rather sophisticated approach to using the overhead projector, with many color illustrations and an extensive bibliography.

Minicalculators in the Classroom, by Joseph R. Caravella (NEA). 1977. 64p. $3.50.

Posters from the Arithmetic Teacher. 9 posters. $2.00.

Imaginative, thought-provoking posters for the elementary classroom; each measures 28.5x36.5 cm.

Other publications worth noting are:

Instructional Aids in Mathematics. 1973. 442p. $17.00.

An illustrated guide to instructional aids, a basis for evaluating their quality and utility, and suggestions for their use as well as ideas for their construction.

Historical Topics for the Mathematics Classroom. 1969. 524p. $14.00.

A substantial treatment of the use of mathematics history in the teaching of mathematics.

Organizing for Mathematics Instruction. 1977. 256p. $10.00.

Discusses alternative teaching approaches such as individualization, survival groups, simulations, and open schools. Emphasizes how to organize for such approaches, deals with all levels of instruction, and gives specific illustrative examples. A non-thematic essay on hand-held calculators is included.

A Bibliography of Recreational Mathematics, by William Schaaf. 1970.
   Vol. 1, 148p.; Vol. 2, 191p.; Vol. 3, 187p. $6.50 each.
   Volumes 1 and 2 list the best of the literature up to 1970. Volume 3
(1973) updates the material and includes classroom games, recreational
activities and a glossary.

Going Metric: Guidelines for the Mathematics Teacher, Grades K-8, by
   Walter W. Leffin. 1975. 48p. $2.50.
   A timely new guide for teachers, giving a history of the metric system.
Discusses the major units, with tips for teaching them. Suggests classroom
activities, with recommended materials and instructions for student-made
learning aids.

NCTM's free catalog — available on request — is a useful buying source for math
laboratories, classroom teachers and libraries. (Some other publications are
annotated independently in this sourcebook.)

KEY PUBLICATIONS

Some of the publications of the National Council of Teachers of
Mathematics are listed here; others are described in the listing in Key Organizations. Most selection aids offered by the ERIC Clearinghouse are also included in
the listing for that organization.

Other sources for mathematics selection aids are teachers' centers —
especially those concerned with mathematics — and professional mathematics
groups, which sometimes hold local workshops on materials. Several educational
publishing houses, most notably Creative Publications (P.O. Box 10328, Palo
Alto, CA 94303) and The Math Group (396 E. 79th St., Minneapolis, MN 55420),
specialize in high-quality math materials. Current catalogs are best for these.
Government agencies and professional groups are good sources on metrication
and math careers.

The printed aids listed here can help in both selecting materials and thinking
through problems related to selection.

Analysis of Elementary School Mathematics Materials. New York: Educational
   Products Information Exchange Institute, 1975. 128p. $20.00. (*EPIE Report*
   69/70).
   This *EPIE Product Report* explains EPIE's method of analyzing instructional materials, applies it to analyzing 32 elementary-school math programs, and
presents conclusions from a readability survey of some major math programs.

A *Supplement to EPIE Report No. 69/70*, prepared especially for California
schools with the cooperation of the San Mateo County Office of Education (Red-
wood City, CA, 1975. 95p.), uses the EPIE format to describe supplementary
math materials approved for use in California schools — including materials for
individualized programs, calculator math, laboratory math, manipulatives, and
metrics.

Catalog of Metric Instructional Materials, compiled by Metric Studies Center, American Institutes for Research. Palo Alto, CA, 1974. $1.50 prepaid; $2.00 if billing is requested. (From P.O. Box 1113, Palo Alto, CA 94302).

This catalog integrates the metric instructional materials of 41 suppliers under seven major headings, with descriptions of their significant features.

Cheap Math Lab Equipment, by Donald A. Buckeye and others. Troy, MI: Midwest Publications, Inc., 1972. 119p. $5.95pa. (From P.O. Box 129, Troy, MI 48099).

Demonstrates ways to stock a mathematics laboratory or an individual learning center with low-cost materials that can be made by teachers, students, or parents. Includes plans and materials lists for 27 items that can be used from first grade to senior high school to teach place value, fundamental operations, number patterns, geometry, mathematical systems, logic, and strategy.

The Compleat Computer, by D. Van Tassel. Palo Alto, CA: Science Research Associates, 1976. 216p. $6.98.

An entertaining, diverse and mind-expanding book that can serve as a structure for organizing a computer literacy course.

Computer Applications in Instruction: A Teacher's Guide to Selection and Use, by Northwest Regional Educational Laboratory. Portland, OR: Northwest Regional Educational Laboratory, 1978. Not yet priced. (From Office of Marketing, Northwest Regional Educational Laboratory, 710 SW Second Ave., Portland, OR 97204).

This guide, designed to inform teachers on the rudiments of computers, includes information on computer hardware, programming languages, ways to use computers in instruction, and ways to evaluate and use computer application materials in the classroom. It includes illustrations, program listings, printouts, and a bibliography, as well as two short simulation units ("Energy" and "CRIMEX").

Curriculum Development in Elementary Mathematics, by Kathleen Devaney and Lorraine Thorn. San Francisco: Far West Laboratory for Educational Research and Development, 1974. $7.95.

Provides overviews, content focus, classroom actions, costs of implementation, evaluation, date developed, source, etc. for nine elementary mathematics curricula, eight developed with U.S. government financing and one by the Nuffield Mathematics Project in England. A helpful guide and comparison model for elementary educators choosing mathematics curricula.

The Fabric of Mathematics, by Mary Laycock and Gene Watson. Rev. ed. Hayward, CA: Activity Resources, 1975. 300p. $15.75.

For each concept, this conceptually-organized resource book provides definitions, objectives, assessments, and learning levels (grades K-9) and incorporates manipulatives, activities, games, and student and teacher references, using only materials that have been examined by the authors, who have a national reputation as math educators. One-hundred pages of appendixes include descriptions and prices of commercial games, manipulatives and activities, as well as information on teacher- or student-made items that can be substituted for these commercial items, plus an annotated list of visuals, a directory of publishers, an annotated list of 200 books on mathematics for students and teachers, a sample assessment checklist, and an index.

This new edition has been completely reorganized and revised; new features are a helpful glossary and "Quick (start-up) Activities."

Games and Puzzles for Elementary and Middle-School Mathematics: Readings from the Arithmetic Teacher, edited by Seaton E. Smith and Carl A. Backman. Reston, VA: National Council of Teachers of Mathematics, 1975. 280p. $6.50; $5.85 members.

Includes more than 100 articles on using games and puzzles in mathematics instruction. Uses include teaching whole numbers, numerations, integers, rational numbers, number theory, patterns, geometry, measurement, logic, and reasoning.

Going Metric: Guidelines for the Mathematics Teacher, Grades K-8, by Walter W. Leffin. Reston, VA: National Council of Teachers of Mathematics, 1975. 48p. $2.50; $2.25 members.

This teacher's guide includes a history of the metric system, tips for teaching the major units, recommendations for materials, instructions for student-made learning aids, and classroom activities.

A Guide to Teaching about Computers in Secondary Schools, by Donald D. Spencer. Ormond Beach, FL: Camelot, 1973. 138p. $12.95.

The three sections of this book deal respectively with curriculum, teaching methods, and administrative uses of computers, with considerable information on teaching strategies, materials and textbooks. The book is intended for practitioner-educators and assumes some knowledge of the subject field.

The I Hate Mathematics! Book, by Marilyn Burns; illustrated by Martha Hairston. Boston: Little, Brown and Co., 1975. 127p. $3.95.

Uses observation and inquiry (on subjects such as sidewalks, shoelaces and toilet-paper cylinders) and mathematical tricks and riddles to introduce complex concepts to children over nine. This is one book in the *Brown Paper School* series by a group of California teachers, writers and artists who prepare books "for kids and grownups to learn from together," which generally combine fun and humor with concepts.

Instructional Aids in Mathematics: 34th Yearbook, by National Council of Teachers of Mathematics. Reston, VA: NCTM, 1973. 442p. $17.00.

This well-illustrated guide is particularly valuable for classroom teachers. It covers criteria for selecting and evaluating many kinds of mathematical instructional aids, including textbooks, other print materials, models, manipulative devices, computers and teaching machines, and projective devices. Its discussion incorporates information on relevant educational objectives, historic backgrounds, and means of construction.

Learning to Think in a Math Lab, by Manon P. Charbonneau. Boston: National Association of Independent Schools, 1971. 51p., plus unpaged section. $2.50.

This book includes a great deal of information on some materials used in math labs, such as scale models, scale drawings, maps, topographic maps, geoboards, shapes, tiles, Cuisinaire rods, kitchen materials, measuring systems, metric materials, thermometers, etc., with interesting comments on how to introduce different materials and what children can be expected to learn from them.

Materials for Individualizing Math Instruction. New York: Educational Products Information Exchange Institute, 1974. 68p. $10.00. (*EPIE Report* No. 65).

In-depth analyses and annotations for 26 sets of commercial materials for grades 1 to 9. It also outlines the distinguishing characteristics of three major models of individualization (traditional, diagnostic, and multiple), demonstrating how certain mathematics materials have been designed to facilitate one or more of these models.

The Math Teaching Handbook, by Persis Joan Herold. Newton, MA: Selective Educational Equipment, 1976. $12.90. (From 3 Bridge St., Newton, MA 01195).

This book, somewhat like *The Fabric of Mathematics*, includes tips and information on materials and teaching in a conceptual framework. Its appendix includes a "typical mathematics course for K-6" compiled from school administrators in 50 states, a glossary, a bibliography, a list of publishers and equipment suppliers, and an index.

Mathematics Projects Handbook, by Adrien L. Hess. Reston, VA: National Council of Teachers of Mathematics, 1977. 48p. $2.00; $1.80 members.

Useful guide for junior and senior high teachers and students for choosing or developing projects; includes an extensive bibliography.

Minicalculators in the Classroom, by Joseph R. Caravella. Washington, DC: National Education Association, 1977. 64p. $3.50. (Also available from National Council of Teachers of Mathematics).

Explores the positive contribution of minicalculators for basic education and offers guidelines for their selection and use.

Teacher-Made Aids for Elementary School Mathematics: Readings from the Arithmetic Teacher, edited by Seaton E. Smith and Carl A. Backman. Reston, VA: National Council of Teachers of Mathematics, 1974. 186p. $5.00.

This book as a whole explores the use of manipulative materials, activities, games, and puzzles in teaching mathematics for understanding whole numbers, numeration, integers, rational numbers, measurement, and geometry. Articles are grouped by these concepts although, of course, many of these aids have multiple applications. The first section, "Teaching Aids: What, How and Why," has three valuable discussions on the appropriate selection and use of teaching aids; Robert E. Reys discusses "what" and provides guidelines and criteria; Allen Bernstein offers criteria and examples ("how"); and Elizabeth H. Fennema in "Models and Mathematics" explains "why." The last chapter on multi-purpose aids has articles on pegboards, child-created games, bulletin boards, mathematics laboratory, and the mathematical functions of charts.

FOR FURTHER READING

*Items marked with an asterisk have further criteria or priorities for mathematics instructional materials.

+ Items marked with a plus have substantial lists of references.

Ahl, David H. *Getting Started in Classroom Computing*. Maynard, MA: Digital Equipment Corp., 1976.

+ Ashley, Ruth. *Background Math for a Computer World*. New York: Wiley, 1973.

Baker, Justine. *Computers in the Curriculum*. Bloomington, IN: Phi Delta Kappa Educational Foundation, 1976. (Fastback 82).

Carpenter, Thomas P., and others. "Results and Implications of the NAEP Mathematics Assessment: Elementary School," *Arithmetic Teacher*, v. 22, no. 6 (Oct. 1975), pp. 438-50.

*Conference Board of the Mathematical Sciences (CBMS) Committee on Computer Education. *Recommendations Regarding Computers in High School Education*. Washington, DC: CBMS, 1972.

Copeland, Richard W. *How Children Learn Mathematics: Teaching Implications of Piaget's Research*. London: Collier-Macmillan, 1970.
Includes a series of teacher-child interviews that serve as a model for discerning what a child knows or is ready to learn.

*Coulter, Myron R. "Reading in Mathematics: Classroom Applications," pp. 95-125 in James L. Laffey's *Reading in the Content Areas* (Newark, DE: International Reading Association, 1972).
Detailed analyses of problems (with some solutions) for elementary mathematics textbooks.

* + Duker, Sam. *Individualized Instruction in Mathematics*. Metuchen, NJ: Scarecrow Press, 1972.

Glennon, Vincent J. "Mathematics: How Firm the Foundation?" *Phi Delta Kappan*, v. 57, no. 5 (Jan. 1976), pp. 302-305.

Hill, Shirley, and others. "Overview and Analysis of School Mathematics, Grades K-12: Issues from the NACOME Report," *Mathematics Teacher*, v. 76, no. 6 (Oct. 1976), pp. 440-68.
Articles by Morris Kline, Ross Taylor and Harold Trimble comment on the NACOME report vis-a-vis revising mathematics curriculum and clarifying the principles of mathematics learning.

Holtz, Michael, and Zoltan Dienes. *Let's Play Math*. New York: Walker & Co., 1973.
Includes suggestions for many materials that can be made at home or in school.

Huff, Darrell. *How to Lie with Statistics*. New York: Norton, 1954.

Johnson, Donovan A. *Paper Folding for the Mathematics Class*. Reston, VA: National Council of Teachers of Mathematics, 1957.

*Kennedy, Leonard M., and Ruth Michon. *Games for Individualizing Mathematics Learning*. New York: Merrill, 1973.
Good introductory chapter on making, storing, and using games. The book as a whole is a well-organized overview of a variety of math games for many purposes, and it provides performance objectives for games dealing with the meaning of numbers, operations, measurement, geometry, probability, and logic.

Lazarus, Mitchell. "Elementary Math and Common Sense," *The Common: A Meeting Place for Education in New England*, Dec. 1977. Reprinted in *EDC News*, Issue 10, pp. 8-9, Fall 1977.

Merrill, Arthur A. *How Do You Use a Slide Rule?* New York: Dover, 1961.

* + National Advisory Committee on Mathematical Education. *Overview and Analysis of School Mathematics, Grades K-12*. Reston, VA: National Council of Teachers of Mathematics, 1975.

National Council of Teachers of Mathematics. *Historical Topics for the Mathematics Classroom*. Reston, VA: National Council of Teachers of Mathematics, 1969.

Nuffield Mathematics Project. *Computers and Young Children*. New York, Wiley, 1972.

Nuffield Mathematics Project. *Pictorial Representation*. New York: Wiley, 1967.

*Pearson, Craig. "Teaching Arithmetic Is More Than Marking 'Right' or 'Wrong'," *Learning*, v. 5, no. 8 (April 1977), pp. 30-37.
Discusses uses and abuses of math tests and the discriminatory criteria of Project TORQUE's tests.

Pederson, Jean J., and Kent Pederson. *Geometric Playthings*. San Francisco: Troubador Press, 1973.

* + Raab, Joseph A. *Audiovisual Materials in Mathematics*. Reston, VA: National Council of Teachers of Mathematics, 1971.

Reys, Robert E. "Comsumer Math: Just How Knowledgeable Are U.S. Young Adults?" *Phi Delta Kappan*, v. 58, no. 3 (Nov. 1976), pp. 258-60.

Rucker, Walter, and Clyde Dilley. *Math Card Games*. Palo Alto, CA: Creative Publications, 1974.

*Rutherford, Millicent. "Some Suggestions for How to Quit Spending in Bars," *Thrust for Educational Leadership*, v. 5, no. 4 (March 1976), pp. 9-10.
Criteria relating to sexist language in math textbooks and problems.

*Schreiner, Nikki. *Games and Aids for Teaching Math*. Hayward, CA: Activity Resources Co., 1972.
A pattern book of successful games and puzzles, with well-thought-out standards and criteria for selecting and using math games.

* + Seidel, Robert J., and others. *Learning Alternatives in U.S. Education: Where Student and Computer Meet*. Englewood Cliffs, NJ: Educational Technology, 1975.

A major section of this thoroughly-researched book is devoted to the background and applications of computer-based learning materials (CBLM). Appendixes include much information on sources.

Seymour, Dale G., and Joyce Snider. *Line Designs.* Palo Alto, CA: Creative Publications, 1968.

*Trueblood, C., and M. Szabo. "Guidelines for Evaluation of Published Metric Materials," *Arithmetic Teacher*, v. 25, no. 5 (Feb. 1978), pp. 46-50.

Warncke, Edna. "If Johnny Can't Read, Can He Compute?," *Reading Improvement*, v. 10, no. 3 (Winter 1973), pp. 34-37.

Yoshino, Y. *The Japanese Abacus Explained.* New York: Dover, 1963.

"When we try to pick out anything by itself, we find it hitched to everything else in the universe."
— John Muir

"If a person is to grow up, he needs first of all access to places and to processes, to events, to records. He needs to see, to touch, to tinker with, to grasp whatever there is in a meaningful setting."
— Ivan Illich, *The Alternative to Schooling*

"The idea ... of living in nature is the most recent acquisition to education. ... the child needs to live naturally, and not only to know nature."
— Maria Montessori, *The Discovery of the Child*

□ □ □

OVERVIEW

During the last ten years, environmental education has been engaged in the task of defining itself and interdependently establishing its content, criteria, and practices. More a theme than a subject discipline, environmental education is highly dependent upon the educational environment. An approach more than a specific content, environmental education may be carried out in most — perhaps all — subject areas.

If the key to affective education is sensitivity to humans, the key to environmental education may be sensitivity to the environment, particularly to local environments including that of the local educational community, whose cooperation is required for effectiveness.

According to the *Editors' Declaration on Interdisciplinary Environmental Education* (Mary E. Hawkins, Chairperson, editor for *Science Teacher*):

> Environmental problems require a comprehensive problem-solving approach and a concerted effort by all disciplines.
>
> For example, if teachers from several study areas attack the same topic at the same time, the students are almost forced to draw the conclusion that there are relationships between these areas or that they are all parts of a whole.
>
> Young people can be adequately prepared to deal with environmental questions only through education that includes all the educational disciplines, the interplay between them, and the recognition that each individual constantly feels and responds to his environment.

In these days of emphasis on basics, some harried educators perceive environmental education as an educational frill. In actuality, however, environmental education has been particularly effective in restoring children's interest in learning — especially in inner-city schools. The environment studied can well be an urban environment. One recent NAEP assessment of political knowledge and attitudes indicated that most students of 9, 13, and 17 years of age were quite interested in learning about pollution and overpopulation (less interested in government, education and transportation).

In Ronald B. Childress' study of environmental education programs, teachers listed "primary" and "secondary" justifications for their programs. Like environmental education itself, these are intricately interdependent. The report is summarized in Childress' "Public School Environmental Curricula: A National Profile," *Journal of Environmental Education*, v. 9, no. 3 (Spring 1978), pp. 2-11. The results are displayed in the chart below.

JUSTIFICATIONS FOR ACTUAL PROGRAMS
(In Order of Frequency)

	% Major	% Contributives
Ecological Justification We need to learn to respect the relationships of interdependent biological and social systems	88	10
Educational Justification EE is necessary knowledge and understanding for today's environmental decisions	79	19
Conservationist Justification Students need to be taught use and development of earth's limited resources	76	19
Relevance Justification Relevant to conditions which sustain life and/or give life meaning	61	31
Aesthetic Justification EE promotes the maintenance of an aesthetically pleasing environment	59	32
Ethical Justification		
Problem-Solving Justification	50	40
Preservationist Justification	50	33
Sociological Justification	49	52
Philosophical Justification	35	41
Rural-to-Urban Justification	33	39
Political Justification	28	45
Techno-Scientific Justification	26	52
Historical Justification	21	48
Economic Justification (Money was available)	16	32
Religious Justification	10	29

Officially the Environmental Education Act (Public Law 91-516) defines environmental education as a process dealing with relationships. It is,

the educational process dealing with man's relationship with his natural and manmade surroundings, and including the relation of

population, pollution, resource allocation and depletion, conservation, transportation, technology, and urban and rural planning to the
whole environment.

Environmental science was defined as the study of real or perceived
environmental problems. Environmental problems, again, were defined as single
problems or groups of problems that involve "consideration or reconsideration of
human value systems and either (or both) natural resources (as human, soil,
mineral, plants, animals, water, air) or social, biological, biophysical, or
biosocial interactions."

The U.S. Office of Education noted in 1970 that practitioners tend to agree
on certain desirable characteristics for good environmental education. These
include:

- a multidisciplinary approach with an emphasis on the interrelationships
  of humans and nature
- a focus on contemporary problems relating to the urban and rural
  environments, both natural and human-created
- incorporation of nonformal as well as formal education processes
- action-oriented activities
- utilization of resources outside the classroom
- development of understanding and attitudes as well as information
- involvement of all age groups
- a design centered on participants, involving each learner/participant in
  choosing priorities for the issues involved and the solutions that seem
  most appropriate, so that participants learn how to learn about new
  situations, and how to weigh alternatives and test solutions.

In another study, "Environmental Education: The Central Need" [*American
Biology Teacher*, v. 35, no. 5 (Nov. 1973), pp. 448-50], Stanley L. Cummings
noted five similar themes in environmental education:

- it does not belong to any one discipline, but is multi-, inter-, and trans-
  disciplinary
- its cultural implications span all ages and affect individuals in all walks of
  life
- it needs to penetrate the human psyche in order to be effective and to go
  beyond understanding in order to effect change
- it is human-centered, works best from students' own surroundings, and
  assumes an obligation to help students integrate learning into their own
  mental constructs
- it depends on actual experience rather than abstract exposure; it is
  experiential rather than textbook oriented; it is knowledge-seeking,
  rather than knowledge-receiving.

RECOMMENDED LEARNING APPROACHES

Similar recommendations on learning approaches emerged from two separate workshops on environmental education held in 1971 (at Bowling Green, Ohio, and Riverside, California) sponsored by the National Science Teachers Association for elementary and secondary environmental education. Their recommendations for selectors are that materials,

- should be interdisciplinary (including social studies, arts, and humanities)
- should be integrational (related to subjects already being taught)
- should be relevant to individuals
- should involve students in sensory and self-directed activities; capitalizing on timely events and student excitement
- should involve parents and community
- should focus on conflicts of interests (considering the full range of complexities behind environmental problems)

With regard to secondary learning approaches NSTA recommends that materials be:

- interdisciplinary
- learner-centered
  - students should work at their own paces
  - activities should be adapted to individual needs and interests
  - include large-group, small-group, and individual tasks
  - students should be involved in selecting problems and planning techniques for solving them
- problem-centered
  - organized around problems rather than content
  - principles and facts should be introduced when needed, not in rigid sequences
  - problems should be well defined, understood by all, and related to students' concerns
  - end product should include alternatives for action

and that the learning approach

- should result in behavioral changes as part of a lifetime continuum
- should integrate affective, psychomotor, and cognitive aspects for balanced learning experiences
- should involve students throughout the entire learning process

V. Eugene Vivian in his *Sourcebook for Environmental Education* (St. Louis: Mosby, 1973) includes ten rather similar criteria for K-12 environmental education. These are abbreviated and summarized below.

Environmental education should,

- develop environmental ethos
- involve every grade from K-12
- include—at all grades—skills in monitoring and reporting on aspects of the environment
- use first-hand sources for all grades
- use problem-solving methods
- employ both multidisciplinary and interdisciplinary approaches
- organize around concepts
- evaluate instruction in terms of student behavior ("ecoaction")
- study healthy as well as sick environments
- consider alternatives and ecoactions

MATERIALS CRITERIA

In practice, according to the survey by Ronald B. Childress on environmental programs in public schools, though instructional materials are garnered from a wide variety of sources, most environmental education materials are developed locally by the teaching staff. According to Childress, the factors exerting the most influence on the selection of curriculum content are:

- student interests
- personal and social needs of students
- teacher interests
- local environmental problems and concerns

Most used instructional strategies are:

- small group projects
- class discussions
- field trips/community resource visits

Least used strategies are:

- computer-assisted instruction
- programmed learning
- behavior/performance contracts

Least used sources are:

- published textbooks
- published curricular programs
- materials developed by state-wide or system-wide committees
- materials from state education agencies

The availability of state-adopted environmental education textbooks and state legislative mandates appears to exert very little influence, though the latter are supposed to be determining.

The practices of environmental educators seem to be congruent with the given criteria, and indicate a curriculum laudably responsive to local conditions and interests. Educators who develop their own materials may be expending more energy than necessary while duplicating both available materials and each other.

Even though many textbooks and published curricular materials are inappropriate or cumbersome, others can be used "as is" or can easily be adapted to local conditions. Environmental organizations and state environmental consultants in particular have a lot to offer local teachers, as do trade books. This chapter will include sources to help educators choose materials congruent with their criteria and adaptable to local conditions.

STATE CRITERIA

In theory at least, environmental program planners and selectors are supposed to meet mandatory legislative requirements for course content. These can usually be translated into checklists for materials. For instance, the ecological and environmental criteria below originally appeared in the California *Education Code*, though they have been slightly rewritten for presentation here. (In California, it is not necessary for all materials to meet all criteria, so long as they conform to others in a reasonable degree.)

CALIFORNIA STATE CRITERIA
(Revised as materials checklist)

Materials should portray the responsibilities of human beings toward a healthy, sanitary environment.

Materials should encourage wise use of human and physical resources.

Materials should portray the interdependence of peoples and their environments.

Materials should identify adverse effects of attempted solutions to environmental problems.

Materials should suggest appropriate means of protecting natural environments.

In application, California programs and materials should be designed to help youngsters develop:

- Awareness of our interdependence with a finite eco-system and the need to preserve its resources and to protect its quality

- Knowledge of the scientific and technological principles governing the interdependence; the economic, social, political factors affecting environmental management; and the effect of human values on environmental quality

- Skills, both individual and social, through which citizens might contribute effectively to the solution of environmental and resource management programs.

INTERDISCIPLINARY SURVEY

Since there is a great deal of emphasis on multidisciplinary materials and coordination, I have included a chart for surveying curriculum materials for environmental concepts and themes so that educators can begin environmental education knowing what is available in the immediate school environment. Ideally, such a survey should be cooperative and interdependent.

INTERDISCIPLINARY ENVIRONMENTAL MATERIALS SURVEY

+ good or extensive materials   ✔ some materials   0 negligible or no materials

Curricular and Subject Disciplines	(Cognitive-Affective Functions)		
	AWARENESS	KNOWLEDGE	SKILLS
Outdoor education			
Mathematics			
Statistics			
Natural sciences			
Physical sciences			
Technology			
Health			
Economics			
Home economics			
Social studies			
Law			
Consumer education			
Political science			
History			
Geography			
Psychology			
Career education			
Humanities			
Literature			
Art and aesthetic education			
Crafts and shop			
Values education			

This chart can indicate whether environment-oriented materials can be located within a school for any or all disciplines. This could involve an item-by-item analysis of, say, social studies materials or library fiction collections or surveys of card catalogs or teachers' recommendations. Materials may be surveyed for theme, approach or subject content. It could also be used as a checklist for buying or evaluating new materials.

THE LOCAL ENVIRONMENT

Starting out with the local environment involves utilization of the immediate physical environment (classroom, school, community), including its human and community resources, its natural artifacts as well as the elements created by humans, and materials created to describe all of these elements. These environmental factors (taken all together) should be selected to develop awareness, knowledge, and/or skills.

Exploration through direct experiences can involve found and/or purchased articles. Some means and materials are:

- direct observations with or without instruments
- observation instruments, e.g.,
    - magnifying glasses
    - surveying instruments
    - microscopes
    - field glasses
- measuring instruments, e.g.,
    - rulers and linear measures (possibly in metric scale)
    - micrometers
    - trundle wheels
- student collections of local items, e.g.,
    - grasses
    - leaves
    - small animals or their habitats
- student-created entities, e.g.,
    - dandelion counts
    - photographs, movies, sketches
    - models
    - snow houses
    - seascapes and cityscapes
    - notebooks
    - tape recordings
    - verbal summaries

Such observations can be helped immensely by "how-to" books on catching insects, exploring your backyard, examining your environment, guides to field trips, etc. Community resources for such explorations include:

- governmental agencies at all levels (from federal offices to local building inspectors)
- parks and park officials
- water and utilities companies
- traffic management
- historical associations
- cemeteries
- scouting and conservation groups
- outdoor education groups
- libraries and museums

Human resources, aside from members or officials of such community groups, include:

- senior citizens
- historians
- representatives of ethnic groups
- botanists
- meteorologists

School environmental factors include:

- the physical plant
- administrative structures and restrictions
- the socio-emotional climate
- demographic, cultural, and economic factors
- resources available for students

Locally-produced print and nonprint materials may include:

- local maps
- guide books
- field trip manuals
- site plans
- local histories
- laws and regulations
- chamber of commerce brochures, promotional slide shows
- local newspapers and news accounts from other sources
- accounts of early settlers
- weather maps
- early names
- current names
- city and county records
- old and new photographs, sketches, movies, and word descriptions of the area
- local collections of such materials

A surprising number of such materials are free or inexpensive. As a bonus, the task of locating such materials inevitably uncovers individuals and groups who could serve as advisers on locating and selecting further environmental educational materials. If local resources include an adequate library or media center, the librarian may provide a list of environment-related materials and/or a demonstration of how to find them in the library.

Since the school community and the community that surrounds the school are so important for environmental education, I have included in For Further Reading a few inexpensive and brief but competent guides for studying the community, by the League of Women Voters and Catharine Williams. My own *Social Studies on a Shoe String* is another guide to using community resources for educational purposes.

TYPES OF MATERIALS

In environmental education the two major cognitive modes are the problem-solving model of social studies and the science process approach. Observation, measurement, experimentation, description, generalization and deduction may be the most typical processes. In terms of Dale's Cone of Experience, environmental education involves direct experience, beginning with the local environment, and concepts, which may best be approached through visualization (pictorial media) and/or verbal (print media) formats. Since environmental education crosses so many subject disciplines, appropriate materials might be in almost any format. Certainly, community and student resources and preferences are important in choosing both media and materials. Simulations are important for student involvement. Environmental fiction has been strongly recommended for arousing feelings and shaping attitudes, as well as for strengthening and broadening life experiences. Media like filmstrips, films, and television programs can also serve these two functions.

Other basic criteria are those of values education, affective education, and aesthetic education. The question of bias and accuracy is also crucial to environmental education, and may be one reason that so many materials are school-made. Certainly free materials in environmental education tend to be suspect and self-serving as, for that matter, are some commercial materials. Free environmental materials may be distributed by notorious polluters, possibly as a sop to conscience or a subtle self-deception. The discussion of free materials in *Media and the Curriculum* is relevant for selecting environmental materials, as are criteria for studying social issues printed in the present work.

The very defects of these free materials can make them valuable primary documents and teaching tools for studying conflicts of interest, ecological viewpoints, and propaganda analysis. Especially at the secondary level, they may be worth acquiring for this purpose. In such cases it is probably best to balance materials from industry and industrial associations with those from advocacy organizations.

The checklist printed below on scope, content, and approach is excerpted from *The Environmental Education Curriculum Analysis Instrument* and reprinted with permission of the ERIC Center for Science, Mathematics, and Environmental Education from *A Review of Environmental Education for School Administrators*, by Stanley L. Helgeson and others (Columbus: Ohio State University, Research Foundation, December 1971).

ENVIRONMENTAL EDUCATION CURRICULUM ANALYSIS INSTRUMENT

Scope:

Social Science:
_____ Economics		_____ Psychology
_____ Geography		_____ Anthropology
_____ Political Science		_____ Sociology
_____ Law		_____ Other (specify)
_____ History		_____

(Analysis form continues on page 70)

Natural-physical science:

_____ Ecology

_____ Biology

_____ Chemistry

_____ Meteorology

_____ Health and medicine

_____ Geology

_____ Physics

_____ Engineering

_____ Physical geography

_____ Agronomy

_____ Other (specify)

_____

Humanistic-aesthetic:

_____ Plastic arts

_____ Music

_____ Literature

_____ Philosophy

_____ Religion

_____ Other (specify)

_____

Content:

Are the materials/program factually sound? _____
Are the materials/program intellectually sound? _____

Problems/issues:

_____ Pollution

          _____ Air

          _____ Water

          _____ Noise

_____ Thermal

_____ Solid Waste

_____ Radiation

_____ Aesthetic

_____ Health

          _____ Physical

          _____ Mental

_____ Resource use

          _____ Renewable

          _____ Non-renewable

          _____ Animal

          _____ Plant

          _____ Mineral

_____ Food production/supply/distribution

_____ Land use

_____ Recreation

_____ Population growth/distribution

_____ Population/resource ratio

_____ Political-legal jurisdictions

_____ Planning

          _____ Urban

          _____ Regional

          _____ Economic development

          _____ Urban problems

          _____ Other (specify) _____

          _____ Non-issue/problem oriented

Scale:

_____ Micro-system (e.g., vacant lot study)

_____ Neighborhood

_____ Community

_____ Metropolitan area

_____ State

_____ Natural or cultural interstate region

_____ U.S. region

_____ National

_____ World region

_____ World

_____ Other (specify)

_____

_____

Approach:

Multi (inter-, cross-, non-) disciplinary approach

_____ Draws from several of the natural-physical sciences (specify which)
_____ Draws from several of the social sciences (specify which)
_____ Draws from both natural-physical and social sciences (specify which)
_____ Based on a single discipline (specify)

Instructional Strategies

_____ Laboratory   _____ Independent study
_____ Field Trips   _____ Role Playing
_____ Exposition   _____ Games
_____ Stories   _____ Simulations
_____ Demonstrations   _____ Group discussions
_____ Questions   _____ Debates
_____ Tests   _____ Surveys and polls
_____ Case studies   _____ Other (specify)
_____ Seminars   _____

The descriptive forms shown on pages 72-73 were used by the Energy Curriculum Inventory (Suite 301, 0224 SW Hamilton, Portland, OR 97201) to describe curriculum materials and reference sources in one environmental education field.

Energy Curriculum Inventory

of

CURRICULUM MATERIALS

Please complete one form for each curriculum item you are describing.
Fill-in items numbered 1-4 and 11.
Check-off the words listed in items numbered 5-10 if they apply.
Please type or print.

1. TITLE & SUB-TITLE

2. AUTHOR(S)

3. IMPRINT Publisher

    Place of Publication

    Date of Publication

4. COST

5. GRADE LEVEL

    ____10-12

    ____7-9

    ____4-6

    ____1-3

    ____K

6. PRINT MATERIALS

    ____Teacher's Guide
    ____Curriculum Guide
    ____Field Trip Guide
    ____Misc. Guide, specify:

    ____Ditto Master
    ____Student Material
    ____Textbook
    ____Workbook
    ____Coloring Book
    ____Comic Book
    ____Enrichment Material
    ____Chart
    ____Pamphlet
    ____Play
    ____Poster
    ____Other, specify:

7. NON-PRINT MATERIALS

    ____Film
    ____8 mm
    ____16 mm
    ____35 mm
    ____Film Loop
    ____Film Strip
    ____Video-Tape
    ___ ___Reel-to-reel
    ____Cassette
    ____Audio-Tape
    ____Reel-to-reel
    ____Cassette
    ____Record (disc)
    ____Slides
    ____Transparency
    ____Flannelgraph
    ____Other, specify:

8. ORGANIZATION

    ____Single Concept
    ____Complete Instr. Unit
    ____Collection of Units
    ____Kit/Package
    ____Multi-Media
    ____Programmed Instr.
    ____Simulation/Game
    ____Other, specify:

9. TESTED ___yes ___no

10. SAMPLE Enclosed

    ____ yes ____no

11. YOUR NAME:

    Address:

    Occupation:

Energy Curriculum Inventory

of

REFERENCE SOURCES

Please complete one form for each reference source you are describing.
Fill-in or check-off all appropriate items.
Please type or print.

TARGET:
Reference sources and/or collections of information
that a specialist could develop into curricula.

1. NAME OF SOURCE

2. ADDRESS

    Street

    City

    State

    ZIP

3. PHONE (   )

4. CHIEF ADMINISTRATOR

5. KIND OF INFORMATION
    ____Technical
    ____General

6. LEVEL OF INFORMATION
    ____Adult
    ____College/University
    ____Jr. College
    ____Career/Vocational
    ____10-12
    ____7-9
    ____4-6
    ____1-3
    ____K

7. MATERIALS ARE:
    ____Available
    ____In Development

8. KIND OF SOURCE (check one.)
    ____Association/Consortium/Union
    ____Bibliography
    ____Book
    ____Business/Industry
    ____Computer Base
    ____Consultant
    ____Directory
    ____Dissertation/Thesis
    ____Educational Program
    ____Energy-focused or -related
        Conservation Guide
    ____Gov't Agency--Federal
    ____Gov't Agency--State
    ____Gov't Agency--Other
    ____In-House Publication
    ____Library
    ____Non-Print, specify kind:

    ____Periodical/Journal
    ____Person
    ____Private Agency
    ____Privately-funded Project/
        Program
    ____Publically-funded Project/
        Program
    ____Public Relations Thrust
    ____Report
    ____Seminar
    ____Workshop
    ____Other, specify:

9. YOUR NAME:

    Address:

    Occupation:

KEY ORGANIZATIONS

While there are many environmentally-oriented organizations in the United States whose publications could be helpful, I have listed only a few—mostly ERIC Clearinghouses and environmental organizations with substantial programs directed toward schools and/or school-age children. Those here are a representative rather than a complete listing.

Other organizations can be found in *Environmental Education: A Guide to Information Sources* and in the *U.S. Directory of Environmental Sources*. The *Directory of Information Resources in the United States: Social Sciences* (annotated in the chapter on free materials in *Media and the Curriculum*) also includes some environmental agencies. Many government agencies are active in environmental education; they can be located through the *Directory of Information Services: Federal Government*, cited in that chapter, and through the ERIC/SMEAC directory, *Environmental Education Activities of Federal Agencies*, or through some documents-finding sources cited in the chapter on government documents in *Media and the Curriculum*.

Conservation and Environmental Studies Center, Inc. (CESC)
Box 2230, Rd. 7
Browns Mills, NJ 08015   (609) 893-9151
The Center, a nonprofit organization, originally funded in 1966 under a Title III grant, is one of a very few projects to continue independent operations. At the present time, funding for CESC's operation comes from contracts with public and private agencies to provide assessments and inventories, teacher training, field studies, demonstration lessons, and school sites and resident environmental experiences. Under the direction of Dr. V. Eugene Vivian, CESC staff have produced curriculum materials in all subject areas, using basic structure that encourages each classroom teacher to incorporate environmental education into many curriculum areas. Most of their curricula have a hands-on orientation. Dr. Vivian himself is the author of a *Sourcebook for Environmental Education* ($5.95), an excellent resource for selectors, which includes a fine chapter on "developing and using instructional materials." Other publications in CESC's substantial curriculum library include *Ecology for Children*, books and learning packets. A publications list is available on request.

Conservation Education Association (CEA)
University of Wisconsin
Green Bay, WI 54302   (414) 465-2137
The Association is a membership organization composed of individuals, organizations and institutions concerned with environmental education. It publishes a quarterly newsletter, bibliographies, guidelines for planning and evaluating programs, lists of films, and other materials.

Its comprehensive annotated bibliography, *Environmental Conservation: A Selected Annotated Bibliography* (which includes books and pamphlets arranged by level and subject, and suggestions for a basic collection) is published by Interstate Printers, Danville, IL 61832. Contact this source for a complete list of Association publications, with current prices.

Energy and Education Action Center (EEAC)
U.S. Office of Education
Room 514, Reporters Building
300 7th St., SW
Washington, DC 20202   (202) 472-7777

The Energy and Education Action Center, established by the Office of Education in collaboration with the Federal Interagency Committee on Education (FICE) promotes all phases of energy-related education on an interagency basis. It is working to establish a reliable data-base for conservation and energy curriculum needs, while attempting to disseminate federal projects on energy education and related materials. It serves as an information center and data distribution network for this purpose.

It also administers a Resource Materials Center that exhibits materials, simulators, games and other educational activities, and supports the development of new curriculum activities that focus on the interrelationships between energy, environment, and engagement.

EEAC's objectives include:

technical assistance to schools

adaptation, identification and dissemination of supplementary curriculum materials dealing with energy

support for teachers' in-service training on energy awareness and conservation

identification and support of programs in career and vocational education on energy-related employment

During 1979, EEAC will collaborate with ERIC Clearinghouse on Science, Mathematics, and Environmental Education to design and organize an information service and to process documents related to energy.

ERIC Clearinghouses

Since environmental education is so multidisciplinary, at least three ERIC Clearinghouses handle significant numbers of documents and materials involving environmental education. Probably all clearinghouses have at least a few items.

**ERIC Clearinghouse for Science, Mathematics, and Environmental
    Education (ERIC/SMEAC)**
1200 Chambers Rd.
Ohio State University
Columbus, OH 43210   (614) 422-6717

This Clearinghouse has a good backup library and issues directories, resource lists, and compilations in the field of environmental education. Some useful materials are listed below.

Teaching Activities in Environmental Education, 1975, by John Wheatley
    and Herbert Coon. 1975. 195p. $4.40. (ED 125 868).
    Includes environmental activities (for all grades K-12) that can be used
in a variety of school settings in many curricular areas.

Review of Research Related to Environmental Education (1973-1976), by
  Herbert Roth. 1976. 58p. $1.95 offset. (ED 135 647).
  One of a series of research reviews, which includes evaluations of
environmental education programs.

A Directory of Projects and Programs in Environmental Education, by
  John F. Disinger. 4th ed. 330p. Dec. 1976. $6.50 offset. (ED 135 669).
  This edition includes summaries of 207 programs and projects, arranged
by states, with some updates and summaries of projects covered in earlier
editions. Most entries include names of contact persons and indications of
materials available.

*Environmental Education in the Urban Setting: Rationale and Teaching
  Activities*, by Herbert L. Coon and Mary Lynne Bowman. 1976. 208p.
  $4.40 offset. (ED 137 140).
  Includes approaches and activities for ecology in an urban setting.

Population Education Activities for the Classroom, by Judith M. Schultz
  and Herbert L. Coon. 1976. 196p. $4.40 offset. (ED 141 178).
  Includes bibliographies, film lists, and tests for 100 population education activities for elementary and secondary schools.

*Environmental Education in Action: Case Studies of Selected Public Schools
  and Public Action Programs*, by Clay Schoenfeld and John F. Disinger.
  1977. 343p. $6.60 offset. (ED 141 185).
  Case studies of 26 action programs and projects, and sets of curriculum
materials.

Affective Instruments in Environmental Education, by John H. Wheatley.
  1975. 16p. $1.10 offset. (ED 147 197).
  Reviews 14 instruments for measuring values and attitudes in
environmental education, with references and citations to additional
instruments.

Water-Related Teaching Activities, by Herbert L. Coon and Charles L.
  Price. 1977. 149p. $4.40 offset. (ED 150 026).
  Most of the activities (77) are related to science; 46 are related to social
studies, with several each related to mathematics, art, language arts, and
music. Materials are arranged by grade level, with a separate section listing
films and filmstrips, water testing equipment, and manufacturers' addresses.

Land-Use Management Activities for the Classroom, by Mary Lynne
  Bowman and John F. Disinger. 1977. 260p. $4.15 offset. (ED 152 541).

Environmental Education Activities of Federal Agencies, by John F.
  Disinger. 1978. 167p. $4.15 offset. (ED 152 481).
  Reports on the educational objectives and activities of 44 federal agencies, with information on products, publications, funding, enabling legislation, etc.

ERIC Clearinghouse for Social Studies/Social Science Education
Social Science Education Consortium
855 Broadway
Boulder, CO 80302   (303) 492-8434
    This clearinghouse has many materials and analyses that deal with the social studies aspects of environmental education. It is considered more fully on page 162.

ERIC Clearinghouse on Rural Education and Small Schools (ERIC/CRESS)
New Mexico State University
Box 3AP
Las Cruces, NM 88001   (505) 646-2623
    The scope of this particular clearinghouse includes outdoor education as well as Mexican-American education, American Indian education, rural education, and small schools. Its newsletter, *CRESS-CROSS*, reports many interesting programs, guides and resources dealing with outdoor education from bicycle touring to camping to exploring such habitats as sea coasts and rivers.

Hatheway Environmental Education Institute
Massachusetts Audubon Society
Great South Road
Lincoln, MA 01773   (617) 259-9500
    The Hatheway Environmental Education Institute, whose staff has been active for 35 years, specializes in inservice teacher training and in developing and collecting curriculum materials in environmental education; its collection is probably the largest in New England. The staff members have long experience as consultants and teachers at federal, state, and local levels.
    The Institute distributes Audubon publications, collects all kinds of environmental materials, and prepares its own publications, including excellent bibliographies of teaching aids.
    The Curious Naturalist (quarterly, $4.00/yr.) is an excellent periodical – with intelligent reviews – for elementary and secondary schools. Margaret McDaniel of the Institute has compiled a useful series of annotated bibliographies entitled *Aids for Environmental Education* ($0.60 each for grades K-3, 4-6, or 7-9; $1.00 for grades 7-14), with two *Updates* at $0.60 each for grades K-6 and grades 7-14. These aids cover about 100 items each in all kinds of media (though mostly in print).
    Other useful bibliographies are *The Energy Crisis—Aids to Study* at $0.60, *Solar Bibliography*, and *Wind Energy Bibliography*, both by J. Scott Tucker, and both $0.25 each.

Institute for Environmental Education
8911 Euclid Ave.
Cleveland, OH 44106   (216) 791-1775
    In its programs and publications, the Institute focuses on first-hand investigations, use of community resources, problem solving, and process-oriented educational methods. It publishes guides and also supplies kits for analyzing watersheds and studying other parts of the environment. Its publications include:
    Turning the Green Machine: An Integrated View of Environmental Systems.
        Oceana, 1978. 320p. $10.00.
        This book, which has received rave reviews, is a primer on the environment which provides an overview of the support systems necessary for life on

planet Earth (water, air, and land) with related discussions of the sources and effects of pollution, plus guidelines and authoritative data for resource planning.

An Environmental Guide for Administrators. 34p. $2.25pa.

Focuses on committees, programs, community interests and resources.

An Environmental Guide for Teachers. 97p. $4.50pa.

Implementation strategies, resources, and ideas for classroom and field-related environmental education.

The Institute's outstanding *Curriculum Activities Guides* at the high school level include guides designed and written by students. Some guides and their prices are:

A Curriculum Activities Guide to Water Pollution and Environmental Studies. 114p. $6.75.

This guide, written by high school students and illustrated by professional draftspersons, tells how to build 22 devices for measuring water quality.

A Curriculum Activities Guide to Solid Waste and Environmental Studies. 146p. $6.76.

A Curriculum Activities Guide to Birds, Bugs, Dogs, and Weather, and Environmental Studies. 138p. $6.75.

Demonstrates population sampling and data gathering, with two major expandable units on birds and weather study stations, and 20 activities designed to teach skills and to raise awareness.

Minnesota Environmental Sciences Foundation, Inc.
5430 Glenwood Avenue
Minneapolis, MN 55422   (612) 544-8971

The Foundation designs and conducts educational programs to inform and to promote citizen response in environmental matters. It writes, tests, and provides reference services on a collection of curricular materials for environmental education.

Its own publications — on such topics as pollution, ecology, energy consumption, values, and life styles — are mostly activity units that include projects with learning objectives, background information, procedures with data sheets, discussion, and follow-up. Their catalog is available without cost.

National Association for Environmental Education (NAEE)
P.O. Box 560931
Miami, FL 33156   (305) 667-0538

This organization of environmental educators promotes and develops programs at all levels, supports research and evaluation of environmental education, and aids in sharing information. It publishes the *Man and Environment* curriculum guides as well as monographs and a monthly newsletter.

Population Reference Bureau
1754 N Street, NW
Washington, DC 20036   (202) 232-2288

The Population Reference Bureau, a privately-funded organization, is an authoritative information source on population dynamics and the environment. It is an excellent resource for population education, which produces inexpensive publications and offers discount memberships to teachers and students. *Interchange*, a bimonthly newsletter for teachers, administrators, curriculum specialists, and others interested in population education, has good reviews of sources and programs. *Population Bulletins* include studies of a wide range of population issues, such as nutrition, affluence, and food resources.

Population Education: Sources and Resources (single copies free, issued at intervals) lists selected population education materials available as of the date of publication.

U.S. Environmental Protection Agency (EPA)

Headquarters Library
401 M Street, SW
Room 2404, PM-213
Washington, DC 20460   (202) 755-0308

This is the headquarters library of a library system which has 28 libraries nationwide, all located in EPA Regional Offices, major laboratories, and program offices, and all focused on environmental pollution. Regional collections emphasize their geographic regions; others emphasize particularly types of pollution, such as noise pollution or pesticide management.

While these library collections are primarily for government officials, all make their collections available to the public. The addresses of branch libraries are listed in the Winter 1979 edition of *Education Libraries* (v. 4, no. 2, pp. 29-31), or can be obtained from the Headquarters Library.

These libraries work cooperatively with EPA's Office of Public Awareness, which prepares and distributes pamphlet literature on environmental issues, from offices in Washington, Boston, New York, Philadelphia, Atlanta, Chicago, Dallas, Kansas City, Denver, San Francisco, and Seattle. These offices also provide access via microfiche to an EPA picture file, DOCUMERICA, that documents the environmental concerns of the United States in more than 16,000 color photographs. Reproductions of selected photographs are available without charge to nonprofit organizations.

U.S. International Environmental Referral Center

c/o U.S. Environmental Protection Agency
401 M Street, SW
Room 2902 WSM (PM213)
Washington, DC 20460   (202) 755-1836

This is the national referral center on the United Nations Environment Program International Referral System, a national and international network which coordinates and develops directories of environmental information sources. The Center has published a *U.S. Directory of Environmental Sources* (2nd ed., 1977) as well as information booklets and brochures. It is meant to provide free referral services and should be a good source for multinational information.

Western Regional Environmental Education Council (WREEC)

c/o Office of Environmental Education
California Department of Education
721 Capitol Mall
Sacramento, CA 95814   (916) 322-4018 and 445-8010

This is a multi-state council (founded in 1970) which includes representatives from the state education departments and resource management persons of 13 Western states; it is intended to develop and coordinate interdisciplinary environmental education in these states. Its major thrust is elementary- and secondary-level programs and activities. It works with states on their educational programs and aids in the exchange of materials, information and expertise providing referral services, consultations, in-service training, and seminars, usually at little or no cost.

In 1973 and 1974 WREEC prepared and published two items that can be most helpful in selecting environmental education materials: *Use This* and *Resource Materials: A Guide to Production and Use*. While these are no longer in print, both have been entered into the ERIC system. *SATISFICE: A Guide for Educational Consultants in Resource Management Agencies*, also out of print but in the ERIC system, has good definitions of environmental education terminology and concepts with good suggestions for coordinating community resources with environmental education.

Project Learning Tree, cooperatively developed with the American Forest Institute, is one sample of a joint industry-educators' program.

KEY PUBLICATIONS

City Mix, compiled by Marda Woodbury, Priscilla Watson, and Nancy Schimmel. Buffalo, NY: D.O.K. Publishers, 1977. 32p. $1.95pa. (A Curriculum Catalyst).

A comprehensive guide to inexpensive materials on city ecology, which lists many other guides and resources—basically for grades 4 to 8.

Energy: A Multimedia Guide for Children and Young Adults, by Judith H. Higgins. Santa Barbara, CA: ABC-Clio Press; New York: Neal/Schuman, 1979. 195p. $14.95. (Selection Guide Series, No. 2).

This convenient guide to energy materials and sources is divided into four parts, dealing with multimedia materials, curriculum materials, selection aids, and other information sources. The first three include 433 numbered annotations; the last section (and chapter) is a guide to periodical indexes; government sources; free-loan and rental films; data bases; and citizen, professional, industrial, and public sources.

The multimedia section—the longest in the book—includes 354 items arranged first by broad subject areas (e.g., coal, oil, wind power), then as print or nonprint, and finally by ascending grade level. That is, easier items are listed first. Subject areas seem well-chosen and are backed by good subject, author, and title indexes. Since the book is so well-done otherwise, I was disappointed not to find more emphasis upon energy use in transportation in general and automobiles in particular. Aside from this major omission, items are well-annotated and well-selected (for clarity, currency, quality, and relevance to the curriculum) from a thorough search of current sources. The annotations in the multimedia section, though brief, are helpful and evaluative. They point out biases, flaws, assets, and educational applications of each item. There are quite a few books that could be used in consumer education courses and/or occupational education courses. Books are chosen to cover both technical and social aspects of energy—at a variety of levels of difficulty. The author seems quite aware of the hazards and values of free materials.

The curriculum materials section—again arranged by grade level—describes 33 curriculum guides, courses, mini-units, manuals, modules, and activity packets. The section on selection aids provides good annotations of periodicals and bibliographies that can be used for accessing or selecting further energy-related materials.

Energy Education Materials Inventory, by Federal Energy Administration. Washington, DC: FEA, 1976. 5v. (ED 133 912—133 916). V. 1, *Print Materials*; V. 2, *Non-Print*; V. 3, *Films*; V. 4, *Kits, Games, etc.*; V. 5, *Reference Sources*.

This comprehensive inventory, prepared under government auspices, covers about 1,000 items in all media, most of which appeared between 1960 and 1975; some are still in print. Though it omits grade levels and is issued in computer-printout format, it is worth consulting because of the breadth of its coverage.

The National AudioVisual Center (NAC) (discussed under Non-Print Media in *Media and the Curriculum*) has a more current and somewhat easier-to-use list of government media in environmental education. NICEM's *Index to Environmental Studies* is noted in the same chapter.

Energy-Environment Materials Guide, by Kathryn Mervine Fowler and Rebecca E. Cawley. Washington, DC: National Science Teachers Association, 1975. 82p. $2.00.

This book, published with a matching *Energy-Environment Source Book* ($4.00), is a selected annotated bibliography of authoritative accessible energy source materials, with three student reading lists arranged by grade level and topics, lists of films and other nonprint media, a survey of energy curricular materials, and more.

Environmental and Outdoor Education Materials Catalog. Updated frequently. $0.75. (From P.O. Box 585, Lander, WY 82520).

An up-to-date, interesting annotated catalog which includes both books and equipment as well as a few ideas and activities—obviously written by people who know the field. A good commercial source for one-stop shopping, at reasonable prices.

Environmental Education: A Guide to Information Sources, by William B. Stapp and Mary Dawn Liston. Detroit: Gale, 1975. 225p. $18.00. (Man and the Environment Information Guide Series).

This comprehensive guide to environmental education sources is a directory which includes lists of reference materials; lists of magazines and newsletters; names and addresses of associations, organizations, and government agencies; funding data; programs and centers.

Guide to Ecology Information and Organizations, by John G. Burke and Jill Swanson Reddig. New York: Wilson, 1976. 292p. $12.50.

An annotated guide to a wide variety of materials that are not too technical (selected primarily for public libraries). Topics or sections include citizen action guides, indexes, periodicals, organizations, reference books, histories, monographs, nonprint media, organizations and government officials, as well as a directory of publishers and producers and a subject-author-title index.

Hunger: The World Food Crisis, by Kathryn Mervine Fowler. Washington, DC: National Science Teachers Association, 1977. 70p. $2.50pa.

Reviews and/or lists a variety of publications, curriculum materials, films, and organizations involved in food and hunger issues, covering materials appropriate for kindergarten to twelfth grade.

Population: An International Directory of Organizations and Information Sources, by Thaddeus C. Tryzyna. Claremont, CA: Public Affairs Clearinghouse, 1976. 132p. $18.75.

This information source describes about 600 organizations concerned with population and family planning — government and non-governmental, national and international; it includes a bibliography of other directories.

Population: The Human Dilemma, by Kathryn Mervine Fowler. Washington, DC: National Science Teachers Association, 1977. 102p. $3.50pa.

This annotated bibliography includes lists for teachers and students on selected, authoritative population literature, a survey of curriculum materials, and a list of organizations active in population issues.

Rain (Journal of Appropriate Technology). 10 issues per year. $10.00. (From 2270 NW Irving, Portland, OR 97210).

This information access journal and reference source comes out almost monthly and includes many ideas and sources which can be adapted to most classrooms. *Rainbook*, from the same source at $7.95, is a one-volume compilation of the best of *Rain* up through the spring of 1977.

Recommended Materials in Environmental Education, compiled by Marda Woodbury. Berkeley, CA: Ecology Center, 1977. 24p. $0.75pa. (From 2701 College Ave., Berkeley, CA 94705).

This annotated bibliography of recommended materials (mostly print or activity-oriented) covers recommended texts, sources of overviews, energy, urban ecology, classroom recycling, pollution, natural history, monitoring kits, gardening, outdoor recreation, and environmental fiction — about 80 items altogether, selected from hundreds more.

A Selected and Annotated Environmental Education Bibliography for Elementary, Secondary and Post-Secondary Schools, by Dr. Jerry F. Howell, Jr. and Jeanne S. Osborne. Morehead, KY: Morehead State University, 1975. 334p. $3.25pa. (From Dr. Jerry F. Howell, Jr., Center for Environmental Studies, UPO 780, Morehead State University, Morehead, KY 40351. Make checks payable to Morehead State University).

A well-done annotated bibliography, with thousands of references, arranged first by topic (e.g., attitudes, careers, conservation, solid waste, technology, and wildlife) and then by grade levels (K-6, 7-9, and 10-14).

FOR FURTHER READING

*Items marked with an asterisk include criteria.

+ Items marked with a plus include additional references.

+ Chicorel, Marietta, ed. *Chicorel Index to Environment and Ecology.* New York: Chicorel Library Publishing Corp., 1975. 2v.

+ Childress, Ronald B. "Public School Environmental Education Curricula: A National Profile," *Journal of Environmental Education*, v. 9, no. 3 (Spring 1978), pp. 2-11.

+ Cummings, Alice, and Dorothy Byars. *Environmental Education: An Annotated Bibliography of Selected Materials and Services Available.* Washington, DC: National Education Association, 1975.

*Cummings, Stanley L. "Environmental Education: the Central Need," *American Biology Teacher*, v. 35, no. 5 (Nov. 1973), pp. 448-50.

+ *Directory of Nature Centers and Related Environmental Education Facilities.* New York: National Audubon Society, 1975.

Heyman, Mark. *Places and Spaces: Environmental Psychology in Education.* Bloomington, IN: Phi Delta Kappa Educational Foundation, 1978. (Fastback 112).

Jernigan, H. Dean, and Linda Wiersch. "Developing Positive Student Attitude toward the Environment," *American Biology Teacher*, v. 40, no. 1 (Jan. 1978), pp. 30-35.

*Kupchella, Charles E., and Margaret C. Hyland. "Essential Curriculum Components in Environmental Education," *Journal of Environmental Education*, v. 8 (Spring 1978), pp. 11-16.

League of Women Voters of the United States. *Know Your Community.* Washington, DC, 1972.
Good questions and analyses for studying any community.

+ Moon, Thomas C., and Barbara Brezinski. "Environmental Education from a Historical Perspective," *School Science and Mathematics*, v. 74, nos. 5-6 (May/June 1974), pp. 371-74.

+ Moore, J. W., and E. A. Moore. "Resources in Environmental Chemistry: An Annotated Bibliography," *Journal of Chemical Education*, v. 52, no. 5 (May 1975), pp. 288-95.

+ Mooy, Leonard H., and Donald L. Stilliman. *The Environmentalist: A Guide to Free and Inexpensive Materials of Environmental Interest.* Santa Barbara, CA, 1973.

Powers, Joyce. "Using Fiction to Teach Environmental Education," *Science and Children*, v. 12, no. 2 (Oct. 1974), pp. 16-17.

+ Rabiega, William A. *Environmental Fiction for Pedagogic Purposes.* Monticello, IL: Council of Planning Librarians, 1974. (Exchange Bibliography No. 590).

* + Sales, Larry L., and Ernest W. Lee. *Environmental Education in the Elementary School.* New York: Holt, Rinehart and Winston, 1972.

*Stapp, William B., et al. "The Concept of Environmental Education," *Journal of Environmental Education*, v. 1, no. 1 (Fall 1969), pp. 30-31.

Stronck, David C. "The Affective Domain in Environmental Education," *American Biology Teacher*, v. 36, no. 2 (Feb. 1974), pp. 107-109.

United States Office of Environmental Education. "A Holistic Perspective for Environmental Education," *Ekistics*, v. 41, no. 246 (May 1976), pp. 252-56.

* + Vivian, V. Eugene. *Sourcebook for Environmental Education*. St. Louis: Mosby, 1973.

Williams, Catharine. *The Community as Textbook*. Bloomington, IN: Phi Delta Kappa Educational Foundation, 1975. (Fastback 64).

Wisniewski, Richard, ed. *Teaching about Life in the City, 42nd Yearbook*. Washington, DC: National Council for the Social Studies, 1972.

Woodbury, Marda. *Social Studies on a Shoe String*. Buffalo, NY: D.O.K. Publishers, 1978.

Wurman, Richard, ed. *Yellow Pages of Learning Resources*. Cambridge, MA: M.I.T. Press, 1972.

THE FEELING DOMAIN
Materials for Affective Education, Bibliotherapy, Mental Health, and Psychology

"Just because his life is often bewildering to him, the child needs to be given the chance to understand himself in this complex world with which he must learn to cope. To be able to do so, the child must be helped to make some coherent sense out of the turmoil of his feelings. He needs ideas on how to bring his inner house into order, and on that basis be able to create order in his life."
— Bruno Bettelheim, *The Uses of Enchantment*

"Knowledge of the political history of issues to which the community is sensitive should be integral to the consideration of affective education. Complex and subtle as systemic and cultural considerations such as these may be, they are every bit as vital as child- and teacher-centered concerns. They must be assessed and reckoned with if affective education is to be considered a trustworthy component of school life and educational process."
— Richard Munger and Mark M. Ravlin, *Furthering the Development of Children in Schools*

" ... the field is amorphous, the goals and objectives immeasurable, and the rhetoric often incomprehensible."
— Diane Divoky (on affective education)

□ □ □

A respect for the feelings of others is inherent in the feeling domain, and sensitivity to the feelings of all individuals involved is basic to adequate selection of materials. As the above quotations imply, selectors need to be concerned not only with the feelings and concerns of teachers and students, but also with those of parents and the community at large. Fortunately, some major advocates of affective education seem especially sensitive to personal factors for teachers and students and to the need for community input into the selection process.

Sensitivity implies local selection at the point of use, based upon immediate needs rather than on mandates for the use of one text or a single approach for large groups of people. Selection is most effective in a context which represents teachers, students, parents, and community—an atmosphere that enhances self-esteem.

Because the feeling domain *is* amorphous and its boundaries unclear, I am treating together in one chapter materials for affective education, bibliotheraphy, mental health education, and psychology. While the last of these areas is perhaps more cognitive than affective and more concept- than effect-oriented—*about* rather than *for*—the subtle and continuous interaction of knowledge, behavior, and experience requires that selection tools for materials in psychology overlap with those for materials in more clearly affective subject areas.

The topics covered in this chapter and their materials also impinge continuously upon other curricular areas, especially on career education, health education, science, social studies, literature, and values education. Since the feeling domain is human and inherently multidisciplinary, affective components and materials are easily integrated into almost any course of study.

Sex education and narcotics education are two areas that could logically be considered subsets of the broad area of psychology, but since their tools and literature tend toward autonomy, I am treating them in separate chapters. These two areas, like health education and nutrition, are areas where science provides a factual basis, which is significantly altered by emotions and by social attitudes. All three aspects must be considered in selecting materials.

Materials for and particularly about disabled persons have large affective components. Teachers in special education or in mainstreamed classes should consult disabled-special education resources (especially those prepared by advocacy organizations) for materials relating to disabilities.

Affective and psychological elements, of course, should be considered for all academic areas, including math, science, reading, social studies, and the arts.

Though psychology (sometimes under the rubric of philosophy) was offered at a few academies and female seminaries as far back as the mid-1800s, even today some teachers and administrators are reluctant to initiate or incorporate affective curriculum. Sometimes they fear community reactions; sometimes they are reluctant to deal forthrightly with areas like emotions and behavior in classroom contexts; sometimes the curricula seem to intrude on privacy; sometimes educators do not know suitable resources.

As far as materials are concerned, however, the situation is actually very favorable. The broad area encompassed in this chapter has an abundance of materials with well-worked-out rationales, theoretical bases, and selection tools. There are at least three organizations collecting and evaluating materials and compiling bibliographies and criteria. Two of these provide ongoing review sources.

It is also an area in which students are genuinely interested and about which they are generally positive, and one for which students have been surveyed on their preferences for content and specific media. It is certainly possible to find or design programs congruent with these preferences.

RATIONALE AND PREMISES FOR AFFECTIVE EDUCATION

One succinct rationale for affective-feeling education is that of the Behavioral Science Education Project (BSEP) whose support for behavioral education rests on the following premises:

- Human experience is an inseparable interplay of cognitive, affective, and behavioral processes.

- An inadequate consideration of any of these processes or neglect of a child's needs for understanding of self and others results in subversion of both the intellectual aims of education and those aims related to positive mental health.

- The numerous findings of the behavioral sciences which are relevant to students and teachers and would be helpful to them can be made available to them in schools.

- Education should include instructional methods which engage the child's affective, cognitive and behavioral processes.

- Clear understanding of one's own and others' behavior is a legitimate basic goal of education.

Certainly affective factors influence student learning. A research study by the U.S. Office of Education, *The Relationship of Self-Concept to Beginning Reading* (No. 377, 1952), indicated that for primary grades self-concept was a better predictor of success or failure in reading than were IQ tests. In Tiburon, California, Dr. Gerald Japolsky brought about dramatic improvement in reading ability in learning-impaired children through group relaxation and guided fantasies.

RATIONALE AND PREMISES FOR PSYCHOLOGY

The premises and aims of psychology differ somewhat in emphasis. Though personal development — students' daily concerns and problems — is dealt with in psychology courses, it is intended there as a means of communicating the basic principles of psychology as a discipline. Self-knowledge — however worthy a goal and however important to students — is part of a broader goal of acquiring reliable knowledge and information on human behavior through scientific observational methods. Discussion and investigation are used to explore issues in a way that encourages critical examination of evidence while protecting diversity of opinion.

One representative psychology curriculum, that of the Human Behavior Curriculum Project, starts from the following premises:

- The psychological study of human behavior is the point of departure for teaching materials.

- Materials should permit the full consideration of interdisciplinary areas, such as sociology, biology, political science, economics and other relevant fields.

- Modules should place students in an experiential and conceptual framework that illustrates human interactions and encourages analysis of behavior.

The content and focus of most precollege psychology courses include materials that contribute to personal development and to a knowledge of the discipline of psychology — though the balance differs. Even at the secondary level, few courses omit materials for personal development, though some emphasize investigative modes.

Most studies show that problem resolution and self-knowledge are major goals of students enrolled in pre-psychology courses. (For specific data see the comprehensive *Teach Us What We Want to Know*, discussed on page 106 of the present work.) In Robert J. Stahl's study, *The Status of Precollege Psychology in Mississippi and Florida* (Columbus: Mississippi College for Women, May 1977) high school students (mostly senior girls) in Mississippi and Florida most often chose the five reasons listed below from twelve suggested reasons for taking psychology courses:

- to help understand and deal with personal problems
- to assist in adjusting to life and in solving life's problems
- to help better understand self and accept self as an individual
- to apply psychological knowledge to understand contemporary problems and society
- to assist in preparing for family future life.

RATIONALE FOR MENTAL HEALTH
AND BIBLIOTHERAPY

While materials for bibliotherapy and mental health may seem largely extraneous to the school curriculum, such materials provide means for self-understanding and emotional growth, as well as comprehension of social issues and abilities to make decisions. They offer individual children opportunities to grow and to solve the problems they may face in life, and they offer groups of children and teachers opportunities to resolve conflict areas that arise from school situations, thus freeing children for more academic pursuits.

Books and other printed materials dealing with feelings and emotions greet children with their own concerns, providing them with ideas they are willing to explore in materials they are willing — sometimes eager — to read. Individual items tend at times to introduce concepts and vocabularies that are meaningful to children as individuals.

Bibliotherapy, a discipline unfamiliar to most educators and to many librarians, is the use of reading materials to promote mental health and to help solve emotional problems, processes which, it is hoped, will occur through universalization and identification, catharsis and insight. Although this particular function of reading has ancient roots, modern bibliotherapy is considered to have been reintroduced early in the twentieth century by the French psychologist Pierre Janet. *The Bookfinder*, listed in Key Publications, includes an extensive bibliography of the field.

Two major approaches are the use of issues-oriented reading lists and of problem-oriented reading lists. *Children's Literature: An Issues Approach* and *Now Upon a Time* (see Key Publications) represent the former; *The Bookfinder* uses the latter. These approaches overlap to a considerable degree, since children's individual problems, confronting say, divorce or racism, may be seen collectively as social issues. The issues-oriented lists provide classroom means for using such books to discuss if not resolve social issues; problem-oriented tools are a bit more oriented toward the needs of individual children.

All of these tools are appropriate for teachers, librarians, and children to use in selecting books for libraries, classrooms, or for their own individual needs — in essence both for individuals and for small groups. My feeling is that wherever possible children could choose such books for themselves, possibly from a thoughtfully preselected collection.

Individual or developmental issues, of course, may be timeless human dilemmas that, as Bruno Bettelheim suggests, can be dealt with through myths and fairy tales. To Bettelheim, fairy tales represent human wisdom, distilled and refined over time, applicable to inner human difficulties. (Tools for locating such works are given in the language arts section of this book; they tend to be organized thematically rather than developmentally.) Fairy tales and myth generally are not perceived as threatening by either parents or school personnel, but they may seem irrelevant. In this case Bettelheim's *The Uses of Enchantment* (Westminster, MD: Random, 1977) may serve as a consciousness-raising device for teachers and parents.

The Mental Health Materials Center, whose products and materials are represented in this chapter, has been selecting mental health materials for a quarter of a century, using rigorous, thoughtful criteria. Since it recommends only eight to ten percent of the materials it evaluates, its recommended materials are apt to be highly valuable when used as suggested. The Center strongly believes in a targeted rather than a shotgun approach.

APPROPRIATENESS

The outline below includes some of the factors which should be considered in designing programs and selecting materials, other than value and authority.

Student Considerations

Developmental appropriateness
    based on knowledge of child development
    ability to think abstractly
    identification of emotional states
    mastery or enabling skills

Previous exposure to similar materials
Attitudes and values
Classroom cultures
Life situations
Preferred learning styles

Teacher Considerations

Competence and knowledge
Attitudes and values—comfort in dealing with affective issues
Preferred teaching styles

Community Considerations
Parental attitudes and life situations
Entire school culture
Available community resources
    people
    places
    things (including materials and sources)

Administrative Considerations and Attitudes

Funds for materials and/or inservice training
Proportion of willing and able teachers
Role and attitude of school psychologists and social workers

In selecting materials, the BSEP considers two questions paramount, aside from the quality of curricula:

• Is the procedure suited to the teacher who will use it—in both personal comfort and skill required?

- Is the technique appropriate for the individual children and for their group interaction?

The BSEP stresses that programs should be situationally specific; materials, "kits" and other aids need to be adapted or "customized" to fit the idiosyncrasies of particular classrooms, schools, and communities.

The following sections of the *Checklist for a New Course in Psychology* — reprinted here with the permission of the Committee on Psychology in Secondary Schools of the American Psychological Association — thoughtfully raise the kinds of questions and considerations that need to be faced in adopting new courses and materials, especially in areas of potential controversy.

CHECKLIST FOR A NEW COURSE IN PSYCHOLOGY

Rationale for Introducing a Psychology Course

What arguments can be presented to substantiate a need for the course?
_____ student interest (perhaps documented by survey data)
_____ specific, immediately useful skills that students could gain from the course: for example, studying more effectively, interviewing for jobs, working with children, listening to other people, evaluating propaganda, learning motor skills more quickly, and interpreting statistics
_____ a need for the course as a part of the school's total academic offering
_____ other

Target Population

What curriculum credit will the course carry?
_____ required for graduation
_____ optional to fulfill a graduation requirement (e.g., one of several courses that meet a requirement for a credit in science)
_____ elective
_____ noncredit
What subject credit will the course carry?
_____ behavioral science
_____ science
_____ social science
_____ social studies
_____ health
_____ other
By what criteria will class composition be determined?
_____ academic ability (high-ability students) low-ability students? a heterogeneous group?)
_____ first come, first served (with a maximum size)
_____ grade level (12th grade only? 11th and 12th grades? all grades?)
_____ deliberate balance (e.g., by age, grade, grade-point average, sex, ethnic background)
_____ other (e.g., prerequisites, career plans)
By what criteria will class size be determined?
_____ same limit that applies to other classes
_____ need for a small class (e.g., for greater individual attention)
_____ special desire for a large class (e.g., to teach a course using a Personalized System of Instruction)
_____ other

Course Content

What orientation or emphasis will be reflected in the course? The orientation may determine in which department the course will be housed — natural science, social science, health, etc. — and thus which subject credit it will carry.

_____ survey of psychology as an academic discipline — an overview of the field, used both as an introduction and as preparation for college courses

_____ experimental method — an emphasis on the scientific methods used in the study of behavior

_____ human development — a focus on a segment of development such as child development and childrearing, adolescence, or aging, or the study of development over the human life span

_____ comparative and physiological psychology — the intensive study of biology and the natural-science aspects of psychology, with a laboratory component

_____ social psychology — the study of the interaction between individuals and their social environment

_____ personality theories — the study of behavior through the theories of Allport, Freud, Jung, Lewin, Maslow, Skinner, etc.

_____ personal growth — an emphasis on self-understanding and personal development

_____ value and ethical development — an emphasis on stages of moral development and moral dilemma discussions

_____ mental health — the study of the behavior and emotions of normal people, to learn ways of living that will improve "psychological health"

_____ other

What factors should be considered in determining the orientation?

_____ student interests

_____ the teacher's academic background and interests

_____ perceived gaps in current course offerings

_____ the goals of the school's program

_____ parental and community concerns

_____ available laboratory facilities

_____ available library facilities

_____ other

What topics might be regarded as controversial by some groups in the community?

_____ behavior modification

_____ drugs

_____ ethnic-group and social-class differences

_____ evolution

_____ family interaction

_____ genetics

_____ human sexuality

_____ psychology of religion

_____ sex-role stereotyping

_____ other

What can be done to minimize the possibility of negative reactions to units on controversial topics?

_____ Discuss the units in advance with school administrators and/or school board members so that they are informed and able to defend the educational value of the units.

_____ Demonstrate that the units are clearly an integral part of the subject matter.

_____ Demonstrate that the units meet an evident student need.

_____ Show that similar material has been successfully taught in neighboring or similar communities.

_____ When appropriate, involve concerned parents and/or community organizations in the planning and presentation of the units.

_____ Other

Teaching Strategies

What teaching strategies are appropriate to psychology instruction?

_____ small-group discussion

_____ lecture-discussion

_____ individualized instruction

_____ programmed instruction

_____ inquiry/inductive teaching

_____ audiovisual presentations

_____ demonstrations

_____ small-group laboratory experiences

_____ individual laboratory experiences

_____ other

(Checklist continues on page 92)

Concerns for Physical Safety

What provisions have been made for dealing with threats to the physical safety of the students?
_____ training of teaching and students in safety procedures (e.g., proper handling of experimental animals) and use of emergency equipment (e.g., eye baths and fire extinguishers)
_____ careful advance planning of field trips
_____ other

Ethical Concerns

What considerations have been given to ethical issues and problems that may arise in connection with instructional activities?
_____ experiments or demonstrations with animals or humans
_____ self-disclosure in class discussion
_____ the questioning of established values (e.g., traditional family structure, importance of competition, etc.)
_____ other
What considerations have been given to the responsibility of the teacher if students turn to him or her for help with their personal problems?
_____ Be aware of the limits of one's preparation and skills; know when the student should be referred to qualified sources of counseling or therapy.
_____ Be familiar with the school's resources for counseling, testing, diagnosis, and therapy.
_____ Be familiar with appropriate resources in the community (mental health centers, peer counselor groups, drug and alcohol councils, Alcoholics Anonymous, public health clinics, etc.).
_____ Other

Community Resources

Have the many related resources in the community been investigated?
_____ agencies and institutions that can serve as sites for field trips and/or use student volunteers for field experience (e.g., hospitals, nursing homes, mental hospitals, prisons, day-care centers, drop-in centers, senior citizen centers, etc.)
_____ psychologists (clinicians, teachers, and researchers) and professionals in related areas available and willing to work with the teacher or the students either in the classroom or on the job (to help plan the course, serve as guest speaker, etc.)
_____ the local public library and nearby college or university libraries and media centers
_____ lectures, films, or special demonstrations on psychological topics at nearby colleges or universities
_____ community and college or university agencies that can provide career guidance and information
_____ other

Qualifications of the Psychology Teacher

What can the teacher do to achieve and maintain competence in teaching psychology in the high school?
_____ Meet the state's requirements for certification in the teaching field of psychology.
_____ Attend workshops offered by state psychological associations, high school psychology teachers associations, or colleges and universities.
_____ Enroll in courses at nearby colleges or universities to maintain and upgrade knowledge of recent developments in psychology.
_____ Read current books and periodicals in the field.
_____ Attend state, regional, and/or national meetings of social studies teachers, science teachers, the American Psychological Association, and the American Association for the Advancement of Science.
_____ Participate in meetings of local psychology teachers associations or meet informally with other high school psychology teachers to share ideas and information.
_____ Other

According to the Mental Health Materials Center curricula can be adapted to a particular audience only if the program exhibits the following:

- awareness of the needs of the audience
- internal consistency for this audience
- appropriate and consistent style
- good organization
- appropriate format
- clarity
- attractive style
- jargon-free style and content

In their complex explication of the world of feelings, *Taxonomy of Educational Objectives: Handbook II, The Affective Domain* (New York: McKay, 1964, pp. 176-84), D. Krathwohl and co-authors included summaries of levels of commitment:

Level 1, *receiving or attending,* is a level where learners are sensitized to the existence of phenomena and stimuli.

Level 2, *responding.* Students may be considered actively attending.

Level 3, *valuing.* Behavior takes on the characteristic of a belief.

Level 4, *organization.* Values are prioritized, related and organized into systems.

Level 5, *value complex.* Actions are consistent with internalized values.

An awareness of the levels of commitment of individual students and groups of students as well as of community groups can facilitate the selection of appropriate materials.

TYPES OF MATERIALS

Since the subject matter of affective education is—one way or the other—human behavior, materials should deal with behavior itself, as well as with concepts and structures that will allow the student to order and to determine his or her own behavior. In terms of Dale's Cone of Experience, direct experience should be involved. Children should also extend their own experience through access to wider experiences—through print and audiovisual modes. Audiovisual modes may have greater immediacy—especially for group experiences (and can be experimental and subjective as well as rational or cognitive). Print materials, over time, allow access to more resources and more individualization. Role-playing, games, and simulations are important for active involvement, vicarious experiences, trying on of roles, and explorations of alternatives. Classroom experiments are important for understanding self and the discipline of psychology. Workbooks can successfully be set up for decision-making or values education.

One informative study by Robert J. Stahl, *The Status of Precollege Psychology in Mississippi and Florida: A Comparative Report* (Columbus: Mississippi College for Women, 1977), compared the materials preferences of psychology students in these two states, allowing them to choose among 15 types of materials. Students checked an average of five items each. Florida students ranked materials in the following order: films/movies, guest speakers, simulation games, materials for classroom experiments, filmstrips, a weekly newspaper, reference service, audio-cassette tapes, different kinds of textbooks, student workbooks, overhead transparencies, materials for slow learners, posters of famous psychologists. The Mississippi students were quite similar, except that they preferred filmstrips to simulation games, and put audio-cassettes ahead of reference service—with a few other minor variations. Textbooks were last on the list, but 12 students in a class without a text wanted one. Students also suggested "other" sources they would like, such as field trips, group talks, a psychology library, sample personality tests, photographs, slides, ink blots, and case studies.

The teachers' preferences for materials were quite like those of the students. They tended to differ a little more on their perceptions of what should be in a psychology curriculum, and their reasons for offering psychology differed slightly from students' motives for taking psychology.

CONTENT CRITERIA

Content assessment and selection criteria have been as well thought out for broad selection as for targeted groups. The BSEP used the following criteria to select resource materials and curricula for review:

- readily available in published form
- accurate in content
- teachable
- attractive
- relevant to the lives and development of children and youth
- appropriate in methodology
- no potentially undesirable side effects

The Mental Health Materials Center, which has actively selected and evaluated mental health program aids since 1953, has refined and defined its evaluative criteria for such materials over the years. Basically, these criteria remain substance, validity, balance, authority, and integrity. The questions/criteria below are reprinted with permission from their *IRC Newsletter*, v. 5, no. 3 (1973-1974 series):

- Is it authoritative? Does it reflect the current best understanding of its subject among competent scholars?
- Does it say something substantial and worthwhile, or is it essentially derivative, a "rehash" of what has been said before?
- Is it as sound as our present state of knowledge permits?
- Is the presentation well balanced, "in the round," maintaining its perspective even if dealing with a limited aspect of a broader theme?
- Does it maintain integrity as an educational tool without recourse to emotional biases, propaganda pressures, or other ulterior motives?
- Is it appropriate to its intended audience?
- Can it be effectively used in a mental health or family life education program—perhaps in a school setting, a training program, a PTA or

other community group, to reinforce a point in counseling, or in some other specific way or ways?

Though these criteria were addressed primarily to mental health professionals, they are equally appropriate for school situations where, unfortunately, trivial or inaccurate materials may be adopted because of supposed appeal.

Finally, the BSEP surveyed both classroom and teacher materials and major approaches in affective education. In the chart below I have matched the approaches they listed with material characteristics that seem appropriate for those approaches.

AFFECTIVE EDUCATION APPROACHES AND MATERIALS

Approaches	Materials Characteristics
Large-group and small-group discussions Decision-making and problem solving Causal understanding of behavior Integration of affective and cognitive areas for self-development	stimulating relevant to interests open-ended child-centered direct experience or convincing vicarious experience role-playing possibilities possibly values orientation
Communications and group process skills	communications/information orientation experiential base

Comprehensive curricula for personal and
  interpersonal adjustment
Psychological curriculum
Self-control curriculum
Awareness of others
Role-playing methods
Enhancing self-concept/self-esteem
Ongoing development of behavioral science
  (based on problems that arise in class)
	classroom/direct experience, possibly supplemented
	  by convincing vicarious experiences
	include concepts of behavioral sciences
	materials to enhance self-knowledge

Values education Moral education	decision-making skills open-ended experiential base
Wide-ranging anthologies	all of above
Growth and development	exceptionally well-matched to individual status and/ or to group norms
Teacher professional growth	all of above

KEY ORGANIZATIONS

The institutions listed below are major organizations that can help in locating and appraising materials for affective education, mental health, and psychology. Many other related organizations are listed and briefly annotated in *A Guide to Mental Health Education Materials* (see Key Publications). The Social Sciences Education Consortium (p. 162) also has materials for affective education.

American Psychological Association (APA)
Clearinghouse on Precollege Psychology and
  Behavioral Science
1200 17th St., NW, Room 209
Washington, DC 20036   (202) 833-7592

This Clearinghouse of the American Psychological Association was established in 1970 to collect and disseminate information on teaching behavioral sciences in elementary schools and psychology in high schools. With the cooperation of another APA agency, the Committee on Psychology in Secondary Schools, these functions have been admirably fulfilled. The Committee and the Clearinghouse provide almost exemplary assistance to educators who wish to select materials in psychology and the behavioral sciences, or to launch or develop courses in these areas.

The Clearinghouse, which operates from a small library of books, surveys, curriculum project materials, guides, and periodical literature, acts as current information and communication and referral source on new programs and materials, names and addresses of local associations and contacts, and similar items.

Its eight-page newsletter, *The High School Psychology Teacher* (formerly *Periodically*) has recently been revised to meet the preferences of its users. Issued five times a year, without cost, during the school year, it includes about 2½ pages devoted to AIDS (Activities, Inquiries and Demonstrations), and additional notes on programs which may generate materials, and a column entitled "In the Reviewer's Opinion," which includes detailed reviews of single items — with student input — as well as broad overviews of fields.

The Clearinghouse also issues and updates bibliographies of materials in its areas of concern. Currently, four free annotated bibliographies are available, including one on *Resource Materials, Course Descriptions, Curriculum Guides and Instructional Units*, and another on *Textbooks*.

Two outstanding background publications are *Teaching Psychology in Secondary School* (1974) by Richard A. Kasschau and Michael Wertheimer (one of a series produced jointly with ERIC Clearinghouse for Social Studies/Social Science Education) and *Psychology Teacher's Resource Book; First Course*, now undergoing revision. Both are reviewed separately in this section.

The Committee on Psychology in the Secondary Schools addresses itself to curriculum development and instruction, inservice and preservice training, certification of teachers — overall to problem areas and improvement of service in teaching psychology at the secondary level. Like the Clearinghouse, it welcomes input from teachers.

The Committee has also prepared a simple, convenient *Checklist for a New Course in Psychology*, which could be a useful model for any group or school considering adding, altering, or reviewing curriculum offerings in any subject. Areas included are rationale, target population, course content, teaching strategies, physical safety, ethical concerns, community resources, teacher qualifications, and instructional materials.

Psychology teachers in high schools who become High School Teacher Affiliates (for $2.50) receive the *APA Monitor* and can subscribe to APA publications at greatly reduced costs.

Behavioral Science Education Project (BSEP)
Ann Arbor Community Services
212 S. Fourth Ave.
Ann Arbor, MI 48108

The Behavioral Science Education Project, which began in 1969, was a Washtenaw County effort to extend the development and use of behavioral science curricula in elementary and secondary schools and to develop means of encouraging teachers and other educators to make available to children and youth in school situations concepts developed by behavioral scientists that will foster understanding of oneself and others and will help all concerned to live and work more effectively in school and out.

To carry out its dissemination, evaluation, development and training efforts, the BSEP evaluated and surveyed literature and materials in this field; field-tested some existing materials; created its own curriculum when needed; and conducted seminars, conferences, study clubs and inservice training for teachers. An Information Resource Center (IRC) contained a library of curricula, teacher resource books, cassettes, phonograph records, journal articles, research reports, lesson plans, course and unit descriptions, project outlines, classroom exercises and techniques, posters, and pamphlets. The IRC has compiled bibliographies and resource guides to the field.

Furthering the Development of Children in Schools, by Richard Munger and Mark M. Ravlin (1977. 44p. mimeo. $2.00), provides valuable assistance in setting up programs, as well as a good bibliography on affective education theory and practice. Two other publications, *Affective Development in Schools* and *Helping Children and Youth with Feelings*, are annotated in Key Publications.

The BSEP has been discontinued as of 1980. For information on its products, contact Dr. William Morse, 3210 School of Education Building, University of Michigan, Ann Arbor, MI 48109.

ERIC Clearinghouse on Counseling and Personnel Services (ERIC/CAPS)
2108 School of Education
University of Michigan
Ann Arbor, MI 48109   (313) 764-9492

ERIC/CAPS, because of its psychological orientation, is probably the best ERIC resource for materials on affective education. Its *Searchlight* bibliography, No. 20, *Psychological and Affective Education* ($1.50, prepaid), provides a 1968-1977 search of the entire ERIC data base on this particular topic. Some materials on needs assessment can also be helpful; *Needs Assessment: Who Needs It?* ($3.00 prepaid), by Donald G. Hayls and Jean K. Linn, uses step-by-step examples of the process. *Searchlight* bibliography No. 21, *Needs Assessment* ($1.50 prepaid), could help educators considering the introduction of affective courses.

Mental Health Materials Center (MHMC)
419 Park Ave., S
New York, NY 10016   (212) 889-5760

This nonprofit educational agency, one of the very few such agencies primarily concerned with materials, was founded in 1953 to help screen and identify the best and most effective mental health materials of all those published. Its expertise is still in the evaluation and effective use of program aids—including publications, films, audiovisuals, videotapes, research findings, conferences, and related services in all areas related to mental health.

MHMC defines mental health to include such areas as alcoholism, drug abuse, sex and family life education, values clarification, health education and, increasingly, the relationships between people and environment. It has collaborated with many child-centered organizations to help deploy educational materials and establish congruent publishing programs, as well as to locate appropriate materials. It can arrange seminars on effective use of materials which delineate principles of selection and program planning, demonstrate creative uses of materials, and help participants develop or improve their own skills.

Its own publications generally bear in some way on the use of materials in mental health programs. Some of these are *Showcase of Mental Health Materials* by Betty Jones ($3.50), a demonstration or how-to program for mental health, and *Memorandum to Discussion Leaders* ($0.25) for discussion leaders who lack training in leading discussions in human relations. *Selective Guide* (see Key Publications), though expensive, is a highly reliable and time-saving guide which eliminates about 90 percent of published materials and points out appropriate audiences and uses for the remainder. Nina Ridenour's philosophy of mental health materials is presented in *Mental Health Education* (see Key Publications). This discussion of principles in the effective use of mental health materials is relevant for teachers interested in mental health or family life education.

Three bimonthly publications update the *Selective Guide: In-Depth Reports, Sneak Previews*, and *News, Notes & Ideas*. The last is prepared by the Washington office of the MHMC and includes updates on related government regulations and legislation, reports on innovative projects, and information on evaluation techniques and program implementation. *Sneak Previews* includes 40 or 50 lively staff film previews per issue, with price, ordering information and rankings on value. *In-Depth Reports* supplements the *Selective Guide* with 10 or 20 recommended items each issue and is, as its title indicates, for in-depth reporting on innovative programs and projects in mental health education.

Mental Health Media Evaluation Project
P.O. Box 1548
Springfield, VA 22151   (703) 978-6975

This project, affiliated with the Mental Health Association, started its media search with 16mm films in 1976 and 1977. During this period it located approximately 1,500 mental health films appropriate for an audience of mental health educators, film librarians, program coordinators, and the general public. About 500 of these were identified as meeting its established criteria: 16mm format, 60 minutes or fewer in running time, informational content applicable to public mental health application, produced since 1966 (unless a classic or unique work), and nationally available for rental, free loan, lease, or purchase.

The Project held the first of its annual film festivals in 1977 to provide recognition for outstanding films in mental health. Its two *Mental Health Association Film Festival Programs*, at $5.00 each, provide information on a good number of films — 83 in 1977, and 60 in 1978.

Its *Comprehensive Resource Guide to 16 MM Mental Health Films* (1977. 120p. $25.00 prepaid; $20.00 to Mental Health Association affiliates) provides annotations and descriptive information on 1,300 films. Its *Evaluative Guide to 16 MM Mental Health Films* (1977. 65p. $15.00 prepaid; single copy free to MHA affiliates) describes 350 recommended films which meet the criteria above, and provides very brief suggestions for use and excerpts from evaluators' comments. Both guides are arranged by title and include brief annotations, descriptive information on length and color, and codes for audience, availability, and sources. Neither includes prices. Subject indexes in the fronts of these two volumes allow access to films under broad categories.

Purchasers of the *Comprehensive Resource Guide* receive six folders per year of distributors' promotional materials advertising new films. A quarterly *Up-Dates* at $25.00 per year ($20.00 for affiliates) provides information on a variety of audiovisuals similar to that included in the *Evaluative Guide*.

The Project is currently emphasizing the evaluation of media other than 16mm films. In general, the materials it locates are more appropriate for secondary school, college, and adult audiences than for teachers at the elementary level, though there are items appropriate for younger audiences.

National Institute of Mental Health (NIMH)
Public Inquiries Section
Room 9−C-05
5600 Fishers Lane
Rockville, MD 20852   (301) 443-4278
Current listings of NIMH publications on such topics as child mental health, aging, crime and delinquency, community mental health, and related subjects are available from the above address. Single courtesy copies of many publications are available from NIMH. Others can be purchased from the Superintendent of Documents, U.S. GPO, Washington, DC 20402.

The NIMH has a National Clearinghouse for Mental Health Information intended primarily for NIMH staff, but available to other professionals at the discretion of its librarian.

KEY PUBLICATIONS

Affective Development in Schools: Resource Programs and Persons, by William
        C. Morse and Richard L. Munger. Ann Arbor, MI: Behavioral Science Education Project, 1975. 95p. $3.00 mimeo.
This BSEP publication contains brief descriptions of representative programs in affective education that were located in a preliminary search. The book essentially is a compilation of survey forms of these programs, alphabetically arranged, with information on name, title, address of program, persons associated with program, affiliations, and starting and termination dates, as well as space for brief description and comments. The survey offers insight on resources and possible approaches. Many of the projects provide a view of their published and forthcoming materials.

The Bookfinder: A Guide to Children's Literature about the Needs and Problems of Youth Aged 2-15, by Sharon Spredemann Dreyer. Circle Pines,
        MN: American Guidance Service, Ind., 1977. 649p. $25.00.
This unique reference work identifies, discusses and categorizes more than 1,000 recent children's books—hardbound books published through 1975—that can help a child or groups of children cope with ordinary or severe life challenges. Most of these books deal with contemporary children. Interestingly, 90 percent are fiction, although the selection criteria were not related to form.

The arrangement of this large book is unusual but convenient, apparently the result of extensive field tests in 1976. It has a split-page format, with annotations of trade books, arranged alphabetically by author and then by title, on the lower part of the page. These annotations provide clear summaries of plots and characters as well as major and sub-themes.

The upper half of the page (essentially a separate volume) includes topical, author, and title indexes, addresses of publishers, and a brief recapitulation of the uses and history of bibliotherapy, with a bibliography of bibliotherapy. The topical index, essentially an index of themes, includes 450 psychological, behavioral and developmental terms which range (alphabetically) from abandonment to work attitude. Other examples are adoption, courage, death, divorce, ethnic/racial prejudice, fantasy, fear, friendship, gender role identity, going to the hospital, loneliness, parents, running away, sex, sibling relationships, and weight control. For each theme there are from one to several dozen books.

The split-page format and flexible binding allow users to keep the subject (or other) index open to a particular topic, while browsing or reviewing specific titles in the annotation section, a convenient time-saving feature.

Overall, this book is a valuable tool which brings to teachers, counselors and school librarians some of the expertise and knowledge of an experienced children's librarian. The annotations and categories are well done, and, while they are not a complete substitute for first-hand knowledge of children's literature, they do provide complete bibliographic access to a great number of well-chosen children's books, with notice of other versions of the work (e.g., braille, filmstrip, paperback, Spanish language).

The books chosen for inclusion were those that deal with real life situations faced by some or all children, and that contain enough information or insight to be worth recommending to children in similar situations.

Children's Literature: An Issues Approach, by Masha K. Rudman. Lexington, MA: D. C. Heath, 1976. 433p. $9.95pa.

This issues-oriented guide, which grew out of the author's theme-centered course in children's literature, has eight chapters dealing with issues important to young — up to age twelve — children in contemporary society: siblings, divorce, death and old age, war, sex, blacks, native Americans, and females. Each of these chapters id divided into six parts: 1) a discussion of the issue, which includes criteria for selecting and using books on this topic; 2) a section discussing the ways particular books relate to this topic; 3) suggestions for teachers (or other adults) to personalize or extend the discussion; 4) suggestions for children, designed to extend their critical reading skills; 5) an annotated list of other sources for adults which deal in some way with relations between books, children and this topic; and, finally, an annotated list of children's books on this topic. (About 1,350 books are annotated in all, with some indication of grade or interest level.)

This book can be used for teaching and could be helpful in assembling theme-centered materials from titles available in public libraries. It is particularly valuable for its selection criteria, its perceptive discussions, and its references for educators. The final chapter on using children's books in reading programs is loaded with suggestions: ideas for implementing programs through grouping, room arrangement, scheduling and record keeping; a stimulating, easy-to-use list of book-centered activities; a discussion of self-selection and self-evaluation; and related references for teachers. Appendix C is a well-annotated bibliography of about 40 other guides to children's literature. Other features are publishers' addresses, lists of award books, an author/illustrator index, a title index, and a good subject index which includes themes and skills.

Coping: Books about Young People Surviving Special Problems: A Bibliography Based on the Acquisitions of EDMARC, by Mary DeWitt Billings. Washington, DC: GPO, 1977. 10p. $1.60.

This short but helpful bibliography of about 100 books is based on books received at EDMARC between January 1976 and April 1977 that received at least two favorable reviews in major review publications. All books included are written for children and deal with contemporary issues such as divorce, working parents, aging, death, running away from home, sex, and child abuse. (Sibling rivalry and handling fantasies are also included in titles for children under seven.) Some mental health categories represented are mental illness, retardation, suicide, severe depression, and dealing with emotions. The entry for each book provides graded levels, a full citation (except for price), and an excellent short description of the book's content. Books are grouped in three broad age-grade groups. Despite the lack of an index, *Coping* is easy to browse.

Discussing Death: A Guide to Death Education, by Gretchen C. Mills and others. 18512 Pierce Terrace, Homewood, IL 60430, ETC Publications, 1976. 140p. $8.50; $5.50pa.

A comprehensive resource and discussion guide for teachers who feel unprepared to discuss death as part of the life cycle. It covers all age ranges from five through high school, and for each includes a brief comment on how children of that age comprehend death as well as concepts which can be developed—providing specific objectives, suggested activities, and relevant books for children to read and discuss.

Another valuable presentation of children's books on death and old age can be found in Masha Rudman's *Children's Literature: An Issues Approach* (Indianapolis, IN: Heath, 1976), on pages 69-113.

Fantasy and Feeling in Education, by Richard M. Jones. New York: Harper, 1968. 276p. $9.50.

Deals with the importance of utilizing emotions and fantasy with educational materials that evoke student feelings and emotions. It provides instances of classroom activities and discussions based on "Family of Man" materials, showing how to evoke content for cognitive and affective growth.

Guide to Mental Health Education Materials: A Directory for Mental Health Educators. National Institute of Mental Health. Rockville, MD: National Institute of Mental Health, 1974. 56p. $0.85. (From GPO, Washington, DC 20402. Single copies free from National Institute of Mental Health, 5600 Fishers Lane, Rockville, MD 20857).

This compact directory offers quick entry into mental health publications (and a few media materials) from 42 commercial publishers and advocacy organizations to professional associations and government agencies. Materials are grouped under subjects, e.g., aging, alcoholism, drugs, racism, recreation, sex. Descriptions include title, price, and sources, sometimes pagination, and occasionally annotations. Most of these publications are inexpensive; some are free. The appendix has addresses and informative annotated descriptions of the issuing agencies.

Helping Children and Youth with Feelings: Affective-Behavioral Science Education Resources for the Developing Self/Schools, by William C. Morse and Richard L. Munger. Ann Arbor, MI: Behavioral Science Education Project, 1975. 57p. $2.00 mimeo.

This bibliography of teaching materials and classroom materials is intended to help classroom teachers select materials for affective education (to enhance normal development, not as a substitute for special education or clinical service). For teachers, it includes books and articles, recommended periodical titles and issues, projects and organizations, and additional resources. Children's materials are represented with a one-page sampling of children's books and annotated outlines of selected curricula based on publishers' descriptions. This useful compilation, which seems thoughtfully selected by people who know the field, is unfortunately marred by inconsistent and sometimes incomplete bibliographic entries.

Human Relations and Values: A Guide to Films, compiled by Carol Jesko, Richard Munger, and Karen Sayer. Ann Arbor, MI: University of Michigan Audio-Visual Education Center, 1976. Unp. (Free from University of Michigan, Media Center, Ann Arbor, MI 48109).

This film list, a cooperative venture with BSEP, annotates and classifies about 175 films dealing with human relationships, with indication of grade level, color, length, course, date, and rental fee from University of Michigan. Typical topics (found in the "A" section) include acceptance of handicaps, acceptance of others, acceptance of self, achievement, adolescence, aesthetic sense, aggression, aloneness, alternatives, anger, anxiety, apathy, assertiveness, attitudes, authority and awareness. Films seem well chosen, well described, and well indexed. For some there is a useful introduction to school use.

Index to Psychology (Multimedia), 3rd ed. Los Angeles: National Information Center for Educational Media, 1977. 1,021p. $47.00.

This comprehensive directory of instructional (nonprint) material has about 18,000 entries on psychology and related areas, such as counseling and guidance, sexual behavior, smoking, drugs and alcohol, attitudes and opinions, sociology, and special education, on all levels from preschool to professional, arranged alphabetically by title and indexed by classified subject. (A fairly high proportion of materials are on adult or professional levels.) Descriptions include title, size and physical description, length, color, producer, distributor, year of release, grade level, and LC catalog card number. A directory of producers and distributors is included.

While this NICEM directory is not at all selective or evaluative, it can be useful in identifying sources and materials. It is updated through NICEM's *Update.*

Mental Health Education: Principles in the Effective Use of Materials, by Nina Ridenour. New York: Mental Health Materials Center, 1969. 116p. $5.00.

A practical and forthright work. Intended for mental health professionals and family life educators, it deals with the effective use of appropriate materials — *how* to use *which* items *where* and with *whom*.

Chapter one gives attention to criteria, ways of distinguishing between education and public relations or popularity and superficiality, and the hazards of free materials. Chapter two, on presentation, has a good discussion of assessing the match between materials and intended audiences. Chapter three provides some guidelines for assessing whether or not materials were effective. Chapter four discusses relationships between programs and materials. Chapter five is a rationale for mental health education and a perspective on mental health itself.

Mental Health in the Classroom. Rev. ed. Kent, OH: American School Health Association, 1968. 44p. $2.50.

This report — prepared by the Committee on Mental Health in the Classroom — uses the simple, handy format of other ASHA publications, with concepts, learning experiences and materials arranged in parallel columns for each grade level. Though dated, the concepts, learning experiences and materials listed in the excerpt reprinted on page 104 are still good starting places for introducing mental health.

Now Upon a Time: A Contemporary View of Children's Literature, by Myra Pollack Sadker and David Miller Sadker. New York: Harper and Row, 1977. 475p. $13.95.

Two university teachers of children's literature cover (mostly contemporary) children's books dealing with life cycles (family, sex, aging, and death), women and minorities in American ecology, humor, war and peace, censorship, and ways to teach issues creatively with literature.

Appendix A has an annotated bibliography of books depicting the handicapped — both fiction and nonfiction — useful to sensitizing children in mainstreamed schools to problems and aspirations of handicapped individuals.

The Psychology Teacher's Resource Book: First Course, by M. Johnson and M. Wertheimer. 3rd ed. Washington, DC: American Psychological Association, 1979. 209p. $6.50pa.

This comprehensive sourcebook for psychology teachers, revised in 1979, provides brief reviews and comparison of textbooks, reading books, and laboratory manuals; a tabulated list of journals including name, address, costs, reading levels, typical article length, descriptions, and recommendations; an extensive list of nontechnical books (such as novels, case studies, biographies) for high school students, classified by problem area; comprehensive guides to broadranging audiovisual materials and reference materials; lists of sources for animals, equipment and supplies; and addresses of organizations apt to provide instructional materials or information for psychology students and teachers. It covers approximately 1,000 items altogether.

Textbooks were evaluated for emphasis, content, and reading levels. Reviewers of books of readings covered quantity of selections, reading level, level of student sophistication, unusual features and interest values.

Page excerpted from *Mental Health in the Classroom*
(Reprinted by permission of the American School Health Association)

THE JOURNAL OF SCHOOL HEALTH   11

GRADE ONE

CONCEPTS	LEARNING EXPERIENCES	MATERIALS
I. Personality structure and development		
Satisfaction in creative activities Importance of cultivating sense of humor and pleasant voice Progress in caring for self and possessions Satisfactions from new experiences	Discuss and develop standards for care of belongings Provide opportunities for pupils to have responsibilities Encourage originality and creativity	Bauer, W. W., et al. *Health for All.* Junior Primer and Book One Kaune, Merriman. *My Own Little House* Thurstone, Thelma and Katharine Byrne. *Mental Abilities of Children* Yashima, Taro. *Youngest One*
II. Interaction of an individual with others, including influences of cultural patterns		
Harmonious relations with brothers and sisters Contributions to family teamwork; taking turns Development of friendships Control of hands and feet Use of "please" and "thank you" Courtesy and kindness to others Participation in solving individual and group problems Respect for rights of others Understanding of various cultural patterns	Provide opportunities for pupils to take turns. wait for teacher's help, etc. Encourage pupils to tell about people, objects, and events in other countries Read stories about people in other countries Teach pupils some words in another language Show approval of acts of kindness and of love	Books about other cultures, holidays, national heroes Barr, Jane. *Good Morning, Teacher* Gramatky, Hardie. *Loopy* Osborne, Ernest. *How to Teach Your Child About Work* Showers, Paul. *Your Skin and Mine* Sound Motion Pictures *The Hare and the Tortoise Yours, Mine, Ours*
III. Socioeconomic status and its influence on mental health		
Consideration for children of different backgrounds	Read stories about children from various kinds of homes Dramatize selected stories	Pictures of children and families of various places Showers, Paul. *Look at Your Eyes*
IV. Emotional climate in home and classroom		
Development of a constructive emotional climate (rapport) through pupil-teacher planning Understanding what is expected, how to work, how to wait, how to play with others Willingness to get help when needed	Read to pupils, then ask them to act out the story Make experience charts dictated by pupils Plan with pupils to make a gift for their parents Develop the respect of the group by asking pupils what *they* think Use indirect remarks such as "We're waiting for someone," in order to retain group control	Kessler, Leonard. *Here Comes the Strikeout* Ridenour, Nina. *Building Self-Confidence in Children* Sound Motion Picture *The Fun of Making Friends* Transcription *Timid Timothy*

Selected Mental Health Audiovisuals. Washington, DC: GPO, 1978. 233p. $2.95.

Lists films, filmstrips, audiotapes, and videotapes in 27 major mental health categories including psychology, animal studies, cognition and perception, learning, community mental health, personality, social issues, treatment, and others. A list of free social welfare films, sources for low-cost film rental, and commercial rental libraries are included.

Selective Bibliography in Behavioral Sciences Resources, by Judith E. Hedstrom. Boulder, CO: Social Science Education Consortium, 1977. 32p. $1.75.

This annotated bibliography of behavioral science resources includes basal curriculum materials, supplementary materials, media and audiovisual materials, games and simulations, teacher resources, associations, organizations, and ERIC documents. All materials were selected for quality, usefulness, recency, and availability—with complete citations including producers' addresses, and Fry readability scores for print materials.

This is one of a series of five bibliographies recently issued by SSEC. The total set (which includes anthropology, world history, economics, political science, and U.S. history) is available for $8.00.

A Selective Guide to Materials for Mental Health and Family Life Education, compiled and edited by Mental Health Materials Center. Rev. ed. Chicago, IL: Marquis Who's Who, 1976. 947p. $45.00. (Free updates available with coupon from *Selective Guide*, MHMC, 419 Park Ave., S, New York, NY 10066).

The 550 items evaluated and summarized in this latest edition of the *Selective Guide* were carefully selected by the editors and consultants of the MHMC in New York as the best of available materials in mental health (about 10 percent of those reviewed). These program items (films, filmstrips, books, pamphlets, leaflets, plays, and others) come from a wide variety of commercial, professional, and government sources with emphasis on current recommendations, though the *Guide* describes many older sensitive and sound titles.

It begins with several useful discussions on effective selection and use of print and nonprint materials in mental health. Materials, mostly for mental health educators and professionals, are arranged by topics which include child growth and development, adolescence, family life—including sex education and aging—and areas of special concern, such as intergroup relations, physical handicaps, developmental disabilities, mental retardation, drug abuse and alcoholism, crime and delinquency, and reference materials. For each item chosen, the *Guide* provides bibliographic detail, source and price, an authoritative evaluation, and suggested audience and uses. Some materials are appropriate for students; many would be appropriate for in-service training for teachers.

Sourcebook on the Teaching of Psychology, edited by P. J. Woods. Roanoke, VA: Scholar's Press, 1973. looseleaf. $22.50. (From P.O. Box 7231, Roanoke, VA 24019).

This looseleaf guide, an outgrowth of the Course Outlines Project of the APA, resembles SSEC's *Data Book* in its looseleaf format and annual updating. Intended for teachers at high school and college undergraduate levels, it includes about 40 course outlines and bibliographies for teaching in 14 traditional areas in psychology and in topical areas like psychology and politics or feminine roles.

Teach Us What We Want to Know, by Ruth Byler, Gertrude Lewis, and Ruth
    Totman. New York: Mental Health Materials Center, 1969. 179p. $3.00.

This interesting document reports a survey of 5,000 K-12 children by the
Connecticut State Department of Education, often using the very words and
recommendations of the children themselves. It contains a wealth of information
on student interests and preferences as well as professional interpretations of the
findings. Four parts cover health interests and concerns (elementary and secondary) and children's interests — at different ages — in such subjects as the body,
nutrition and food, exercise, physical education, safety and first aid, mental
health, sex education, and emotional development.

Teaching Human Beings: 101 Subversive Activities for the Classroom, by
    Jeffrey Schrank. Boston: Beacon Press, 1972. 192p. $7.95; $3.45pa.

This book includes 101 interesting classroom activities dealing with
unorthodox areas such as hidden assumptions, violence and the violated, learning
about death, and subversive activities; most activities are appropriate for a wide
range of age levels elementary and older. For most topics it suggests background
readings with lists of related books, films and filmstrips.

Teaching Psychology in Secondary Schools, by Richard A. Kasschau and
    Michael Wertheimer. Washington, DC: American Psychological Associa-
    tion, and Boulder, CO: ERIC Clearinghouse for Social Studies/Social
    Science Education, 1974. 64p. $2.50.

This publication is part of a parallel series on trends in social science education commissioned by ERIC/ChESS. It covers, interestingly, the history and
philosophy of secondary psychology courses, certification of teachers, and
includes a solid appendix on resources. There is a very sensitive and informative
chapter on psychology curriculum materials, with commentary on the difficulties
inherent in evaluating such curricula.

The Uses of Enchantment: The Meaning and Importance of Fairy Tales, by
    Bruno Bettelheim. New York: Knopf, 1976. 328p. $12.50.

Bettelheim's book is an impassioned and scholarly presentation of the values
of fairy tales as growth experiences for children, prepared under a grant to
explore the contributions of psychoanalysis to education. To Bettelheim, an
educator and therapist, fairy tales are mirrors reflecting inner human development. This book examines some popular fairy tales in terms of the developmental
stages and tasks they represent and shows their meaning and application to
children. The principles demonstrated here can help teachers and librarians
perceive, assess, and recommend similar stories.

What Makes Me Feel This Way? Growing Up with Human Emotions, by Eda
    LeShan. New York: Macmillan, 1972. 128p. $4.95.

A book — for children — on the whole range of feelings, including those
which children do not like to talk about or do not understand. An invitation for
children to explore their own feelings and, if they want, to talk about them with
adults or friends. Covers the difference between feeling and knowing, what happens when feelings are not allowed, letting feelings show, feelings that confuse,
dreams and daydreams, understanding grownups, and feelings that come later.

FOR FURTHER READING

Several more extensive bibliographies are cited in the text. These include items prepared by ERIC/CAPS, the end bibliography in BSEP's *Furthering the Development of Children in Schools* and bibliographies incorporated in MMHC and APA publications.

*Items marked with an asterisk include criteria.

+ Items marked with a plus include additional references.

* + Baskin, Barbara H., and Karen H. Harris. *Notes from a Different Drummer: A Guide to Juvenile Fiction Portraying the Handicapped.* New York: Bowker, 1977.
   Provides detailed critical analyses of 400 fiction works dealing with physically and mentally disabled persons and lists additional nonfiction and curriculum-related titles. Includes criteria for further selections.

+ Bernstein, Joanne E. *Books to Help Children Cope with Separation and Loss.* New York: Bowker, 1977.
   Includes 1,400 recommended books classified by such broad topics as family deaths, adoption and foster placement, divorce and separation, loss of mental and/or physical functions, and general concerns about death. Annotations of individual titles cover age and reading levels as well as therapeutic values.

Buchholz, Ester S. "The Proper Study for Children: Children and Their Feelings," *Psychology in the Schools*, v. 11, no. 1 (Jan. 1974), pp. 10-15.

Canfield, J., and H. Wells. *100 Ways to Enhance Self-Concept.* New York: Prentice-Hall, 1976.

Castillo, Gloria A. *Left-handed Teaching: Lessons in Affective Education.* New York: Praeger, 1974.

Chase, L. *The Other Side of the Report Card: A How-to-do-it Program for Affective Education.* Pacific Palisades, CA: Goodyear, 1975.

+ Horner, Catherine T. *The Single-Parent Family in Children's Books....With an Appendix on Audiovisual Materials.* Metuchen, NJ: Scarecrow Press, 1978.

Kagan, Jerome. *Understanding Children: Behavior, Motives and Thought.* New York: Harcourt, Brace, Jovanovich, 1971.

Krathwohl, D., and others. *Taxonomy of Educational Objectives: The Classification of Educational Goals, Handbook II, Affective Domain.* New York: McKay, 1964.

Maas, J. B. "Selecting Audiovisual Materials for Teaching in the Behavioral Sciences," *Behavioral and Social Science Teacher*, v. 1, no. 1 (Fall 1973-1974), pp. 69-71.

Mattocks, Arthur I., and Charles C. Jew. "The Teacher's Role in the Development of a Healthy Self-Concept in Pupils," *Education*, v. 94, no. 3 (Feb.-March 1974), pp. 200-214.

Morimoto, Kimo. "Notes on the Context for Learning," *Harvard Educational Review*, v. 43, no. 2 (May 1973), pp. 245-47.

Munger, Richard, and Mark M. Ravlin. *Furthering the Development of Children in Schools*. Ann Arbor, MI: Behavioral Science Education Project, 1977.

Querashi, M. Y., and R. R. Zulli. "A Content Analysis of Introductory Psychology Textbooks," *Teaching of Psychology*, v. 2, no. 2 (April 1975), pp. 60-65.

Ready, D., and S. Simon. *Humanistic Education Sourcebook*. Englewood Cliffs, NJ: Prentice-Hall, 1975.

Ringness, T. *The Affective Domain in Education*. Boston: Little, Brown, 1975.

+ Rubin, Rhea Joyce. *Bibliotherapy Sourcebook*. Phoenix, AZ: Oryx Press, 1978.

Stahl, Robert J. *The Status of Precollege Psychology in Florida from 1970-71 through 1974-75: A Report of a Longitudinal Study*. Gainesville, FL: P. K. Yonge Laboratory School, 1976. (Research Monograph No. 22).

Stahl, Robert J. *The Status of Precollege Psychology in Mississippi and Florida: A Comparative Report*. Columbus: Mississippi College for Women, May 1977.

Thompson, J. *Beyond Words: Nonverbal Communication in the Classroom*. New York: Citation, 1973.

Vallett, R. *Affective-Humanistic Education*. Belmont, CA: Fearon, 1975.

SELECTING MATERIALS FOR
HEALTH EDUCATION

"When we start looking at issues such as human biology, there is suddenly a great deal of disagreement about the information to which people should have access."
— Janet Hanley Whitla, Director, School and Society Program, Education Development Center, Newton, MA

"We need to get people to live differently if we are going to influence their health."
— Leonard Syme, School of Public Health, University of California, Berkeley

□ □ □

Several topics that logically could be part of health education — sex education, nutrition, and narcotics education — are treated separately in this cluster of chapters on health-related education. Though some of the criteria and many of the problems are the same, they were treated separately because independent guides, sources, and criteria make this seem a more convenient approach. These three topics — which could also be discussed with mental health education — involve both knowledge (scientific facts) and attitudes, as does health education itself.

Health education is considered an applied science that draws from the disciplines of psychology, biology, medicine, social sciences, and environmental sciences. In schools, it may be taught as part of physical education, consumer education, family life education, science (particularly biology), or psychology courses, or as part of fire safety week or driver education. But, philosophically, health education, like much of modern medicine, has been more concerned with disease than with health.

According to Anne Castile and Stephen Jerrick's survey of *School Health in America* (Kent, OH: American School Health Association, 1976), many states have legislative or other mandates that require (or forbid) particular parts of health education; about 35 states require instruction on drugs, alcohol and/or tobacco; 8 states require venereal disease education; 16 states have some sort of requirement on safety education; 11 demand some kind of nutrition education; and mental health education is required in 13, education on diseases in another 13, community health in 10 states, environmental health in 8, family life or sex education in 7, personal health education in 10, anatomy and physiology in 5, dental health and/or oral hygiene in 7, consumer health education in 8, education in growth and development in 6, health careers in 4, and first aid in 6. The descriptions of course are overlapping and variable, not necessarily logical.

Still, these varied requirements — confusing though they are — reflect some sort of public and legislative consensus that it is important to allot time during the school year to affect some aspects of the future health behavior of students and adults. These fragmented approaches, unfortunately, do not permit a continuing, comprehensive, pertinent program — reaching all students in all grade levels — that might succeed in developing or changing health habits.

According to surveys and assessments, students are quite interested in, and relatively well informed on, health facts. Health education, indeed, is one of the brighter areas tested by the National Assessment of Educational Progress, though even here, because of the "controversial" nature of sex education, the NAEP did not attempt to question 17-year-old students on their knowledge of topics like birth control, family planning, prenatal care, or venereal disease. Their study, *Checkup*, however, found that most students of 17 knew comparatively many facts about good health practices, accident prevention, and emergency health care, though young adults of 24, questioned on the same topics, consistently knew more. This consistent difference between 17-year-olds and young adults suggests that, quite likely, a good proportion of health knowledge is acquired outside the school. Even though the factual basis is high compared to other subjects tested, health education in schools is limited by a restricted and/or inconsistent curriculum. Areas that seem to need substantial improvement include emergency care, drug and alcohol use, and contraception.

In health education there is also an obvious gap between belief and action. (Smoking, for example, is pandemic—and increasing—among high school youths, even though 90 percent believe that it is harmful—or at least believe that this is the acceptable answer.)

Though few schools have comprehensive health programs, somewhere in their buried archives of passed resolutions almost every organization concerned with health and education has recommended a comprehensive health education program—based on student needs—from preschool or kindergarten to twelfth grade, complete with specified times, adequate budgets and adequate teachers. Organizations recommending such time and materials allocations include the National Education Association; the American Alliance for Health, Physical Education, Recreation and Dance; the American Association of School Administrators; the National School Boards Association; the National Congress of Parents and Teachers; and medical associations such as the American Public Health Association, the American Dental Association, the American School Health Association, and the American Medical Association. The recommendations of the latter may be typical.

The Department of Health Education of the American Medical Association suggests that a professionally-directed health education program should offer opportunities for students to:

- discuss problems, issues, and topics of interest to them
- obtain accurate information on crucial areas such as drug abuse, nutrition, venereal disease, human sexuality, obesity, alcoholism, mental health, self-medication, and smoking
- become interested in health and safety aspects of daily activities
- learn how one's health status is related to health behavior
- practice skills in understanding, interpreting, and evaluating health information
- develop a critical attitude toward advertising of health services and products
- experience a sense of responsibility for personal, family and community health
- gain understanding of growth and development from conception through adolescence
- explore the processes through which social values are acquired and the ways in which they can affect health

- examine attitudes, values and beliefs that they hold and that other students hold
- develop and maintain relationships with others
- use relevant problems in developing critical thinking and decision-making skills

These recommendations are consistent with student needs as well as with the health concerns of 5,000 K-12 students as revealed in *Teach Us What We Want to Know* (reviewed in the chapter on the feeling domain).

Other areas that should probably be included in current health education are:

- environmental origins of world health trends
- environmental sources of disease, including cancer
- occupationally-induced diseases
- health toll of affluent diets and life styles
- social policies that permit undernutrition and poor sanitation
- prenatal nutrition
- child-rearing practices

Aside from commercial materials, a wide range of inexpensive, free, and/or free-loan materials are available from voluntary and professional health agencies and from governmental organizations. Most lung associations, for example, will lend out models of lungs, while comparable models, charts, recordings, games, and pictorial materials are available from other voluntary and governmental agencies. *Media and the Curriculum* provides information on some sources for such materials. these materials are apt to be authoritative, but, of course, should be subjected to reviews and criteria as should other free and inexpensive materials.

Since textbooks cannot possibly treat all topics with adequate depth, these materials—and other printed materials—are needed for comprehensive coverage. For health, it is important to include current periodicals, pamphlets, reference materials, and books that reflect and express unorthodox viewpoints on topics like health hazards and holistic health. There is, indeed, a wealth of materials to be incorporated into the curriculum, if someone or some group is responsible for that curriculum. In many schools the school nurse is by far the most knowledgeable person for suggesting sources and for appraising accuracy and reliability. She or he can also suggest direct experiences and materials that should be used when possible. These might include thermometers and other health and first-aid supplies, health appraisal materials such as eye charts, stop watches for fitness tests, etc.

Other local sources are local medical groups, medical schools, and voluntary health organizations which are often aware of, or even developers of, health education materials. To assure community support and continuity, relevant groups at all levels should be consulted.

Studies show that parental support and involvement in health education can contribute substantially to the success of programs. This help is forthcoming in many situations. *He-Stra* (AAHE's publication, see Key Organizations) estimated that during 1976 and 1977 the National PTA—largely through its Comprehensive School/Community Health Education Project—devoted more than 5,000 eight-hour working days and more than $300,000 worth of materials and services to improve health education. In this era of back-to-basics and low budgets for materials, we particularly need this kind of parental and community involvement to help health education programs meet their potential.

KEY ORGANIZATIONS

Other organizations active in health education are listed in related chapters on social studies, the feeling domain, sex education, nutrition education, etc. The *Directory of National Organizations Concerned with School Health*, issued by the American School Health Association, is the basic guide for still others.

American Medical Association (AMA)
Department of Health Education
535 North Dearborn Street
Chicago, IL 60610   (312) 751-6588
The purpose of this six-person department of the AMA is to disseminate accurate scientific information on health issues to the general public. It issues a substantial number of low-cost pamphlets and booklets at quantity discounts. Some materials of interest to educators and students include pamphlets and booklets on topics like safety, first aid, alcoholism, smoking, environmental medicine, nutrition, aging, physical fitness, and school health. The Department has also issued ten very interesting pamphlets on sex education at prices which range from $0.24 to $1.00 each. These, and most of its other materials, can easily be incorporated into the curriculum, although they were not specifically designed for this purpose.

Materials are listed in two publication lists, designed respectively for 1) educators and physicians, and 2) medical consumers. Both include items that can be used in health education.

Above and beyond its pamphlet dissemination, the Department of Health Education will answer mailed or telephoned queries on topics related to health and will conduct computer searches of medical data banks (such as MEDLINE, TOXLINE, AVLINE) for a relatively low ($15.00) charge.

This department works with other organizations, like the National Education Association, with which it prepared an authoritative *Suggested School Health Policies* ($1.95) covering health programs for the handicapped and health aspects of physical education as well as more obvious aspects of school health policies.

Why Health Education in Your School?, 1977 ($0.45), includes both rationale and resources for health education.

American School Health Association (ASHA)
1521 South Water
Kent, OH 44240   (216) 678-1601
The American School Health Association—founded in 1927—is the only national professional organization solely concerned with the health of the

school-aged child. It is composed of health educators as well as school nurses, school physicians, dentists, nutritionists, and others. ASHA strives to promote comprehensive and constructive school health programs through health services, health instruction, and promotion of a healthy school environment. It establishes guidelines for standards of excellence and competency for its own members, and serves as the professional liaison among the disciplines in the field of school health, cooperating with local, state, and national organizations in behalf of all school health personnel.

Its publications include authoritative publications on health education, sex education, narcotics education, school health, and mental health from a developmental viewpoint.

> *Directory of National Organizations Concerned with School Health.* Updated at intervals. $3.50; $3.00 members.
>
> Includes current information on approximately 150 organizations concerned with school health, including addresses, purposes, telephone numbers, meetings, publications, subdivisions, sections, etc.

> *Health Instruction: Suggestions for Teachers*, 1977. 90p. $3.00pa.
>
> This interim curriculum guide has many references and suggestions for developing health education experiences for children K-12.

> *Mental Health in the Classroom*, 1968. 44p. $2.50pa.
>
> Useful presentation of behavioral characteristics of students (nursery school to college age) and the appropriate experiences and (often outdated) resource materials.

> *The Journal of School Health* (10 issues/year) is included with membership, and is probably the best single source of information on means of evaluating materials. A *Topical Index* to the *Journal* is available for $3.00 ($2.50 for members). Reprints are available at $0.20 per page ($1.00 minimum order).

Association for the Advancement of Health Education (AAHE)
American Alliance for Health, Physical Education,
 Recreation, and Dance (AAHPERD)
1900 Association Drive
Reston, VA 22091   (703) 476-3460

Though the National Education Association took official cognizance of the importance of having an NEA unit dedicated to the health of school children back in 1894, the AAHE did not begin its independent official existence until 1974. It is a membership organization of health professionals and educators which attempts to serve as liaison agent with other organizations interested in health education, with health professionals generally, and with community groups and educators. It investigates curriculum needs, develops resources, provides information on these and other resources, and develops criteria for health education programs and policies.

One of its journals, *Health Education* (6 issues/year; $20.00), includes reviews of new books, instructional aids, equipment, and supplies, as well as information on innovations and teaching strategies. Current issues include broad articles on the impact of media on health education, content areas in health education for disabled persons, means of understanding and working with power structure in schools, relationships between health education and the social sciences, and similar topics. Though this is a fairly expensive publication, it should be available somewhere in the school district as a source of information on trends and materials.

Other publications which are helpful as guides to materials are:

Consumer Health Education Resource Unit for Junior High Grades, 1971. 20p. $0.75.
This booklet suggests content and teaching ideas for consumer health classes.

Evaluation Instruments in Health Education, Rev. 1969. 32p. $1.00.
This annotated bibliography includes knowledge, attitude and behavior tests for all grades up to first-year college.

Other materials are listed separately in Key Publications.

KEY PUBLICATIONS

See also Key Publications in *Media and the Curriculum* and in health-related topics in this work.

Health: A Multimedia Source Guide, by Joan Ash and Michael Stevenson. New York, Bowker, 1976. 185p. $16.50.
This annotated guide lists and describes 700 groups and organizations that provide information on issues related to health matters. These include associations, research institutes, and foundations; media producers and distributors; book dealers; governmental agencies; pharmaceutical companies and other industrial companies; and libraries or information services. It includes subject and source indexes as well as an index to sources of free and inexpensive health materials.

National Directory of Safety Films. Chicago: National Safety Council. Frequently updated. $4.95pa. (From 444 North Michigan Ave., Chicago, IL 60611).
A comprehensive listing of about 1,000 available films and filmstrips dealing with all aspects of safety. This catalog, updated fairly frequently, provides content summaries, sources, turning time, and release date for the materials it lists, but not price or specific grade levels.

The Council also distributes free flyers on school safety that can be consulted for the safety hazards of toys, school equipment, laboratory materials, playground equipment, and theater sets.

FOR FURTHER READING

*Items marked with an asterisk include criteria.
+ Items marked with a plus include lists of references.

Reprints of the *Journal of School Health* can be obtained from the American School Health Association at $0.20 per page ($1.00 minimum).

Block, A. R. "How to Handle Curriculum Controversy: Legal Perspective," *National Elementary Principal*, v. 57, no. 2 (Jan. 1978), pp. 35-41.

Bowen, R. O. "The Effect of Informal Dissemination of Health Information," *Journal of School Health*, v. 42, no. 6 (June 1972), pp. 342-45.

*Byler, R. V. "Teach Us What We Want to Know," *Journal of School Health*, v. 40, no. 5 (May 1970), pp. 252-55.

Castile, Anne S., and Stephen J. Jerrick. *School Health in America: A Survey of State School Health Programs*. Kent, OH: American School Health Association, 1976.
Provides, with tables, an overview of school health programs and a state-by-state survey which covers agencies and persons responsible for school health education and services, school environment standards, certification requirements, and "immediate plans for improving school health programs."

Cushman, W. P. "An Overview of Approaches to Curricula and Course Construction in Health Education," *Journal of School Health*, v. 39, no. 1 (Jan. 1968), pp. 14-20.

Fodor, J. T. "A Conceptual Approach to Curriculum Development in Venereal Disease Education," *Journal of School Health*, v. 43, no. 5 (May 1973), pp. 303-306.

Glass, L. H., and C. E. Campbell, "Venereal Disease Education: A Comparison of Programmed and Conventional Instruction," *Journal of School Health*, v. 35, no. 7 (Sept. 1965), pp. 322-27.

Hardt, D. V. "Health Curriculum: 370 Topics," *Journal of School Health*, v. 48, no. 1 (Jan. 1978), pp. 656-60.

"Health Education Texts and Supplements," *Curriculum Review*, v. 16, no. 3 (Aug. 1977), pp. 167-79.

Hoyman, H. S. "Models of Human Nature and Their Impact on Health Educatation," *Journal of School Health*, v. 44, no. 7 (Sept. 1974), pp. 374-81.

*Hurt, T. "Conventional Versus Systems and Linear Versus Intrinsic Models for Developing Self-Instructional Materials for Health Education," *Journal of School Health*, v. 42, no. 9 (Nov. 1972), pp. 542-47.

*Lennon, M. L. "Selection of Family Life Education Materials Used in the Chicago Public Schools," *Journal of School Health*, v. 42, no. 4 (April 1972), pp. 233-38.

* + Miller, D. F., and others. "The Readability of Junior High School Health Textbooks," *Journal of School Health*, v. 44, no. 7 (Sept. 1974), pp. 382-85.

National Assessment of Educational Progress. *Checkup: A National Assessment ment of Health Awareness among 17-Year-Olds and Young Adults.* Denver, CO: NAEP, 1978.

"On Philosophical Direction for Health Education," Special Feature Issue, *Health Education*, v. 9, no. 1 (Feb. 1978).
    Fourteen articles and an introduction deal with the philosophical implications and directions of health education.

* + Osborn, B. M., and W. Sutton. "Evaluation of Health Education Materials," *Journal of School Health*, v. 34, no. 2 (Feb. 1964), pp. 72-73.

Pelz, D. R. "A Representative Panel of Teachers Evaluates a Voluntary Health Agency's Classroom Materials," *Journal of School Health*, v. 40, no. 9 (Nov. 1970), pp. 502-504.

Rogers, H. R. "The Multi-Media Approach to Health Science," *Journal of School Health*, v. 42, no. 6 (June 1972), pp. 329-30.

* + Rubin, Milton, and others. "An Instrument to Measure Effectiveness of Oral Health Education Curricula," *Journal of School Health*, v. 48, no. 3 (Feb. 1978), pp. 108-110.

Scheer, J. K., and C. Williams. "Shopping for the Best Text," *Health Education*, v. 8, no. 6 (Nov.-Dec. 1977), pp. 26-27.

Specter, G. J. "School Newspapers as a Source of Health Information," *Journal of School Health*, v. 38, no. 10 (Dec. 1968), pp. 695-97.

Woody, R. H. "Educational Television Programming and School Health," *Journal of School Health*, v. 44, no. 5 (May 1974), pp. 246-49.

SELECTING MATERIALS FOR NARCOTICS EDUCATION

This chapter will consider materials on some voluntarily ingested harmful substances—alcohol, tobacco, and narcotics—though curricula could well be enlarged to consider the involuntary poisons or medical hazards to which we are subjected in modern life. However, other toxic substances are considered under the general rubric of health education. Food overdoses and misuse are considered under nutrition. The social aspects of addiction may be covered in social studies materials; materials relating to the personal implications of addiction or overuse can be located through the tools and sources suggested in the chapter on the feeling domain, particularly the Mental Health Materials Center.

Since people take drugs (tobacco and alcohol) to change the way they feel, drug education must be affective to be effective. Generally, young people take drugs to feel happy—or less unhappy; to escape from pain, stress or frustration; to remember or to forget; to be acceptable or to be sociable; to escape boredom; or to satisfy curiosity. In certain communities peer pressure is a very important component, so ideally, programs need to involve communities to be effective.

Above all, drug education must deal with feelings, not merely information. The National Institute on Drug Abuse, in a free pamphlet, *Drug Abuse Prevention* (1977. 20p. Available from 5600 Fishers Lane, Rockville, MD 20857), suggests that drug abuse programs (and, implicitly, materials) need to encompass the following approaches and objectives:

- improving decision-making skills
- improving communication
- improving interpersonal relationships
- improving health education and health habits
- providing accurate information on drugs and their reactions, balanced with an understanding of why people use drugs
- encouraging the young to respect themselves
- releasing the imagination, curiosity, creativity, and compassion that are natural expressions in young people
- including community resources—knowledge, generations, heritages, cultures
- altering attitudes that equate drug and alcohol abuse with sophistication or maturity
- altering attitudes which are overly harsh on drug users

The program might also consider the peer pressures and the advertising pressures that affect consumption, and materials should, of course, be developmentally appropriate. These perspectives are important for education on tobacco and alcohol as well.

To the present, materials have often been so heavy-handed and moralistic that they have failed to change attitudes and behavior even though they may have succeeded in supplying information. Particularly for elementary students, there have been relatively few materials available, and those available tended to be of relatively poor quality. But, Gail Milgram, the Director of Education of the Rutgers Center of Alcohol Studies, believes that—at least for alcohol education—materials are finally improving in number and quality.

With this increase in the availability of quality materials should arise perspectives which will bring these materials into the learning program. One of the clearest approaches is that of the curriculum in the American School Health Association's *Teaching about Drugs*, which arranges content, materials, activities and objectives under student developmental levels. The chart on page 119 is reprinted by permission of the American School Health Association.

Since many materials are issued by government agencies, the chapter on government documents in *Media and the Curriculum* suggests some appropriate sources—for example, free subject bibliographies by the Superintendent of Documents. Other voluntary and government agencies will supply free or free-loan materials to schools.

KEY ORGANIZATIONS

Other organizations are listed in the chapters on health and the feeling domain. Still others can be found in directories of governmental and voluntary organizations.

American Social Health Association (ASHA)
260 Sheridan Ave., Suite 307
Palo Alto, CA 94306 (415) 321-5134

Founded in 1912, ASHA is a national voluntary organization carrying on a continuous campaign against drug abuse and venereal disease. It places great emphasis on research, public information, and education, and disseminates information. It is currently working with schools and community groups to secure the inclusion of education on venereal disease in school curricula. A complete listing of publications is available from their headquarters office.

National Clearinghouse for Alcohol Information
1776 E. Jefferson St.
    Mailing address:
    P.O. Box 2345
    Rockville, MD 20852 (301) 468-2600

This governmental organization, somewhat analogous to the National Clearinghouse on Drug Abuse Information, also supplies free pamphlets and posters on alcoholism. Its media guide, *In Focus: Alcohol and Alcoholism Media* (1977. 73p. Free), describes and lists about 300 media items (films, filmstrips, slides, video recordings) on alcohol and alcohol-related topics. This is revised and updated through a monthly announcement service.

National Clearinghouse for Drug Abuse Information (NCDAI)
P.O. Box 1635
Rockville, MD 20850 (301) 443-4426

(Text continues on page 120)

ASHA'S CURRICULUM FOR TEACHING ABOUT DRUGS

Late Adolescent Years

Objectives	Content	Learning Activities	Resources and Materials*
A. To understand the wide-spread use of drugs in modern living.	1. Legitimate drug products are medical tools to be used for specific purposes. a. Extensive use in medical practice. (1) To prevent, control, and treat illness and disease. (2) To extend life. (3) To relieve pain. (4) As adjunct to psycho-therapy. (5) To diagnose ill-ness and disease. (6) To facilitate surgery, e.g., anesthetics, anti-hypotensives, immuno-suppressants. b. Self-medication. (1) To relieve minor aches and pains. (2) To combat fatigue. (3) To induce sleep. (4) To alter mood. (5) To supplement diet. (6) To regulate body functions. (7) To improve appear-ance. 2. Social acceptance of the use of drugs and chemicals is widespread. a. Extensive use of pre-scription medicines. b. Extensive use of nonpre-scription medicines for minor aches, pains, etc.	Invite a physician to discuss the use and misuse of pre-scription and nonprescription medicines. Discuss how to differentiate between minor aches and pains and those that need medical attention. Discuss the individual's responsibility when using nonprescription medicines. e.g., the need to follow the manufacturer's directions for use. Analyze the term social ac-ceptance. Evaluate the social acceptance of alcoholic beverages. How important it is? How exten-sive?	**Books:** Houser, Norman W., Rich-mond, Julius, Drugs: Facts on Their Use and Abuse, Scott, Foresman and Co., 1900 E. Lake Ave., Glen-view, Ill., 60025 (Student). Proger, Samuel, The Medi-cated Society, Macmillan Co., 866 Third Ave., New York, N.Y., 10022 (Student). Resource Book for Drug Abuse Education, National Clearinghouse for Mental Health Information, Super-intendent of Documents, U.S. Government Printing Office, Washington, D.C., 20402 (Teacher). **Pamphlets:** McCarthy, Raymond G. and Pascuitti, John J., Facts About Alcohol, No. 5-842, Science Research Asso-ciates, Inc., 259 E. Erie St., Chicago, Ill., 60611 (Student). Read the Label on Home Medicines, The Proprietary Assn., 1700 Pennsylvania Ave., N.W., Washington, D.C., 20006 (Student).

*Resources have been evaluated and selectively chosen for the con-tent area where they appear. Final choice of desirable materials must be made by the teacher.

NCDAI, created in 1970, is now the major federal resource for public inquiries on drug abuse programs and related activities. It has two major functions: first, it operates an information bank and referral center with information on all persons and programs concerned with drug abuse at all levels. Teachers with questions can contact NCDAI and receive information without charge. Second, it produces and distributes publications on drug abuse information, as well as directories of drug-abuse resource people. An excellent education packet of selected materials on drug abuse (including school curricula, bibliographies and catalogs) is available without charge to teachers.

It also supplies a substantial list of government *Publications for Researchers, Community Workers, Educators, Concerned Public.* Free, relevant publications are: *Primary Prevention in Drug Abuse: An Annotated Guide to the Literature* (1977), and *The Rap Kit—Resources for Alternative Pursuits* (1975).

Its computerized information system covers media as well as print materials.

National Council on Alcoholism (NCA)
733 Third Ave.
New York, NY 10017   (212) 986-4433

Established in 1944, the Council works for the prevention and reduction of alcoholism through education, rehabilitation and community services, and serves as a national clearinghouse of information on therapeutic and preventive programs. NCA also supports research and provides consultation to national, state and local agencies (both governmental and voluntary) and to schools, professional organizations and other institutions. Some relevant publications are:

Alcohol. You Can Help Your Kids Cope: A Guide for the Elementary School Teacher, by Peter Finn. 1975. 11p. $0.30.
Provides information on ways to integrate alcohol education into elementary school programs. Reprinted from *Instructor*, Nov. 1975.

What Is Alcohol Education?, 1975. 4p. $0.25.
Basic guidelines for educators. Briefly discusses goals, approaches and techniques.

Resource Guide for Alcohol Education, 1976. 68p. $4.50.
Includes outlined factual information about alcohol use and misuse, with discussion stimulators, related bibliography and suggested audiovisual aids.

Alcohol Information Kits. For students, $1.50; for educators, $2.25.
These special kits contain material by members of the professions and disciplines to which the particular kits are addressed. The authors have, for the most part, been engaged in dealing actively with the problems of alcoholism in relation to the special aspects discussed. These kits are particularly valuable for the special committees of local councils on alcoholism and for institutes and conferences.

Rutgers Center of Alcohol Studies
Rutgers University
New Brunswick, NJ 08903   (201) 932-3510
    The Center of Alcohol Studies is an interdisciplinary unit of Rutgers University that conducts community and laboratory research, a Summer School of Alcohol Studies, and year-round training courses. The Center documents all the scientific and scholarly literature on alcohol problems through a *Classified Abstract Archive of the Alcohol Literature* (CAAAL) which now contains abstracts on cards on more than 20,000 documents arranged according to 94 main categories and 92 subtopics. Educators who wish to peruse headings on alcohol education can locate these cards at 100 depositories around the country. (Addresses may be obtained from the Center.) Their *Journal of Studies on Alcohol* includes about 100 original articles a year, as well as abstracts and reviews of more than 1,500 items annually, with a classified list of current references in each issue. The Center has a substantial publishing program on alcohol, including educational aspects. Some relevant publications are:

> *What Is Alcohol? and Why Do People Drink?*, by Gail G. Milgram. 24p. $1.00.

> "What Shall We Teach the Young about Drinking?," by Robert D. Russell. *Popular Pamphlets on Alcohol Problems* (No. 5). $0.25.

> *Exploring Alcohol Questions*, by R. G. McCarthy. $0.45.
>   Six leaflets, illustrated. For Grades 7 and up.

> *Philosophies for Educating about Alcohol and Other Mood-Modifying Substances; Personal or Social Controls*, by R. D. Russell. $0.35.

> *Drug Education; a Review of Goals, Approaches and Effectiveness, and a Paradigm for Evaluation*, by G. N. Braucht and others. $0.50.

> *A Descriptive Analysis of Alcohol Education Materials*, by Gail G. Milgram. $0.30.

KEY PUBLICATIONS

Alcohol Education Materials: An Annotated Bibliography, by Gail Gleason Milgram. New Brunswick, NJ: Rutgers Center of Alcohol Studies, 1975. 304p. $15.00pa. *1979 Supplement*. ca.300p. $15.00pa. (From Rutgers Center of Alcohol Studies, New Brunswick, NJ 08903).
    These helpfully evaluative annotated bibliographies of printed materials for alcohol education are based on materials in the collection of Rutgers Center of Alcohol Studies supplemented by a thorough search for relevant materials. Items covered include books (hardback and paperback), curriculum guides, pamphlets, leaflets, periodicals, and other items, with information on audience, concepts, orientation, and summaries of contents which evaluate each item in terms of content, presentation, readability, and whether or not it meets the needs for which it was designed. The 1975 bibliography covers 873 items for teachers and students at all levels, arranged by author and title with full bibliographic information

(including price, when available), with indexes by title and audience level (high school students, teacher, etc.), type of publication, and content level (high school student, teacher, etc.), type of publication, and content of text (as highway safety, sociology of drinking, etc.). The *1979 Supplement* will also have about 900 evaluations.

A Bibliography of Drug Abuse Including Alcohol and Tobacco, by Theodora Andrews. Littleton, CO: Libraries Unlimited, 1977. 306p. $15.00.

A current work that provides critical annotations of 725 books on all aspects of drug abuse including reference works and authoritative treatments of such topics as prevention and prevalence, social and psychological aspects, and religious uses and implications. It has been strongly recommended for both high school and public libraries.

Drug Abuse Films, by Joan Grupeonoff for the National Coordinating Council on Drug Education. 3rd ed. Chicago: American Library Association, 1973. 126p. $5.00pa.

Systematic review of more than 200 drug abuse films and other media of the 1960s and early 1970s on the dual criteria of scientific accuracy and conceptual integrity. Of the more than 200 media items reviewed, only 32 (mostly films) were fully recommended. Others were rated objectionable for one (specified) reason or another. Selection guidelines are credited on page 9. Evaluations and information are quite full.

Drug Education: A Bibliography of Available Inexpensive Materials, compiled by Dorothy P. Wells. Metuchen, NJ: Scarecrow Press, 1972. 111p. $6.00.

A guide to materials particularly useful for secondary schools with budget problems. It lists and describes about 400 free and inexpensive items, including some teaching guides, posters, charts, glossaries and comic books, from about 100 publishers. Though some of the publications are undoubtedly out of print, this book is valuable for the names of the issuing agencies, and indicates the types of materials that are apt to be available. Publications are sorted into general, government and reprint areas, and arranged by publishers. While this excludes information on alcohol and tobacco, other items are well covered.

An Evaluation of Alcohol Education Materials in Elementary, Junior High School and Senior High School Textbooks as Related to Student Needs, by D. L. Paul. Kalamazoo: Western Michigan University, 1964. 21p. Paperback (thesis); price not available.

This thoughtful thesis evaluates 32 textbooks for their treatment of alcohol, describing which areas of alcohol are covered and how well they are covered. In general, the study found that textbook coverage was poor, especially at the elementary level. There was little information on alcohol in elementary science texts; the reasons for drinking, for instance, were rarely covered, even though students express interest in this aspect of alcohol education.

Learning about Alcohol: A Resource Book for Teachers. Washington, DC: Association for the Advancement of Health Education, 1974. 200p. $2.95pa.

This resource book, with contributions from educators, physicians, and sociologists, is designed to aid teachers in selecting appropriate approaches and materials for alcohol education in current schools and classrooms. It includes an extensive listing of teaching media and sources.

Resource Book for Drug Abuse Education. Washington, DC: Association for the Advancement of Health Education, 1970. 124p. $1.50.

Summarizes factual information on major abused drugs and suggests techniques for communicating this information to young people.

Student Values in Drugs and Drug Abuse, by Sister Mary Virginia Sztorc, C.S.S.F., Haverford, PA: Catholic Library Association, 1976. 32p. $2.00.

This series of annotated bibliographies covers books for teenage readers, books and materials for parents and teachers, and educational media (films, sound filmstrips, recordings—disc and tape). Good source materials for programs on drugs and drug abuse with a values-clarification approach.

Teaching about Drugs: A Curriculum Guide, K-12. 2nd ed. Kent, OH: American School Health Association, and Washington, DC: Pharmaceutical Manufacturers Association, 1972. 216p. $4.00pa.

Part I, the curriculum, based on concepts, includes suggested materials based on developmental levels. Part II includes review papers, teaching aids, glossaries, charts, references, and color illustrations.

FOR FURTHER READING

Note: Theodora Andrews' *Bibliography of Drug Abuse Including Alcohol and Tobacco*, among others (see Key Publications), is an excellent source for locating further knowledge.

Bland, H. B. "Problems Related to Teaching about Drugs," *Journal of School Health*, v. 39, no. 2 (Feb. 1969), pp. 117-19.

Braxton, E. R., and R. J. Yonker. "Does Being Urban, Poor, Black, or Female Affect Youth's Knowledge and/or Attitudes Relating to Drugs?," *Journal of School Health*, v. 43, no. 3 (March 1973), pp. 185-88.

English, G. E. "The Effectiveness of Emotional-Appeal Versus Fact-Giving Drug Educational Films," *Journal of School Health*, v. 42, no. 9 (Nov. 1972), pp. 540-41.

Smith, H. W., and F. J. Meyer. "Parent and Teacher Attitudes toward and Knowledge of Drug Abuse," *Journal of School Health*, v. 44, no. 3 (March 1974), pp. 152-55.

THOUGHT FOR FOOD
Selecting Materials for Nutrition Education

"We are what we eat."

□ □ □

Nutrition education is a small, adaptable educational area related to many curriculum subjects and is one that has some well-thought-through criteria. It can be taught as part of science, health education, home economics, or consumer education. Food customs — including our own — are intimately related to cultures. Typically, multicultural or bicultural courses, particularly those for younger children, include recipes and "foods from many lands" or cultures. The search for food and the development of new food has played and continues to play important roles in human history. For example, the search for spice routes was a major reason for many early explorations, and our American political institutions were undoubtedly strongly affected by the mass emigration of Irish citizens following the Irish potato famine. The "food chain" or cycle, is, of course, a basic environmental concept.

The food industry, one of our largest industries, should probably be considered within economics and political science curricula as well as within consumer education courses. Both our daily diet and the entire economic-social structures of agricultural countries (not only banana republics) are intimately related to our corporate food giants.

Their viewpoint (better living through chemistry) and their productions also tend to dominate nutrition education. To start with, American children get a great deal of misleading information about foods and nutrition from commercial television. Supposedly, by the age of 18, a student has typically spent 18,000 hours in front of his or her television set, as compared to 15,000 hours in school classrooms. According to broadcast industry statistics, 75 percent of the TV commercials that children are exposed to are food related, with the money spent inversely related to food value and quality. Their school-directed publications — attractive, if self-serving freebies — are also suspect. In a subject area where funds for materials are low, and many teachers are not too knowledgeable, these publications are often accepted with gratitude and used rather uncritically. Though there is much that is useful in these publications, they should be examined by both teachers and students with all criteria suggested for free materials. If enough of them are acquired, specific biases may tend to even out. (Dairy producers promote milk; cereal manufacturers believe in a hearty — cereal — breakfast.)

Many corporate publications and older nutrition frameworks as well are based on concepts of a daily consumption of a "basic four" that have been shown to be outmoded and inadequate by the hearings of the U.S. Senate's Select Committee on Nutrition and Human Needs. Older curricula should be revised in terms of the Committee's publication, *Dietary Goals for the United States* (2nd ed., 1977).

Other authoritative government documents sources on diet can be obtained (often free) from the U.S. Consumer Information Center in Pueblo, Colorado, and from other government documents sources listed in the chapter on government documents. Some other sources considered relatively authoritative are the National Academy of Sciences, the National Research Council, and the Food and Nutrition Board. State or local agricultural or nutrition extension agencies are often good sources of ideas and materials for nutrition education. Their materials — generally prepared as teaching tools for low-income adults — are often usable as is, or are easily adaptable for school situations. These materials include some interesting games and simulations as well as informational materials; curriculum guidelines; easy-to-prepare, nutritious recipes; etc.

Since food is an affective area, nutrition education materials should include direct experiences with cooking and tasting (smelling and looking at) foods, as well as abstract visual and printed materials on foods and nutrition. Cooking courses are a good means of combining food knowledge with math, language, health, multicultural, and science experiences, such as measuring (why not in metric?), following directions, empathizing, studying effects of heat and time on materials, etc. Cooking is also a pleasant and memorable way to spend an afternoon.

If climate, time and space permit, gardening is another pleasurable activity stemming from nutrition education, that involves math (measurement), following directions, planning, sequence, biology, concepts of time and consequence, as well as nourishment. Students of all kinds (inner city, suburban, gifted, retarded, etc.) have shown positive responses in learning and attitudes toward both gardening and cooking.

Food itself (raw or processed) is a prime teaching material that can be eaten, examined through the senses, under a microscope, or through chemical and bacterial analysis. Food can also be explored through art — student pictures, photographs, food still lifes of the masters.

Every community offers opportunities for field trips and experts — some of whom may produce instructive materials as well as food. Some possibilities are farms, agricultural agents, fish hatcheries, food testing laboratories, all types of food stores and factories, canneries, food brokers and distributors, and the garbage collectors who process the debris from our food cycle. Resource people can range from dentists and nutritionists to tea tasters, food chemists, and food bureaucrats. School cooks and dietitions and the school lunch programs are obvious resources.

Other direct experiences in nutrition education could include animal and plant experiments involving food; environmental studies of local food chains and suppliers, or of the waste (if any) in one's own school lunchroom; taste experiments; or writing exercises involving food. These should be selected for involvement and congruence with objectives. They may at times require some science materials, often only homemade or inexpensive materials.

Printed materials and charts should be selected for accuracy, currency, clarity and freedom from bias. If they are biased, critical-thinking concepts and consumer-education concepts should be incorporated with nutrition concepts. Media materials should be selected for relevance and accuracy, or students should be required to sift out their probable biases or viewpoints.

The two excerpts below are taken from an *Instrument for Use in the Analysis of K-12 Nutrition Curriculum Guidelines*, which can be used to analyze many kinds of nutrition education materials. This copyrighted outline is reproduced here with the permission of the Society for Nutrition Education and the National Nutrition Education Clearinghouse. It is not to be reproduced elsewhere without written permission from the Clearinghouse.

INSTRUMENT FOR USE IN THE ANALYSIS OF
K-12 NUTRITION CURRICULUM GUIDES[1]

Developed by Christine Go, Nutrition Education Consultant

Note: Although this instrument is intended for analyzing K-12 nutrition curriculum guides, it is also suited to analysis of other instructional resources in nutrition, e.g., college texts.

I. GENERAL QUESTIONS

A. This curriculum has been developed by:
   1. school educators _____
      a. local _____ b. state _____ c. federal _____
   2. non-profit _____
      a. educational _____ b. subject matter _____ c. food commodity _____
   3. private/commercial industry _____
      a. educational _____ b. food _____
   4. university/extension _____
      a. local _____ b. state _____ c. federal _____
   5. other (explain) _____

B. The curriculum's primary focus is:
      nutrition education _____
      home economics _____
      health education _____
      consumer education _____
      school food service _____

C. The guide is intended for:
      K-12 _____   5-8 _____
      K-6 _____   7-12_____
      K-3 _____   7-9 _____
      1-8 _____   9-12_____
      4-6 _____   other (explain) _____

D. Is this guide recommended or required by the state:
      yes _____ no _____ does not indicate _____

E. Does the guide contain:

	yes	no
rationale	_____	_____
objectives	_____	_____
concepts	_____	_____
learning activities	_____	_____
evaluative measures	_____	_____
supplementary references	_____	_____

_____

[1]*Prepared as a part of a contract from National Dairy Council, 6300 N. River Rd., Rosemont, IL 60618.*

II. CURRICULUM DESIGN AND LAYOUT

A. Is the guide:
   easy to follow _____   other (explain) _____
   fairly understandable _____
   confusing, ambiguous _____

B. Does the guide include a student supplementary reference section:
   yes _____   no _____

   If yes:
   appendix   _____
   bibliography   _____
   resource lists   _____
   booklets   _____
   glossary   _____
   other (explain)   _____

C. Does the guide include a teacher supplementary reference section:
   (*"Teacher supplementary references" is a broad term used to include the possible answers found in the previous question.*)

   yes _____   no _____

   If yes:
   _____ resource lists
   _____ nutrition principles/information
   _____ 1. a separate section aside from the concepts and learning activities
   _____ 2. integrated along with the concepts and learning activities
   _____ lesson sheets (audiovisuals, dittoes, etc.)
   _____ other (stuffed toys, charts, posters, badges, parent leaflets)

D. Does the guide recommend or require:
   _____ attendance at required previous training sessions before using the guide
   _____ other previous education qualifications
   _____ no background knowledge
   _____ training sessions during the use of the guide
   _____ no indication of the above

III. CONTENT/CONCEPTS

Do the concepts included in the guide emphasize the following:

_____ 1. The way a food is handled influences the amount of nutrients in the food, its safety, appearance, taste and cost; handling means everything that happens to food while it is being grown, processed, stored, and prepared for eating.

_____ 2. The food we eat enables us to live, to grow, to keep healthy and well, and to get energy for work and play.

_____ 3. Food is made up of certain chemical substances that work together to interact with body chemicals to serve the needs of the body.

_____ 4. All persons, throughout life, have need for about the same nutrients, but in varying degrees.

_____ 5. Food use relates to the cultural, social, economic, and psychological aspects of living as well as to the physiological.

_____ 6. The maintenance of good nutrition involves a knowledge of where the public can contact community nutrition resources.

_____ 7. Food plays an important role in the physical and psychological health in individual families.

_____ 8. Food plays an important role in the physical and psychological health of a society or nation.

_____ Provisions are made to introduce to students the types and responsibilities of various nutrition/food-related careers.

V. LEARNING ACTIVITIES

A. Is there a stated learning approach in the guide:
yes _____   no _____

B. Are there any statements of rationale in explanation of the suggested/recommended learning activities:
yes _____   no _____

C. Do the learning activities supply appropriate practice and exposure for the behavior outlined in the objectives:
frequently and consistently _____
occasionally   _____
rarely   _____

D. Are there any statements or procedures designed in the learning activities to provide students with immediate knowledge of their learning progress:
yes, consistently and frequently _____
yes, but only periodically   _____
yes, but very seldom   _____
no   _____

E. Does the guide employ:

	yes	no
1. a good number of different types of learning activities (6 or more)	_____	_____
2. a few types of learning activities (1-6)	_____	_____
3. primarily one type of learning activity	_____	_____

F. Is there a sequence/correlation between one learning activity and the next:

	frequently	occasionally	rarely	never
1. logical order	_____	_____	_____	_____
2. random order	_____	_____	_____	_____
3. from simple to complex	_____	_____	_____	_____
4. errorless discrimination	_____	_____	_____	_____
5. chronological order	_____	_____	_____	_____
6. from general to specific	_____	_____	_____	_____
7. geographical order	_____	_____	_____	_____

"logical order"—activities do not necessarily have to be dependent on others, but arranged together they fall into an understood pattern or sequence
"from simple to complex"—one activity is dependent on another
"errorless discrimination"—tasks are sequenced in such a manner that the student should move from step to step without making errors. This technique is used in some types of programmed instruction.
"general to specific"—a breakdown of a general concept into specifics

G. Are the instructions for the teachers concerning the learning activities:

	frequently	occasionally	rarely	never
1. specific and clear	_____	_____	_____	_____
2. general	_____	_____	_____	_____
3. vague	_____	_____	_____	_____
4. provide additional background information for each activity	_____	_____	_____	_____
5. provide no background information for learning activity	_____	_____	_____	_____

H. Are the materials used in learning activities:

	frequently	occasionally	rarely	never
1. available within the local community	____	____	____	____
2. available through special arrangements/ordering procedures	____	____	____	____

I. How much do the educational materials used in the learning activities cost:

	frequently	occasionally	rarely	never
1. 0-$5	____	____	____	____
2. $6-$10	____	____	____	____
3. $11-$20	____	____	____	____
4. $21-30	____	____	____	____
5. $31-$40	____	____	____	____

J. Are the learning activities suitable for classroom use:
generally _____
occasionally _____
seldom _____
never _____

K. Do the activities employ different media techniques in their presentation:

	frequently	occasionally	rarely	never
1. films/videotapes/slides	____	____	____	____
2. cassettes/tapes	____	____	____	____
3. graphs/charts	____	____	____	____
4. posters/pictures	____	____	____	____
5. displays/bulletin boards	____	____	____	____
6. textbooks	____	____	____	____
7. pamphlets/booklets/books	____	____	____	____
8. learning center/packets	____	____	____	____
9. field trips	____	____	____	____
10. special speakers	____	____	____	____
11. animals/plants	____	____	____	____
12. food preparation/taste	____	____	____	____
13. science experiments	____	____	____	____
14. arts/crafts	____	____	____	____
15. newspaper/magazines	____	____	____	____

L. What learning methods approaches are used in the activities:

	frequently	occasionally	rarely	never
1. teacher-centric	____	____	____	____
2. pupil-centric	____	____	____	____
3. group participation	____	____	____	____
4. individual participation	____	____	____	____
5. rote learning	____	____	____	____
6. lecture/class discussion	____	____	____	____
7. problem solving	____	____	____	____
8. values clarification	____	____	____	____
9. role-play/games/riddles	____	____	____	____
10. reports/projects/surveys/debates	____	____	____	____
11. community resources	____	____	____	____

M. What types of learning experiences are suggested:

	frequently	occasionally	rarely	never
cognitive	____	____	____	____
psychomotor	____	____	____	____
affective	____	____	____	____

N. Are students given the opportunity to assess:

	frequently	occasionally	rarely	never
1. their own personal nutrition habits	____	____	____	____
2. the nutritional status habits of a larger group	____	____	____	____

"Nutritional status of a larger group" is anyone other than the student himself (e.g., ethnic groups, socioeconomic groups, the class, teens, the elderly).

O. How often are other subject areas integrated with the study of nutrition:

	frequently	occasionally	rarely	never
1. arts/crafts	____	____	____	____
2. foreign languages	____	____	____	____
3. language/arts/English	____	____	____	____
4. math	____	____	____	____
5. physical education	____	____	____	____
6. sciences	____	____	____	____
7. social sciences	____	____	____	____
8. music	____	____	____	____
9. health	____	____	____	____
10. career education	____	____	____	____
11. child development	____	____	____	____

P. Are the learning experiences designed with different student abilities in mind:

frequently _____   never _____
occasionally _____   no formal indication _____
rarely _____

If so, does the guide include learning experiences and/or suggestions for:

	frequently	occasionally	rarely	never
1. students with learning disabilities	____	____	____	____
2. students of average abilities	____	____	____	____
3. students of advanced abilities	____	____	____	____

Q. Do the learning activities specify:
1. which specific grade level they correspond to _____
2. which grade range they correspond to _____

VI. SOCIAL CONCERNS

A. Does the guide encourage student awareness of current nutrition policies, trends, and controversies where and when appropriate:

	frequently	occasionally	rarely	never
1. Diet vs. growth & health	____	____	____	____
Diet vs. physical appearance	____	____	____	____
Diet vs. exercise/obesity	____	____	____	____
Diet vs. weight loss techniques	____	____	____	____
Diet vs. physical performance	____	____	____	____
Diet vs. mental development	____	____	____	____
Diet vs. life growth patterns	____	____	____	____
Diet vs. peer acceptance	____	____	____	____
Diet vs. health problems/ malnutrition	____	____	____	____

	frequently	occasionally	rarely	never
2. World food supplies/shortage	___	___	___	___
Malnutrition/hunger in USA	___	___	___	___
Malnutrition/hunger outside USA	___	___	___	___
Food wastage/recycling	___	___	___	___
New food sources for future	___	___	___	___
Food feeding programs	___	___	___	___
Food protection agencies	___	___	___	___
Reliable community nutrition resources	___	___	___	___
Food related legislation	___	___	___	___

Contemporary issues related to those listed above can be found below:
new food sources for future—protein substances, soybean substitutes, seaweed
food feeding programs—food stamps, commodity foods, aged feeding programs
food protection agencies—e.g., USDA, FDA, local health departments
reliable community nutrition resources—FAO, American Heart Association, UNICEF, Red Cross, Consumer Action Groups, Planned Parenthood, University Extension

	frequently	occasionally	rarely	never
3. $ management, comparative food prices	___	___	___	___
Meal planning	___	___	___	___
Snacks	___	___	___	___
Food preparation	___	___	___	___
Food safety	___	___	___	___
Food processes	___	___	___	___
Food industry techniques and practices	___	___	___	___
Convenience foods	___	___	___	___
Food/nutrition labeling	___	___	___	___
Unit pricing/date coding	___	___	___	___
Food additives/enrichment	___	___	___	___

Contemporary issues related to those listed above can be found below:
$ management/comparative food prices—shopping tips, consumer policies, comparing food prices
meal planning—meal examples for breakfast, lunch, dinner
food preparation—actual food preparation, cooking, recipes
food safety—food handling, staphylococcus, diseases
food processes—the route food takes from the farm to the dinner table
food preservation—canning, freezing, etc.

	frequently	occasionally	rarely	never
4. Food patterns/nutritional status:				
Low income	___	___	___	___
Middle income	___	___	___	___
High income	___	___	___	___
Ethnic/cultural groups	___	___	___	___
Religious groups	___	___	___	___
Elderly	___	___	___	___
Adults	___	___	___	___
Pregnant women	___	___	___	___
Adolescents	___	___	___	___
Preschool/elementary children	___	___	___	___

(Outline continues on page 132)

	frequently	occasionally	rarely	never
5. Psychological aspects of nutrition/food patterns	___	___	___ ___
Food misinformation	___	___	___ ___
Food advertising	___	___	___ ___
Vegetarians	___	___	___ ___
Health/natural foods	___	___	___ ___
Etiquette/manners	___	___	___ ___
Food in history	___	___	___ ___
Dental care	___	___	___ ___
Nutrition-related careers	___	___	___ ___
Other: special diets	___	___	___ ___

Contemporary issues related to those listed above can be found below:
psychological aspects of nutrition/food patterns — myths, old wives tales, eating vs. emotions
food misinformation — food faddism, food quackery
food advertising — public media
health/natural foods — organic foods, vitamin supplements
special diets — e.g., low sodium, low fat diets, therapeutic

B. Are there any learning activities designed to encourage student awareness of reliable nutrition resources in the community:
   several instances (6 or more) _____   a few _____
   some instances _____   none _____

"Reliable nutrition resources in the community" refers to sources of information through which the general lay public can obtain sound nutrition information.

C. Specify those community resources:

	frequently	occasionally	rarely	never
1. school food service	___	___	___ ___
2. other school services	___	___	___ ___
3. health organizations	___	___	___ ___
4. professional medical personnel	___	___	___ ___
5. parent involvement	___	___	___ ___
6. university extension	___	___	___ ___
7. public media	___	___	___ ___
8. government agencies	___	___	___ ___
9. other community sources	___	___	___ ___
10. food industry	___	___	___ ___

Community resources related to the general categories listed above can be found below:
other school services — library
health organizations — Red Cross, FAO, WHO, hospitals, American Heart Assn.
professional medical personnel — doctors, dentists, nurses
public media — radio, TV, newspapers
government agencies — USDA, FDA, Public Health Depts.
other community sources — zoo, museum, consumer action, Better Business Bureau
food industry — supermarkets, farms, dairy, canneries, bakeries, graneries

D. Is there any stereotyping:

	Sexual	Cultural
to a large extent	___	___
to a small extent	___	___
free of stereotyping	___	___
discourages stereotyping	___	___

"Discourages stereotyping" — This possible answer has been included to assess whether any sampled guides have made conscious efforts to discourage sexual and/or cultural typecasting.

E. Do the learning activities:

	Socioeconomic	Cultural
frequently incorporate various kinds of values into the lessons	_____	_____
occasionally incorporate various kinds of values into the lessons	_____	_____
rarely incorporate various kinds of values into the lessons	_____	_____
never incorporate various kinds of values into the lessons	_____	_____

This question has been designed to determine whether different socioeconomic and/or cultural factors and values are integrated into learning experiences in addition to placing them in separate lesson units.

VII. EVALUATION

A. This guide contains:
   no evaluation measures _____
   evaluation measures _____

B. Evaluation measures are:
   frequent and consistent _____
   occasional _____
   rare _____

C. Evaluation measures are:
   pre-test procedures _____
   post-test procedures _____
   both pre- and post-test procedures _____

D. Are there instructions for presenting the evaluations (pre- and post-tests) in the guide:
   yes _____   no _____

	frequently	occasionally	rarely	never
If yes:				
1. specific	_____	_____	_____	_____
2. general	_____	_____	_____	_____
3. vague	_____	_____	_____	_____

EVALUATIVE/SUMMARY MEASURES OF THE FIVE POINT RATING SCALES[1]

I. Concepts/Content (C/C)

5	4	3	2	1
Presents sound scientific nutrition principles; clearly stated; introduced with consideration of the abilities of students		Presents sound scientific nutrition principles, but may have a few discrepancies; may be ambiguous or introduced in a manner beyond or below student activities		Biased in its presentation of nutrition facts and principles/ irrespective of scientifically proven and agreed upon principles; often very ambiguous; poor wording; irrespective of student ability

[1]*Adapted by permission from M. J. Eash, **Developing an Instrument for Assessing Instructional Materials**, Curriculum Theory Network Monograph Supplement, The Ontario Institute for Studies in Education, 1972.*

2. Goals/Instructional Objectives (G/IO)

5	4	3	2	1

G/IO correspond to concepts; clearly stated; consistent throughout conceptual framework; useful for teacher; appropriate to the abilities of students		Average, some G/IO are met; some not thoroughly covered; some missing; some inappropriate for teacher and students; inconsistent, choppy		Many are vague, unclear, missing, superficially covered; stated ambiguously; often student is unable to meet the G/IO due to the guide's inability to meet the student's level of understanding and skill

3. Learning Activities/Approach (LA/A)

5	4	3	2	1

LA/A correspond to G/IO and concepts; excellent use of teacher/student participation; offers a variety of LA; easy and adaptable set of LA for the classroom; provides the teacher aids and background information appropriate to LA; utilizes the LA to a thorough and broad extent; integrates other subject areas		Does not always correspond with the G/IO; predominance of teacher participation; may offer a small variety of LA; sometimes vague in its purpose, directions and background information; does not always present concepts thoroughly and in depth; integration of other subjects occasionally		Often deviates from stated G/IO; totally teacher dominated; offers only one kind of LA method; LA inappropriate to the stated G/IO; directions, purpose and background materials often vague and confusing to teacher; very little integration of nutrition into other subject areas

4. Social Concerns (SC)

5	4	3	2	1

Covers a wide variety of current issues concerning nutrition (i.e. obesity, malnutrition, future food resources, ethnic nutrition status, etc.) in accordance with student ability; presenting these concerns free of misconceptions or stereotypes; integrating these issues into various lessons as well as presenting the issues in units of their own		Covers only a few current issues, may not consider the maturity and skill of its users; may have a few misconceptions; has a few units on these subjects but makes no effort to integrate the concerns with different lessons		Makes no effort to include any social concerns; often includes much nutrition misinformation and stereotyping; does not consider the abilities and skills of its students

5. Evaluation (E)

5	4	3	2	1
Helpful suggestions and methods in evaluating LA for the teacher; as it appropriately corresponds with the learning package; provides several kinds of evaluative measurements frequently and consistently throughout		Some evaluative measures, but directions are vague; they do not always correspond with the information presented in LA; offers only a few evaluative measurements; evaluates often on a superficial basis		No suggested evaluations; or measures are inappropriate

6. Organization (O)

5	4	3	2	1
Excellent organization; concepts presented in logical sequence and easy to understand and follow; provides enough information for teacher to follow		Organization is confusing at times, while understandable during others; the scope may be somewhat limited and not detailed enough for teacher to carry out IO and LA		Illogical sequence; does not provide enough structure to give teacher information to build an instruction design; inconsistent in its organization

KEY ORGANIZATIONS

Other relevant organizations are listed in the chapters on consumer education, free materials, television, and government documents in *Media and the Curriculum,* and in the chapters on environmental education, science, and social studies in this work. The Nutrition Foundation's *Index of Nutrition Education Materials* lists many more.

Center for Science in the Public Interest (CSPI)
1757 S St., NW
Washington, DC 20009   (202) 332-9110
A public service (Nader-like) organization which has issued some attractive and well-researched publications on food and nutrition education that nicely balance out corporate offerings. They include a monthly magazine, *Nutrition Action* ($10.00/yr.), which includes news, activities, and reviews.
Other productions are:
Creative Food Experiences for Children, by Mary Goodwin, 1974. 191p. $4.00 (quantity discount).
Well set up for teaching with activities, games, recipes, and facts.

Focus on Food, 1977. 4p. tabloid. $0.15 each (quantity discount).

Nutrition Scoreboard. Book and chart. 1975. $1.75.

School Lunch Action Guide, 1976. 12p. $0.50.

Scoreboard to Better Eating, by Michael F. Jacobson and Sandra Kageyama. 102p. $2.50pa.

Food and Nutrition Information and Educational
Materials Center

National Agricultural Library, room 304
U.S. Department of Agriculture
10301 Baltimore Blvd.
Beltsville, MD 20705   (301) 344-3719

The purpose of this organization is to disseminate information on food and nutrition to individuals managing child nutrition programs and to those engaged in teaching nutrition to children. The Center was developed by the Food and Nutrition Service of the National Agricultural Library. Its collection includes books, pamphlets, films, tapes, manuals, and programmed instructional materials. Its publications include semiannual book catalogs of loan materials, brochures, bibliographies and guides to audiovisual materials in food and nutrition. These are free to individuals engaged in nutrition education as long as the supply lasts.

The organization provides free search services to target audiences, lends materials, and makes referrals to other information sources.

National Nutrition Education Clearinghouse (NNECH)

2140 Shattuck Ave., Suite 1110
Berkeley, CA 94704   (415) 548-1363

The National Nutrition Education Clearinghouse is a service of the Society of Nutrition Education, a membership organization committed to promoting nutritional well-being through education, communication, and applied educational research.

The NNECH maintains a Clearinghouse Collection library of more than 8,000 items useful to nutrition educators, selected from a wide variety of sources, and abstracted, evaluated, and cross-referenced in 80 categories. The Clearinghouse staff maintains an on-going publication program compiling and publishing bibliographies, reference works and teaching/counseling materials, based on materials reviewed and evaluated by qualified nutritionists, using NNECH's own evaluation instrument.

The Society can make special arrangements to compile bibliographies for particular courses of instruction, to survey or test teaching materials, or to review these materials during their developmental phases.

Current materials are reviewed in their quarterly *Journal of Nutrition Education* ($15.00/yr. for individuals; $20.00 for institutions; $2.00 more in Canada). This publication also includes feature and research articles, commentary on policies, planning, legislation and government, perspectives on controversial issues in nutrition and consumer education, as well as program ideas, teaching tools, and motivational techniques. The *Journal* reviews books, current research, and curriculum materials.

Generally their publications provide authoritative selections and annotations for materials on a wide range of nutrition topics, ranging from obesity through vegetarianism to nutrition during pregnancy, infant nutrition, and mass media aspects of nutrition. All of these might be appropriate for some educational programs in some school situations. The publications listed below are more obviously relevant to educational needs and purposes. (The costs provided are non-member costs. Members of the Society are entitled to a 20 percent discount.)

Audiovisuals for Nutrition Education, 1975. 28p. $4.00.
Evaluative reviews of more than 170 audiovisuals. Lists media type, audience level, availability, and prices, with three indexes: author/publisher, title, and subject.

Basic Nutrition Facts, 1975. 16p. $3.00.
Over 100 sources of sound nutrition information including textbooks, popular books, pamphlets, bibliographies, reading/resource lists, audiovisuals, journals, and magazines.

Elementary Teaching Materials and Teacher References, 1975. 19p. $3.00.
More than 150 entries in all media which are divided into 11 categories according to type of materials.

Instrument for Use in the Analysis of K-12 Nutrition Curriculum Guides, 1976. 16p. $2.00.
May be used as an evaluation tool for curriculum guides and texts.

Nutrition Education, K-12 Teacher References: Concepts, Theories and Guides, 1976. 20p. $3.00.
Extensive compilation of 149 background references for teachers, including books, curriculum guides, bibliographies, journal articles, periodicals, and audiovisuals. Previous edition was entitled *General Teacher References.* Author/title index.

Nutrition Information Resources for Professionals, 1978. 15p. $0.50.
This concise resource for professionals in nutrition education and related fields has guidelines for finding reliable information sources and evaluating educational materials. Nearly 100 entries are listed -- organizations, reliable nutrition books, pamphlets and popular magazines with reliable information, nutrition journals, and government and trade publications.

Secondary Teaching Materials and Teacher References, 1977. 25p. $3.00.
An aid for teachers of grades K-12, this resource has more than 200 entries in six categories of materials and references.

Nutrition Foundation, Inc.
Attn: Office of Education and Public Affairs
888 17th St., NW
Washington, DC 20006   (202) 872-0778
The Nutrition Foundation is a nonprofit public institution in existence since 1941, created and founded by leading companies in the food industry and allied

industries. Its focus has been on the scientific, technical, medical, and clinical aspects of nutrition. It has long been concerned with medical education in nutrition and nutrition education at the post-secondary level. Though considered authoritative, its ties to the food industry are reflected in its outlook and publications.

Some relevant publications appropriate for elementary and secondary programs include:

Index of Nutrition Education Materials, Rev. ed. 1977. 237p. $8.50pa.
>A well-arranged, easy-to-use index, which simplifies the problems of locating nutritional information. It uses separate color-coded sections for publications, teaching aids, major sources, state and regional offices, and provides a directory of major nutrition information centers. The section on "teaching aids" includes some materials in braille and foreign languages. These teaching aids are arranged alphabetically by title under categories like additives, alcohol, community health service. Audience, price, source, and address are included for each item.

>While many materials are for professionals and adults, a fair proportion can be used in elementary and secondary schools.

>It has a good directory of nutrition-related organizations that might supply additional materials — health agencies, voluntary agencies, state nutrition services, film libraries, U.S. Department of Agriculture, etc.

>As compared to the materials directories of the NNECH, this is less specific and lacks evaluative annotations. It does, however, excel in arrangement and numbers of items.

Nutrition Education in a Changing World, by Pennsylvania State University, 1978- . "Early Childhood," 29 units. 409p. $9.00. Elementary (1-3), 8 units. 220p. $6.00. Elementary (4-6), not yet paged. Unit 1, $6.00; Units 2-3, $8.00; Units 4-5, $8.00; Units 6-8, $8.00.

KEY PUBLICATIONS

Hunger: The World Food Crisis, by Kathryn Mervine Fowler. Washington, DC: National Science Teachers Association, 1977. 65p. $2.50pa. (Also available as ED 142 394).
>Materials here were selected to be "appropriate for classrooms." They include free-loan films and low-cost items.

FOR FURTHER READING

*Items marked with an asterisk include criteria.
+ Items marked with a plus include lists of references.

* + American School Food Service Association. *Nutrition Education: Catalyst for Change.* Denver, CO: ASFSA, 1973.
>They also authored an undated + *Bibliography of Nutrition and Nutrition Education* ($1.00).

*Kratky, Patricia, and Lois Haigh. *Making Nutrition Education Count*. White Bear Lake: Minnesota Instructional Materials Center, 1975. (Available for $12.95 from 3300 Century Ave., N, White Bear Lake, MN 55100).

*Project Head Start. *Nutrition Education for Young Children: A Guide for Teachers and Aides*. Washington, DC: Project Head Start, 1977. (Single copy free from Nutrition Department, Project Head Start, P.O. Box 1182, Washington, DC 20013).

* + U.S. Senate Select Committee on Nutrition and Human Needs. *Dietary Goals for the United States*. 2nd ed. Washington, DC: GPO, 1977.

SELECTING MATERIALS FOR
SEX AND FAMILY LIFE EDUCATION

"In numerous polls and studies, most young people assert that they are dissatisfied with the sex education that they have received—from whatever sources they have received it. They express a desire to learn more than biological facts, to discuss problems that may have no easy answers with an informed and sympathetic teacher, to come to grips with an increasingly sex-oriented society so that they can make the right decisions at the right times."

"A child begins receiving sex education from the moment he is born."
> —National Education Association, "What Parents Should Know about Sex Education in the Schools"

"Even though many educators and citizens see a distinct need for including sex education in the public school curriculum, it seems no one can agree on how it should be taught, where it should be taught, and by whom it should be taught."
> —Elizabeth Mooney, *The School's Responsibility for Sex Education*

"Sex education is not a packaged curriculum that can be purchased and plugged in like an electric appliance."
> —Derek L. Burleson, "Guidelines for Selecting Instructional Materials in Sex Education, *Journal of Research and Development in Education*, Fall 1976

□ □ □

OVERVIEW

Sex education is a controversial hotbed that many educators try to avoid, even though students are certainly interested, and 72 percent of parents, according to recent attitude polls, believe that sex education is an appropriate role for schools. Though efforts have been made since the 1920s (and probably before) to establish sex education programs in American schools, even today (perhaps more often than not) curricula and materials for sex education, if they are included at all, are taught at inappropriate levels and ignore current values, current dilemmas, and current realities. Some curricula and materials do not seem to be in touch with any realities. Our failure, overall, to deal adequately with this important area may contribute to children's alienation from schools.

In certain perspectives, sex education should be an easy subject since sex is such an interesting and crucial aspect of everyone's life. As a topic, sex education can fit logically into many established curricula: into health education, home economics, social studies, biology, psychology, and values education, as well as into curricula for conflict resolution and decision making. Since it is so important and intimately tied up with our emotions and values it is a subject that cannot be exclusively approached through facts, figures, or exposition, but must encompass values and attitudes and a great deal of human experience.

Our values, however, tend to determine the facts that we include. In a period when sex roles for both men and women are changing, sex education materials may present rather rigid or stereotyped sex roles. Sometimes sex education is limited to education on reproduction—and even there the male role may be almost completely disregarded. Some states or districts specifically exclude human reproduction as a topic for biology. Some school districts with high rates of teenage pregnancies or venereal disease limit their sex education courses to skimpy courses in reproduction at the sixth-grade level. Junior high librarians in these schools who try to fill the gap with books that deal honestly with sexuality feel exposed and vulnerable, "in solitary splendor on the hot seat," unsure of support from district or principals if an irate parent complains.

Derek Burleson, whose guidelines on materials will be summarized later, suggests that the first step in sex education programs before purchasing materials is to devote "time and energy" to clarifying objectives, involving parents and community, training staff, and planning the curriculum. Since sex education is such a sensitive human issue, the approaches and criteria delineated in the chapter on the feeling domain seem particularly appropriate.

It is a difficult area for educators, at all levels. Individual principals, superintendents, teachers and school librarians have all certainly faced criticism and/or lost jobs because of their selection or backing of programs and materials in sex education.

There are, however, many rationales for sex education (many of which are incorporated into the end bibliographies in this chapter). The parents who are popularly believed to oppose treatment of this subject do in fact approve it in the vast majority of cases. Our largest parental organization, the National PTA, with the cooperation of the Bureau of Health Education, is currently compiling an overview of sex education programs and resources to help local groups develop appropriate sex education programs. Their compilation, still in progress as of this writing, will eventually include a useful guide with:

- an overview of major sex education organizations, programs and resources
- bibliographies of major sex education studies
- summaries of pertinent state laws and other mandates
- descriptions of current sex education programs
- listings of other materials and resources

The information source on the status of this program is Pauline Carlyon, National Congress of Parents and Teachers, 100 North Rush St., Chicago, IL 60611. Such an official action by the PTA should eventually do much to defuse any remaining parental opposition to sex education programs per se and to help resolve the dilemmas of what to include.

CRITERIA FOR SELECTION

One useful set of criteria (for print materials), devised by Masha K. Rudman, begins with the premise that the aim of sex education is to make the student informed and comfortable about his or her sexuality and the processes of sex. Sex materials, according to Rudman, Burleson and the American School Health Association, should start from students' developmental levels. Rudman suggests that materials should transmit appropriate amounts of information, since either overloads or insufficient facts can cause anxiety. Vocabulary, similarly, should be informative and non-threatening. She prefers accurate dictionary terms rather than vernacular or euphemisms, but in any case vocabulary should be consistent with the presentation, in an approach that maintains dignity. Materials should acknowledge and value sexuality in all human beings, and present both the enjoyment and the problems. Materials should communicate values clearly, indicate that there are many attitudes and sets of attitudes, and avoid moralizing and perpetuating myths. Opinions should be identified as opinions. To develop responsibility, materials should indicate consequences of behavior and deal honestly with negativity and aggression. If problems are presented, they should be realistic, while solutions should be feasible. Materials for either sex should include information on both sexes, as well as materials on homosexuality. Materials should avoid stereotypes on capability, interest, arousability, and behavior norms. Illustrations also should avoid stereotypes and prurient or demeaning humor.

Though most evaluations are for print, media, and pictorial materials, available sex education aids range from anatomically-correct dolls for young students to anatomical models for high school students. The use of either can considerably increase understanding simply by being available.

Burleson suggests that educators who wish to use instructional materials that contain explicit photographs and language, need well-developed rationales worked out before materials are selected, not after the fact. For selecting materials as a whole, Burleson suggests that:

- instructional objectives should be clearly and precisely stated before the selection of materials (Goals may include imparting information, improving communication, or developing personal values.)

  (Media and materials should then be selected for congruence with goals and objectives.)

- materials should be appropriate for the physical, intellectual and social maturity of intended audiences (It is better to anticipate a stage than delay materials until after the fact.)

- materials should be accurate, complete, and up to date

- materials should recognize varying points of view (with arguments presented pro and con)

- value positions should be made explicit in introductions to books and/or in accompanying promotional materials

- instructional materials should avoid rigid sex stereotyping

- instructional materials should have supportive resources, such as manuals, discussion guides, and bibliographies, as well as philosophies and rationales

- selection process should involve both parents and youth

Elizabeth Mooney's Fastback on the *School's Responsibility for Sex Education* (Bloomington, IL: Phi Delta Kappa Education Foundation, 1974) has an interesting section surveying the strengths and weaknesses of sex education programs in terms of vocabulary, responsibility, health and disease, human and animal reproduction, social aspects of relationships, development of masculine and feminine roles, love and sexual arousal, individuality and value systems.

To improve sex education, she advocates continuing programs set in developmental contexts that:

- incorporate emotional or street vocabularies as well as scientific vocabularies

- incorporate sociological data on various life styles

- teach about sexual health within the context of total human sexuality and response

- make specific comparisons and contrasts between human sexual relations and animal sexuality

- develop units on social relationships during the social-structuring years of 11 to 15

- allow opportunities to discuss sex-object choices with accurate information and objectivity (to develop a self-perceived level of comfort with oneself and others)

- include extensive discussion of self-image (or self-love) and its importance in sustained interpersonal relationships

- provide careful and objective delineation of religious and cultural teachings and expectations regarding sex (including anthropological materials)

- contain extensive discussion of the processes involved in developing individual value systems

One criterion, implicit rather than fully explicit in these sets of criteria, is that sex education materials should be designed to allow (but not compel) time and space for discussions, for student comment and questions. Since sex education courses are attitudinal as well as informational, it is important that they be taught by adults who are comfortable with their own sexuality and thoroughly at ease teaching sex education courses.

Burleson's recommendation that parents, students, teachers and community be consulted in the selection process is probably the single most important determinant in avoiding ugly struggles over such emotional issues as homosexuality, life styles, and sexual options. Since instructional materials are tangible, they can easily focus anxiety and reaction, unless their uses and rationales have been fully aired with all parties involved.

KEY ORGANIZATIONS

Organizations listed in the chapters on health and the feeling domain have excellent resources. The Mental Health Materials Center and the American Medical Association, for example, are two organizations that, respectively, review and produce high-quality materials.

National Council on Family Relations
1219 University Ave., SE
Minneapolis, MN 55414   (612) 331-2774
    The National Council on Family Relations is engaged in counseling, educa-
tion, and research in the field of family relations. It works from a substantial collection of materials on family relations and issues bibliographies and resource
guides that draw from this collection. Their most substantial bibliography, *Family Life: Literature and Films*, is entered in this chapter in Key Publications.
Other relevant materials are an *Inventory of Marriage and Family Literature*, an
inventory of more than 3,000 articles, by David Olson and Nancy Dahl, available
from IMFL Project, Family Social Science, 310 North Hall, University of Minnesota, St. Paul, MN 55108 ($13.95; $9.95pa.), and Rebecca Smith's *Resources
for Teaching about Family Life Education*, at $6.00.
    The Council's materials focus basically on marriage and family life and are
excellent resources for this area.

Sex Information and Education Council of the U.S. (SIECUS)
137 North Franklin St.
Hempstead, NY 11550   (516) 483-3033
    Founded in 1964, SIECUS is a nonprofit, voluntary organization devoted to
the understanding of human sexuality as an aspect of individual and social
health. It focuses upon human sexuality as a positive factor in the total physical,
emotional, and mental health of the individual and his or her effective function-
ing in society. SIECUS is not in any way associated with the federal government.
As a basic resource on sexuality, it serves as a clearinghouse for information on
materials and organizations working in the field of human sexuality and sex
education. It also serves as consultant on program planning and problem areas
for community agencies, religious institutions, schools, colleges, researchers, and
others. It creates and distributes original books, study guides, and specialized
annotated bibliographies. Some of the latter are distributed free, or rather inex-
pensively. Its Resource Library offers a reference and research source.
    Its bimonthly, *SIECUS Report*, available at $10.00 per year and edited by
the prestigious Mary S. Calderone, includes pertinent articles, reviews of current
materials, and important news in sex education and sex information.
    Some other publications, appropriate for school use, are published and
distributed by the Human Sciences Press, 72 Fifth Ave., New York, NY 10011.
Some were produced jointly with other educational associations. They include:

Packet A: Sex Education and Moral Values. 9 items. $15.95. (Order 4584).
    Deals with the development of morals and values and education in
values within the context of human sexuality programs.

Packet B: Parents as Sex Educators. 14 items. $18.95. (Order 4592).
    Contains materials to increase parents' own understanding and appre-
ciation of human sexuality to assist them in passing on this understanding to
their children.

A Resource Guide in Sex Education for the Mentally Retarded, by SIECUS,
    and the American Alliance for Health, Physical Education, and Recrea-
    tion. New York: Human Sciences Press, 1971. 55p. $3.50pa.
    An overview of curriculum concepts and content with sample lessons
and a detailed list of written and audiovisual materials, coded by difficulty
level and topic.

A Bibliography of Resources in Sex Education for the Mentally Retarded, 1973. 24p. $3.50pa.

This bibliography includes resources for parents and professionals as well as materials for use with mentally retarded individuals themselves.

Film Resources for Sex Education, by Derek L. Burleson and Gary Barbash, 1976. 52p. $4.95pa.

An annotated guide to about 200 recent films (1960s to 1975) and other audiovisual materials for use in sex education programs in school or community settings. Each listing includes the recommended audience level, description, distributor, and sale and rental prices. Most annotations appeared in earlier SIECUS publications.

Sex Education and Family Life for Visually Handicapped Children and Youth, by SIECUS, and the American Foundation for the Blind. New York: Human Sciences Press, 1975. 86p. $4.00pa.

This resource guide covers some special learning problems relating to the psychosexual growth of the visually handicapped, with an extensive annotated bibliography of resources in print, large type, braille, talking books, cassettes, and audiovisuals.

KEY PUBLICATIONS

Other publications are included in the chapters on health and the feeling domain.

Conceptions and Misconceptions: Sexuality in Children's Books. Oakland, CA: Association of Children's Librarians of Northern California, 1978. 34p. $2.00pa. (From Cynthia King, Fresno County Public Library, 2420 Mariposa St., Fresno, CA 93121).

This bibliography, prepared for the Association of Children's Librarians' Institute on Sexuality in Children's Fiction, Berkeley, California, April 13, 1978, annotates and evaluates about 120 books on sex for preschool to eighth grade, including non-fiction (mostly) and fiction, dealing with birth, reproduction, puberty, sexual identity, sexuality, sexual tensions, and relationships. These books—mostly trade books (not pamphlets or audiovisuals)—were examined by 18 ACL members on criteria of 1) readability, 2) accurate sexual descriptions, detailing all aspects of reproduction, 3) contemporary and positive viewpoints, 4) biologically informational language, 5) warm and personal attitudes, 6) illustrations: precise, labeled and accessible to our multicultural society. Books were closely examined for their treatment of such subjects as homosexuality, masturbation, abortion, premarital sex, sex roles, contraception, and marriage as optional.

The annotations, which cover books rejected as well as books recommended with and without reservations, are extremely helpful in delineating contents and approaches, limitations and assets of books discussed, and grade levels for each book.

Books are arranged by level (primary, intermediate, junior high) and under broad topics—birth and reproduction, puberty and adolescence, relationships—with an author-title index at the end.

This booklet, intended for parents, teachers, counselors, and pediatricians as well as librarians, is a good guide for use as well as for selection. Though the citations do not include prices, they do indicate which books are available in paperback.

Family Life, Literature and Films: An Annotated Bibliography, by Minnesota Council on Family Relations. Minneapolis: Minnesota Council on Family Relations, 1972. 375p. $6.50 plus $0.50 postage. *1974 Supplement*. 244p. $6.50 plus $0.50 postage. Both for $12.00 plus $0.75 postage. (From Minnesota Council on Family Relations, 1219 University Ave., Minneapolis, MN 55414). (Also available as ED 118 234 and ED 118 235).

These substantial bibliographies include descriptive annotations of films, records, tapes, literature, and other teaching aids arranged by 13 broad areas: 1) theoretical, historical, and cross-cultural perspectives; 2) male and female roles; 3) sexuality and sex education; 4) reproduction and family planning; 5) adolescence and youth; 6) pre-marriage considerations; 7) marital and family process; 8) family crises; 9) child development and parenthood; 10) middle and later years; 11) self-growth and personal potential; 12) social issues and the family; and 13) the aims and methods of family life education. They also include lists of related periodicals, publishers, information sources, and producers and distributors of audiovisual materials.

Growth Patterns and Sex Education: A Suggested Program for Kindergarten through Grade 12. Kent, OH: American School Health Association, 1967. 138p. $2.75pa.

Though this program, and its update (below), could be more current in both content and materials suggested, it is very well organized. Arranged by grade level, it provides for each grade comment, typical student questions, concepts and attitudes, and teachable materials, interestingly integrated. While this guide has no specific religious orientation, it should be highly acceptable to family-oriented and religiously-oriented schools and communities.

Growth Patterns and Sex Education: An Updated Bibliography, Pre-School to Adulthood. Kent, OH: American School Health Association, 1972. 52p. $2.25pa.

This 28-chapter annotated bibliography is arranged by media and by audience and ranges from dissertations and professional journals to kits, charts, slides and models—all in all a comprehensive listing of the best available materials of 1972.

FOR FURTHER READING

*Items marked with an asterisk include criteria.
+ Items marked with a plus include lists of references.

+ Brewer, Joan Scherer. "A Guide to Sex Education books: Dick Active, Jane Passive," *Interracial Books for Children Bulletin*, v. 6, nos. 3 and 4 (1975), pp. 1, 12-13.
Incisive review of 15 sex education books; includes an analysis of their general attitudes and their treatment of topics like bisexuality and homosexuality.

Burkart, J., and A. E. Whaley. "The Unwed Mother: Implications for Family Life Educators," *Journal of School Health*, v. 43, no. 7 (Sept. 1973), pp. 451-54.

*Burleson, Derek L. "Guidelines for Selecting Instructional Materials in Sex Education," *Journal of Research and Development in Education*, v. 10, no. 1 (Fall 1976), pp. 79-82.
Thoughtful yet concise guidelines, procedures, and cautions for selecting sex education materials in school settings. Recommends using materials prepared for educators, with manuals and discussion guides.

*Butts, June Dobbs. "Sex Education: Who Needs It?," *Ebony*, v. 32, no. 6 (April 1977), pp. 96-100.
Discusses sex education in context of street culture and commercial exploitation of sexual violence. Believes that sex education should include feelings and empathy, be *personal, present day*, and *positively reinforced*.

* + Child Study Association of America. *What to Tell Your Child about Sex*. Rev. ed. New York: Pocket Books, 1974.
Good background for selection, with an excellent discussion of children's sexual development up to age 17, questions and answers, and an annotated bibliography.

Core, Deborah L., and others. *Towards a Healthy Gay Presence in Textbooks and Classrooms*. Urbana, IL: National Council of Teachers of English, 1976. Cassette.
Eighty minutes of speeches sponsored by the NCTE Gay Caucus; some concerned with the problems of the gay presence in society, others with attitudes toward homosexuality in various literary traditions. Janet Hooper notes the absence of sexual minority materials in textbooks.

Dearth, P. B. "Viable Sex Education in the Schools: Expectations of Students, Parents, and Experts," *Journal of School Health*, v. 44, no. 4 (April 1974), pp. 190-93.

*Hull, Virginia, ed. *Sex Education and the Schools*. New York: Harper and Row, 1967.
Reports interesting and still-enlightening exchange between Mary Calderone, Alan Guttmacher, Millicent McIntosh, and Richard Unesworth; includes their approaches and recommendations for conveying healthy attitudes and information.

* + *Issues in Children's Book Selection*. New York: R. R. Bowker, 1973.
Includes three very relevant articles, two entitled "Sexuality in Books for Children," by Josette Frank and Barbara Werbsa, and "The Maturation of the Junior Novel: From Gestation to the Pill," by Lou Willett Stanek.

+ Maynard, Richard. "Feature Films for Sex Education," *Media and Methods*, v. 9, no. 3 (Nov. 1972), pp. 43-46.
Twenty-two films, previewed by the *Media and Methods* staff. Same issue, pp. 48-49, has Sandra Soehngen's "Sex Education: Who Needs It?"

*Mooney, Elizabeth. *The School's Responsibility for Sex Education*. Bloomington, IL: Phi Delta Kappa Educational Foundation, 1974. (Fastback 47).

National Education Association. *What Parents Should Know about Sex Education in the Schools.* Hyattsville, MD: American Education Week, 1977. Thoughtful flyer—available at $1.50 for 30.

Parcel, G. S., and D. L. Kenepp. "The Status of State Policies Concerning Birth Control Education," *Journal of School Health*, v. 42, no. 10 (Dec. 1972), pp. 614-17.

Rudman, Masha K. "Sex," pp. 145-70 in *Children's Literature: An Issues Approach.* Lexington, MA: D. C. Heath, 1976.
Discusses ways to utilize trade books (children's literature) to convey attitudes toward and information about sex to children up to age 12; includes activities, criteria for selection and use, and ways to use fiction and nonfiction, with an annotated list of references for adults and intelligent critical evaluations of about 60 books for children.

Uslander, Arlene, and Caroline Weiss, with the editors of *Learning Magazine. Dealing with Questions about Sex.* Palo Alto, CA: Learning Handbooks, 1975.
Another developmentally-organized book that provides specific answers to some questions children ask from kindergarten through junior high.

+ Wells, Dorothy. "Venereal Disease," *Library Journal*, v. 99, issue 15 (Sept. 16, 1974), pp. 2126-31.
Suggests 46 inexpensive pamphlet sources.

Woody, J. D. "Contemporary Sex Education: Attitudes and Implications for Childrearing," *Journal of School Health*, v. 43, no. 4 (April 1973), pp. 241-46.

SELECTING MATERIALS FOR
SOCIAL STUDIES AND SOCIAL SCIENCES

"All of us, young and old, female and male, need new skills and attitudes. We all need to acquire and practice a variety of forms of humane, human interaction skills. We all need to acquire and practice the skills of identifying those problems the solution to which will enhance humankind's quality of life."

> —John D. Haas, "Worthwhile Futures: You Can't Get There from Here," *Link*, May 1978

"One might say ... that in any given learning situation teaching materials should be drawn from (1) broadly social and highly controversial issues of the culture; (2) knowledges, values, and attitudes of students; and (3) relevant data of the social sciences."

> —Maurice T. Hunt and Lawrence E. Metcalf, *Teaching High School Social Studies*, 1968

"The social studies ... have been criticized for both their excesses and lapses. Although the fault-finding varies with the critic, there seems to be widespread agreement that the typical program suffers from an exaggerated preoccupation with the past and from undue factual detail."

> —Louis Rubin, *Curriculum Handbook*, 1977

"One of the interesting questions in studies of human learning is whether new information should be presented first as a rule and then by example—ruleg—or first as examples, then the rule of principle—egrule. Ruleg appears to be a bit faster, egrule a bit deeper. Why deeper? Because the opportunity for intuitive leaps is greater when one seeks to induce form—a rule or principle or generalization—from that which is unformed."

> —Arthur Welesley Foshay, "Intuition and Curriculum," *Link*, March 1978

□ □ □

CONCEPT TEACHING

In certain ways, selecting instructional materials for the social studies and social sciences is a relatively easy task. Historians, librarians, teachers, and scholars have produced, individually and/or through professional organizations, a number of competent guides reviewing, annotating, and/or recommending a wide spectrum of programs and materials. Organizations of social science educators, in particular, have provided compilations, frameworks, criteria, and guidelines to aid in selection. State frameworks, too, offer substantial guidance in the social studies, though these are not always perceived as welcome or helpful.

From other perspectives, selection can be difficult. The social studies—social science continuum is, at best, an uncertain eclectic hodgepodge incorporating, among other fields, geography, economics, history, political science, anthropology, and psychology—all presumably reflecting some common principles and scholarly discipline. Despite their supposed concern with the social, social studies/social science courses seem remote and irrelevant to many students. The separate fields, again, call on different skills and need to be evaluated according to different standards. "Social science skills" embrace the disparate skills of reading, writing, map reading, math and statistics, inductive thinking and decision making—tasks range from visual and motor skills to manipulation and the ability to work with values and ideas. Some social sciences/studies, such as geography, are closely tied to measurable physical reality; others require an understanding of human nature (human feelings and actions). The factual content can be enormous. The complex interrelationship makes it exceedingly difficult to prepare instructional objectives or outlines that are measurable, straightforward, intellectually respectable, and truly relevant.

Concept teaching—through social science concepts—has been strongly recommended by both the National Council for the Social Studies and the Social Science Education Consortium as a means or nexus for organizing the facts in social science disciplines and correlating these varied disciplines. Lacking these, the social studies can seem exceedingly diffuse.

Our incomplete social studies revolution of the 1960s—which introduced new media, new programs, new textbooks, paperbacks and simulation games—was intended to increase students' skills in analysis and in clarifying values, as well as their stores of knowledge.

However, according to our latest national assessment of social studies and citizenship as reported in *NAEP Newsletter* in October 1978, the 9-, 13-, and 17-year-olds tested in 1976 showed rather low accomplishments for skills and knowledge though their attitudes seemed more promising; at least 70 to 80 percent of all groups indicated a concern for the well-being and dignity of others. Whether our students' rather low accomplishments overall represent a failure of the old or the new social studies is not clear. (It may simply reflect a decline in materials budgets.) Perhaps our actual social studies may be an uneasy amalgam that succeeds at neither didactic nor heuristic teaching. Whatever the cause, evaluation studies of specific new social studies materials indicate—in many cases—relatively high student achievements and increased comprehension.

Though the national assessment tests primarily treated facts and interpretations, low student scores may possibly indicate the difficulties we experience in teaching subject areas that require thought and value decisions. Without a context, the facts and interpretations of social studies are hard to remember and apply. Unlike, say, grammar or addition, social studies as a curriculum area does not lend itself to drill and repetition.

Still, a Fall 1978 survey of 36 major social studies publishers by Donald Schneider and Roland Van Sickle indicated that—so far as the 27 publishers who responded were concerned—the market was dominated by single back-to-basics hardback texts, primarily chosen for readability. History was still chronological and narrative; geography dealt with names and places, physical geography, and map and globe skills as well as reading skills. With some exceptions at the secondary level, the responding publishers reported decreased demand for broadening and humanizing social studies. They considered materials dealing with inquiry, ethnic studies, women studies, values or career orientation, to be of limited interest.

Within history's basic chronological narrative framework, there are, admittedly, attempts to enrich the cultural and social contexts, to emphasize the role of the average person—essentially to personalize history. At the secondary level, the publishers indicated some increased growth in world geography, global studies, psychology, and sociology, and some inclusion of law-related content. In consumer economics, there was increased emphasis on consumer problems and decision making, though decision making is not particularly emphasized in political science.

Since each discipline of the social studies/social sciences has its own content (often specified by state frameworks), this chapter will emphasize some methods and criteria for selecting instructional materials for treating concepts and problem solving. Obviously, the clear presence and quality of concepts are not the only criteria for social studies materials. For current materials, currency, accuracy, and authenticity are highly important—though there are productive ways to utilize inaccurate materials. For history, concepts must be balanced with chronology; for geography, with measurement and other math and science concepts.

Some areas, like sex education and narcotics education, involving social and affective concerns as well as scientific information are treated in separate chapters. Legal education and multicultural education are also treated separately, more for convenience than from philosophical considerations.

Barry Beyer and Anthony Penna, who wrote the summary chapter of *Concepts in the Social Studies* (Washington, DC: National Council for the Social Studies, 1971) suggest that:

> In concept-teaching content must be viewed as a *vehicle*, not as an end in itself. The content of a lesson must be viewed primarily as a way of helping learners conceptualize about a particular idea or thing. The real substance of the lesson and in fact the basic cognitive objective must be a specific concept.

According to these authors:

> Purposeful conceptualizing requires more than a textbook. The personal experiences of the student play an important role—as data banks and as perceptual screens—in any conceptual learning. But so, too, do other media. There is in all conceptualizing an important affective dimension, a dimension of feeling or experiencing. It is almost impossible to develop this dimension in a classroom setting without the use of audio and visual media, media which can help the student become involved in experiences about which he is trying to conceptualize. The use of multi-media is an essential tool of effective concept-teaching—not in the sense of "show and tell" nor as merely supplemental to a lesson, but the use of multi-media as an integral part of the teaching-learning experience.

Social science concepts might be described as cognitive abstractions that can be applied to classes or groups of objects, occurrences, ideas, or recurring situations that have common qualities or characteristics. For example, a geographic concept might be "mountains"; a political concept could be "democracy" or "elections." Concepts, then, may be simple or complex, and can be related to each other through hierarchies or flow charts. Social science concepts are mental filing systems and sets of associations which should, hopefully, enable us to process and organize new experiences and information in a changing world. The concept of "nation," for example, can be used in understanding new nations or changing nations, if commonalities are clearly perceived. Stereotypes are, in essence, false or partially false concepts. These abound in social studies instructional materials.

APPROPRIATE MATERIALS

The introductory quotation by Arthur Foshay from "Intuition and Curriculum" poses the question of whether learning should be presented from rule to example (ruleg), or example to rule (egrule). Foshay concluded that ruleg was faster and egrule deeper. Clearly, both are needed in social studies, and require somewhat different materials. To incorporate both, social studies materials need to include abstract materials, direct experiences, and materials at all other ranges on Dale's Cone of Experience.

For egrule we need materials—beyond print— to build up children's backgrounds of experiences—particularly for younger children, children with limited experiences and those—at any age (possibly some of the time, for some subjects only)—still in the concrete operations stages. At all ages, pupils need to work with at least some positive and negative examples of whatever they are conceptualizing.

Textbooks, if well done, can supply overviews, ranges, and illustrations of concepts in their exposition of history, geography, and other social disciplines. For this to be more than book learning, students require other experiences to flesh out these concepts and make them memorable and real. These experiences might include fiction, films, art, role playing, simulation exercises, or actual observation or participation. Particularly in the primary or preschool grades, students need concrete experiences to develop their skills in comparing, contrasting and studying cause and effect or before and after.

While middle-grade children still need concrete experiences, they can also work with pictures, films, historical records, historical fiction or anecdotal accounts that represent realities. Later, in the high school years, most students still need some concrete or near-concrete experiences, though they are prepared increasingly to work with abstract print materials to infer, to judge logical consistency, to distinguish degrees of certainty, and to relate values to evidence. For high school students, media materials are appropriate as are factual materials in printed form: reference books (atlases, yearbooks, histories, encyclopedias for compiling and locating facts); pamphlets and magazines for currency and range of viewpoints; and books as supplements. There is a great deal of printed realia in the social studies—e.g., sample ballots, income tax forms, political advertisements and posters—which can aid in the saturation in data considered important for fact-based intuitive learning. Replicas of historical documents, as compiled into portfolios like the *Jackdaw* series of Grossman publishers, are useful for historical backgrounds and are easy to store and integrate into curriculum areas. These usually include document facsimiles, overviews, reading lists, and lesson plans.

Historical fiction and science fiction are two literary genres that can also enliven social studies and social issues for many. They may be most usable for areas overlooked in standard texts—from women's roles in the west to nuclear terror. Hannah Logasa, who compiled several guides to historical fiction, claims that this genre can convey the flavor of a period as no text can. She believes that students reading historical fiction enjoy and absorb facts and flavors that they would never get from history texts—about the costumes, cultures, literature, manners, architecture, daily lives, daily food, ways of travel, inventions, ideas, and beliefs of credible humans from other periods, with whom they can identify, thereby establishing a sense of historical continuity. In a similar way, science fiction postulates the future. Science fiction novels, stories, and movies present some current dilemmas in gripping form. Librarians, English teachers and sci-fi fans have compiled guides to make these materials accessible—often with adequate reviews and finding devices. Historical fiction, actually, is quite accessible—by time periods—through library card catalogs. These two literary genres encourage inexpensive individualization and student selection, though teachers must provide appropriate means of incorporating them into curriculum. These are, essentially, interdisciplinary materials.

Pictorial media use concrete representations to aid abstractions. Such tangible items as maps, globes, charts, diagrams, and time-lines are important tools for understanding social studies and social science concepts. Pictures, too—especially photographs—can provide important evidence of at least the surface appearance of realities and conflicts. Still pictures, which can be perused and re-examined, may be better and cheaper teaching devices than motion pictures which move on by, though the latter, of course, better demonstrate interactions and movements of people. Both provide concrete backgrounds and help students sharpen their powers of observation. Comprehension of maps, charts, and chronological devices such as time lines is a basic social science literacy skill, which can be correlated, developed, and reinforced through appropriate interdisciplinary materials that relate mathematics to social studies.

Games and simulations provide students with involvement in situations paralleling real life and real decision making. They are an appropriate means for broadening experience and are discussed more fully in the chapter on games and simulations in *Media and the Curriculum*. Social science educators in many ways have been pioneers in developing educational simulations. Real-life games and sports from other cultures can be one means of broadening experiences; these can be located in the chapter on games. Art and music projects, too, can draw on other times or cultures for cross-cultural inspiration.

Many kits for studying histories or cultures contain not only replicas of documents, but either real artifacts or replicas of artifacts; others contain pictures. Both are useful for direct experiences and amplifying reading.

Artifacts and skilful replicas can also be viewed first hand at museums, whose teaching roles are often seriously neglected in the social studies. My brief guide, *Social Studies on a Shoe String* (Buffalo, NJ: DOK Publishers, 1977), suggests ways to use local cultural institutions such as museums, newspapers, local government, and historical societies to create a low-cost, lively curriculum in the social studies. Three other useful guides to local resources have been compiled by Ellen Barnes, Catharine Williams, and Richard Wurman. These are all listed in For Further Reading. Books, like Thomas Weinland and Donald Protheroe's *Social Science Projects You Can Do* (Englewood Cliffs, NJ: Prentice-Hall, 1973) and David Weitzman's *My Backyard History Book* (Brown Paper School Book, 1975) also provide teachers and students means of using their own communities as teaching resources.

The National Council for the Social Studies, a Key Organization, has prepared some brief guides for using local history. Many other do-it-yourself guides are available from the American Association for State and Local History, 1400 Eighth Ave., S, Nashville, TN 37203. Local and interdisciplinary materials can also be used as source materials for social studies concepts. (According to some research, students tend to be most interested personally in what we would consider interdisciplinary areas.)

Some broad cross-disciplinary social science concepts that might be used are the following, selected by social scientists (Robert Fox and others) at the Social Science Education Consortium:

- Conflict and cooperation
- Identity and membership
- Deviation and conformity
- Power and influence
- Dependence, independence, and interdependence
- Socialization and development
- Change and equilibrium
- Resource identification, development, and utilization.

The chapter on science materials also includes many suggestions for science-social studies interdisciplinary concerns, such as health and medicine, war and data processing. Like environmental education, social studies is naturally a multi-disciplinary field whose materials come from many curriculum areas.

SPECIFIC CRITERIA

In using concepts rather than content to organize experience and information, we must proceed for each subject, through the school years, with carefully structured sequences of concepts that move from simple to complex and from broad distinctions to fine distinctions. At each grade, for each subject, or for children of varying abilities, we need to make decisions about which concepts, which problems or what content to include. Some criteria for choosing concepts emerge from professional opinion, classroom experiences, and student interests. Ideally, concepts should be:

- important for particular disciplines
- useful in making sense of problems
- meaningful or relevant to students, or
- capable of helping students make future experiences meaningful
- applicable to particular content

Criteria for problems, similarly, are based on currency, urgency, personal interest, personal and societal need, as well as on content and concepts. Some suggested criteria are that problems should be:

- significant, for some of the reasons above
- relevant to students (possibly a value dilemma for students)
- related to core concepts in the social sciences and/or in other domains of knowledge (e.g., physical, biological, technical, literary, artistic, etc.)

According to Jean Fair, for both concepts or problems it is easier to develop thinking skills where materials:

- are perceived by children as related to their own lives
- contain structures, cues and props to make thinking easier
- have an appropriate emotional content (lack of feeling or, conversely, too much feeling may militate against thinking)
- do not rely solely on print format, but include ample, directed experiences
- use modes appropriate to students' ages and development

Since our twentieth century society has no dearth of problems, it is relatively easy to find social studies materials for problem solving, a teaching approach advocated by Richard Gross and Raymond Muessig in *Problem-Centered Social Studies Instruction* (Washington, DC: National Council for the Social Studies, 1971), who claim that students learn best when they are actively considering problems. (The following list is reprinted by permission of the National Council for the Social Studies and Raymond H. Muessig.)

For problem solving, appropriate materials should

- be problem centered, acknowledging existence of conflicts and problems
- present a variety of points of view, allow or encourage exposure to opinion and propaganda
- include materials from advocates and advocacy organizations
- attempt to balance out opposing viewpoints
- present many forms of primary documents — photographs, records, first-hand accounts, on-spot recordings, documentary films, and videotapes, if needed and available
- include trade books and trade magazines
- utilize and rely on reference and research tools, such as reference books, periodical indexes, library card catalogs (and possibly computer bibliographic tools)
- present sufficient data — from authoritative sources and advocacy organizations — to allow students to describe and explore points of view and form own hypotheses
- utilize government and organizational statistics, if needed
- include open-ended materials

To use these materials and to use social studies media effectively, students need training in analysis, problem-solving methods, and social studies skills. In fact, training in some or all of the skills below has been shown to improve students' comprehension and understanding of social studies materials. (Values clarification exercises have also been helpful.)

- Problem-solving methods
- Defining problems
- Logical analysis
- Propaganda analysis (the use of rhetorical devices to persuade)
- The historical method, and the nature and limitations of evidence
- The limitations, uses, and understanding of statistics
- Map reading skills
- Interpretation of graphs, charts, pictures, tables, and legends
- Library research methods, including dictionary use and social studies reference books such as gazetteers
- Information sources
- Awareness of their own biases and limitations

These problem-solving learning skills are logically part of the curriculum of language arts (critical reading and interpretation), psychology, art, and mathematics, as well as of social studies. When skills like critical reading are taught in social studies, they should ideally be related to the texts and materials used. That is, the vocabulary should be chosen from words in texts or independent reading. Map instruction should be used with maps chosen to introduce countries or regions.

Readability formulas assess mainly sentence length and word familiarity, rather than the concept level which is so important in social studies. Nonetheless, social studies texts have been studied and found, often, to be rather difficult to read. Herber suggests that the range of readability levels within a text is more indicative of its potential difficulty than the average readability score. His survey of reading research in the social studies leads him to conclude that teacher intervention is more important than vocabulary control for student understanding of materials. He believes social studies texts may be the best functional vehicle for teaching reading skills for social studies students. Of course students should also have training in using the mass media (especially newspapers) and social studies realia (like official notices and ballots) since these will be their primary sources.

The Cloze procedure, described in the chapter on readability in *Issues and Policies*, has been suggested as a quick way to check students' ability to handle diverse social studies reading materials. (Every fifth word of a passage is replaced with a blank; if students can fill in 44 percent of the blanks correctly, they should be able to handle these materials.)

Many important social areas—such as sex or conflict—are taboo in educational materials for certain communities, possibly because of tradition or fear of community reactions. Cries of outrage are less likely in adopting social studies curricula or materials:

- if educators are aware of the resources, interests, and needs of their local communities
- if communities are consulted in establishing educational priorities
- if community resources are used as fully as possible
- if problems and concepts are truly significant to students

- if chosen materials are successful in teaching facts as well as concepts and attitudes
- if mechanisms are established to facilitate community interactions

(Other suggestions are available in the chapter on the feeling domain in this book and in the treatment of parent-community input in *Issues and Policies.*) Arthur Foshay's guidelines for *Coping with Community Controversy* (Boulder, CO: Social Science Education Consortium, 1974) suggest that controversy over curriculum change can be turned to advantage if controversies are examined and understood rather than avoided or suppressed.

Free and inexpensive materials abound in the social studies, where they are particularly valuable in dealing with controversial topics. Such materials — largely pamphlets, pictures or posters, and free rental films — come from many sources: corporations, all levels of government, advocacy organizations, political parties, and special interest groups. Even though their objectivity may be suspect, they are excellent sources. The guides and guidelines in the chapter on free materials in *Media and the Curriculum* provide some sources and some selection criteria.

The following criteria, reprinted with the permission of the National Council for the Social Studies, may be useful to incorporate into selection policies for selection and defensive purposes. It is taken from Dr. C. Benjamin Cox's *The Censorship Game and How to Play It*, Bulletin 50, National Council for the Social Studies, 1977, pp. 28-29, and is not to be reprinted without permission.

CRITERIA FOR EVALUATION OF TEACHING MATERIALS USED IN THE STUDY OF CURRENT ISSUES

1. Relevance of material:
   a. Is the material related to the objectives of the course or the unit?
   b. Is the material related to the issue being studied?
   c. Is the material adaptable to the range of reading ability of the students? In case of supplementary material, it may properly be too easy or difficult for the majority of the class.
   d. Is the material used as a basic text or as supplementary material?
      (*Note:* Supplementary material of a biased nature is rightfully used in order that various sides of an issue may be considered by the students. A basic text should be expected to meet criteria of objectivity and fairness that cannot be applied to all supplementary material.)

2. Balance and objectivity:
   a. Is the material factually accurate?
   b. Does the author distinguish between unsupported generalizations and generalizations based upon objective data?
   c. Are opinions distinguished from statements of fact?
   d. Is the material written in an objective, well-balanced manner?
   e. Does the author indicate that there are conflicting theories or opinions on the issues under discussion?
   f. Can use of the material help students to develop sound methods of weighing evidence and evaluating conclusions?
      Note: If the material in question does not meet the criteria outlined in (2), its use may still be justified. The following questions concerning the way in which it is used would then be pertinent:
      1) Have students been provided with a variety of supplementary materials written from divergent points of view?
      2) Are students aware of the nature and purposes of the organization publishing the materials?
      3) Have the students been helped to analyze the partisan nature of the material and its lack of objectivity and balance?

3. Likelihood of contribution to democratic citizenship:
   a. Can use of the material arouse interest in issues that confront American citizens today?
   b. Can use of the material help in developing an appreciation of democratic ideals?
   c. Can use of the material help in developing an understanding of democratic procedures for solving problems that confront individuals, groups, and communities?

3. (cont'd)
   d. Can use of the material aid in developing understanding of the rights of the individual in American society?
   e. Can use of the material help develop understanding of the obligations of the individual in American society?
   f. If the material treats situations that may be regarded as failures or shortcomings of our democracy, does it point out constructive ways for dealing with these situations within the framework of our Constitution?
      Note: If the material in question does not meet the criteria outlined in (3), its use may still be justified. The following questions concerning the way in which it is used would then be pertinent:
      1) Is the material provided in order to illustrate an undemocratic point of view?
      2) Has the teacher called attention to ways in which the material fails to uphold democratic ideals and practices?

The following relatively brief teacher evaluation form for social studies materials is based on an evaluation form designed to collect teachers' comments on classroom use and implementation. It is adapted from *A Guide to Selected Curriculum Materials on Interdependence, Conflict and Change*, prepared for the Center for Teaching International Relations by the Center for War/Peace Studies (now the Center for Global Perspectives) (New York, 1973. Unpaged).

TITLE

Authors

Publisher

Availability

Cost

* * * * *

Recommendations and Description Based on Teacher Use
The information below is based on the following teacher use

    ____ teachers, ____ students

    Grade levels

    Portion taught

Recommended Placement

Teaching Time

Suggested Preparation Time

Helpful Supplementary Materials

I   Description
    A Comments

       Focus

       Subfocus

    B Key concepts

    C Goals and Objectives

(Form continues on next page)

II Abilities required
    A Reading level

    B Skills

Use of	None	Moderate	Heavy
charts			
graphs			
tables			
maps			
inquiry/hypothesizing			
discussion			
value judgments			
simulation			
role-playing			
independent projects			
reading			

III Teachers' comments on motivation effectiveness

IV Additional comments

The Social Science Education Consortium has developed a compact but informative reporting information checklist which covers descriptive substantive characteristics, teaching strategies, and evaluation information. This Information Checklist is reprinted on page 160 with the permission of the Social Science Education Consortium.

The State of California has developed a rather concise report format for social studies materials evaluation (reprinted by permission on page 161).

INFORMATION CHECKLIST FOR MATERIALS IN THE SOCIAL SCIENCES

PROJECT IDENTIFICATION
CURRICULUM
SPECIFIC TITLE

DESCRIPTIVE CHARACTERISTICS		*SUBSTANTIVE CHARACTERISTICS*		*STRATEGIES EMPLOYED & EVALUATION INFORMATION*	
PUBLISHER		AREA OF POLITICAL SCIENCE		STRATEGIES	
AVAILABLE FROM		Political Theory		*Teacher-Student Action*	
Project		Public Law		Direction	
Publisher		International Relations		Exposition	
GRADE LEVEL & STRUCTURE		Comparative Government		Stories	
K-3		American Political Behavior		Pictures	
4-6		National		Demonstrations	
7-8		Local		Questions	
9 (Civics, Am. Gov't., Am. Hist., World Cult., Prob. of Dem., Int. Rel., Soc. Sci./Soc. St.) 10 11 12		CONCEPTS		*Resource-Student Action*	
		Legitimacy		Student Materials	
		Authority		Films	
		Power		Filmstrips & Slides	
SUBJECT AREA		Decision-Making		Records	
		Leadership		Tapes	
(Anth., Econ., Geog., Hist., Pol. Sci., Sociol., Soc. Sci./ Soc. St.)		*Citizenship*	Representation	Transparencies	
			Voting	*Teacher-Student Interaction*	
MATERIALS			Socialization	Discussion	
Student Materials			Interest Groups	Questions	
Teacher Guide			Participation	Case Studies	
A-V Kit			Parties	Seminars	
Tests		*Human Rights*	Freedom	*Student-Student Interaction*	
FORMAT			Equality	Role Playing	
Curriculum			Natural Rights	Games	
One-year course			Conscience	Simulations	
Semester			Justice	Group Discussions	
Units			Duty	Debates	
Issues		*Change*	Development	*Student-Resource Interaction*	
MEDIA UTILIZED			Modernization	Readings	
Student Materials			Stability	Laboratory	
Case Studies		*Conflict*	Pressure	Documents	
Readings			Violence	Independent Study	
Maps			Resolution	Film Loops	
Charts			Revolution	Programmed Instruction	
Films & Filmstrips		Institutions		Artifacts	
Records		Bureaucracy			
Tapes		Sovereignty		EVALUATION	
Transparencies		Law		Field Tested	
Artifacts		ISSUES		TYPES OF SCHOOLS	
Other		Civil Rights		Urban	
		Violence		Suburban	
1 *Incidentally used*		Right to Dissent		Rural	
2 *Considered, but not of prime concern*		Political Security		RESULTS	
3 *Occasionally recurring theme or intensively studied for short periods*		Social Security			
		Quality of Life		Cognitive Attainment	
		Pollution		Skill Attainment	
4 *Continuously recurring theme*		Overpopulation		Affective Attainment	
5 *Dominant theme*		Poverty & Welfare		MATERIALS REVISED BASED ON RESULTS	
* *Not available for analysis*		International Peace & Law			
		Drug Use & Abuse			

EVALUATION FORM
SOCIAL SCIENCE FRAMEWORK, K-12

CALIFORNIA'S REPORTING FORMAT FOR EVALUATION OF SOCIAL STUDIES MATERIALS

KEY: E - EXCELLENT
G - GOOD
F - FAIR
P - POOR

CIRCLE ONE CATEGORY THAT IS MOST DESCRIPTIVE OF THE EVALUATOR

A. Elementary Teacher   C. Elementary Principal   E. College or University   G. Student
B. Secondary Teacher   D. Curriculum Specialist   F. Lay Public   H. Board of Education

NAME OF COUNTY_____

	E	G	F	P
1.0 COMMUNICATION (Is the document understandable?)				
1.1 Vocabulary, Plain Language				
1.2 Sentence Structure				
1.3 Clarity of Ideas				
1.4 Organization of Ideas				
1.5 Overall Comprehension				
2.0 GOALS				
2.1 Relevancy				
2.2 Applicability				
2.3 Inclusiveness				
3.0 PROGRAM GOALS				
3.1 Relevancy				
3.2 Applicability				
3.3 Inclusiveness				
4.0 ILLUSTRATIVE LEVEL OBJECTIVES				
4.1 Cognitive				
4.2 Affective				
4.3 Relevancy				
4.4 Applicability				

	E	G	F	P
5.0 CONTENT ANALYSIS (Is there balance in these general areas?)				
5.1 Flexibility				
5.2 Concepts & Generalizations				
5.3 Content Focuses				
6.0 INTERDISCIPLINARY CONCEPTS				
6.1 Relevance				
6.2 Significance				
6.3 Usefulness				
7.0 ARE CONCEPTS FROM EACH OF THE DISCIPLINES REPRESENTED? (Are all areas adequately treated?)				
8.0 PROCESS-METHODOLOGY				
8.1 Inquiry				
8.2 Didactic				
8.3 Lecture (Data Giving)				
8.4 Group Activities				

COMMENTS: Indicate additions, deletions or expansion of present topics. Please be specific. Include page number and rationale for changes. (Use back)

KEY ORGANIZATIONS

Note: Many other worthwhile sources for social studies/social sciences materials are listed in the revised edition of the *Directory of Information Resources in the United States: Social Sciences*, compiled by the National Referral Center, Science and Technology Division, Library of Congress (Washington, DC: GPO, 1974).

ERIC Clearinghouse for Social Studies/
    Social Science Education (ERIC/ChESS)
    and
Social Science Education Consortium (SSEC)
855 Broadway
Boulder, CO 80302   (303) 492-8154

The SSEC, which sponsors ERIC/ChESS, is a nonprofit organization intended to improve the quality of social science education at all levels. More than some other ERIC clearinghouses, ERIC/ChESS specializes in collecting and analyzing teaching materials in its extended fields of interest. SSEC maintains an Educational Resources Center—a "hands on" center with a total of 5,500 new social science project materials: innovative textbooks, multimedia kits, games and simulations, a professional library, and reference materials. SSEC also offers workshops to train individuals and groups in the analysis and use of social studies curriculum materials and methods.

It also offers a $20.00 (two week) computer search to help locate social studies curriculum materials for particular grade levels and topics. The price is only $10.00 if fewer than 10 citations are found, and the money is refunded if the user is not satisfied. The charge is $0.10 extra for each citation after the first 50. Duplicate copies of popular curriculum materials topics are often available at popular prices, as are other about-to-be-discontinued materials.

SSEC has developed several substantial instruments for analyzing curriculum materials, among them *The Curriculum Materials Analysis Instrument* by Irving Morrisett and others (1971. 129p. $4.50), with a shorter (31p.) form available for $1.15; an *Ethnic Studies Materials Analysis Instrument* (1975. 22p. $1.95), essentially a modification of the Curriculum Materials Analysis System covering format, realism and accuracy, society and the individual, and intercultural understanding; and a *Career Education Materials Analysis Instrument*, discussed in the chapter on work.

SSEC has also provided massive compilations to analyze and/or compare curriculum materials in social studies, including the *Social Studies Curriculum Materials Data Book* (annotated under Key Publications) and *Materials for Civics, Government, and Problems of Democracy*, by Mary Jane Turner (1971. 199p. $4.25pa.).

The Consortium has an impressive series of publications which cover all aspects of social studies from environment to career education, including behavioral sciences, citizenship, history, legal education, anthropology, U.S. and world history, future studies, ethnic studies, and values education. It is also a resource on simulation games. In addition it compiles many selective bibliographies at rather low prices (some are cited as Key Publications). A complete list of publications is available on request.

The SSEC now houses an ethnic heritage program which has funded more than 250 projects in training, curriculum materials, and dissemination since 1977. Since these are relatively unknown, the Clearinghouse is planning to identify, assemble, analyze and code these projects and related materials during 1979.

SSEC's newsletter, *Link* ($5.00 a year for 5 issues), is an excellent information source on conferences, publications and trends in social studies education. ERIC/ChESS' newsletter, *Keeping Up*, is sometimes incorporated within *Link*. Sample copies can be obtained by request (attention *Keeping Up*).

Institute for Political and Legal Education (IPLE)
c/o Educational Improvement Center-South
207 Delsea Drive
RD 4, Box 209
Sewell, NJ 08080   (609) 228-6000

The IPLE has designed a series of social studies programs to provide middle school, high school and adult education students with practical experiences and understanding of political and governmental processes. Though the programs are developed for New Jersey, they can, according to the U.S. Office of Education, be used in other locations.

They are, essentially, activity-centered, community-based programs. The IPLE approach stresses 1) the acquisition of cognitive knowledge and affective skills, 2) student participation in classroom and school activities through role-playing simulation games, and 3) student participation in local and state agencies or other community organizations. Secondary curriculum areas deal with political processes, governmental and organizational structures, and law-related concerns.

Curriculum materials, which may be purchased at cost, include resource information and teaching techniques. Some recommended high school manuals are: *Voter Education* ($8.00); *State Government: The Decision Making Process* ($10.00); *Individual Rights* ($6.00); *Fair Trial v. Free Press* ($2.75); *Juvenile Justice* ($16.00); and *Law and the Family* ($5.00). Supplementary curriculum booklets cover such topics as lobbying, model congress, *Community Research Techniques* ($1.75), county, state and local government. Filmstrips cover some of these topics. All materials have been validated. *Approaches to Political/Legal Education — An Implementation Guide* ($10.00) includes good discussions of organization, grantsmanship, and use of community resources. An organization brochure and a complete list of materials are available on request.

National Council for the Social Studies (NCSS)
2030 M St., NW, S400
Washington, DC 20036   (202) 296-0760

NCSS is a professional organization for teachers, supervisors, administrators and other educators in the fields of history, political science, sociology, economics, social studies, and education at every level — elementary through university. Regular membership includes subscriptions to its journal, *Social Education*, and its newsletter, *The Social Studies Professional*, as well as receipt of three *Bulletins*, selected special publications, a discount for NCSS's Annual Meeting, and other membership benefits; comprehensive membership includes all of the above, plus an additional three *Bulletins*. *Social Education* itself is an excellent source of reviews for all sorts of media.

NCSS *Bulletins* are a carefully-edited series of paperback books, averaging around 130 pages in length, which combine topicality with thoroughness; they are valuable for reference, browsing, research, and classroom use. Some recent titles include:

Competency-Based Teacher Education (Bulletin 56, 1978; $5.95pa.)

Social Studies Curriculum Improvement (Bulletin 55, 1978; $5.50pa.)

Teaching of World History (Bulletin 54, 1978; $5.50pa.)

Social Studies and the Elementary Teacher: Promises and Practices (Bulletin 53, 1977; $4.95pa.)

Building Rationales for Citizenship Education (Bulletin 52, 1977; $4.95pa.)

The NCSS *How-to-Do-It Series* (no. 2) comprises pamphlets designed to fit into a three-ring binder; they aim to provide a practical and useful source of classroom methods and techniques for elementary and secondary social studies teachers, with guides for using such media as simulations, newspapers, bulletin boards, and motion pictures. The four most recent titles of this new series are: "Using Questions in Social Studies" (no. 4, 1977; $1.00), "Reach for a Picture" (no. 3, 1977; $1.00), "Effective Use of Films in Social Studies Classrooms" (no. 2, 1977; $1.00), and "Improving Reading Skills in Social Studies" (no. 1, 1977; $1.00).

NCSS *Yearbooks* (discontinued with the forty-seventh *Yearbook* in 1977) provided wide perspectives on broad topics, often with substantial lists of resources. Its *Position Statements* are also valuable for selectors. Two useful titles are *Curriculum Guidelines for Multiethnic Education* (1976. $2.50pa.), and *Social Studies Curriculum Guidelines* (1971. $1.50pa.).

Other publications are cited separately. A complete list is available on request from the publications office of the NCSS at 1515 Wilson Blvd., Suite 101, Arlington, VA 22209.

KEY PUBLICATIONS

Many other relevant materials are included or can be found in the chapters on games and print materials in *Media and the Curriculum*. Social studies materials are continually reviewed by the *Curriculum Review*. Prime materials for controversial issues are available through *Alternative Sources*. The *History Teacher* has very competent reviews of textbooks and readers, while the *Journal of Geography* reviews new books and maps.

Concepts in the Social Studies, edited by Barry K. Beyer and Anthony N. Penna. Washington, DC: National Council for the Social Studies, 1971. 95p. $2.70 pa. (Bulletin 45).

This compilation explores the nature and implications of concepts and the reasons and methods for teaching concepts. Part II, which provides a rationale for teaching concepts in the social studies, is particularly helpful for selectors in detailing the process and the means for conceptualization and their implications for teaching. Most of the questions, outlines and discussions can be applied to materials and programs, and should greatly help in selecting and analyzing materials for conceptual teaching in this subject area, or in developing a general educational policy.

Constructing a Community System Based Social Science Curriculum, by John W. Muth and Lawrence Senesh. Denver, CO: Social Science Education Consortium, 1977. 147p. $6.00.

This state-of-the-art paper discusses how and why to use communities as laboratories for social science teaching and has many activities for children.

Controversial Issues in the Social Studies: A Contemporary Perspective, edited by Raymond H. Muessig. Arlington, VA: National Council for the Social Studies, 1975. $8.75 (45th *Yearbook*).

An eight-chapter publication with 13 contributors, which does not evade controversy. Some especially interesting articles are chapters entitled "Should Traditional Sex Modes and Values Be Changed?" and "Should the Study of Death Be a Necessary Preparation for Living?" Overall, a good background for controversy.

The Creative Social Studies Teacher, edited by Paul H. Tedesco. New York: Bantam, 1974. 257p. $1.25pa.

Many of the ten articles in this paperback suggest specific tools and tactics for teaching social studies courses with paperbacks and other trade books. Topics include cultural pluralism, the Third World, American history, economic education, and the future. One article deals with simulation games in American history. Most of these articles suggest specific titles and approaches for each topic.

Developing Decision-Making Skills, edited by Dana G. Kurfman. Arlington, VA: National Council for the Social Studies, 1977. 279p. $9.95 (47th *Yearbook*).

This *Yearbook*, one of several NCSS *Yearbooks* on social studies skills, treats decision making as the context within which the more traditional social studies skills are discussed and considered. Some of these skills, naturally, are emphasized more than others. This book provides thorough treatment of the social studies skills of analysis, application, evaluation, obtaining and interpreting information, as well as discussions of the affective characteristics necessary for good decision making. The teaching strategies, models, checklists, and readings throughout are quite pertinent to the task of selecting materials. Some outlines and checklists can be adapted almost without change.

Developing the Library Collection in Political Science, by Robert Bartlett Harmon. Metuchen, NJ: Scarecrow Press, 1976. 198p. $7.50.

This well-classified, indexed selection device for political science materials is aimed toward small- to medium-sized public libraries and junior college libraries. It seems useful, as well, for high school and junior high school libraries and for social science teaching, having a good chapter on general selection sources, and good annotations of selected reference books and periodicals.

Evaluation Studies on "New Social Studies" Materials, by Karen B. Wiley and Douglas P. Superka. Boulder, CO: Social Science Education Consortium, 1977. 124p. $4.50 mimeo.

This compilation of reports brings together in one convenient place abstracts of research and evaluation studies performed on 68 new social studies materials;

these could be very useful for individuals selecting among new social studies programs. Some of these studies correlate particular courses of study with student achievement. For some curricula (the "Family of Man," for example) there is quite a respectable amount of research. The competent annotations are alphabetically arranged under project titles, with separate indexes for subjects, grade levels, investigators, authors, editors, and publishers.

Films on the Future: A Selective Listing, by Marie Martin. Washington, DC: World Future Society, 1977. 68p. $6.00pa. (From World Future Society, 4916 St. Elmo Ave., Washington, DC 20014).

An interesting annotated listing of about 250 films for intermediate and secondary education on such topics as cities, food, forecasts, population, human values, ocean sciences, and science fiction, providing information on source, length, and (sometimes) rental costs. The World Future Society also publishes *The Futurist*, a monthly publication that lists and reviews materials dealing with the future—mostly at the high school and adult level—and offers discounts on future-oriented books through its book service.

Intercom. New York: Center for Global Perspectives, 1959- . 5 issues/yr. $6.00; single issues $1.75. Quantity discount. (From 218 E. 18th St., New York, NY 10003).

This resource tool began with introducing educators to the problems of war, peace, conflict, and social change with the idea of promoting constructive alternatives consistent with global values. Issues are gold mines of resources on particular topics, with maps, overviews, suggested discussion issues, comprehensive guides to organizational sources, and well-annotated lists of appropriate materials, often from relatively unknown sources. These annotated listings—of consistently high quality—include print, programs, and audiovisual materials. They offer more to high school and college teaching then to elementary teaching, though some issues concentrate on elementary resources. Two recent issues deal with *Building Social Studies through Language Arts* and *Culture's Storehouse: Building Humanities through Language Arts*.

Internationalize Your School, by Richard P. Hall and others. Boston: National Association of Independent Schools, 1977. 35p. $2.00pa.

This handbook on internationalization includes model curricula (with suggested materials for each) for five alternate approaches to global studies. Other items are criteria for selecting "study abroad" programs, with an annotated directory of international programs. Most valuable, perhaps, is an annotated source list of about 45 organizations active in international education and/or global studies; some are prime materials sources; others have developed programs.

Materials for Civics, Government, and Problems of Democracy: Political Science in the New Social Studies, by Mary Jane Turner. Boulder, CO: Social Science Education Consortium, 1971. 199p. $4.25pa.

A systematic comparative survey of 49 not-quite-so-new political science curriculum packages, with comparative information on 1971 costs and availability, contents, educational objectives, teaching strategies and evaluations.

Notable Children's Trade Books in the Field of Social Studies, by a Joint Committee of the Children's Book Council and the National Council for Social Studies. New York: Children's Book Council, annual listing. (Single copy free from CBC for $0.24 stamped self-addressed large envelope. From CBC, 67 Irving Place, New York, NY 10005).

This valuable yearly annotated list of notable children's books in the social studies appears annually in *Social Education* and is available from the CBC in May.

Preparing to Teach Political Science: Sources and Approaches, by Mary Jane Turner. Boulder, CO: ERIC Clearinghouse for Social Studies/Social Science Education and Social Science Education Consortium, 1974. 29p. $1.50 mimeo.

This paper identifies some major approaches to understanding political phenomena and suggests curriculum materials to implement each approach. It also suggests periodicals that include background information and/or ideas for classroom content and strategies; tools for locating additional curriculum materials; and bibliographies of political sources that contain more detailed and explicit examination of how political learning takes place. Altogether, this tool helps teachers and librarians locate materials consistent with local objectives and student needs.

Reading for Young People: The Great Plains, by Mildred Laughlin. Chicago: American Library Association, 1979. 159p. $7.50pa.

This is the first of a regional series of annotated bibliographies, *Reading for Young People*, intended to introduce selected materials dealing with the unique cultural heritage of national regions such as the Great Plains. This particular guide—selected and annotated by a committee of librarians from Kansas, Nebraska and the Dakotas—includes 368 books that reflect—in fact and fiction—the culture of the Plains Indians, the adventures of those who followed the Santa Fe and the Oregon trails, and the lives of the settlers.

Selections range through fiction, poetry, folk tales, music, and drama to biography and other informational guides. Annotations provide evocative quotes from the book along with resumés that summarize content and scope and suggest approximate grade levels and list bibliographic information. The appendix identifies additional audiovisual materials appropriate for a study of the Great Plains.

This series of guides would seem to be extremely helpful for selecting books to add depth and interest in history and social studies for all regions of this country.

Selective Bibliography in Anthropology and World History Resources, by Alice Vigliani. Boulder, CO: Social Science Education Consortium, 1977. 29p. $2.00pa.

Selective Bibliography in Economics Resources, compiled by Judith Hedstrom. Boulder, CO: Social Science Education Consortium, 1977. 34p. $1.75pa.

Selective Bibliography in Political Science Resources, compiled by Judith E. Hedstrom. Boulder, CO: Social Science Education Consortium, 1977. 37p. $2.00pa.

Selective Bibliography in United States History, compiled by Juan E. Ramos and Barbara Crevling. Boulder, CO: Social Science Education Consortium, 1977. 37p. $2.00pa.

These four bibliographies were prepared by ERIC/ChESS to provide information on new trends and materials in secondary social science education. Each bibliography includes basal and supplementary curriculum materials—print, non-print, games or simulations—plus teacher resources, associations and organizations, and ERIC Documents. Materials were chosen on the criteria of quality, usefulness, availability, and recency. Annotations provide information on the content focus and/or instructional approaches of items included. Citations include addresses, sources, and the Fry readability score for print items.

Social Studies Curriculum Development: Prospects and Problems, edited by Dorothy McClure Fraser. Washington, DC: National Council for the Social Studies, 1969. 333p. Out of print. Reprint available. $40.20pa.; $13.40 microfiche. (From University Microfilms International, 300 North Zeeb Rd., Ann Arbor, MI 48106).

This compiled yearbook is organized around the critical decision-making areas of curriculum reform, with illustrative materials drawn from various projects in the belief that it is the teacher's role to select significant content appropriate to learners at various stages of maturity within the content of established purposes. Includes criteria for selecting, developing, and evaluating materials and programs, with models for analysis of materials and classroom interactions.

Social Studies Curriculum Materials Data Book. Boulder, CO: Social Science Education Consortium, 1971-1977. 3v. $75.00, looseleaf format. Annual $10.00.

This ongoing evaluative summary of curriculum materials in the social studies now includes more than 500 analyses of materials from federally-funded social studies projects, textbooks, games and simulations, supplementary materials, and teacher resources. The latest annual paperbound update can stand alone as a resource for current materials.

Data sheets include an overview (rationale and general objectives); description of the format, elements and costs; time required to implement the materials; intended users; characteristics required of intended users; explanations of necessary teaching or gaming procedures; evaluation data; and relevant information from social sciences. Subject areas include traditional studies and new curriculum areas, as well as multidisciplinary and interdisciplinary studies.

Teaching Local History: Trends, Tips and Resources, by Fay D. Metcalf and Mathew T. Downey. Boulder, CO: Social Science Education Consortium, 1977. 103p. $3.75pa.

Although this is primarily a state-of-the-art paper, it includes a variety of teaching suggestions and activities, and a complete chapter on local history resources. Other chapters cover using the community as historical resource, local economic history, family history, history of local art and architecture, and folklore.

Teaching Youth about Conflict and War, edited by William A. Nesbitt, Norman Abramowitz, and Charles Bloomstein. Washington, DC: National Council for the Social Studies, 1973. 101p. Out of print. Reprint available. $12.80pa.; $6.00 microfiche. (From University Microfilms International, 300 North Zeeb Rd., Ann Arbor, MI 48106).

This book is designed for classroom use, and provides the teacher with a background essay covering various approaches to the problem of war; an exploration and analysis of the conceptual and value frameworks involved; and a lucid exposition of how the various elements and dynamics of The Robbers' Cave experiment can be related specifically to values and concepts discussed earlier in the book. This section contains discussion questions. The book also includes a number of suggestions for additional teaching units for different grade levels, and a substantial section annotating resources, organizations, and curriculum projects.

World History in Juvenile Books: A Geographical and Chronological Guide, by Seymour Metzner. New York, Wilson, 1973. 356p. $12.00.
  A comprehensive geographical and chronological listing of more than 2,700 trade books for elementary and junior high, including both fiction and non-fiction. Provides full bibliographical information and brief annotations for books whose contents are not clearly conveyed by their titles.

FOR FURTHER READING

*Items marked with an asterisk include criteria and/or checklists.
+ Items marked with a plus include substantial lists of references.

* + Barnes, Ellen, and others. *Teach and Reach: An Alternative Guide to Resources for the Classroom*. Syracuse, NY: Human Policy Press, 1974.

* + Center for Teaching International Relations (now the Center for Global Perspectives). *A Guide to Selected Curriculum Materials on Interdependence, Conflict and Change*. New York: 1973.

+ Cline, Ruth K. J., and Bob L. Taylor. "Integrating Literature and 'Free Reading' into the Social Studies Program," *Social Education*, v. 42, no. 1 (Jan. 1978), pp. 27-31.

*DuVall, Charles R. *A Study of the Measured Readability Level of Selected Intermediate Grade Social Studies Textbooks*. 1971. (ED 051-049).

* + Estes, Thomas S. "Reading in the Social Studies: A Review of Research since 1950," pp. 177-90 of James L. Laffey's *Reading in the Content Areas*. Newark, DE: International Reading Association, 1972.

*Fersh, Seymour. *Learning about Peoples and Cultures*. Evanston, IL: McDougal, Littell & Co., 1974.

Foshay, Arthur. *Coping with Community Controversy: Guidelines for Introducing New Social Studies Programs*. Boulder, CO: Social Science Education Consortium, 1974.

Fraser, Dorothy McClure. *Stimulating Techniques for Teaching Social Studies: Using Components of the Britannica Knowledge Retrieval Center*. Chicago: Encyclopaedia Britannica, updated at intervals.

*+ Hall, Susan J. *Africa in U.S. Educational Materials: Thirty Problems and Responses*. New York: School Services Division, African-American Institute, 1977, c1976. 62p.

*Hart, Richard L., and Victor W. Shapiro. "The NCSS Curriculum Guidelines: Dissemination and Utilization," *Social Education*, v. 39, no. 2 (Feb. 1975), pp. 92-95.

Herber, Harold L. "Reading in the Social Studies: Implications for Teaching and Research," in James L. Laffey's *Reading in the Content Areas*. Newark, DE: International Reading Association, 1972.

Hollister, Bernard C., and Deane C. Thompson. *Grokking the Future: Science Fiction in the Classroom*. Dayton, OH: Pflaum/Standard, 1973.

+ Johnson, Roger E. *How Reliable Are Our Elementary Social Studies Texts?* Anaheim, CA: International Reading Association, 1970. (ED 043 459).

*Katzer, Jeffrey. *Evaluating Information: A Guide for Users of Social Science Research*. Reading, MA: Addison-Wesley, 1978.

*King, David C. "Social Studies Texts: How to Recognize Good Ones and Survive Bad Ones," *Learning*, v. 5, no. 5 (Jan. 1977), pp. 38-41.

*Kurfman, Dana G. "Choosing and Evaluating New Social Studies Research," *Social Education*, v. 36, no. 7 (Nov. 1972), pp. 775-82.
Includes two teacher evaluation forms and one student evaluation form.

Larkin, James M., and Jane J. White. "The Learning Center in the Social Studies Classroom," *Social Education*, v. 38, no. 7 (Nov./Dec. 1974), pp. 698-710.

+ Logasa, Hanna. comp. *Historical Fiction: Guide for Junior and Senior High Schools and Colleges*. Brooklawn, NJ: McKinley, 1968.

*Long, Barbara Ellis. "Using the Behavioral Sciences as a Focus for Social Studies—a String for the Beads," in *Teaching Social Studies in Urban Schools*. Reading, MA: Addison-Wesley, 1972.

Lunstrom, John P., and Bob L. Taylor. *Teaching Reading in the Social Studies*. Newark, DE: International Reading Association, 1978.

* + Michigan State Department of Education. *A Study of Elementary and Secondary Social Studies Textbooks; Part I, The Textbook Report; Part II, The Textbook Reviews*. Lansing, MI: 1973. (ED 077 788).

* + "Model for Analyzing Curriculum Materials and Classroom Transactions," in *Yearbook, 1968*. Washington, DC: National Council for the Social Studies, 1968.

*Peters, Charles W. "Evaluating Social Studies Materials: Readability Formulas Are Not the Only Answer," *Social Studies*, v. 63, no. 2 (March/April 1977), pp. 70-77.

Schneider, Donald O., and Ronald Van Sickle. "How Textbook Publishers View Social Studies in the Schools," *Social Education*, v. 43, no. 6 (Oct. 1979), pp. 461-65.

Standard Oil Company (Indiana). *Organizations Providing Business and Economic Education Materials or Information*. Chicago: Standard Oil Company (Indiana), 1979.

+ Sutherland, Zena. *History in Children's Books: An Annotated Bibliography.* Brooklawn, NJ: McKinley, 1967.

Weinland, Thomas, and Donald Protheroe. *Social Science Projects You Can Do.* Englewood Cliffs, NJ: Prentice-Hall, 1973.

Williams, Catharine. *The Community as Textbook.* Bloomington, IN: Phi Delta Kappa Educational Foundation, 1975. (Fastback 64).

+ Woodbury, Marda, and others. *Social Studies on a Shoe String.* Buffalo, NY: DOK Publishers, 1977.
Listing of inexpensive community and print resources.

Wurman, Richard S. *The Yellow Pages of Learning Resources.* Cambridge, MA: MIT Press, 1972.
Many suggestions of persons and places to observe and learn from.

SELECTING MATERIALS FOR LEGAL EDUCATION

During the last ten years, along with an increase in crime and litigation, we have had an explosion of interest in law-related curricula — often spearheaded by law enforcement agencies and lawyers, individually or through legal associations. Often these programs are supported by funding from outside regular school funds. Many curricula are excellent. Most tend to combine theory and practice in desirable proportions. Many build upon affective concerns.

In *Law in the Curriculum* (Bloomington, IN: Phi Delta Kappa Educational Foundation, 1978), Murry Nelson suggests that law concerns can easily be integrated into high school courses in economics, sociology, anthropology, current history, and consumer education. Other areas which could easily incorporate law concerns are science, health, environmental education, and nutrition. Elementary subjects that offer opportunities to include law are world history, regional cultures — and, of course, such affective concerns as divorce, adoption, and rights of the handicapped. Law, of course, is an integral part, or should be, of courses in citizenship education, career education, consumer education, sex education, narcotics education and political accountability. Since the adoption of the Twenty-Sixth Amendment, 18-year-olds eligible to vote need background to understand our legal and political processes.

Proponents of law education consider understanding of law as basic a skill as reading, writing, and arithmetic. Legal skills are, essentially, skills that may be needed to deal effectively with the constraints and opportunities of modern society.

Law lends itself well to direct-experience education through an involvement with the local community and with the experiences of students or their friends and family.

On the basis of a thorough study of curricula, in *Law-Related Education in America* the Youth Education for Citizenship recommends that successful law education should:

- encourage the inquiry method of instruction
- encourage role-playing exercises
- seek to develop and implement field-learning experiences
- endeavor to use the governance of the school as a model of justice
- present legal issues realistically, acknowledging conflict and controversial issues

As they put it:

Traditional courses in civics and government ... present a romantic myth of the American legal system, in which the ideals of democracy are confused with the realities of politics. Law-related curricula can help solve this problem by raising issues which are relevant to students and posing questions concerning the practical problems of achieving justice which can fully engage their intelligence.

Law is a subject that can be well taught through concepts, which can be adjusted and made more complex as students advance in years and understanding. Proponents of law education, for example, believe that such concepts as "leadership," "responsibility," "rules," and "fairness" are appropriate for students in grades K-3, while the slightly more complex concepts of "justice" and "rights and responsibilities" can be taught at upper elementary grades.

For teaching law, we have available a substantial quantity of relatively high quality materials. The Youth Education for Citizenship (YEFC), a special committee of the American Bar Association, has done an outstanding job of collecting information on these programs, as have some other Kay Organizations.

KEY ORGANIZATIONS

Many other organizations are listed in the *Directory of Law-Related Education Projects* published by Youth Education for Citizenship.

Correctional Service of Minnesota
1427 Washington Ave., S
Minneapolis, MN 55454   (800) 328-4737 and (612) 339-7227

Correctional Service of Minnesota is a non-profit United Way agency, whose purpose is to develop and distribute law-related materials throughout the United States at a reasonable cost. Its specialties are junior and senior high law education, police training and in-service training for corrections. It offers in-service training to educators as well as curriculum design and implementation.

Its Law Enforcement Resource Center publishes an excellent free catalog in tabloid format, which has descriptions and blurbs for such law-related materials as newspapers, discussion and simulation games, visuals, multi-media materials, pamphlets, books, rental films, sound filmstrips, and professional reading. *INSIGHT—A Law-Related Newspaper* ($15.00/classroom set of 35 copies), for secondary students and teachers, is based on the premise that law education is too important not to be exciting. It, too, is in tabloid format, and attempts—rather successfully—to combine style and substance.

It includes news, feature articles, study questions, classroom activities, maps, charts, cartoons, and resources organized around special themes/issues of interest to students.

National Street Law Institute
605 G St., NW
Washington, DC 20001   (202) 624-8217

The National Street Law Institute is an outgrowth of a Georgetown University Program that taught law courses through high schools in the District of Columbia, juvenile and adult correctional institutions, and community-based programs. It is now sponsored by a consortium of universities in Washington, DC, and is still operated to develop curriculum materials and programs to teach law to laypersons. Its special strengths, as its name implies, are introduction to law, criminal law, juvenile law and correctional law; it is also interested in family, housing, individual rights and consumer rights.

It provides technical assistance, teacher training programs, workshops and conferences, as well as materials development. Its publications include a national text, *Street Law: A Course in Practical Law* (1975. $5.95) and *Street Law: A Course in the Law of Corrections* (1976. $3.50), both published by West Publishing Company, Mineola, NY 11501. These are both well-developed, validated curricula for students of high school age and older.

Youth Education for Citizenship (YEFC)
American Bar Association
1155 East 60th St.
Chicago, IL 60637   (312) 947-3966

YEFC was created by the American Bar Association in 1971 to foster effective, high-quality programs of law-related education in our nation's elementary and secondary schools — to prepare students for participation in a democracy by helping them gain better understanding of our legal system. Its goal is to have law taught systematically at every grade from kindergarten through high school. It is a national clearinghouse for information as well as a facilitative agency cooperating with lawyers, educators, and parents to develop law-related programs on a community basis. YEFC conducts workshops, develops and evaluates programs, and compiles resource guides of existing programs and materials.

It has produced excellent, comprehensive, well-organized compilations of curriculum materials, which are kept up to date by a periodical *Update on Law-Related Education* ($5.00 for 3 issues a year). *Update* has regular sections on curriculum materials and teaching strategies, as well as discussions of such areas as recent Supreme Court decisions, recent legal developments, opposing views on controversial issues, and articles on such topics as sports and the law.

Its *Directory of Law-Related Education Projects* (3rd ed., 1978. 122p. $2.00pa.) describes the subjects, activities and materials of nearly 400 state and national projects in law-related education. Projects are arranged state-by-state with a separate section for national projects.

Publications on materials include:

Bibliography of Law-Related Curriculum Materials (1976. 116p. $1.00pa.). Well organized, with annotations that include grade level and educational applications; discusses more than 2,000 books and pamphlets for teacher reference and grades K-12.

Gaming: An Annotated Catalogue of Law-Related Games and Simulations (1975. 32p. $1.00pa.).
Careful, well-organized descriptions of more than 130 games and simulations.

Media: An Annotated Catalogue of Law-Related Audio-Visual Materials (1975). 79p. $1.00pa.).
Describes more than 400 media items — mostly films, filmstrips, and tapes for law-related education in grades K-12.

These low-cost publications are available at discount rates for quantity or combination offers.

KEY PUBLICATIONS

Other comprehensive guides, published by the Youth Education for Citizenship (YEFC) and the Correctional Service of Minnesota, are included under Key Organizations.

Handbook of Legal Education Resources, compiled by Mary Jane Turner. Boulder, CO: Social Science Education Consortium, 1977. 225p. $7.00.
This comprehensive guide to teaching materials in legal education analyzes and classifies materials according to objectives (or categories): the role of law in society; concepts related to law; constitutional law and civil rights; criminal law and the criminal justice system; contemporary issues; and substantive law.
These materials are presented in formatted descriptions that provide information on the developers, publishers, publication dates, grade levels, cost, and availability. Separate bibliographies deal with commercial materials, children's literature with legal content, and ERIC documents.

FOR FURTHER READING

Nelson, Murry R. *Law in the Curriculum.* Bloomington, IN: Phi Delta Kappa Educational Foundation, 1978. (Fastback 106).
Includes substantial lists of references.

SELECTING MATERIALS FOR
MULTICULTURAL EDUCATION

"We have made of this world a neighborhood, and now we are challenged to make of it a brotherhood."
— Martin Luther King, Jr.

"Multicultural education is education which values cultural pluralism ... Multicultural education affirms that schools should be oriented toward the cultural enrichment of all children and youth through programs rooted in the preservation and extension of cultural alternatives ... Education for cultural pluralism includes four major thrusts: (1) the teaching of values which support cultural diversity and individual uniqueness; (2) the encouragement of the qualitative expansion of existing ethnic cultures and their incorporation into the mainstream of American socio-economic and political life; (3) the support of explorations in alternative and emerging lifestyles; and (4) the encouragement of multiculturalism, multilingualism, and multidialectism."
— American Association of Colleges for Teacher Education

"The Native American must be a living part of the study of American history, social sciences, citizenship, and world history from first grade on."
— Jeannette Henry, *Textbooks and the American Indian*

"Empathy ... is the capacity to see oneself in the other fellow's situation."
— Daniel Lerner, *The Passing of Traditional Society*

□ □ □

OVERVIEW

Unlike such social studies courses as geography, economics, and history, multicultural education does not stem from a recognized academic discipline. It stems, rather, from the civil rights movement and a somewhat nebulous peace-international movement. In a way, it extends the criteria for fairness and bias to programmatic areas and is conceptually related to bilingual-bicultural programs.

Ethnic heritage studies programs were codified in the Education Amendment of 1972, Section 504, which authorized for all students of the nation "an opportunity to learn about the differing and unique contributions to the national heritage made by each ethnic group." The ultimate intent was to contribute to "a more harmonious and patriotic populace."

Frameworks for ethnic studies have been established by the professional bodies listed as Key Organizations in the chapter on social studies, as well as by other professional organizations — like, for example, the National Council of Teachers of English, The National Education Association, and the Association for Supervision and Curriculum Development.

Other conceptually-related guidelines were laid down earlier by individual and group proponents of internationalism and global perspectives. In different editions of *The World of Children's Literature*, Anne Pellowski, now at the Information Center on Children's Cultures, surveyed children's literature from an international perspective, reported efforts to foster the creation of relevant materials, and suggested standards for validity. Other post-World War II organizations, like Unesco and the International Youth Library, engaged in the same task.

The rationales for multicultural education include improved self-concept, knowledge of one's own culture or heritage, and, ultimately, appreciation of diversity. Conceptually, international or intercultural education follows a continuum away from cultural steroetypes toward awareness of superficial or highly-visible cultural traits, awareness of subtle or significant features, and awareness of how another culture perceives its members. This latter shift in perspective goes well beyond intellectual understanding or factual knowledge.

For both multicultural or international education, materials—so far as possible—should be valid or free from stereotypes. Too often, unfortunately, a patronizing if well-meaning set of stereotypes replaces a more hostile set. In many cases, romantic stereotypes emphasize customs for the most part discarded, extremes of wealth or poverty, simple virtues, rural or village life, ignoring current or historic realities. Basic social and cultural values of other societies are often downplayed or omitted when they are disturbingly different from ours. Ethnic heritage education sometimes does justice to the original cultures but ignores the American experiences of particular cultures and their interactions with our history. This may be particularly true for Asian Americans, native Americans, Mexican Americans, and black Americans.

In most cases, the best judges of accuracy or validity are individuals who participate in a culture, particularly if they are scholars or educators as well as actual members. They are, naturally, well aware of stereotypes that are applied to them, and how well or badly they fit and feel. Ethnic organizations, such as the American Indian Historical Society and the Asia Society, have provided an excellent service for educators in surveying textbooks for accuracy and perspective. Their criteria are thoughtful and helpful—and should be applied by others choosing materials that deal with these two groups.

My preference in general is to choose materials that have been selected by groups that include both librarians and ethnic representatives. Librarians are valuable in selecting materials for literary quality and appeal to children; ethnic groups in surveying validity. Educators, of course, may be experts on whether materials will work in their classrooms.

In recent years, ethnic organizations have had a tendency to establish headquarter facilities complete with archives and libraries. For example, the American Jewish Historical Society has an office, a library, and a Jewish Media Service, and is currently establishing a Jewish Film Archive and Study Center to include all non-print materials relevant to the American Jewish experience. The American Italian Historical Society is interested in establishing a similar headquarters. This chapter's Key Organizations include a few such groups; others can be located through L. Wynar's *Encyclopedic Directory of Ethnic Organizations in the United States* (Littleton, CO: Libraries Unlimited, 1975). I would suggest these organizations as prime sources for information on their cultures in this country. Similarly, consulates, embassies and trade organizations are good sources of information on their own countries or areas—although their materials may be colored by a desire to attract tourists or investments. Travel agents' materials, often free and interesting, are distorted by the same considerations. Such things as maps and statistics, of course, tend to be accurate. Our own government and the United Nations are also good sources on other countries and regions and on international statistics.

Some organizations—such as the Japanese American Curriculum Project (see Key Organizations), the Afro-American Publishing Company, or Inter-Culture Associates—combine two functions. They are simultaneously commercial distributors and ethnic experts. The Afro-American Publishing Company, for instance (910 South Michigan Ave., Suite 556, Chicago, IL 60605), includes materials for implementing or reinforcing black or integrated studies for every grade level and for most curriculum areas. The company's materials include audiovisual materials; books for beginning readers; toys, games, and read-to books for younger children; and records and reference books for older children. Interculture Associates, Box 277, Thompson, CT 06277, has similar materials for Africa and Asia, with picture sets, study prints and actual artifacts, and provides access to inexpensive materials by publishers from these countries.

Catalogs from ethnic publishers and producers are a good way of locating materials that have been pre-selected as adequate by an interested group. Often the items have not been reviewed elsewhere; often they are not included or emphasized in catalogs of larger distributors. Such groups, if adequately financed, have the advantages of smallness and specialization, and are interested in meeting user needs and supplying good service.

Foreign publishers of children's materials can be located through library tools, as well as through *Multicultural Resources for Children* (see Key Organizations). The Information Center on Children's Cultures includes English-language books by foreign publishers. School departments of different countries can also be good sources of educational materials. The New Zealand Department of Education, for example, has issued excellent booklets on Pacific Island cultures and Asian cultures, well set up for school use.

Since cultures embrace all aspects of our lives, multicultural curricula can embrace all subject or curriculum areas, from arts and crafts through physical education, music, folklore, literature, science, and mathematics. Arts and crafts courses could use techniques or art forms (e.g., bead work or weaving) from other countries; physical education, the sports and games from other countries and cultures; language arts, the literature, mythology and literature forms (e.g., haiku) of other cultures; social studies, their governments, economics and value systems; math, math games and counting systems; and science, the history and concepts of science, medicinal plants, means of building, etc. Bringing multicultural education into these areas makes them more real and meaningful, and extends both our knowledge and our empathic understanding. Some of the book-finding tools listed in the chapter on the feeling domain can also be useful for selecting materials that relate to the emotions and the lives of children and adults of other cultures.

In the terms of the Cone of Experience, for empathic understanding, it is desirable to have some direct experiences, activities, or contacts. Otherwise materials can run the gamut, so long as they are accurate and convey verisimilitude. Books may be the most accessible, best-indexed sources, but pictures in some form, whether posters or movies, are equally important.

INSTRUMENTS AND CRITERIA

Instruments for analyzing instructional materials in multicultural or pluralistic education have been designed by the National Education Association, the Social Science Education Consortium, and the Ethnic Heritage Center for Teacher Education. These are cited in For Further Reading. Excellent criteria for

Asian materials were designed by the Asia Society and are included in *Asia in American Textbooks* (see Key Publications). Similarly excellent criteria on American Indians are available in *Textbooks and the American Indian*, published by the American Indian Historical Association (see Key Organizations).

The following school surveys were developed by the Oakland Public Schools in order to determine the areas in which classroom teachers would need training in order to select multicultural materials and to integrate them into classroom instruction.

TRAINING IN SELECTION OF MATERIALS AND ACTIVITIES FOR CLASSROOM USE IN A MULTICULTURAL APPROACH TO EDUCATION

Need Additional Training	No Additional Training Needed	When selecting learning materials for a multi-ethnic approach to education,
		1. Do you know where to go, whom to contact, what commercial catalogs and/or book review resources to examine?
		2. Are you knowledgeable of ethnic themes which would be relevant to minority and other students for materials selected?
		3. Can you recognize continuing stereotypes of people (racial, ethnic, sex-role, class, etc.), actual and implied, in teaching-learning materials?
		4. Can you refocus, in examining learning materials, on omissions of ethnic and racial peoples from materials content?
		5. Are you able to point out picture inaccuracies, visual stereotypes of people in learning materials?

TRAINING IN INTEGRATING MATERIALS AND ACTIVITIES RELATING TO SPECIFIC ETHNIC GROUPS

Need Additional Training	No Additional Training Needed	In integrating your curriculum to begin work towards district goals,
		1. Can you identify and select teaching themes around which to develop an ethnic and/or multi-ethnic unit?
		2. Can you specify subject areas (language arts, math, fine arts, physical education, etc.) which can be transformed into integrated education by incorporating racial and ethnic minority information?
		3. Can you use innovative and creative delivery systems (manipulative materials, audio-visual kits, resource personnel, etc.) to incorporate multi-ethnic learning values, even though they may need to be teacher-made?
		4. Can you integrate racial and historic anniversaries of various ethnic and racial groups into your curriculum?
		5. Can you, in teaching social sciences today, present curriculum from ethnic and racial perspectives?
		6. Can you include visual materials of racial and ethnic minorities as "part-and-parcel" of your classroom environment?

(Survey continues on page 180)

Need Additional Training	No Additional Training Needed	
		7. Can you regularly use ethnic publications such as newspapers and magazines as an educational resource?
		8. Can you organize a multi-cultural or cross-cultural curriculum around a theme or issue such as citizenship?
		9. Can you revise your teaching techniques to accommodate different learning styles relating to cultural conditions?

The following short form (pages 181-84) is taken from the *Ethnic Studies Materials Analysis Instrument* and reproduced here with permission of the Social Science Education Consortium. The long form (SSEC publication 179, 1975) is 18 pages long and covers product characteristics, general educational quality, ethnic heritage content, adaptability to conditions of use, and overall evaluation.

ETHNIC STUDIES MATERIALS
ANALYSIS INSTRUMENT – SHORT FORM

FORMAT

1. Do the materials show and discuss different ethnic groups relating to each other, or are groups shown in isolation?

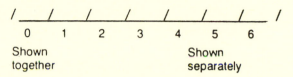

Shown
together

Shown
separately

2. Do the materials show actual examples of the language/dialect of the ethnic group?

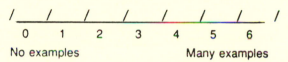

No examples

Many examples

3. Do the materials emphasize actual photographs and pictures rather than illustrations?

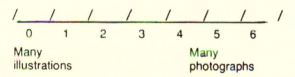

Many
illustrations

Many
photographs

REALISM AND ACCURACY

4. How accurate are the historical facts presented in the material?

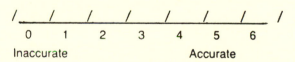

Inaccurate

Accurate

(Short form continues on page 182)

5. Do major omissions distort the historical accuracy of the materials?

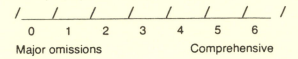

0   1   2   3   4   5   6

Major omissions   Comprehensive

6. How free of bias is the overall content of the materials?

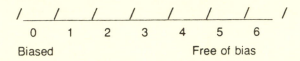

0   1   2   3   4   5   6

Biased   Free of bias

7. To what extent do the materials stereotype members of the ethnic group?

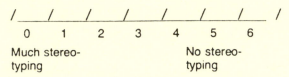

0   1   2   3   4   5   6

Much stereo-   No stereotyping   typing

8. Do the materials portray a diversity of life styles within the ethnic group?

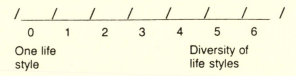

0   1   2   3   4   5   6

One life   Diversity of
style   life styles

9. Is the ethnic group presented from only one viewpoint or from many points of view?

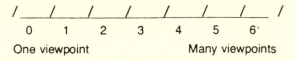

0   1   2   3   4   5   6'

One viewpoint   Many viewpoints

10. To what extent do the materials portray the influence of the ethnic group on life in the United States?

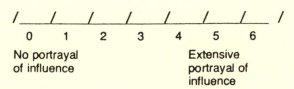

0   1   2   3   4   5   6

No portrayal   Extensive
of influence   portrayal of
                        influence

11. Do the materials emphasize the ethnic group's heroes to the exclusion of its average members?

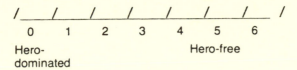

Hero-
dominated   Hero-free

DEVELOPMENT OF INTERCULTURAL UNDERSTANDING

12. To what extent do the materials promote student understanding of the universality of human joys and problems?

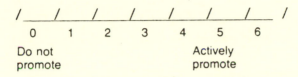

Do not   Actively
promote   promote

13. To what extent do the materials promote the concept of assimilation (groups "melting" together in society until they become indistinguishable)?

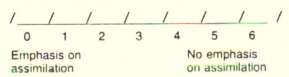

Emphasis on   No emphasis
assimilation   on assimilation

14. To what extent do the materials promote the concept of ethnic pluralism (groups living together in harmony and mutual respect while maintaining separate identities)?

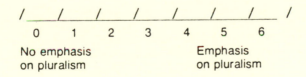

No emphasis   Emphasis
on pluralism   on pluralism

15. To what extent do the materials promote students taking pride in their own ethnic groups?

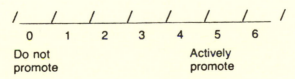

Do not   Actively
promote   promote

(Short form continues on page 184)

16. To what extent do the materials promote student appreciation of all ethnic groups?

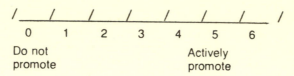

	0	1	2	3	4	5	6

Do not
promote

Actively
promote

OVERALL EVALUATION

17. In general, how sound is the substantive content of these materials?

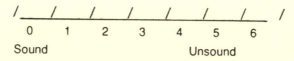

	0	1	2	3	4	5	6

Sound

Unsound

18. In general, how innovative are these materials?

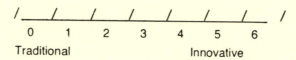

	0	1	2	3	4	5	6

Traditional

Innovative

19. In general, of what quality are the physical and technical presentations of the materials?

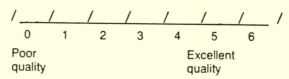

	0	1	2	3	4	5	6

Poor
quality

Excellent
quality

20. In general, to what degree would you recommend these materials be used?

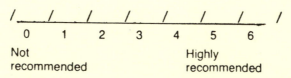

	0	1	2	3	4	5	6

Not
recommended

Highly
recommended

KEY ORGANIZATIONS

Many other potentially valuable ethnic organizations are described in L. Wynar's *Encyclopedic Directory of Ethnic Organizations in the United States* (Littleton, CO: Libraries Unlimited, 1975) which provides information on altogether about 16,000 organizations representing 80 ethnic groups.

Those listed here are eclectic, authoritative, or responsible sources with expertise and/or current awareness of school needs. The Social Science Education Consortium also has an ethnic project which is described in the chapter on social studies under the ERIC Clearinghouse on Social Studies/Social Sciences. Lists and criteria prepared by the Association for Childhood Education International are good for materials for younger children. The ACEI is treated as a Key Organization in the last chapter of *Issues and Policies*. The Key Organizations listed in the chapter on Fairness and Bias in the same book are, of course, active in this area, as are the Key Organizations for Bilingual/Bicultural Education.

American Indian Historical Association
1451 Masonic Ave.
San Francisco, CA 94117   (415) 626-5235
This overworked and underfinanced group of native American scholars, historians, activists and educators—founded in 1964—has produced some impressive publications, without benefit of federal funding. Currently, unfortunately, due to this lack of funding, their research library is in storage. Even without it, their publications—about 30 in all—combine authenticity, scholarship, and educational know-how.

These publications include a quarterly magazine, *The Indian Historian* ($7.00) and *Wassaja*, a monthly national newspaper ($10.00/yr.) of Indian America, loaded with information on education, litigation, book reviews, federal awards, and other news. The *Weewish Tree*, an excellent, authentic magazine for young people, is available for $6.50/yr. for seven issues. Jeannette Henry's *Textbooks and the American Indian* ($5.00, edited by Rupert Costo) is a model of how to go about evaluating ethnic books. It reviews state history texts as well as national texts—more than 300 altogether—for accuracy, extent of coverage and contributions. At the time it was issued, at least one commercial publisher tried to have it suppressed. The Association's *American Indian Reader* series, now in five volumes, sells for $22.50 a set, or $5.00 each. Volumes cover anthropology, history, education, literature, current affairs, and Indian treaties. They are currently preparing an *Index to Literature of the American Indian* to cover information from 1974 through 1980.

The Association of Chinese Teachers (TACT)
1-15 Waverly Place
San Francisco, CA 94108   (415) 863-2282
TACT is a membership organization composed basically of Chinese American educators in the San Francisco Bay Area, formed in 1969 to address the needs of schools from the Chinese-American perspective. They serve as advocates for educational areas of concern such as bilingual education and English language instruction, and have been actively developing curriculum materials to reflect the Chinese American experience.

Two on-going projects, funded by federal monies, include a program for developing and disseminating curriculum materials, The Project for Cross-Cultural Understanding, and a Children's Television Project intended as a series of five multicultural children's television programs for Chinese American children.

Their publications and filmstrip sets, which are well adapted for educational and multicultural criteria, include a reading anthology for children of 9 to 12, *Chinese Americans, Past and Present* ($2.95, quantity reduction), and *Teacher's Guide and Activity Sheets*. *Chinese Americans* includes 20 reading selections, fiction and non-fiction, covering historic and contemporary Chinese American experiences. TACT's *Chinese Americans: Realities and Myths* ($49.95) is a filmstrip set, with four filmstrips, cassettes in English and Cantonese, an anthology, and a teacher's manual. *Understanding Chinese Americans* (three filmstrips, two English cassettes and a teacher's guide all for $35.00) is an effective tool for cross-cultural understanding and inservice education.

**Center for Information and Resources in
    International Studies (CIRIS)**
Council for Intercultural Studies and Programs
60 East 42nd St.
New York, NY 10017   (212) 972-9877
This organization is devoted to developing teaching materials on Asia, Africa, and the Third World—largely for use at the college undergraduate level. Some of their materials, which include bibliographies, syllabi, course outlines, reading lists, audiovisual materials and paperback books, seem appropriate for secondary students. Their periodical, *Intercultural Studies Information Service*, comes out nine times a year.

**ERIC Clearinghouse on Rural Education and
    Small Schools (ERIC/CRESS)**
Box 3AP
New Mexico State University
Las Cruces, NM 88003   (505) 646-2623
ERIC/CRESS is responsible for acquiring, indexing, abstracting and disseminating information related to all aspects of the education of American Indians and Mexican American migrants, as part of its responsibility for keeping up with information on small schools, schools in rural areas, and outdoor education.

The ERIC Clearinghouse on Social Studies/Social Science (ERIC/ChESS) has additional materials on multicultural education.

Ethnic Heritage Center for Teacher Education
American Association of Colleges for
    Teacher Education (AACTE)
One Dupont Circle, Suite 610
Washington, DC 20036   (202) 293-2450
The Ethnic Heritage Center was established at the Washington Headquarters of the AACTE in July 1975, with federal funding from Title IX of the Elementary and Secondary Education Act. With a national advisory council, it is intended as "a national focus for the development of policies, activities and programs to enable teachers to function more effectively in multicultural settings."

Its function is to acquire, analyze, and disseminate materials and programs in ethnic studies. It also plans to issue papers and prepare bibliographies and learning packages for teacher education and Leadership Training Institutes. Essentially, it reviews materials that might be useful in training teachers.

It collects studies, reports, curriculum guides, textbooks, bibliographies, non-print materials, and literature as well as materials from Ethnic Heritage-funded projects and materials from professional organizations. As of April 1978, it had collected about 2,500 such items and was engaged in cataloging and abstracting these documents. At that time it had no knowledge of courses in materials selection for multicultural materials, though it had completed a survey in multicltural and bilingual courses in a *Directory of Multicultural Education Programs in Teacher Education Institutions.* Another publication, *Multicultural Education and Ethnic Studies in the United States* (1976. 175p. $4.00pa.), is an analysis and annotated bibliography of selected ERIC documents.

Information Center on Children's Cultures
United States Committee for UNICEF
331 E. 38th St.
New York, NY 10016   (212) 686-5522

This information center—part of the education and information services of the U.S. Committee for UNICEF—works from a multilingual collection of educational materials on children in other countries, chiefly designed for the use of children from pre-school to about the age of 14. Its resources include more than 10,000 books; more than 10,000 photographs; 500 toys; and 100 periodicals; plus pamphlets, films, filmstrips, records, children's art, games, musical instruments, and others.

It has prepared an impressive assortment of brief annotated bibliographies of materials about and for children and cultures. These are particularly strong on countries and areas in Asia, Africa, Latin America and the Middle East, where materials are apt to be sketchy. Items included on these lists are carefully chosen for authenticity and appeal to children. These lists are available in return for a large, self-addressed, stamped envelope for about $0.15 in postage for each 5 pages.

Other short (2-5 pages) lists cover general international and multicultural topics, like *Arts and Crafts around the World* (3p.), *Games from around the World* (2p.), *Pen Pals and Other Exchanges* (2p.), *Songs and Dances of the World* (5p.), *Sources of Children's Books from Other Countries* (3p.), and *Spanish and Spanish-English Books*, among others. There are some mini-units available at similar low prices: *What's in a Name?* (1p.), *Development* (energy sources) (1p.), *Masks around the World* (1p.), and many others. Most of these lists are updated every year or so.

The Information Center cooperates with the Committee's School Services Division which develops and distributes educational materials to improve global and intercultural educational programs. School Service materials—authentic, accurate, and inexpensive—include multilingual puzzles, kits for teachers and students, display materials, books, records, slide sets, and filmstrips. These are listed in the free publications catalog of the United States Committee for UNICEF. Send a self-addressed stamped envelope for the separate order-description sheet of the Information Center.

Japanese American Curriculum Project, Inc. (JAPC)
414 East Third St.
P.O. Box 367
San Mateo, CA 94401   (415) 343-9408

The JAPC, established in 1969, is a nonprofit educational corporation staffed by volunteer Japanese American educators. It develops and disseminates Japanese American and Asian American curriculum materials, including books, filmstrips, records, activities materials, etc., with a concentration on Asian experiences in the Americas. Without any federal funding, JAPC provides authoritative inservice training, assistance in developing curriculum, as well as a resource library for students and teachers and a retail, mail-order bookstore. All materials are chosen for authenticity and relevance to the needs of educators.

The Project's exhibits, consultants, and demonstrations of Japanese American and Asian American curriculum materials are available to educational institutions and the general public. Its library has teacher curriculum guides from many school districts, as well as a thoughtful selection of books, pamphlets, periodicals, newspapers, filmstrips, kits, and games. The Project has also issued some excellent bibliographies.

Its retail bookstore (mail order and drop in) is a comprehensive outlet for selected quality material on Asian American education, with new items added weekly; a catalog is available on request.

Middle East Studies Association of North America, Inc. (MESA)
New York University
Hagop Kevorkian Center for Near Eastern Studies
Washington Square
New York, NY 10013   (212) 598-2400

MESA, an international organization founded in 1966 by American and Canadian scholars, was intended to facilitate communication among these scholars and to promote high standards of authorship and instruction on the geographic area that runs from Morocco to Pakistan and from Turkey to the Sudan. The emphasis is primarily upon materials in the humanities and social sciences dealing with the period beginning with the rise of Islam. This organization has commissioned two interesting studies of Middle East topics in secondary school materials, each available at $2.50 prepaid. William J. Griswold's *The Image of the Middle East in Secondary School Textbooks* found that the majority of secondary school texts "contained factual errors, perpetuated stereotypes in political and social description, oversimplified complicated issues, listed outcomes while ignoring causes and provided moral judgements on the actions of nations in the guise of factual history." This book includes suggestions for classroom activities as well as syllabi on Islamic history and the four Arab-Israeli wars.

A second report, *American Images of the Middle East Peoples: Impact of the High School*, by Dr. Michael Suleiman, analyzed the result of a questionnaire mailed to high school teachers of world history in six states, to assess teachers' awareness of their textbooks' coverage of the Middle East. Most of these teachers were unaware of their textbooks' biases.

Multicultural Resources
Room 120, North Science Building
California State University of Hayward
Hayward, CA 94542

Permanent mailing address:

Box 2945
Stanford, CA 94305

This comprehensive library-exhibit collection consists of about 10,000 recent items and is still encountering the vicissitudes it has experienced since its origin in 1969. It is currently stored at California State University, Hayward. It is set up as a resource for research, reference, and curriculum development. It has an excellent section of tools for selecting ethnic materials, most of which are listed in its most recent bibliography: *Multicultural Resources for Children*, by Margaret S. Nichols and Peggy O'Neill (1977. 205p. $5.00pa.). This guide, like the collection itself, is arranged by major culture areas: black, Spanish-speaking, Asian-American, Pacific Island, and native American. For each of these areas the collection includes folk tales and legends, materials for young children, art and music, children's books, popular readings, high interest/low vocabulary materials, social studies materials and series, bilingual materials, pictures, posters, maps, study prints, periodicals, games, simulations, and examples of creative productions by children in all cultures. There is good representation of foreign publishers and organizations, especially those from Africa, Asia, Mexico, the Philippines, Samoa, South America and Spain, who are listed in the directory of *Multicultural Resources*. Materials in the collection and in the bibliographies were chosen to increase understanding and appreciation of various cultures and to help develop and reinforce positive images for minority youth. The bibliography includes more than 200 items on evaluating multicultural materials. Though individual items are not generally annotated or indexed by subject in the bibliography, the collection and resultant bibliographies are conveniently arranged for browsing. Citations include latest known prices.

Two other inexpensive bibliographies prepared by the Center, *Multicultural Bibliography for Pre-School through Second Grade* and *Multicultural Materials: A Selected Bibliography*, treat, respectively, references of materials for young children and resources for parents and teachers. Other resource lists are prepared from time to time.

This precariously funded collection may be one of the most comprehensive, well-rounded and current multicultural collections available. The founders, through years of dedicated work and persistence, have established contact with many publishers and producers who forward relevant materials as they are issued. Now in storage (as of summer 1980) with an uncertain future, it may be integrated into the library collection of California State University at Hayward.

KEY PUBLICATIONS

Some equally—or more—important key publications are subsumed under Key Organizations. I would particularly recommend Multicultural Resources' *Multicultural Resources for Children* for educational materials. For authentic current reading lists on almost any country or area of the globe I would recommend the inexpensive lists compiled by the Information Center on Children's Cultures.

Africa in U.S. Educational Materials: Thirty Problems and Responses, by Susan J. Hall. New York: School Services Division, African-American Institute, 1977, c1976. 62p. $3.00pa. (From African-American Institute, 833 United Nations Plaza, New York, NY 10017).

Surveys 30 common problems in educational materials dealing with Africa; these can also be used as criteria for selecting and evaluating other items.

The African-American Institute also distributes a free pamphlet, *African Resources for Schools and Libraries*, which lists and sometimes annotates recommended organizations, distributors, reference books, films, maps, poster sources, periodicals, etc. on Africa.

Akwesasne Notes. Roosevelttown, NY: Mohawk Nation. 5 issues/yr. Donation requested. (From Mohawk Nation via Roosevelttown, NY 13683).

This award-winning publication in tabloid newspaper format is the official publication of the Mohawk Nation at Akwesasne and is co-published by the Program in Indian Studies of the State University of New York at Buffalo. It provides current reporting and analysis of issues from a native American perspective and reviews and sells books on issues relating to native Americans. Areas include poetry, politics, history, biography, story telling, crafts, and culture.

It has its own small publishing house, which is indexed in *Alternative Press Index*, and produces posters and calendars as well as books and pamphlets.

American Indians and Eskimos: A Selection Guide for Children and Young Adults, edited by Mary Jo Lass-Woodfin. Chicago: American Library Association, 1977. 254p. $20.00.

This selection guide for children's librarians assesses quality (by rating scale) and reading level (by grade range) for 750 titles that deal in some way with either historic cultures or current conditions of native Americans. Books are arranged alphabetically by author and indexed for contents; annotations assess insight and historic accuracy. This guide is valuable not only for pointing out some worthwhile books, but also for calling attention to inaccurate or incomplete portrayals. The book is bibliographically complete, with prices given for books still in print.

The Arab World: A Handbook for Teachers, by Ayad Al-Qazzaz, Ruth Afifi, and Audrey Shabbas. Berkeley, CA: Arab World Consultants, 1977. $5.00pa. (From NAJDA, Box 6051, Albany, CA 94706).

This handbook for teachers began in response to a request from California's Textbook Commission to study the portrayal of Arabs and Arab-Americans in elementary and junior high school textbooks. The end product has exceeded that original detailed survey and provides an analysis of the fullness and accuracy of Arab portrayals in 24 social studies texts currently used in California schools. It also includes explanations of 15 key subjects; 17 reprints of source materials on the Arab world; and a resource guide that suggests some books, audiovisual materials, and sources of free materials. Arab World Consultants are also developing multimedia materials to teach elementary school children about the Arab world.

Asia in American Textbooks: An Evaluation, by the Asia Society. New York: Asia Society, 1976. 36p. Free. (From 112 E. 64th St., New York, NY 10021).

This book distills the results of an intensive survey conducted by the Asia Society with help from the Ford Foundation on how Asia is depicted in American school textbooks. The study surveyed 306 social studies texts used in the 50 states as of 1975, supplemented by titles supplied by classroom teachers in an effort to evaluate materials that were actually being used. Materials were reviewed by Asian scholars and teachers. The survey questions dealt with:

- accuracy and authenticity
- underlying assumptions and approaches
- attitudes toward Asian life and cultures
- use of primary Asian sources and humanistic materials (e.g., literature, fine arts, historical documents, etc.)
- style and tone
- format and illustrations
- attitudes toward women
- qualifications of authors and consultants

Asian Americans: An Annotated Bibliography for Public Libraries, by Asian American Librarians Caucus. Chicago: American Library Association, 1977. 47p. $2.50.

This basic purchasing list for public libraries includes titles for both adults and children covering major Asian American groups: Chinese Americans, Japanese Americans, Korean Americans, and Filipino Americans.

Aspects of Jewish Life: A Selected and Annotated Bibliography of Books and Multimedia Materials, by Hannah Grad Goodman. New York: Jewish Book Council, 1974. 111p. $2.00pa.

This multimedia bibliography seems to be set up for programs or assemblies on topics of Jewish interest, with materials categorized (sometimes duplicated) in 39 alphabetical topics. Though the materials are representative rather than comprehensive, the program orientation assures a good balance of all types of media: books, paperbacks, films, kinescopes, filmstrips, recordings, musical scores, sheet music, song books, royalty and non-royalty plays, exhibits, and cassettes. Materials listed range from 1917 through 1974; most books seem to be still in print; addresses are given for sources of other materials.

Building Ethnic Collections: An Annotated Guide for School Media Centers and Public Libraries, by Lois Buttlar and Lubomyr R. Wynar. Littleton, CO: Libraries Unlimited, 1977. 434p. $18.50.

This guide to ethnic materials is directed toward school media centers to introduce multicultural educational curricula and to establish well-balanced collections to support such curricula. It provides reference sources on ethnicity, as well as print, non-print, and reference materials on 42 ethnic groups—altogether 1,186 annotated items, with a substantial number of items on teaching methodology and ethnic curriculum. The reference works include guides, bibliographies, encyclopedias, statistical sources and directories. For each ethnic group, titles are arranged in five basic categories: reference, teaching and curriculum, non-fiction, literature and fiction, and audiovisual materials. Bibliographic descriptions are complete with paging, price, and approximate grade ranges. The book has author, title and audiovisual indexes, plus an alphabetical directory of audiovisual producers. The table of contents serves as a subject index.

Titles were selected largely through a comprehensive survey of ethnic publications in print, paying special attention to major current bibliographies and reference publications. Other items stemmed from ethnic groups and ERIC searches. Additional materials were chosen selectively on the criteria of currency (availability for purchase), existence of favorable reviews in standard media selection tools, and balance for grade level and type of medium, plus a few classic materials, which seem to be of permanent value.

Ethnic American Minorities: A Guide to Media and Materials, edited and compiled by Harry A. Johnson. New York: R. R. Bowker, 1977. 204p. $15.95.
This guide — intended for teachers, students, librarians, and administrators — combines in one volume discussion of certain American ethnic minorities and annotated lists of selected media materials. For four major groups — Afro-Americans, Asian Americans, native Americans and Spanish-speaking Americans, it includes a brief, apparently authoritative background on the history and educational needs of each, followed by annotations of relevant media materials, arranged by medium. These include films, filmstrips, slides, transparencies, audio recordings and cassettes, video cassettes, pictures, posters, and graphics. The items here, chosen by personal examination for the most part, seem interesting and well-selected. The fifth section, a rather dubious catch-all for "other" minority groups, omits the introductory essay and, though limited in size, does not seem particularly well selected — though items were chosen, like the others, from a pool of 300 selected producers and distributors. Items in the first four groups were selected with the assistance of ethnic educators on the criteria of availability, authenticity, relevance, and suitability for children and youth. The fifth section unfortunately was not subjected to this in-depth evaluation.
Citations provide price, release date, source, technical information, and a coded indication of grade level, whose key I could not locate; fortunately, it was an easy code to crack. There is a title index, a directory of sources, and a good subject index which makes it easy to locate relevant items under topics like music, musical instruments, or women.

Ethnic Studies Handbook for Librarians, by Frances Haley and others. Boulder, CO: Social Science Education Consortium, 1979. 67p. $5.00pa.
This collection of resource materials and activities for libraries and classrooms includes information on how to set up ethnic learning centers.

Good Reading for the Disadvantaged Reader: Multi-Ethnic Resources, Champaign, IL: Garrard, 1970. 201p. $4.25pa.
These ethnic reading materials, selected to help children develop positive ethnic identities, have been graded for readability according to Spache or Dale-Chall formulas. Ethnic groups included are native Americans, blacks, Mexican Americans, Puerto Ricans, and Asian Americans. This guide has author and title indexes.

Guide to Free-Loan Films about Foreign Lands. Alexandria, VA: Serina Press, 1975. 283p. $12.95pa.
Provides synopses and sources for approximately 3,000 films available on a free-loan basis from more than 75 foreign governments, airlines, and other sources. Materials, arranged by country, include some excellent resources on art and history, as well as films on customs and culture, sports, music, travel,

science, international relations, etc. Most films have English sound tracks; others might be useful for bilingual or foreign language classes.

Multi-Ethnic Media: Selected Bibliographies in Print, coordinated by David Cohen for the Office for Library Service to the Disadvantaged, American Library Association. Chicago: American Library Association, 1975. 33p. $2.00pa.

This book, intended as a source book for developing ethnic collections in public schools, emphasizes blacks, native Americans and Mexican Americans, with annotated references to relevant bibliographic essays, bibliographies and some information sources.

Native American Arts and Culture: A Resource Directory, by Laurie Nogg Adler. Denver, CO: Western States Arts Foundation, 1977. 85p. $3.00pa. (From Western States Arts Foundation, 428 East 11th Ave., Denver, CO 80203).

This biblio-directory, a detailed listing of support sources for native American cultural projects, includes suggestions for preparing grant applications. It describes foundations, art and cultural sources, state and federal agencies, religious organizations, information sources, publications, fund-raising workshops, and native American interest groups.

Reading Ladders for Human Relations, edited by Virginia M. Reid. 5th ed. Washington, DC: American Council on Human Relations, 1972. 346p. $10.50; $4.50pa.

The major ladders in this series (originated by Hilda Taba) are: creating a positive self-image, creating a sensitivity to the feelings of others, appreciating different cultures (ethnic, religious, regional, and world), extending insights into different life styles, and adjusting creatively to change. Within each of these themes, books are arranged by maturity level and then listed alphabetically by author.

Other criteria used in selection were:

- Books which contain the essentials of all good literature: plot, content, theme, characterization, and format.

- Books which, through text or illustration, belittle no people either through condescension, deprecatory statements, or ridicule.

- Books which are natural and convincing instead of those which are contrived and which suggest superficial treatment in solving the difficult problems humans face.

- Books whose illustrations supplement the text in adding content or contributing to the mood.

- Books which recognize minority groups' participation in and contribution to the history and culture of our country.

- Books which prevent the carrying forward of old prejudices and stereotypes into the new generation.

- Books which can help each reader realize his or her identity, appreciate his or her individuality, and respect his or her heritage.

- Books containing subject matter appropriate to the age—non-fiction which is accurate and meaningful, and fiction which is true to life and has a valid theme.

- Books no longer in print are included because they may still be found in libraries, and increased demand for and use of these books might possibly bring them back into print.

FOR FURTHER READING

A substantial bibliography of more than 200 items on evaluating multicultural materials is available in *Multicultural Resources for Children*, published by Multicultural Resources. *Building Ethnic Collections* (see Key Publications) also includes many relevant items.

*Items marked with an asterisk include criteria.
+ Items marked with a plus have substantial lists of references.

*Banks, James A. *Teaching Ethnic Studies: Concepts and Strategies.* Washington, DC: National Council for the Social Studies, 1973.

*Banks, James A. *Teaching Strategies for Ethnic Studies.* Boston: Allyn & Bacon, 1975.

+ Byler, Mary Gloyne. *American Indian Authors for Young Readers: A Selected Bibliography.* New York: Association on American Indian Affairs, 1973.

*Castan, Frances. "The Great Instructional Materials Game," *Scholastic Teacher, Junior/Senior High Teacher's Edition*, Supplement to February 5, 1973.

Casteñada, Alfredo, and Tracy Gray. "Biocognitive Processes in Multicultural Education," *Educational Leadership*, v. 32, no. 3 (Dec. 1974), pp. 203-207.

*Deslonde, James. *Assessment of Needs for Achieving a Culturally Pluralistic Environment.* San Francisco: Far West Laboratory for Educational Research and Development, 1973.

* + Dunfee, Maxine. *Eliminating Ethnic Bias in Instructional Materials: Comment and Bibliography.* Washington, DC: Association for Supervision and Curriculum Development, 1974.

*Dunfee, Maxine. *Ethnic Modification of the Curriculum.* Washington, DC: Association for Supervision and Curriculum Development, 1970.

Fitzgerald, Frances. *America Revised.* Boston: Little, Brown, 1979.

* + Garcia, Ricardo L. *Fostering a Pluralistic Society through a Multi-Ethnic Education.* Bloomington, IN: Phi Delta Kappa Educational Foundation, 1978. (Fastback 108).

Gold, Milton J., and others, eds. *In Praise of Diversity: A Resource Book for Multicultural Education.* Washington, DC: Association of Teacher Educators, 1977.
Includes useful vignettes of some ethnic groups.

+ Grant, Carl A., and Gloria W. Grant. "Multicultural Education and Instructional Materials," *in* Carl A. Grant's *Multicultural Education: Commitments, Issues and Applications* (Washington, DC: Association for Supervision and Curriculum Development, 1977).

+ Grant, Gloria W., ed. *In Praise of Diversity: Multicultural Classroom Applications.* Omaha, NE: Teacher Corps, Center for Urban Education, University of Nebraska, 1977.
  Fifty-one activities in social studies, language, science, math, and art, with supplementary activities and backup resources for many.

*Harvey, Robert G. *An Attainable Global Perspective.* New York: Center for War/Peace Studies, 1973.

MacCann, Donnarae. "Children's Books in a Pluralistic Society," *Wilson Library Bulletin,* v. 51, no. 2 (Oct. 1976), pp. 154-62.

+ Michigan University Audiovisual Center. *Film Resources on Japan.* Washington, DC: U.S. Office of Education, 1975.
  Annotated guide to 355 films and 204 filmstrips.

*National Education Association. *Checklist for Selecting and Evaluating U.S. History Textbooks.* Washington, DC: National Education Association, 1973.

*National Study of School Evaluation. *Evaluation Guidelines for Multicultural/ Multiracial Education, Designed Primarily for Secondary Schools.* Arlington, VA: NSSE, 1973.

Newman, Katharine, comp. *A Reading List of Ethnic Books in Print.* Los Angeles: University of California, Los Angeles, Department of English, 1979.
  Includes the works of nearly 500 writers.

* + Pellowski, Anne. *The World of Children's Literature.* New York, Bowker, 1968.
  Good summary section on internationalism in children's literature with references and criteria.

*Rinne, Carl H. "Criteria for Evaluating Curriculum Materials in Human Relations," *Educational Leadership,* v. 32, no. 1 (Oct. 1974), pp. 37-40.

*Smith, Gary R. *Evaluation Unit: An Experimental Unit.* Denver: Denver University Center for Teaching International Relations, 1976. (ED 125 995).

*Social Science Education Consortium. *Ethnic Studies Materials Analysis Instrument.* Boulder, CO: SSEC, 1975. (Publication 1979).

+ Social Science Education Consortium. *Materials and Human Resources for Teaching Ethnic Studies: An Annotated Bibliography.* Boulder, CO: SSEC, 1975.

+ Stanford, Barbara Dodds, and Karima Amin. *Black Literature for High School Students.* Urbana, IL: National Council of Teachers of English, 1978.
  Includes literature units, articles on teaching, and an historical survey, as well as activities and many bibliographies.

*+Stensland, Anna Lee. *Literature By and About the American Indians: An Annotated Bibliography for Junior and Senior High School Students.* Urbana, IL: National Council of Teachers of English, 1973.
A substantial bibliography of myth, legend, fiction, drama, biography, autobiography, history, anthropology, archeology, music, arts, crafts, modern life, and problems, with study guides to selected books.

+Tanyzer, Harold. *Reading, Children's Books, and Our Pluralistic Society.* Newark, DE: International Reading Association, 1973.

*Task Force for Evaluation of Instructional Materials. "Racial and Sexual Bias in Textbooks: Guidelines for Selection," *Educational Media Yearbook, 1975-76.* New York: Bowker, 1975.

*Troper, Harold. "Multiculturalism in the Classroom: Pitfalls and Options," *The History and Social Science Teacher,* v. 12, no. 1 (Fall 1976), pp. 3-7.
Part of a special issue on "Multiculturalism in the Curriculum."

*Wolsk, D. "New Approaches to Education for International Understanding: Report from an International Co-operative Project of Associated School Teachers Using a Socio-Affective Approach," *International Understanding at School* (published by Unesco, Paris, France), no. 35 (June 1973), pp. 41-47.

+Wynar, L. R. *Encyclopedic Directory of Ethnic Organizations in the United States.* Littleton, CO: Libraries Unlimited, 1975.
Provides information on 1,600 organizations representing 80 ethnic groups.

SELECTING FOREIGN LANGUAGE AND
BILINGUAL MATERIALS

Since the sources and criteria for foreign language and bilingual materials overlap so extensively, I am, for the sake of brevity, treating bilingual and foreign language materials in one combined chapter. While the classrooms and teachers' problems can be vastly different, there are similar considerations and sources for selecting materials for these two educational situations. Both have cultural and linguistic elements. Both require authentic, accurate representation of the culture whose language is used or studied; both require some logical, sequential materials to develop linguistic ability.

At least in theory, both require a wide variety of materials in many media:

- reading materials providing for different student abilities, interests, strengths and achievement levels

- diagnostic tests

- English-language materials dealing with the language group or country whose language is being studied

- some classical "literary" works from that language, possibly in English and/or in the original language (children's versions may be appropriate — if sensitively prepared and faithful to the concepts and feelings of the original) — should include some contemporary authors

- foreign language periodicals and newspapers (maybe designed for children, but not necessarily)

- dictionaries

- slides, posters, postcards and other pictorial representations of countries and individuals who speak the language being studied or used

- representation of art works from the culture and language being studied

- recordings and/or cassettes (with authentic accents and pacing) in the language being studied

- other available high-quality audiovisual materials depicting the relevant cultural/language group

- printed or other information on school life in the culture being studied

- some available means of representing the music of the culture being studied, e.g., authentic recordings or song books

- toys and games, food, and festival materials from the culture/country being studied; supplemented by appropriate books, e.g., cookbooks, reference books on holidays, etc.

- other realia, such as flags, dolls, models, stamps, coins, calendars, art works, and crafts from the country being studied, supplemented by reference books

- travel materials, possibly free, as railroad schedules, maps, advertisements, travel literature, and folders
- motivational displays using these and other materials
- personal contact with individuals of or from that culture, through parents' groups, ethnic groups, travel agencies, embassies, pen pal exchanges, etc.
- foreign language flash cards and games (e.g., Bingo or Scrabble)
- teacher-made materials for drill and individualization.

Other aspects can vary. The origins and rationales for foreign language study and for bilingual education are quite different. While there is a large element of enrichment in bilingual, bicultural education, it stems largely from justice and necessity (since possibly 10 percent of children currently in American schools do not use English as their primary language). It is oriented toward survival and is primarily directed toward children who are perceived as disadvantaged or underprivileged. Often these children test out rather low in school achievement tests. The National Assessment of Educational Progress Development is currently pilot testing a Spanish language assessment program in the New York City area to see whether linguistic barriers are significant factors in lowered Hispanic achievement.

Foreign language instruction, on the other hand, probably depends upon college entrance and graduation requirements for its continuance. It stems, perhaps, from an upper-class or finishing school view of culture, augmented by the trend toward internationalism that followed World War II and then by Sputnik. Many materials in current use were subsidized—in part or in full—with funds from the National Defense Education Act, which designated six languages as "critical" and supported both foreign language teaching and the teaching of English as a second language.

Whatever the virtues of bilingual or foreign language mastery, very few American high school students (and relatively few college students) actually succeed in reaching any degree of competence or fluency in a foreign language—possibly because these are really not perceived as essential or important by most students. In Europe, where multilingualism has been perceived as more advantageous, public schools succeed to a far greater extent in teaching foreign languages. While there are current ambitious training programs for bilingual teachers, most credentialed teachers now employed in schools lack expertise in the foreign languages and cultures needed in contemporary bilingual education.

The Bilingual Education Act of 1968 defined bilingual-bicultural education as education in two languages and the use of these two languages as media for instruction—for any or all of the school curricula. This should include a study of the history and culture associated with the student's mother tongue. Bilingual education is supposed to develop self-esteem and a sense of participation in both cultures in participating children. Ideally it should enrich and preserve cultural and human resources and create better human relationships among different groups and individuals in participating schools. Current research suggests that bilingualism can be helpful to developing children—both cognitively and socially.

By fiat, then, bilingual programs involve teaching *in* a language, teaching *of* a language, and teaching *about* (and/or with) a culture. This might be a *root* culture (like Taiwanese or Chinese) or an *ethnic* culture (like Arab-American, Japanese-American). The cultural components and criteria are about the same as the cultural criteria in the chapter on multicultural materials, and should involve contemporary as well as historic aspects of the culture. Ideally they should encompass all aspects of a culture: personal, social, religious, linguistic, intellectual, scientific, and aesthetic—hopefully all coordinated with the rest of the school program. It would seem to require a very individualized curriculum, with carefully selected materials—chosen to be appropriate to the student and community mix and the language skills of the students and teachers.

Unfortunately, the theoretical value of such programs is limited by the availability of both teachers and high quality materials. Where our traditional foreign language classes clustered about classic, well-studied European languages—largely French, Spanish and German—bilingual education may demand instant expertise in languages few practicing teachers have formally studied—languages from the Middle East or the Philippines, native American languages, or Vietnamese.

If teachers or materials are scarce or if students come from many language groups, English as a second language (ESL) is a means of teaching students just enough English to attempt school instruction in English. A transitional bilingual approach teaches children in their own language until the time when they have mastered sufficient English to participate more fully in school programs. In maintenance bilingual approaches, students are given instruction in their own primary language and English, possibly up to or through high school, with school subjects either divided between the two languages or taught in both. The reciprocal bilingual approach is the only truly bilingual approach. With this, both non-English-speaking and English-speaking children receive instruction in each others' languages.

The San Jose Area Bilingual Consortium, a group of ten districts in Santa Clara County, California, suggested a checklist of desirable characteristics for bilingual education. These were reprinted as "Ten Characteristics of a Good Bilingual Classroom" in *Forum*, July 1978, and are available from the Consortium at 1605 Park Ave., San Jose, CA 95126. The Consortium suggests that a bilingual classroom provide:

- evidence of instruction in language arts in the dominant language, including
    language development
    reading
    oral expression
    writing skills
    with appropriate instructional materials

- evidence of subject area instruction in the dominant language, including
    math
    social sciences
    language and health
    with appropriate instructional materials

- evidence that culture is included in all aspects of the instructional program

- evidence that the classroom environment (e.g., bulletin board, etc.) reflects the culture and learning of two languages

- evidence of equal status for the dominant language demonstrated through available written materials
- evidence of parent participation
- evidence of suitable adult role models in both languages

While these are appropriate goals for bilingual education classes, they are not easily achieved.

William Francis Mackey's excellent "Checklist of Variables in Evaluating Bilingual Education" is incorporated in his chapter on "The Evaluation of Bilingual Education" in Bernard Spolsky's *Frontiers of Bilingual Education* (Rowley, MA: Newbury House, 1977). Mackey suggests careful examination of such things as:

- purposes and priorities of programs
- characteristics of students
  e.g., languages spoken by students
    at home
    among themselves
    at school
    out of school
- grasp of second language(s)
- exposure to and choice of other languages, through
    television and radio
    parents and relatives
    printed materials
- characteristics of community (especially parents)
    parental attitudes and language preferences
    place of origin
    social and income levels
    period of time at that level
    length of time and stability in this community
    whether community is heterogeneous or homogeneous
    size, density, and isolation of community
    relation to other communities
    access to materials (e.g., libraries, museums, cultural centers)

Even for Spanish-speaking children, our largest bilingual group—who are involved in possibly 80 to 90 percent of bilingual programs—there are numerous, subtle problems in locating and selecting materials. Problems are similar—but usually greater—with materials for other language groups.

Since the problems with Spanish-language materials may be representative, I will outline some briefly. To start with, these children are not part of one large, homogeneous group—linguistically or culturally. Linguistically, there are many different varieties of Spanish spoken in the New World, since different countries were settled by men from different parts of Spain at a time when the Spanish language differed considerably from province to province. As a consequence, Spanish spoken by individuals from, say, Cuba, Puerto Rico, or Mexico differs considerably. Spoken Spanish in each of these areas is also affected by native American languages. The Spanish of Mexico, for example, is influenced by the Aztec language. The differences are greatest in the words used most frequently by young children, since household words, terms for food and cooking, children and clothes are often the words that were used by native American mothers. Where the flora and fauna of the New World differ from those of Spain, vocabularies vary extensively. For example, terms for such commonplaces as bananas and peanuts differ in most Latin American countries.

As a consequence, it is exceedingly difficult for publishers to develop Spanish-language materials or kits that are equally effective for Spanish-speaking children in, say, California, Texas, Florida and New York. (It is even more difficult, of course, to locate materials in Tagalog.) It is particularly difficult to obtain authentic teaching materials for the young children who need them the most. The more universal these materials attempt to be, the less authentic they are for specific cultures.

If we try to turn to publishers in foreign countries for authentic and appropriate materials, we encounter problems in locating dealers — as well as problems with school purchasing procedures and foreign currencies. But books like Leonard Wertheimer's *Books in Other Languages* and other items listed in Key Publications do offer guidelines and short cuts to facilitate such purchases.

In general, children's book publishers in Latin American countries produce what we would consider to be exceedingly flimsy books — usually well below our general standards for durability. These are generally produced in what we would consider to be exceedingly limited editions. As a consequence, buyers of library books and suplementary reading materials need to rebind or process many items before use, and/or need to buy multiple copies before attractive books go out of print. However, since most children's materials published in Latin America are placed in "collections" with similar formats, if one is familiar with a particular "collection" one can predict the price, appearance, size, format and typeface of all books in that collection.

Librarians who like to purchase from reviews of books or lists of recommended books have less assistance with foreign-language books than with English-language books. Some classics excepted, children's books published in Latin America and Spain are not apt to be reviewed and evaluated before editions are exhausted. Once we stray from a few classic authors, it is difficult to evaluate the cultural authenticity of materials, though authors like Isabel Schon and institutions like Proyecto Leer (see Key Organizations) offer assistance. Aside from annotated book lists and a few book importers who allow book examination on the premises, there are few opportunities to examine or review books before purchase. Despite these disadvantages, foreign language trade books are an important resource; they usually represent their own country's language and customs far more authentically than textbooks published in English-language countries. Also, they can be important for foreign language teaching.

Textbooks published in foreign countries — especially Latin American countries — have other biases. One study of Spanish-language materials located 88 illustrations involving males and two involving females. Mothers, of course, always work in the home. One text asked (in Spanish): "What does your father do?" and "How does your mother occupy her time?" Other Latin American texts incorporate what we would consider religious bias, with suggested exercises that involve mass or religious vestments. In these books, poor people are often portrayed as dark, hungry, or ignorant. If such books must be used out of necessity, they usually require some means of discussion or amplification.

For bilingual teaching there may be equal—if different—problems in using American-published textbooks, aside from language difficulties. The bibliographies and reviews in the chapters on textbooks and fairness and bias in *Issues and Policies* and in the chapter on social studies in the present work, document the fact that our textbooks—particularly our language and history textbooks—tend to exclude or distort the roles and works of many or most minority groups. The contributions and cultures of minorities may also be underrepresented in the pictures, displays, music, records, games, and field trips used in North American schools.

Other selection concerns are bilingual and cultural. Some bilingual concerns are:

- difficulty of vocabulary (for age/grade levels)

- appropriateness (in terms of idioms, clichés, words and expressions) for particular groups

- appropriateness of sentence structure for age/grade levels and for cultural groups or subgroups

- appropriateness of language morphology for intended use of materials

- appropriateness of language syntax for intended use of materials

- whether language is:
  authentic or not authentic
  formal or informal
  regional or universal

Some cultural concerns are:

- cultural contexts

- quality and value of comments on cultural issues

- authenticity of presentations of cultures and culture groups

- freedom from stereotyping

- objective depiction of social issues

- objective depiction of political issues

- objective depiction of religious practices

These considerations are generally relevant for foreign language instructional materials, particularly those that involve cultural values.

Unfortunately, foreign language instruction offers teachers relatively few opportunities for choice and selection, since publishers have expanded their "textbooks" to packages that may incorporate audiotapes and/or recordings, picture cards, workbooks, films, posters, tests, and other materials—all presumably integrated and sequentially organized for optimal learning.

According to California's thoughtful *Foreign Language Framework* (1972), substantial problems can be encountered in eclectic selection of materials for foreign language instruction. According to this framework, students who start the study of a foreign language should be able to expect "sequential and continuous" progress in that language whether it is taught by one teacher at one school or by many teachers at many schools. From the point of view of this framework, even teachers who believe they can create superior learning opportunities by combining or adapting lessons or sequences from different packages may be short-changing their students by not covering all the content in the dominant package. This viewpoint holds that, ideally, all teachers in each school, each district, and among districts should mutually agree upon one single textbook or textbook package to assure continuity.

This approach is probably fairly acceptable to many foreign language teachers who have been accustomed to working with the same textbooks as other teachers of the same language. However, since modern textbook packages are so extensive, teachers in this situation now have very few opportunities for selection and individualization—even for supplementary materials. Proponents of individualizing language instruction would of course attempt to provide a greater choice of materials.

In both bilingual and foreign language instruction, selection is complicated by professional controversies on the relative merits of speaking or reading mastery and the extent to which the programs should incorporate information on and artifacts from the culture whose language is being studied. The cultural component is greater in bicultural education, where in many cases there are controversies about cultural authenticity. Obviously, positions on these issues affect the choice of materials.

Still another problem in selecting materials for foreign language instruction is that the grade or age at which language instruction begins differs considerably in different schools and different states. (Some districts are not consistent among schools; other districts offer early instruction but fail to support it subsequently.) Depending upon the age, interests and language abilities of students, appropriate materials would differ considerably even if student exposure to other languages was consistent.

KEY ORGANIZATIONS

Other important organizations for cultural aspects are listed in the chapter on multicultural resources.

Asian American Bilingual Center
2168 Shattuck Ave., 3rd Floor
Berkeley, CA 94704   (415) 848-3199
The focus of this center is on core curricula for Asian bilingual and multicultural education. It also has reproduced an annotated listing of materials and programs suited for most major Asian language groups, *A Directory of Asian American Bilingual Programs in the United States*. It also produces a free newsletter on center activities which helps update this field.

Center for Applied Linguistics (CAL)
3520 Prospect St., NW
Washington, DC 20007   (202) 298-9292

CAL, an important center for research and development in applied linguistics, has a scope that covers bilingual education, foreign language teaching, language testing, ESL, and the use of language for special purposes; it also relates linguistics to other disciplines. Its major publication, *Linguistic Reporter* ($6.00/yr. for 9 issues during the academic year), provides news on recent developments in these fields. Its new book series, *Language in Education: Theory and Practice* ($40.00 for a minimum of 12 titles), provides practical guides, topical discussions, and annotated bibliographies in book format, with titles like *Directory of Foreign Language Service Organizations, Vocabulary Presentation and Review, Classroom Language,* and *Current Approaches to the Teaching of Grammar in ESL.*

CAL publishes a series of textbooks in the Vietnamese language at $6.00 per book. These include arithmetic for grades 1 to 3; science, grades 1 to 5; readers to grade 5; national history, grades 2 to 4; and *80 Games.* Its *Vietnamese Refugee Education Series* includes phrase books, cassettes, handbooks for teachers, and a *Selected Annotated Bibliography for Teaching English to Speakers of Vietnamese* (1975. $2.50pa.). They have also issued a videotape series, mostly for adult refugees. CAL operates a National Indochinese Clearinghouse and technical assistance from this address, with a free hot line, (800) 336-3040.

According to its *Indochinese Refugee Alert Bulletin*, the following *Refugee Education Guides* are now available without charge: *A Selected, Annotated Bibliography of Materials for Teaching English to Indochinese Refugee Adults, A Selected Bibliography of Dictionaries* (1978) and other annotated bibliographies of materials for adult students from Laos and Cambodia.

Since 1974, the Center has been the site of the ERIC Clearinghouse on Languages and Linguistics. Information on its accessions is published in approximately 40 state and national language publications.

Desegregation Assistance Center (LAU)
Office of Equal Educational Opportunity
Division of Technical Assistance
400 Maryland Ave., SW
Washington, DC 20202   (202) 245-8484

This Desegregation Assistance Center provides entree into the nine LAU Centers funded under Title IV of the Civil Rights Act of 1964 to provide assistance to elementary and secondary school districts to meet the special education needs of students who speak limited English. Some of these have substantial collections of materials.

Dissemination and Assessment Center for
Bilingual Education (DACBE)
7703 North Lamar Blvd.
Austin, TX 78572   (512) 458-9131

This particular National Dissemination and Assessment Center specializes in materials for Spanish-speaking and native American bilingual education. Its free catalog documents its ambitious programs in both publishing and dissemination. Some publications on materials and programs are:

CARTEL: Annotations of Bilingual Multicultural Materials. Name differs slightly. V. 1-4. Cumulative issues, v. 1-3/$3.70pa. each. V. 4, 1977-78. $2.50pa.

Unfortunately, the current volume, volume 4, is the last volume planned for this excellent annotated bibliography of bilingual and multicultural materials in many languages, complete with intelligent reviews, grade level codings, author, title, and subject indexes. It is a model worth copying.

Guide to Title VII Bilingual Bicultural Programs, 1978-79. 7th Annual Directory. $7.50pa.

This guide, now in its seventh edition, provides access to bilingual education programs funded through the Elementary and Secondary Education Act for the current school year. It includes the addresses of basic programs as well as information on national networks and centers, and various awards and fellowships.

Modern Language Association (MLA)
62 Fifth Ave.
New York, NY 10011   (212) 741-5588

The MLA was founded in 1883 to promote study, criticism and research on modern languages and literature including both English and foreign languages. MLA's Foreign Language Program has played an important role in advancing the study and teaching of languages other than English, often cooperatively with the Association of Departments of Foreign Languages (ADFL) or with the American Council on the Teaching of Foreign Languages (ACTFL).

Its annual *International Bibliography* is a leading continuing bibliography of books and articles on modern languages and literatures. Volume 2 covers "Other Literatures," including General Romance, French, Italian, Spanish, Portuguese and Brazilian, Romanian, General Germanic, German, Netherlandic, Scandinavian, Modern Greek, Oriental, African, and East European.

Resources include publications, conferences and bulletins. Some other relevant publications (out of many) are:

Developing Language Curricula: Programmed Exercises for Teachers. 1970. 78p. $7.00. (Available from ACTFL).

These basic principles of language analysis can be used in classrooms with non-English-speaking children.

Options for the Teaching of Foreign Languages, Literatures and Cultures, compiled by Warren C. Born and Kathryn Buck. 1979. 293p. $8.95pa. (Available from ACTFL).

A curriculum survey conducted by the MLA.

Russian Language Study in 1975: A Status Report, edited by Joseph L. Conrad. 1976. 74p. $3.50pa.

Includes an overview on the teaching of Russian in American high schools.

Textbooks in German, 1942-1973: A Descriptive Bibliography, compiled by Kathryn Buck and Arthur Haase. 1974. 172p. $10.25.

A classified annotated list of books published in the U.S. for elementary, secondary, and college classes.

Textbooks in Spanish and Portuguese: A Descriptive Bibliography 1937-1970, compiled by Marta de la Portilla and Thomas Colchie. 1972. 128p. $9.00.

Lists of 16 categories of books published in the U.S. for high school and college students whose first language is English, with works on Hispanic culture as well as language teaching.

National Assessment and Dissemination Center (NADC)
49 Washington Ave.
Cambridge, MA 02140   (617) 492-0505

NADC, a project sponsored by Lesley College in Cambridge, MA, and the Fall River Public Schools, distributes a substantial list of publications developed by language and bilingual groups; these materials are very well described and annotated in the Center's free catalog. The quarterly, *Bilingual Journal* ($5.00/yr.; $1.25 per issue), includes reviews of programs and pertinent materials (mostly French and Portuguese) as well as comprehensive articles on significant topics and developments in bilingual education.

Native American Materials Development Center
407 Rio Grande Blvd., NW
Albuquerque, NM 87104   (505) 242-5222

This Center provides services for native American bilingual, bicultural programs, currently largely concentrated on Southwest native languages, Navajo in particular. It provides direct access to Navajo curriculum materials (including some in English) as well as referral services for locating other native language bilingual materials.

National Clearinghouse for Bilingual Education (NCBE)
1300 Wilson Blvd., Suite B2-11
Rosslyn, VA 22209   (703) 522-0710 and (800) 336-4560

(American Indian) Field Office
407 Rio Grande Blvd., NW
Albuquerque, NM 87103   (505) 842-9857

(Asian American) Field Office
530 Oak Grove Ave., Suite 107
Menlo Park, CA 94025   (415) 321-8118

NCBE, mandated by Congress in 1977 and funded by the Office of Bilingual Education and the National Institute of Education, works out of the Offices of the InterAmerican Research Institute under a three-year contract to develop information services in bilingual education to meet the needs of the bilingual education community. Aside from the two field offices and the toll-free hotline listed above, NCBE serves as an information source on other agencies engaged in bilingual education, and offers a limited number of free on-line searches to locate materials on bilingual education in 80 computerized data banks. It is also working on its own computerized data system to process information that deals in any way with bilingual education. Search forms are available from the Clearinghouse itself and from cooperating centers in the Title VII network. Free references and referral services are available by mail and phone.

Its free monthly newsletter, *Forum*, includes current news articles with information on legislation, research, events, people and programs. Recently *Forum* has featured helpful portraits of other centers.

Some publications that provide information on materials are:

Bibliography of English as a Second Language Materials: Grades K-3, 1978. 20p. $1.50.
Includes lists of ESL texts, readers, tests, reference, and supplementary materials.

Bibliography of English as a Second Language Materials: Grades 4-12. 1978. 54p. $2.75.
Similar in scope, but more materials.

Resources in Bilingual Education: A Preliminary Guide to Government Agency Programs of Interest to Minority Language Groups. 1978. 62p. $3.50.
Useful information on government programs and funding sources relating to minority language education.

Sources of Materials for Minority Languages: A Preliminary List. 1978. 35p. $2.75.
Suggests materials sources for a wide variety of languages, as well as embassy contacts for securing additional information.

NCBE Selected Accessions List (monthly). Free.
A useful listing of significant materials received by the Clearinghouse during the previous month.

Proyecto Leer

1736 Columbia Rd., NW, Suite 107
Washington, DC 20009   (202) 265-3275
Proyecto Leer, now funded by the Ford Foundation, was founded in 1967 by Martha Tome, a trained librarian and refugee from Cuba, who saw the need for identifying "elementary books and other reading and instructional materials in Spanish for children and adults appropriate for school and public libraries." Today Proyecto Leer works from a base of more than 15,000 titles, with slightly changed scope and objectives. It now attempts to:

- Evaluate and review recreational and educational materials in Spanish and ethnic literature in English for children and adults

- Train librarians and teachers in selecting and ordering materials for Spanish-speaking students

- Work with schools, libraries and community programs to make these materials available.

Two means of extending its services are a traveling collection of 2,000 titles available for workshops, and a *Bulletin* which provides annotated listings of Spanish language books and books related to Hispanic culture, along with lists of sources, publishers, magazines, conferences, etc. The *Bulletin* is issued somewhat irregularly, because of budget and time constraints, although the project attempts to publish it twice a year.

KEY PUBLICATIONS

(The emphasis on Spanish-language materials reflects available sources.)

An Annotated Bibliography of Title VII French Project-Developed Instructional Materials, 1970-1975, developed by the National Materials Development Center for French/Portuguese. Bedford, NH: NMDC/FP, 1976. 50p. $1.25pa. (Available from National Assessment and Dissemination Center in Fall River, MA).

Materials developed through bilingual French programs from 1970 to 1975 are grouped here as audiovisuals, comprehensive curriculum guides, fine arts, French as a second language, games, language arts, mathematics, health and physical education, reading and readers, science, social studies, and tests. Annotations provide grade levels as well as indications of appropriate curriculum areas.

El Banco del Libro Recomiendo (Series). Caracas, Venezuela: El Banco del Libro, 1973?- . $21.00/set. (From Banco del Libro, Departamento de Publicaciones, Apartado 10914, Caracas 101, Venezuela).

Bibliographies of recommended spanish-language children's books issued in mimeographed format by the Venezuelan Department of Education, with some indexing. Books are categorized by grade levels, subject and reading levels. Volume 3 deals with ecology.

Bibliography of Instructional Materials for the Teaching of French: Kindergarten through Grade Twelve, by the French Bibliography Committee. Sacramento, CA: California State Department of Education, 1977. 149p. $1.50pa. (From Bureau of Publications Sales, California State Department of Education, P.O. Box 271, Sacramento, CA 95802).

This bibliography annotates a variety of materials designed to increase cultural awareness and/or language fluency. This bibliography, like previous bibliographies in Portuguese, German and Spanish, includes textbooks as well as filmstrips, grammars, maps, pictures, readers, slides, tapes, and transparencies—primarily arranged by subject matter to facilitate location by topics. These are extremely selective bibliographies with each item reviewed by at least two or as many as sixteen committee members. Materials are coded for subject categories, language interest levels, maturity levels, and types of materials. It provides a helpful matrix for comparing and analyzing materials, as well as addresses of sources.

Similar bibliographies available from the California State Department of Education, Bureau of Publications Sales, are:

Bibliography of Audiovisual Instructional Materials for the Teaching of Spanish. 1975. $0.75pa.

Bibliography of Instructional Materials for the Teaching of Portuguese. 1975. $0.75.

Bibliography of Spanish Materials for Students, Grades Seven through Twelve. 1972. $0.65.

Bibliography of Language Arts Materials for Native North Americans, Bilingual, English as a Second Language and Native Language Materials, 1965-1974, compiled under the direction of Karen Abbey. Los Angeles: American Indian Studies Center, University of California, 1977. 283p. $4.00pa.

The bibliography of this book includes more than 1,000 items suitable for use in native and bilingual education — grammars, dictionaries, reading books, etc. — arranged under languages. It also includes helpful discussions of specific language difficulties and grammatical categories, as well as straightforward information and suggestions on teaching and working with cultural differences.

A Bicultural Heritage: Themes for the Exploration of Mexican and Mexican-American Culture in Books for Children and Adolescents, by Isabel Schon. Metuchen, NJ: Scarecrow Press, 1978. 164p. $7.00.

The emphasis here is on culture, with descriptions and evaluations for students from kindergarten through grade 12. These are classified within five thematic areas — customs, life styles, heroes, folklore, and key historical developments — and then by age/grade ranges — kindergarten through second, third to sixth, and seventh to twelfth.

Evaluations include outlines or discussions of goals and learning, themes, specific ideas, and suggested follow-up activities, as well as a personal evaluation for each title, with recommended titles starred. The book provides author and title indexes.

The appendix has three articles: on selecting Spanish language books in the U.S.; on the scarcity of young people's books in Mexico; and on the unexplored wealth of materials from Spain.

Bilingual Education Resource Guide, compiled by Carmel Sandoval and Susan Gann. Washington, DC: National Education Association, 1977. 120p. $4.50.

This information packet for bilingual educators has two selective bibliographies for Mexican American and native American students. The 17-page native American bibliography is particularly valuable for listing other bibliographies and including selected materials from such organizations as the Navajo Curriculum Center and the Navajo Reading Study, as well as background information, analysis of state programs, information on funding and grants for programs, addresses of general assistance centers and teacher education programs. This is loaded with names, addresses and telephone numbers of contact persons and programs.

The bibliographies, though not extensive, were chosen by Joe Gonzales, materials coordinator of Southwest Bilingual Education Training Resource Center, as readily available representative materials, with some items chosen for cultural and/or historical importance.

El Boletin: Books of Mexico. Monthly/flyer. Tijuana, Baja California: E.D.I.A.P.S.A. (Free from P.O. Box 597, San Ysidro, CA 92073).

This is a free occasional flyer supported and distributed by a committee of the Mexican government interested in developing Mexico's book trade and publishing industry.

Books in Other Languages: How to Select and Where to Order Them, edited by
Leonard Wertheimer and Mary Cerre. 3rd ed. Ottawa, Canada: Canadian
Library Association, 1976. 129p. $15.00. (From Order Department, 151
Sparks St., Ottawa, Ontario K1P5E3).

This selection tool for Canadian librarians covers all languages spoken in
Canada. Its source section, in particular, could be useful for school personnel in
language and multi-ethnic programs in the United States and in Canada.

*Books in Spanish for Children and Young Adults: An Annotated Guide/Libros
Infantiles y Juveniles en Español: Una Guia Anotada*, by Isabel Schon.
Metuchen, NJ: Scarecrow Press, 1978. 155p. $7.00.

A guide for selecting Spanish-language books by Hispanic authors for
children of preschool through high school years. Most books in this guide were
published after 1973; most came from Argentina, Chile, Colombia, Costa Rica,
Cuba, Ecuador, Guatemala, Mexico, Peru, Puerto Rico, Spain, Uruguay, and
Venezuela.

Books are intended to present the life styles, folklore, heroes, history, fiction, poetry, theater, and classical literature of Hispanic cultures as they are
expressed by Hispanic authors. Most books are readily available in some Spanish-
speaking countries. All were in print as of January 1978.

The descriptive and evaluative annotations designate outstanding, marginal
and non-recommended titles, and assign tentative grade levels. Indexes cover
authors, titles and subjects. Appendixes provide names and addresses of
"reliable" book dealers in Spanish-speaking countries and of U.S. book dealers
who specialize in Spanish-language books.

Chinese Cultural Resource Book (For Elementary Teachers), by Irene Kwok,
with the Chinese Pilot Program. San Francisco: San Francisco Unified
School District, 1975. 324p. $3.50pa. (Available from National Assessment
and Dissemination Center in Fall River, MA).

Materials for the social science curriculum, grades K to 6, written in English
and Chinese, are intended as ethnic heritage resources. The book includes 206
stories, poems, songs, games, art projects, and recipes correlated with five major
Chinese festivals.

Latino Materials: A Multimedia Guide for Children and Young Adults, by
Daniel Flores Duran. New York: Neal Schuman; Santa Barbara: ABC-Clio,
1979. 249p. $14.95. (Selection Guide Series No. 1).

This annotated guide to Latin American materials, intended for librarians
and educators, covers books, films, and journals selected for accuracy, cultural
relevance, vocabulary, artistic merit, and presentation of positive role models
without stereotyping, sexism, or racism. The book is in four sections: one section
of critical essays, one on general resources, one on Mexican American resources,
and one on Puerto Rican resources. Each of these is subdivided into elementary,
secondary, and professional materials and further divided into books, films, and
(sometimes) journals; 473 items altogether. The annotations are helpfully
descriptive and critical, with adequate details and comparative data, as well as
full bibliographic information, price, and distributors (for films). The book
includes a glossary and an annotated directory of publishers and producers, as
well as good subject and author-title indexes.

Master Locator Booklet for Classroom Materials in TESL, by Adolf Heike. Bloomington: Indiana University Linguistics Club, 1975. 119p. $4.05pa. (Also available as ED 123 929). (From 310 Lindley Hall, Indiana University, Bloomington, IN 47401).

A substantial checklist that includes texts, audio recordings, films, filmstrips, graphics, and manipulatives for teaching English as a second language, as well as materials for TEUP (teaching English to the underprivileged). Citations provide source, price, author, publication date, and publisher, but omit grade levels, format details, running time, and the release dates of visual materials.

Material Development Needs in the Uncommonly Taught Languages: Priorities for the Seventies. Arlington, VA: Center for Applied Linguistics, 1975. 90p. $3.95pa.

Reprints the proceedings of a conference sponsored by the U.S. Office of Education that dealt with current and future priority needs for instructional materials in this important area. Some articles and recommendations deal with "Languages for the World of Work," "African Languages," "Amerind and Creole Languages in the Americas and the Caribbean," and many others.

Options and Perspectives: A Sourcebook of Innovative Foreign Language Programs in Action, K-12, by F. William D. Love, and others. New York: Modern Language Association of America, 1973. 361p. $3.00pa. (From 62 Fifth Ave., New York, NY 10011).

An organized and detailed presentation of 51 innovative foreign-language programs for elementary and secondary schools with information on materials and costs. The latter details, unfortunately, are probably made obsolete through inflation. A new *Options for the Teaching of Foreign Languages, Literatures and Cultures* was to be issued in 1979 ($8.95pa.).

Selector's Guide for Bilingual Education Materials. New York: EPIE Institute, 1976. 3v. $20.00 each; $10.00 for members. Vol. 1, *Spanish Language Arts*; Vol. 2, *Spanish "Branch" Programs*; Vol. 3, *The Status of Programs in Chinese, Japanese, Korean, and Vietnamese.* [EPIE *Reports* 73, 74 and *Special Report* (unnumbered).]

In these three reports, all issued in 1976, EPIE explores and evaluates Spanish-language and Asian-language materials with its usual thoroughness. Volume 3, a *Special Report*, funded by the National Institute for Education, includes appendixes and an initial chapter dealing with philosophies, implications and criteria for selecting Asian-language instructional materials for bilingual classrooms.

A Survey of Materials for the Study of the Uncommonly Taught Languages, by Dora E. Johnson, and others. Arlington, VA: Center for Applied Linguistics, 1976-1977. Set of 8, $26.50; any three, $10.50; $3.95 each.

This one-of-a-kind annotated bibliography series is an important cross-disciplinary materials resource for everyone concerned with teaching uncommonly-taught languages. The eight different sections include more than 5,000 entries in or for 500 languages and dialects; these range from teaching materials to dictionaries. Each section focuses on a major geographic area and is arranged by language and language groups within that area. While the main purpose of this bibliography was to compile materials to help English-speaking adults learn obscure languages, the materials chosen can be used to facilitate language learning in many other ways. Section titles are: 1) Western Europe/Pidgins & Creoles (European Based), 1976, 34p.; 2) Soviet Union, 1976, 42p.; 3) The Middle East & North Africa, 1976, 42p.; 4) South Asia, 1976, 41p.; 5) Eastern Asia, 1976, 39p.; 6) Sub-Saharan Africa, 1977, 80p.; 7) Southeast Asia & the Pacific, 1976, 72p.; 8) North, Central & South America, 1977, 80p.

A Teacher's Notebook: French, by National Association of Independent Schools. Boston: Author, 1974. 46p. $2.00pa.

This notebook, prepared by the members of the NAIS French Committee, covers what to teach, which materials to use, and how to test the teaching, and includes many practical aids for all stages. The lists of materials, texts, and various programs are representative and meaningful, while short enough to be convenient. Items were selected on the collective judgment of a five-person committee, which also provided working criteria for texts for various grades. Lists include addresses and sources, though not prices; annotations are brief but helpful.

A Teacher's Notebook: German, by National Association of Independent Schools. Boston: Author, 1974. Paged in 11 sections. $1.00pa.

This quick reference, primarily for new teachers, covers realia, visual aids, basic library, journals, testing, and curriculum.

A Teacher's Notebook: Latin, by National Association of Independent Schools. Boston: Author, 1974. 81p. $2.00pa.

Based on the experience and/or acquaintance of a six-member committee and on current availability, this guide to the teaching of Latin covers textbooks, criteria for tests, and comprehensive and easy-to-use lists of relevant films, filmstrips, slides, posters, pictures, recordings, maps, replicas, student publications, recommended source books, and professional organizations. Citations include sources, addresses, and 1974 costs.

A Teacher's Notebook: Russian, by National Association of Independent Schools. Boston: Author, 1973. 37p. $1.00pa.

Includes a classified directory of materials sources and media centers for Russian, as well as nine other articles dealing with topics like eclectic, direct, and linguistic methods for teaching Russian; Audio-Lingual Method (ALM) Materials; and other suggestions for effective Russian programs.

A Teacher's Notebook: Spanish, by National Association of Independent Schools. Boston: Author, 1973. 45p. $1.00pa.

This notebook integrates classroom suggestions and course outlines with appropriate textbooks for beginning, intermediate, and advanced students. It includes a simple test outline and an excellent chapter on teaching aids, with annotations of sources, lists of journals, radio programs in Spanish, related associations and the like. A final chapter suggests titles for a basic library.

FOR FURTHER READING

*Items marked with an asterisk include criteria.

+ Items marked with a plus include substantial lists of references.

+ "Bilingual-Bicultural Education: Policies, Programs, and Research," Special issue of *Education and Urban Society*, v. 10, no. 3 (May 1978).

*Booth, Venita. *Guidelines for Implementing Individualized Instruction in Foreign Languages*. Corpus Christi, TX: Corpus Christi Independent School District, 1973.

* + California State Department of Education. *Bilingual-Bicultural Education and English-as-a-Second Language Education: A Framework for Elementary and Secondary Schools*. Sacramento, CA: CSDE, 1973.

* + California State Department of Education. *Foreign Language Framework*. Sacramento, CA: CSDE, 1972.
Appendix B (pp. 101-107) consists of "Guidelines for Evaluation of Foreign Language Instructional Materials"; pp. 116-18 include "Criteria for Evaluation of Pupil Textbooks, Teachers Editions, and Teachers Manuals"; pp. 118-19 have "Criteria for Evaluating Visual and Auditory Elements of the Foreign Language Materials Program."

+ Conner, John W. *Japanese Culture in the United States of America*. Sacramento, CA: California State University, Sacramento, Department of Anthropology, 1977.

* + Derrick, William M. *Early Immersion Language Learning Programs*. Princeton, NJ: Educational Testing Service, Office of Minority Education, 1978.

+ Dorry, Gertrude Nye. *Games for Second Language Learning, Grades K-12*. New York: McGraw-Hill, 1966.

+ Evans, G. Edward. *Bibliography of Language Arts Materials for Native North Americans*. Los Angeles: University of California, Los Angeles, 1977.

* + Garcia, Ricardo. *Learning in Two Languages*. Bloomington, IN: Phi Delta Kappa Educational Foundation, 1976. (Fastback 84).

* + *Instructional Materials Selection Guide: Bilingual/Bicultural ESL*. Los Angeles, CA: National Dissemination and Assessment Center, California State University, Los Angeless, 1978.

Lambert, Wallace E. "Cognitive and Socio-Cultural Consequences of Bilingualism," *Canadian Modern Language Review*, v. 34 (1978), pp. 537-44.

Lambert, Wallace E., and others. "Some Cognitive Consequences of Following the Curricula of the Early School Grades in a Foreign Language," pp. 259-67 in *Monograph Series of Language and Linguistics*, edited by James E. Alatis. Washington, DC: Georgetown University Press.

+ Lovett, James, and Ted Snyder. *Bilingual Materials for Mathematics*. Columbus, OH: ERIC Clearinghouse on Science, Mathematics and Environmental Education, 1979.

*Moser, Alba I. *Individualized Instruction for the Bilingual Classroom*. Newport Beach, CA: Chess and Associates, 1975.

National Center for Education Statistics. *Geographic Distribution, Nativity, and Age Distribution of Language Minorities in the United States*. Washington, DC: GPO, 1977.

*+Okawa, Tetsu. *Study of Curriculum Development and the Treatment of Materials in Classrooms*. Washington, DC: U.S. Office of Education, 1979.
This survey, not yet in print as of June 1979, was a mail and site survey of availability, needs and gaps in bilingual education materials and the means by which these are dispersed to classrooms.

"Other Languages," Special issue of *McGill Journal of Education*, v. 13, no. 2 (Spring 1978).

+Rivers, Wilga M. *Teaching Foreign-Language Skills*. Chicago: University of Chicago Press, 1968.
Deals thoroughly with practical aspects of teaching a foreign language, and can be useful also to the teacher of English as a second language.

+Sanchez, Alberto R. *Chinese Culture in the United States of America. An Annotated Bibliography*. Sacramento, CA: California State University, Sacramento, Department of Anthropology, 1977.

*Sanders, Anthony R. *Creating Materials for Bilingual-Bicultural Learning Centers*. Newport Beach, CA: Chess and Associates, 1975.

+*Sourcebook of Equal Educational Opportunity*. 2nd ed. Chicago: Marquis, Academic Media, 1977.
Loaded with statistical and other information on groups often denied equal educational opportunities, including native American, Asian and Pacific American, disadvantaged white ethnic, and Hispanic. Part I provides an overview of U.S. population characteristics and an excellent review of racial (and sexual) stereotypes in texts and other media.

Spolsky, Bernard, and Robert Cooper, eds. *Frontiers of Bilingual Education*. Rowley, MA: Newbury House Publishers, 1977.
Includes chapters of evaluation, policy, history, psychology, philosophy, and international aspects of bilingual education.

*Tobier, Arthur, ed. *Teaching Bilingual Children*. New York: Workshop Center for Open Education, 1974.

+Treuba, Henry T., comp., with Juan Moran, and others. *Bilingual Bicultural Education for the Spanish Speaking in the United States: A Preliminary Bibliography*. Champaign, IL: Stipes, 1977.

*+Women on Words and Images. *Sexism in Foreign Language Textbooks*. Princeton, NJ: WOWI, 197?

+Yates, Barbara, ed. "Special Issue on Bilingual Education," *Education Libraries*, v. 4, no. 3 (Spring/summer 1979), pp. 53-68.
This special issue covers the 1978 Bilingual Education Act, as well as directories of library organizations serving ethnic groups and data bases for bilingual education.

SELECTING MATERIALS FOR THE
LANGUAGE ARTS

"The attitude and habits which the classroom teacher displays toward reading books other than texts are important in the eyes of students."
— Ruth K. J. Cline, "Integrating Literature and 'Free Reading' into the Social Studies Program," *Social Education*, January 1978

"Critical reading requires the application of every reading skill, lively practice in meaningful situations, and an opportunity to react creatively."
— Ruth C. Cook and Ronald C. Doll, *The Elementary School Curriculum*, 1973

"It is the English teacher's job to make as many points of views and beliefs, to make as much information available to students as he can, and then help the student, to the extent of the teacher's ability, to find his way among them."
— Roy Alin, President, Washington State Council of Teachers of English

□ □ □

OVERVIEW

This chapter deals largely with the selection of materials for teaching reading, since reading is, from an educational perspective, the most basic of the language arts. (In a developmental sense, of course, language, the spoken word, comes first.) The chapter includes some evaluation standards and criteria for reading programs and materials, as well as some sources, guides and aids for selecting other language arts materials. Since the focus is on materials for formal reading and language arts programs, related subjects such as book selection, books as a genre, children's literature and books in schools are covered more fully in the chapter on print materials in *Media and the Curriculum*. That chapter, consequently, is important for language arts, reading and English teachers. Readability is treated separately in *Issues and Policies*.

Reading or the teaching of reading is paradoxical in a sense. As we spend more time and money, develop more experts, and focus more closely on the process of reading, we fail somehow to improve our teaching of reading in schools. My own belief, as parent, librarian, reader, and observer of readers, is that reading abilities (like abilities in speaking) develop more from actual reading than from instruction in reading. In my experience both adults and children understand materials better when they read materials that interest them. In educational terms, successful reading depends upon interest and motivation; comprehension is strongly related to content. This viewpoint is corroborated by comparative research in some countries that succeed better than we in teaching and encouraging reading. In Japan, England, and Israel, where literacy levels are substantially higher than in the United States, reading instruction emphasizes parental involvement and the publication of materials for students' diverse reading interests. David Harmon notes in the July-August 1975 issue of *National Elementary Principal* that these countries—which use standardized reading tests far less than we—put considerably more effort into determining children's interest areas. He believes that our reading tests that test only motor and cognitive factors and ignore content (affective areas) cannot be accurate.

Though we are not a nation of readers (the majority of adults do not read one book per year), parents and teachers stress (in two senses) the teaching of reading, though teachers, especially elementary teachers, are often not heavy readers themselves.

One fairly recent study on student attitudes toward literature (in the April 1974 issue of *American Education*) reported that most students at all ages had predominantly positive views of literature and that almost all read some materials voluntarily in their free time, though less than they did in the past. This reservoir of goodwill should be more fully tapped in our teaching approaches and materials selection policies for reading and language arts. But, on the contrary, student verbal achievement and reading achievement have shown continuing if not consistent decline over the last 18 years — a period in America marked by many other kinds of stress.

Each expert has his or her own explanation for this phenomenon. The *Wirtz Report*, in its two-year investigation to account for lowered SAT scores over 14 years, issued a five-page *List of Hypotheses Advanced to Explain the SAT Score Decline*, by Yvonne Wharton. Major categories were:

- changes in the schools (curriculum factors, instructional policies, teacher factors, student factors)

- changes in society (family, religion, civil rights, crises in values, national priorities, economics, labor movement in education, technological changes)

- changes in the population

- problems with the tests

The Wirtz Advisory Panel ultimately concluded that about one-half of the score decline was probably due to the changing composition of the students seeking entrance to college; the remainder was attributed to the proliferation of elective courses, lowered standards, easier textbooks, increased television viewing, diminution of learning motivation, and familial/social changes — a multitude of reasons.

I tend to agree with the panel's hypothesis that the increase in television watching over the sixties (one hour more per student per day, on the average) not only took time away from other pursuits but also affected some children's approaches to processing information. Daniel Fader in *The New Hooked on Books* (see Key Publications) remarked that students who spend six hours a day watching television may be basically different in intellect from students who spend time in other ways, and may require different teaching approaches. Our easier textbooks, similarly, may be part of a vicious cause-and-effect cycle. While they are a response to lower verbal skills, their use may tend to contribute to diminished verbal skills.

It may be that children today are refusing to be bored. While we concentrate on *how* to teach youngsters to read, we may not provide them with anything they wish to read. Some approaches to teaching reading seem counter-productive, whatever their paper success. Many children, for example, are thoroughly turned off by programmed reading; others by phonics drills.

In the *Elementary School Curriculum* (Boston: Allyn and Bacon, 1973), Ruth Cook and Ronald Doll reported a follow-up study of two equated groups of 25 children in the same community. One group was taught by heavy drill in a synthetic phonics program; the other learned through easy, meaningful materials with an analytic approach to word recognition. Logically enough, the first group tested higher in word recognition tests; the second was significantly ahead on reading for meaning. When they checked the circulation records of the nearby public library (which had a summer reading program), they found that *all* 25 children in the second group were readers (some very heavy readers) and that one child only from the first group withdrew a book.

Paul Copperman, who documents our decline in literacy in an angry polemic, *The Literacy Hoax* (New York: Morrow, 1978), ascribes our failure largely to experiments in education and our abandonment of reading textbooks in the elementary schools. This latter is inaccurate. Whether or not we have experimented in education, we have *not* abandoned reading texts. A survey reported by Cook and Doll indicates that more than 85 percent of elementary teachers used basal readers. It is unlikely, in any event, that school materials are solely responsible for our decline in verbal abilities. By the eighth grade, students who have been formally taught through the same tools frequently vary in reading ability, spelling mastery, writing skills and verbal capacity from fourth through twelfth grade levels. (Presumably their use of time outside school varies considerably.) Some students succeed because of or despite our materials and methods of instruction. Others do not. Boys, who consistently test lower on the average than girls in verbal ability, have a harder time learning to read. Typically, boys fill our remedial reading classes.

Factors that correlate with success in teaching reading have been frequently identified. These are apt to be affective forces, rather than drills or specific reading texts. Some factors are: parental involvement, the presence of reading materials in the home, emotional atmosphere in school and home, student self-esteem, and the quality of interaction between students and teachers.

Several studies confirm that the presence of a variety of materials is an important variable. Other studies, including the *California School Effectiveness Study* and the *Michigan Cost-Effectiveness Study*, indicate that students are most successful in learning to read when teachers choose more materials for their own classrooms. Presumably, these materials are selected to meet the needs of specific children.

Other factors that have been identified as contributing to learning reading are programs such as movement education, music education and elementary science programs, such as SCIS. Presumably, these may involve improved coordination, ability to work sequentially, improved oral attention, observation, or classification—perhaps a more interesting curriculum.

The overwhelming majority of studies on individualizing reading show that students—at all ages, from all social levels—learn to read better when they choose materials that interest them. Their selections, typically, differ widely in theme, content, variety, and vocabulary—from prescribed materials students encounter in basal readers and assigned readings.

The variety encompasses not only different kinds of literature and media, but materials about many types of characters and situations, by authors of varying styles, temperaments and attitudes toward experience. Materials may arise from different times, locations, cultures, and experiences. These materials may again be related to different curriculum areas in addition to their personal appeal.

Multicultural materials, for example, might contribute to self-esteem, knowledge, variety, and classroom atmosphere. Well-written animal books might contribute to science knowledge and literary appreciation in addition to reading skills.

Fader's *New Hooked on Books* uses much anecdotal evidence to support his conclusion that children read much more and far better when they themselves select their own reading materials. (Paperback books are ideal, according to Fader.) He believes that children should not only have their choice among available preselected materials, but should also actually select the materials to be purchased.

Phyllis Anderson Wood is another who believes that children learn to read by reading. In an article appearing in *Catholic Library World* (July-Aug. 1977) she asserts that the teacher's main task is helping match students to appropriate learning materials. As Wood (author and high school English skills teacher for academically disadvantaged students) puts it: "The most effective tool (in teaching English) has been putting the right book in the right hand at the right moment." For her, the reading experiences should be fun first of all and should lead to a feeling of success and mastery. For students who have experienced failure in reading, an encounter with this "right book" may be a turning point, the start of a healing process or a process of growth, and this is not likely to occur if the book is not emotionally affective.

Wood's quest for the "right books" led her to authorship. Others who share her views may find assistance in selection in the principles, criteria and aids in my chapter on the feeling domain. MECRE's *Source Book of Evaluation Techniques for Reading* includes a relatively unsophisticated *Interest Inventory Record* on pages 90-92 that provides a useful starting place for learning student interests.

STUDENT SELECTION AND INDIVIDUALIZATION

This chapter, the chapter on books in *Media and the Curriculum*, and the chapter on individualization in *Issues and Policies* all provide tools to help teachers who are willing to attempt teaching reading and language arts with books of their own choosing. Several of the titles in the chapter on the feeling domain in the present work are also valuable for this purpose.

The *New Hooked on Books* in particular has many accessible mechanisms for self selection by students. Sam Duker's *Individualized Reading* (see Key Publications) provides detailed research to back the feasibility of this method. According to Duker, individualized reading involves, ideally:

- self-selection of instructional materials
- self-pacing, with each child proceeding at his or her own rate
- reading skills taught only to those who need them, when needed, individually or in ad hoc groups
- teaching and diagnosis carried out through teacher-pupil conferences
- sharing of reading experiences to broaden everyone's experiences

While individualization can be done with basal readers, Duker finds that, in general, individualizing is not too compatible with basal approaches. It requires, above all, flexible teachers. The research reports summarized in Duker's book indicate that self-selection and individualized reading are the methods most likely to raise reading scores for all kinds of students at all grade levels.

The *Recommendations for Improving Reading Instruction* printed below arise from the perspectives that early childhood educators are philosophically congruent with perspectives of Duker, Fader, Zimet and Wood. This joint statement of concerns and recommendations is the concensus of a group of educators from the following organizations: American Association of Elementary/Kindergarten/Nursery Educators, Association for Childhood Education International, Association for Supervision and Curriculum Development, International Reading Association, National Association for the Education of Young Children, National Association of Elementary School Principals, National Council of Teachers of English. (These concerns and recommendations have, of course, implications for materials selection as well as for content and programs.)

RECOMMENDATIONS FOR IMPROVING READING INSTRUCTION:
Pre-First Grade

CONCERNS:
1. A growing number of children are enrolled in pre-kindergarten and kindergarten classes in which highly structured pre-reading and reading programs are being used.
2. Decisions related to schooling, including the teaching of reading, are increasingly being made on economic and political bases instead of on our knowledge of young children and of how they best learn.
3. In a time of diminishing financial resources, schools often try to make "a good showing" on measures of achievement that may or may not be appropriate for the children involved. Such measures all too often dictate the content and goals of the programs.
4. In attempting to respond to pressures for high scores on widely-used measures of achievement, teachers of young children sometimes feel compelled to use materials, methods, and activities designed for older children. In so doing, they may impede the development of intellectual functions such as curiosity, critical thinking, and creative expression, and, at the same time, promote negative attitudes toward reading.
5. A need exists to provide alternative ways to teach and evaluate progress in pre-reading and reading skills.
6. Teachers of pre-first graders who are carrying out highly individualized programs without depending upon commercial readers and workbooks need help in articulating for themselves and the public *what* they are doing and *why*.

RECOMMENDATIONS:
1. Provide reading experiences as an integrated part of the broader communication process that includes listening, speaking, and writing. A language experience approach is an example of such integration.
2. Provide for a broad range of activities both in scope and in content. Include direct experiences that offer opportunities to communicate in different settings with different persons.
3. Foster children's affective and cognitive development by providing materials, experiences, and opportunities to communicate what they know and how they feel.
4. Continually appraise how various aspects of each child's total development affects his/her reading development.
5. Use evaluative procedures that are developmentally appropriate for the children being assessed and that reflect the goals and objectives of the instructional program.
6. Insure feelings of success for all children in order to help them see themselves as persons who can enjoy exploring language and learning to read.
7. Plan flexibly in order to accommodate a variety of learning styles and ways of thinking.
8. Respect the language the child brings to school, and use it as a base for language activities.
9. Plan activities that will cause children to become active participants in the learning process rather than passive recipients of knowledge.
10. Provide opportunities for children to experiment with language and simply to have fun with it.
11. Require that pre-service and in-service teachers of young children be prepared in the teaching of reading in a way that emphasizes reading as an integral part of the language arts as well as the total curriculum.
12. Encourage developmentally appropriate language learning opportunities in the home.

Single copies of this statement are available free with a self-addressed, stamped envelope from International Reading Association, 800 Barkdale Road, Newark, DE 19711. Bulk copies are available at cost.

USING FRAMEWORKS FOR SELECTION CRITERIA

Typically, state or district frameworks provide policies and overviews as well as general statements that can be transformed into criteria. In California, for instance, the 1973 *Framework in Reading for Elementary and Secondary Schools* suggests a variety of factors to consider in selection. Since these factors seem rather typical of framework statements, I have transformed them into an outline to use in selecting or evaluating materials.

FACTORS IN SELECTING INSTRUCTIONAL MATERIALS IN READING

	Poor			Excellent	N/A
Relationship of materials to district curricular objectives					
Provision of continuous learning experiences through all levels					

Variety of materials to match differences in student:
    learning abilities
    interests
    achievements
    maturity levels
    cultural and language backgrounds					

Variety of materials to reflect pluralistic experiences:
    cultural
    racial
    ethnic
    religious
    age
    sex					

Materials that recognize multisensory approaches to learning					
Materials that provide diagnostic tools					
Materials for self-instruction					
Materials for individualized instruction					

Materials well related to the reading process, that recognize:
    oral basis of language
    relationships among listening, speaking, writing,
        and reading comprehension
    relationship of background experiences to reading
        comprehension
    contributions of linguistic science
    application of reading abilities to content areas in
        the curriculum					

High quality in
    writing style
    organization
    physical attractiveness
    durability					

Teachers' guides that are practical and valid					

According to this same *Framework*, materials for effective reading instruction should include:

- textbooks
- tradebooks
- periodicals
- language and word games
- filmstrips
- films
- slides
- recording tapes
- charts
- study prints
- manipulative materials
- models and realia

The developers of this framework also recommended both teacher-produced and student-produced materials, and systems compiled from a variety of materials—selected for particular purposes. *Evaluation Criteria for Junior High Schools*, by the National Study of Secondary School Evaluation, adds these:

- pamphlets
- paperback books
- library books for different reading levels and interests
- newspapers
- dictionaries
- usage handbooks
- indexes to fiction and non-fiction
- *Reader's Guide*
- books of quotations
- teacher-prepared guides
- class sets of good literature
- class sets of language arts texts
- school spelling lists and books
- vocabulary study texts
- diagnostic tests and materials
- radio
- television
- recordings
- transparencies
- maps
- pictures
- up-to-date reading lists

This latter source suggests grading these materials for variety, quality and quantity. Record-book combinations and cassette-book combinations are also popular with young children.

These lists may be combined into a checklist for teachers or schools that wish to survey the adequacy of instructional materials for reading and the language arts in their classrooms, schools and districts. Few schools, unfortunately, have adequate ranges of materials.

This apparently extensive list could be extended still further to include perhaps more music and artifacts, such as songbooks or rhythm instruments, since musical activities increase auditory perception. One report, for instance, by the Lake County (California) Intermediate Education District, included songs and rhythm activities as vehicles for improving reading skills in problem readers. All students developed an interest in reading, while 75 percent showed significant gains, particularly in auditory discrimination, syllabification, understanding of vowels and consonants, and improved comprehension and attitudes toward reading. In addition, films, filmmaking, and other media activities have also proven successful in increasing language and reading skills. Joseph M. Conte and George H. Grimes (in *Media and the Culturally Different Learner*, cited in the For Further Reading list) also strongly recommend multisensory approaches and locally-produced materials for teaching reading. Their book is a good presentation of how and why to select such media.

Other titles in the Key Publications list in this chapter also address this issue, by suggesting tools, ways of attracting funds for purchasing such materials, and ways to create one's own. The chapters and sources on media and pictorial materials in *Media and the Curriculum* might also be helpful for educators who wish to extend their range of language arts materials to records, tapes, films, and other media.

MATERIALS FOR "RELUCTANT READERS"

Because of increasing illiteracy, we have seen a decided increase in "high interest-easy reading" lists from publishers, English teachers, volunteer groups, and public libraries. In general, lists developed by publishers are partial, while those developed by theorists may or may not have appealing books. The better lists are generally those developed by remedial reading teachers and public libraries. Public library lists usually have a wider reading base—more books from which to select and more readers to provide input. Lists by remedial reading teachers provide more depth and more analysis of the fewer books they select.

Readability as determined by formula is a most inadequate means of selection, and should not be the sole determinant. The following list, adapted from one designed by Mildred Dorr for the Cleveland Public Library's Adult Education Department, seems as usable as any. It includes factors of appearance, content, style and vocabulary that are equally important.

CONSIDERATIONS IN SELECTING BOOKS FOR RELUCTANT HIGH SCHOOL READERS
(Underline relevant items for book under consideration.)

APPEARANCE
1. Looks like an "adult" book:
   cover, contents, size, shape, title
   reading or grade level inconspicuous if present
   not a "one sentence to one line" page arrangement

2. Does not look too "hard" to read:
   "thin" book, easy-to-handle size
   amount of written material on page small
   page broken into smaller units or parts
   type sharp and clear, larger in size than that used on this page
   well-spaced letters, wide margins
   generous paper

3. Has many graphic illustrations:
   realistic, appealing to readers addressed
   accurate, useful
   well placed to help explain text
   diagrams, drawings, graphs, charts, maps, other_____
   in color, black and white, both

STYLE AND VOCABULARY
1. Vocabulary:
   adult in tone, related to readers' experiences
   as simple as possible to cover subject adequately
   repetition of the familiar

2. Simple sentence structure

3. Short sentences:
   average sentence length 7-8 words (easiest reading)
   average sentence length 10-12 words (easy reading)

4. Short paragraphs:
   average of not more than 6-8 sentences per paragraph

5. Style:
   clear, direct, interesting, stimulating, not patronizing

CONTENT
1. Subject:
   of immediate, present interest
   ideas and situations with which reader can identify
   easy-to-comprehend facts and information
   self-explanatory; no body of pre-established knowledge needed
   helps clarify pre-established knowledge
   in sufficient depth to be useful
   accurate, up to date, timely
   promises to arouse awareness, deepen interests, broaden horizons
   also provides enjoyment, relaxation, humor, inspiration

2. Includes:
   glossary, index, table of contents, suggestions for further reading
   exercises, review, comprehension tests, directions for teachers (if desired)

COGNITION

Even for cognitive reasons, students need to go beyond the simplified vocabulary and sentence structure used in standard texts. NAEP assessments of representative young Americans at ages 9, 13, and 17 indicate that students perform fairly well on simple written assignments and are fairly adept at creative writing, but are "in trouble" when it comes to "expressing complex ideas through logical, structured writing."

The cognitive areas mentioned in the chapter on cognition in *Issues and Policies* are important here. The SOI Institute mentioned in that chapter has designed an interesting reading workbook as well as a list that categorizes intellectual tasks in remedial reading according to Guilford's Structure of Intellect model. Under "cognition," for example, we have such things as alphabetizing or picture classification; "evaluation" would include abbreviations, related words, and rhymes; "memory" would include definitions, misspelled words, and mnemonics; "convergent production" might include scrambled sentences and parts of speech; and "divergent production" might include composition and similes. In the Peabody system of language development, the significant categories are considered to be:

- classification
- fluency
- critical thinking
- describing
- imagining
- following directions
- listening
- memory
- patterning
- relationships

Ruddell's communications model includes both cognitive and affective factors:

- oral and written language forms
- meaning
- interpretation
- memory and feedback
- affective mobilizers
- cognitive strategies

MECRE's *Source Book of Evaluation Techniques for Reading* includes a critical thinking checklist on page 89.

Diagnostic teaching tools are another cognitive analysis approach more often used in special education, individualizing, and grouping than in initial selection. These, like other learning disabilities inventories, may be used to analyze the strengths (or, more likely, the weaknesses) of children of varying learning abilities for individualized selection as well as for instructional purposes.

One tool that may be useful is Evelyn Searls' *How to Use WISC Scores in Reading Diagnosis*, part of the *Reading Aid Series* of the International Reading Association (1975. $3.00). This provides a concise summary of relationships between scores on the Wechsler Intelligence Scale for Children and children's reading skills.

Typically, each publisher's series has worked out its own tables and charts of cognitive factors. These should probably be viewed critically and carefully to see if materials in fact do and are what is claimed. The list of process verbs in the *Issues and Policies* chapter on cognitive criteria, may be helpful in analyzing questions and activities. Six basal readers are already compared in the analysis chart of *Milton Bradley's Reading Plan* (see Key Publications) which compares these series on 61 behavioral skills grouped into five major categories:

- decoding skills
- structural skills
- vocabulary skills
- comprehension skills
- study skills

Their chart, of course, can be used to analyze other reading series and other reading materials.

Tools listed in the chapters on special education and commercial retrieval systems in *Issues and Policies* are good for locating materials for cognitive tasks.

ROLES AND NEEDS

Depending upon students, reading programs, and school philosophies, different individuals will be active in selecting materials or reading programs. Somewhat different materials might be selected by different people for:

- team teaching
- departmentalized grouping
- differentiated staffing
- multigrade classrooms
- special groups
- schools with or without adequate libraries and/or learning resource centers

Ideally, some materials at least should be chosen near the point of use, by individual teachers, librarians, students and, possibly, parents and community representatives. For materials in the language arts, librarians with their expertise on books and their knowledge of recent materials have important functions, as do literature experts and reading specialists. (Library finding tools are most helpful for individual selection and buying guides.) The list below indicates, in a general way, some appropriate roles for each.

EDUCATORS' ROLES IN THE TREATMENT OF READING MATERIALS

Classroom Teachers' Roles
- assess student reading abilities and interests
- diagnose student strengths and weaknesses
- recognize learning modalities of individual students
- know own best teaching styles
- choose materials appropriate for individual characteristics of students and own teaching style
- make appropriate materials accessible
- prescribe reading materials when necessary or appropriate
- communicate with parents
- exhibit own love of reading
- work with other teachers (especially content area teachers) to make reading a school priority
- as needed, produce and design own materials

Reading Specialists' Roles
- communicate with parents and educators
- train and assist paraprofessionals
- evaluate, select, and prepare materials
- design and coordinate reading records
- be resource person for whole school and staff

Librarians-Media Persons' Roles

- correlate library/media center and its resources with curriculum needs and expressed needs of students and teachers
- select and evaluate materials on basis of quality, individual appeal and correlation with curriculum
- act as resource consultant for students and faculty
- assist teachers and students in selecting new materials to order
- assist teachers and students in selecting appropriate materials from existing collection
- design instructional experiences based on library materials (especially on research, locating materials, free reading)
- arrange materials for maximum accessibility
- publicize materials for maximum utilization
- serve as source of information on students' reading and hobby interests
- produce materials, as needed

These roles, of course, may be modified by individual circumstances.

QUANTITATIVE STANDARDS

The National Council of Teachers of English has certain qualitative and quantitative standards for materials for English. These include:

1) Room libraries of approximately 500 selected titles should be provided for every English classroom, and a resource center should be provided that includes periodicals, microfilm readers, typewriters, class sets of books, and materials for student use.

2) The English faculty of each school should select its own books and develop its own materials.

3) Every department should have an English center to house its professional library and teaching materials collection, its file of teacher-prepared materials that have been found effective, its audio-visual equipment, and its work space for teachers.

CENSORSHIP

Censorship is an important problem for English teachers—particularly at high school levels. It might be increased with free selection or student selection policies. While these do not force individual students to read particular materials, they do allow them options from which to choose—a situation which is seen as menacing by some parents and some communities.

Probably the best defense against censorship is a well-thought-through selection policy—revised as needed—and devised with some continuing mechanism for community input. Research evidence as to the educational value and efficacy of free-selection policies (from such books as Duker's *Individualized Reading*) should be made available to committees or groups drawing up selection policies. Teachers selecting or assigning books for classes of students or individual students should have a conscious—preferably written—rationale for selecting and teaching particular books. Librarians similarly should have some conscious, articulable reasons for their selections beyond literary value and favorable reviews.

CRITERIA FOR SELECTION

Robert B. Ruddell's *Reading-Language Instruction: Innovative Practices* (Englewood Cliffs, NJ: Prentice-Hall, 1974) includes an excellent set of "Criteria for Examining Reading Systems." These systematic, practical and conceptually sound criteria cover skill development and content in great detail, with some attention to components (format), instructional approaches, outstanding characteristics and weaknesses. Skill development and content include language-based approach, decoding skills, literature as response, the author's craft, and evaluation. Derived from his five-part communications model, these criteria are simple to apply and allow for a wide variety of materials.

The taxonomy reprinted below are revised from Roger Farr et al., *Taxonomy of Evaluation Techniques for Reading Programs* and issued as *Sourcebook of Evaluation Techniques for Reading Programs* by James Laffey and Carl Smith. It is reprinted here with the permission of Laffey and Smith and the Measurement and Evaluation Center in Reading Education, Indiana University. Some of MECRE's checklists deal with social class experiences, development, balance, validity, and illustrations.

MECRE PRACTICAL FORMAT CHECKLIST

Do the physical aspects of the material present an inviting and attractive format which adds ease of reading?

1. Is the book durably bound in order to hold up under normal classroom use?
   Yes _____ No _____ Comment_____

2. Are the pages easy to turn?
   Yes _____ No _____ Comment_____

3. Are the materials light enough for easy manipulation?
   Yes _____ No _____ Comment_____

4. Does the overall appearance of the book provide appeal to the age group of the child?
   Yes _____ No _____ Comment_____

5. Is the paper heavy enough to adequately hold the print without showing through?
   Yes _____ No _____ Comment_____

6. Is the paper off-white and dull in finish so that reflection of light by the pages is reduced to a minimum?
   Yes _____ No _____ Comment_____

7. Is the print black enough to show up well under adequate lighting?
   Yes _____ No _____ Comment_____

(List continues on page 228)

8. Is the print large enough to accommodate each age group without unnecessarily taxing the eyes, while at the same time not appearing childish?

Yes ____   No ____   Comment_____

9. Does the type of print ensure against letter confusion?

Yes ____   No ____   Comment_____

10. Is the print well balanced with the margins, illustrations & leadings (space between the lines) on the page?

Yes ____   No ____   Comment_____

11. Are pages variously arranged and artistically balanced?

Yes ____   No ____   Comment_____

12. Is the distance between lines wide enough to break the printed pattern?

Yes ____   No ____   Comment_____

13. Are the lines of print of an appropriate length for ease in reading?

Yes ____   No ____   Comment_____

14. Are the margins of sufficient width to allow the child to hold the book without covering part of the print?

Yes ____   No ____   Comment_____

15. Does the book open flat to allow the child to read from a flat surface?

Yes ____   No ____   Comment_____

16. Are the paragraphs short and concise with smooth transitions?

Yes ____   No ____   Comment_____

17. If a basal series is being used, does the teacher's manual correspond well with the child's book?

Yes ____   No ____   Comment_____

MECRE CHECKLIST OF READING INTEREST

Does the material provide for appeal to a variety of interests and develop deep and permanent interests in reading?

1. Is the material interesting to children of the age, sex, and background for which it is intended?

Yes ____   No ____   Comment_____

2. Are differences between interests and rate of development between boys and girls taken into account?

Yes ____   No ____   Comment_____

3. Are differences in interest related to intelligence and socioeconomic background considered?

Yes ____   No ____   Comment_____

4. Do the materials have built-in motivational devices and activities related to the child's interest?

Yes ____   No ____   Comment_____

5. Do the materials have an attractive format and illustrations which will hold the child's interest?

Yes ____   No ____   Comment_____

6. If a basal reading series is being used, does the teacher's manual provide the teacher with techniques for motivating the child to read through tapping his interests?

Yes ____   No ____   Comment_____

7. Are the materials helping to satisfy the child's needs (e.g., make him feel worthy, accepted, useful, etc.)?

Yes ____   No ____   Comment_____

8. Are exceptional children kept interested in the reading program in the following ways:
   a. Is the gifted child kept interested in reading by being given enrichment activities?

   Yes ____   No ____   Comment_____

   b. Is the underachiever given a lot of easy materials at his independent level so that he is not overwhelmed by the reading process (at his frustration level)?

   Yes ____   No ____   Comment_____

9. Do the materials relate to the interests the child has in his own subculture?

Yes ____   No ____   Comment_____

10. Do the materials inspire the child to learn (i.e., arouse curiosity; portray knowledge about the world around him; utilize his interests, needs, and concerns)?

Yes _____   No _____   Comment_____

11. Are literary techniques used to involve the child in what he is reading (e.g., excitement, suspense, humor, etc.)?

Yes _____   No _____   Comment_____

The following criteria for supplementary textbooks were adapted from *Evaluating Library Resources for Elementary School Libraries* by Mary Gaver and Marian Scott (East Brunswick, NJ: ssh press, 1962). Supplementary textbooks were defined here as any books used in addition to basic texts and provided in quantity, usually for specific instructional purposes.

CRITERIA FOR SUPPLEMENTARY TEXTBOOKS

CRITERIA	RATING		
	Superior	Average	Inferior
Interest	very high interest content	some interest and appeal	lacks challenge and interest
Vocabulary	controlled vocab., pitched slightly below basal reader	not carefully controlled	no control or control so rigid as to be uninteresting
Subject Span	great variety	some variety	little or no variety
Format	outstandingly attractive	acceptable but not eye-catching	dull or poor
Recency	copyrighted in last five years	five to ten years old	more than ten years old
Compatibility	connecting link between basal reader and curric. subjects	some incidental tie-ins with curriculum	unrelated to curriculum
Challenge	up to date and/or challenging	ideas with little challenge	no new or challenging ideas
Readability	easily mastered	acceptable	too easy to develop ability, or so difficult as to discourage
Flexibility	can be used in individualized programs	can be used with groups	useful only as class text

KEY ORGANIZATIONS

International Reading Association (IRA)
800 Barksdale Rd.
Newark, DE 19711   (302) 731-1600

This non-profit membership organization is open to reading teachers and specialists, parents, administrators, librarians, and all others interested in improving reading instruction. It forwards this goal through three main thrusts — publications, meetings, and affiliates.

Its publications program includes about ten to twenty monographs a year and three major periodicals: *Reading Teacher*, for elementary teachers; the *Journal of Reading*, for secondary, adult, and college reading; and the *Reading Research Quarterly*, a scholarly quarterly concerned with research and theory. Individual membership, at $15.00 a year, includes one of these three journals. A $20.00 membership includes two journals, *Journal of Reading* and *Reading Teacher*, both published eight times a year, from October through May. Both periodicals provide reports on ERIC/RCS materials and reviews of instructional materials. The February 1978 issue of each included an extensive list of "New Materials on the Market," compiled by Hilda Stauffer using information supplied by publishers and producers. These materials were coded for type (format), reading difficulty, interest level, and skills developed.

Beyond these valuable periodicals, the IRA publication program — which offers discounts to members — issues nine series, including:

Reading Aids (practical suggestions for classroom teachers) with such titles as —

> *Reading and the Bilingual Child* ($3.00)
> *Improving Reading in Science* ($3.50)

Monographs such as —

> *Reading in the Content Areas*, by James Laffey

Annotated Bibliographies with titles like —

> *Sources of Good Books for Poor Readers* ($0.75)
> *Individualized Reading* ($0.75)
> *Reading Programs in Secondary Schools* ($0.75)
> *Assessing Reading Behavior: Informal Reading Inventories* ($2.00)
> *Case Studies in Reading* ($0.75)

Convention Publications such as —

> *Reading Interaction: The Teacher, the Pupil, the Materials* ($5.00)

Some other IRA materials are listed as Key Publications; others are incorporated in other chapters of this book.

National Council of Teachers of English (NCTE)
1111 Kenyon Rd.
Urbana, IL 61801   (217) 328-3870

The NCTE is a non-profit membership organization, the world's largest subject-matter association, with 100,000 members — mostly teachers, administrators, and institutions. Its focus is the concerns of English and language teachers at all levels — elementary, secondary, and college. It aids these through advice, guidance, professional meetings, and a substantial body of publications. It is also the headquarters office of the ERIC Clearinghouse on Reading and Communication Skills.

Its wide-ranging members have their choice of three grade-level sections as well as special-interest groups (e.g., adolescent literature), and committees that deal with such professional concerns as sexism, censorship, students' right to learn, teachers' right to teach, classroom practices, and curriculum. NCTE has been in the vanguard on the issues of sexism and censorship—logically enough, since high school English teachers as a group are vulnerable and exposed. NCTE groups hold more than 20 separate conventions, conferences, institutes and workshops each year, whose proceedings are often reproduced and excerpted in print or cassette format.

Its membership includes a choice of three professional journals, *Language Arts, English Journal*, and *College English*, addressed respectively to elementary, secondary, and college teachers. All include valuable materials on theory, classroom practices, and current issues, as well as reviews of instructional materials.

Its 1977-78 catalog of professional publications (free on request) included more than 400 items, mostly in print or cassette format, with a few literary maps. Its wide-ranging professional output includes useful policy positions on censorship, sexism, and the like; annotated book lists and resource guides; classroom ideas; materials for reading, composition, poetry, language, and drama; ESL materials; dialect materials; reference aids; and materials on media. Most of these offerings—readily accessible in its well-arranged and well-indexed catalog—have some bearing on materials selection. A few of the more relevant are listed here. Others are incorporated as "Key Publications."

Publications (Print)—

Censorship, edited by Marion Gleason (1969. 47p. $2.25)

Censorship and the Values of Fiction, by Wayne Booth (1964. 12p. $0.50)

Classroom Practices in Teaching English: Responses to Sexism, edited by Oida H. Clapp (1977. 150p. $4.95)

Inventing and Playing Games in the English Classroom: A Handbook for Teachers, by Ken Davis and John Hollowell (1977. $6.50)

Women and Girls, edited by Iris Tiedt (1977. 105p. $3.00)

Cassettes—

Ideology, Censorship and Textbook Adoptions, by George Hillocks and Charles Suhor (1976. 59 minutes. $6.00)

Sexism in Reading Materials, by Doris Gunderson and Norma Wilson (1975. 60 minutes. $6.00)

NCTE also serves as headquarters for the ERIC Clearinghouse on Reading and Communication Skills (ERIC/RCS) which, like other clearinghouses, culls professional literature, publishes relevant materials in microfiche format, and prepares abstracts for *Resources in Education* (*RIE*) and *Current Index to Journals in Education* (*CIJE*).

The Clearinghouse examines literature reviews, research reports, conference papers, project and program reviews, curriculum guides and descriptions, and periodical literature in its areas of concern. Most important perhaps are materials produced by state education departments and school districts. The scope includes all aspects of reading—psychomotor, cognitive and affective—as well as professional materials related to reading guidance, classroom techniques, identification, diagnosis, and reading improvement. It covers English as a native language—as a symbol system, and in relation to speaking, listen-writing, and reading literature. Journalism education includes the creation, interpretation, and evaluation of journalism in all media. Speech sciences include theater, oral interpretations, public speaking, rhetoric, group interaction, and media presentations.

This Clearinghouse maintains quality control of documents through joint evaluation committees set up with other cooperating organizations like the International Reading Association, the Speech Communication Association, the Journalism Education Association, and others.

As might be expected from its language specialization, ERIC/RCS publications are quite extensive. One useful booklet series is the *TRIP Series* (Theory and Research Into Practice) which uses research as a basis for classroom-oriented practices. A typical title is *Structuring Reading Activities for Reading Classes* (1976. $1.95, with quantity discount).

ERIC/RCS issues bibliographies in many formats, including convenient annotated bookmark bibliographies of resources on topics like creative dramàtics, improving self-concept through reading, teaching guides for reading teachers, etc. These bibliographies select appropriate resources from professional conferences, commercial publishers, private organizations, educational associations, school jurisdictions, and state departments of education.

Right to Read Program
Information and Materials Branch
Administrative Services Division
U.S. Office of Education
Washington, DC 20202   (202) 245-8387

The Right to Read Program—founded in 1970—is an umbrella program that uses three strategies to assure literacy for school children and adults in the U.S. Its basic dissemination strategies are the establishment of demonstration programs, designation of Right to Read states, and support of national impact programs and special-emphasis projects.

It has produced materials to aid in teaching reading and achieving literacy. Some are for sale by the U.S. Government Printing Office. Others are distributed without charge. In addition to the items below—single copies of which are available free—the program has produced brochures, briefing papers and IRA briefing reports, which give information concerning all aspects of the Right to Read effort, as well as five Right to Read posters created by Morrie Turner, the cartoonist who created the *Wee Pals* King Syndicate comic strip.

HANDBOOKS

Right to Read Assessment and Planning Handbook ($2.35. GPO Stock No. 017-080-01390-8).
"A step-by-step process for systematically planning a reading program."

Tutor-Trainers' Resource Handbook ($1.90. GPO Stock No. 1780-01334).
"For planning, development and administration of a volunteer tutor program."

Tutor Resource Handbook for Teachers ($0.75. GPO Stock No. 1780-01332).
"For effective utilization of tutors by classroom teachers."

Tutors' Resource Handbook ($2.15. GPO Stock No. 1780-01333).
"For tutors to develop their roles both inside and outside [the] classroom."

MANUALS

Developing the Leadership Role. "A resource book for principals."

Leadership: Principals and Reading Programs. "Practical and specific suggestions to both elementary and secondary personnel."

Right to Read Administrator Leadership Clinics. "Illustrating that the effectiveness of Right To Read Programs [is] directly related to the leadership skills possessed by the principal."

Parents' Kit for Children's Pre-Reading Activities.

Reading Aids and Ideas for Parents.

Reading Assessment Scale, "That All May Read." "For the reading teacher (to accompany *Right to Read Assessment and Planning Handbook*)."

OTHER AIDS AND MATERIALS

Right to Read Summer Kit. "An aid for those interested in developing reading programs as part of their summer activities for children."

The First Four Years of Right to Read, by Ruth Love Holloway. "A detailed summary of the development of the Right to Read effort."

The Reading Crisis in America ($0.40. GPO Stock No. 1780-011310). "An illustrated brochure that dramatizes the reading problem in the U.S."

KEY PUBLICATIONS

I have not included standard reference tools in English, such as guides to plays, short stories, poetry, historical fiction, etc., which are excellent finding devices for teachers at all levels. Christine Wynar's *Guide to Reference Books for School Media Centers* (Littleton, CO: Libraries Unlimited, 1973) and its *Supplement* (1976) include a good assortment of these. These tools, logically arranged and annotated, are used far less than they should be in selecting materials.

Assessment Problems in Reading, edited by Walter H. MacGinitie. Newark, DE: International Reading Association, 1973. 101p. $4.50 ($3.00 members).

Deals with a wide spectrum of assessment problems in reading and indicates ways to improve instruction through more effective assessment of the pupil, teachers, classroom organization, and instructional materials.

Chicorel Index to Poetry: Poetry on Discs, Tapes, and Cassettes. New York: Chicorel, 1972. 443p. $60.00.

Indexes 700 collections of poetry in audio formats, with information on contents, subjects, label and number, price, and release date. Indexes are by author, individual titles, first line of poetry, and performer.

Effective Reading Programs: Summaries of 222 Selected Programs, by the Right to Read Effort, U.S. Office of Education. Washington, DC, 1975. 251p. $6.95. (Distributed by the National Council of Teachers of English).

This catalog describes more than 200 reading programs that were in operation for at least two years and that were effective in raising reading scores. Programs are coded so that more detailed descriptions can be obtained through the ERIC system.

Enrichment Ideas, by Ruth Kearney Carlson. 2nd ed. Dubuque, IA: William C. Brown, 1976. 166p. $2.50pa.

Provides teaching ideas and lists of children's books, on topics related to language, with a good section on ways to plan and organize reading—for example: free reading, bibliotherapy, contracts, self-selection. Language topics include: "miracle of language," "wonderland of words," "Oriental culture," "creative literature," "loneliness," plus a new chapter on controversial issues in children's literature. This last section explores many issues that are examined in this book and its companions: racial and sexual stereotyping, death and violence in children's books, book selection and censorship, handling of religion, etc. One enrichment idea that is applicable to the present chapter is for children to read and evaluate controversial books.

Federal Funds for Reading: NAVA Special Report, by Mary Ernst, edited by Kathleen M. Springer. Fairfax, VA: National Audio-Visual Association, 1977. 88p. $6.00pa. (prepaid).

This reasonably current compilation describes 18 federal programs that provide funds for reading and for materials to implement reading, and includes analyses of plans for spending money in 1978.

The guide begins with a NAVA survey of state legislation on competency. The bulk of the book is organized by programs: elementary and secondary, early childhood, higher education, adult education, and library programs. Part journalistic and part directory, it provides names and addresses of contact persons and grant recipients, as well as easy-to-understand accounts of the purposes and apparent trends in various reading programs. There is an understandable emphasis on funds for audiovisual expenditures.

Gateways to Readable Books: An Annotated Graded List of Books in Many Fields for Adolescents Who Are Reluctant to Read or Find Reading Difficult, by Dorothy E. Withrow, Helen B. Carey, and Bertha M. Hirzel. 5th ed. New York: H. W. Wilson, 1975. 299p. $12.00.

The fifth edition of this classic resource—for slow, retarded and reluctant readers—includes more than 1,000 titles of trade books in categories like careers, adventure, minorities, sports, and community problems. Entries include bibliographic information, fairly good annotations, and an indication of reading difficulty (generally a professional consensus). Books range in difficulty from pre-primer to eighth-grade levels. It does include some popular titles and titles of other book lists for reluctant readers. Other helpful sections discuss and suggest reading texts, books in series, simplified dictionaries, magazines and newspapers. There is a reading level index in addition to the usual author and title indexes.

Getting People to Read: Volunteer Programs That Work, by Carl B. Smith and Leo C. Far. New York: Dell, 1973. 238p. $2.95pa.

This idea book and source book includes discussions of successful age-level programs for children of all ages—pre-school to high school, with information on organization, evaluation, and roles of tutors. It includes sample lesson plans and an extensive bibliography of supportive reading.

Good Reading for Poor Readers, by George D. Spache. 9th ed. Champaign, IL: Garrard, 1974. 303p. $5.75pa.

The ninth edition of this well-known guide lists approximately 1,800 titles for remedial reading, arranged under broad categories, with brief annotations and bibliographic descriptions but no prices (though reading and interest levels are indicated). Materials include trade books, simplified books, textbooks, magazines, series, programmed materials, games, and visual aids. The first four chapters discuss ways of choosing books to match children's abilities and needs, and present a survey of readability formulas. Appendixes include Spache's readability format (with a criticism of the reliability of Fry's graph) as well as author and title indexes and a directory of publishers.

A Guide to Information Sources for Reading, compiled by Ronnie M. Davis. Newark, DE: International Reading Association, 1972 (reprinted 1975). 158p. $5.00pa.; $3.50 for members. (From IRA, 800 Barksdale Rd., Newark, DE 19711).

This slightly outdated guide provides a convenient, comprehensive survey to research and reference materials on all aspects of reading, with entries that involve instructional materials; handbooks, and guides to materials; annotated bibliographies and compilations of materials; and inventories of projects and activities. One particularly valuable section is its title guide to the reading-related conferences and proceedings of 19 educational organizations.

The guide in general is an explication of reference books, directories, indexes, associations, journals, etc., that are useful in research in reading. It provides brief annotations to reading information sources, to some important general reference sources, and to intelligently-selected resources in related areas like education, medicine and behavioral sciences. Unfortunately, since the information is current as of 1972, it provides limited access to the materials of the 1970s.

A Guide to Post-Classical Works of Art, Literature, and Music Based on Myths of the Greeks and Romans, by Ron Smith. Urbana, IL: National Council of Teachers of English, 1976. 24p. $1.90pa.

This convenient guide lists a variety of works in art, music and literature, based on Greek or Roman mythology. These are separated by category and arranged alphabetically according to the key person, event, or place in the myths. A separate bibliography lists secondary sources on the adaption of classical myths by artists, writers and composers.

Handbook for Storytellers, by Caroline Feller Bauer. Chicago: American Library Association, 1977. 400p. $15.00.

This unusual handbook for teachers, librarians, parents, and volunteers demonstrates ways and means to use media effectively in presenting stories to audiences of all ages—from pre-school to seniors. It indicates how to relate media—such as film, music, puppetry, crafts (and magic)—to stories and how to create these media as needed. It includes a variety of subject bibliographies for choosing stories for all occasions. Though this book was intended primarily as a program aid and includes a few sample storytelling programs, it has many other school applications for subject units, class projects, and individualization.

High-Interest-Low Vocabulary Reading Materials, compiled by Thomas E. Culliton and others. Boston: Boston University School of Education, 1978. $3.00. (Reprint of February 1978 issue of the *Journal of Education*). (From 765 Commonwealth Ave., Boston, MA 02215).

This annotated bibliography, a supplement to the original *High Interest-Low Vocabulary Booklist* which appeared in 1957, is, like its predecessor, designed to help select materials for students who have difficulty reading up to grade levels. Generally, materials were chosen with interest levels considerably higher than the vocabulary level (which ranges from grades one through eight). This list has five graded bibliographies on interest topics: birds, animals, biographies, sports, and social problems. (An earlier *1967 Supplement* was curriculum-related.) Essentially, the list includes a number of attractive books of good quality. "Interest" here was determined not only by subject but by such factors as size of book, use of personal pronouns, size of print, spacing, length of line, arrangement, and pictures. Vocabulary levels were determined through techniques devised by Botel, Fry, and Dale-Chall. Other factors affecting inclusion were sentence structure and degree of abstraction. Annotations, which are informative rather than provocative, include interest levels for each book.

How to Teach Reading with Children's Books, by Jeannette Veatch, illustrated by Warren Goodrich. New York: Teachers College Bureau of Publications, 1964. Unpaged. $0.75. (From Columbia University Bureau of Publications, Teachers College, New York, NY 10027).

This simple booklet, which looks like a child's book, provides step-by-step instructions for using trade books to teach reading in classrooms.

I Read, You Read, We Read; I See, You See, We See; I Hear, You Hear, We Hear; I Learn, You Learn, We Learn, compiled by American Library Association, Library Service to the Disadvantaged Committee. Chicago: American Library Association, 1971. 104p. $2.00pa.

This book list (an outgrowth of an earlier booklet prepared for the Office of Economic Opportunity) is still a useful selection tool despite its date and its cumbersome title. Fourteen hundred books, seemingly chosen to appeal to children who think they do not like books, are categorized into four broad age groups: pre-school, 5 to 8, 9 to 11, and 12 to 14. While most titles appeared prior to 1970, most of the books are available in libraries and most should still appeal to the target groups.

Independent Reading, Grades One through Three: An Annotated Bibliography with Reading Levels, by Gale S. Jacob. Williamsport, PA: Bro-Dart, 1975. 86p. $3.95pa.

This excellent reference source for teachers, parents, and librarians is an annotated bibliography of 850 books rigorously examined for appeal (content and format), literary merit, accuracy (if non-fiction), and Spache reading level. (This particular format makes fine distinctions of months within reading levels so that each book cited is assigned to a half-grade reading level.)

Slightly more than one-half of the books were published after 1970, though the bibliography does include a few classics which go back to the thirties. Almost all are in print, and most should be easily located in libraries. Books are categorized in 29 diverse subjects which seem to correspond reasonably well to primary reading interests, like animals, arts, crafts, family relationships, nature study, sports, transportation, etc. Extensive cross references are used in the table of contents and in the body of the work. There is an author-title index as well as a separate reading-level index. Information includes 1975 prices and sources. Altogether convenient and helpful.

Individualized Reading: An Annotated Bibliography, by Sam Duker. Springfield, IL: C. C. Thomas, 1971. 209p. $10.75.

Though not quite current, this meticulously-annotated, well-indexed, comprehensive bibliography is an invaluable tool for anyone who wants to attempt to individualize reading through student (self) selection at any grade level. It summarizes a great deal of research and classroom experiences with annotations sufficiently precise and detailed that the gist of each approach is apparent. According to the research reports summarized here, individualized reading resulted in improved reading scores and comprehension in the overwhelming majority of cases.

Issues in Evaluating Reading, edited by Stanley F. Wanta. Arlington, VA: Center for Applied Linguistics, 1977. 63p. $4.95pa.

This collection of articles deals with content, forms and uses of reading tests and with the evaluation of reading.

Literature and Young Children, edited by Bernice E. Cullinan and Carolyn W. Carmichael. Urbana, IL: National Council of Teachers of English (also distributed by American Library Association), 1977. 192p. $7.95.

This book by specialists in children's literature identifies educational objectives relating to children's literature and demonstrates different methods of increasing language development and reading ability, nurturing imagination, and encouraging authentic, satisfying emotional responses through such literature. It suggests ways to use pantomime, puppetry, and dramatics to present stories and poetry, and includes a study on measuring the impact of literature through children's verbal and non-verbal responses. An annotated bibliography of 100 books was tested on many children.

Middle Schools Literature Survey, compiled by William G. Dexter. Boston: National Association of Independent Schools, 1977. Unpaged. $2.00.

This is a title-author listing of literature books currently used in fifth through ninth grade classes in 126 independent schools across the country, with separate lists for Dickens and Shakespeare, and asterisks on books which were "particularly successful." There is a final, seven-page title-author listing of these books at the end, which indicates the grade or level in which these books were especially successful.

Milton Bradley's Reading Plan: Materials for Use with Major Reading Management Systems and Basal Reading Programs, compiled by John Pescosolido. Springfield, MA: Milton Bradley Company, 1976. 22p. Free. (Send letter on school letterhead). (From Milton Bradley Company, Springfield, MA 01101, Attn: Advertising Department).

While the ultimate purpose of this interesting and convenient brochure may be to facilitate the sale of Milton Bradley reading aids, it includes helpful charts that can be used to compare and analyze basic reading tests as well as criterion-reference systems. In essence, these charts correlate 60 specific skills (presented as behavioral objectives) with tests from criterion measurement systems intended to measure these skills with appropriate educational materials from Milton Bradley.

The 61 behavioral skills are very well thought out, and they encompass a variety of testing strategies and allow for alternatives. They are grouped in five broad categories: decoding skills, structural skills, vocabulary skills, comprehension skills and study skills.

This booklet analyzes the Ginn Reading 360, Harper and Row Design for Reading, Holt Basic Reading System, Houghton Mifflin Reading Program, Macmillan Reading Program, and Scott Foresman Reading Systems. It could be used to analyze and compare other texts as well. It would seem to be a good diagnostic instrument for assessing needs and prescribing reading for individual students or groups of students, and hence a useful tool in individualizing.

This publication, like some others by Milton Bradley, includes concepts, suggestions, and information that transcend the usual boundaries of the materials catalog genre. Criterion-reference systems analyzed include Cooper-McGuire Word-Analysis Test, McGuire-Bumpus Diagnostic Comprehension Test, Diagnosis: An Instructional Aid (Science Research Associates), Mountain Valley Teacher Support System in Reading, Prescriptive Reading Inventory, Criterion Reading, and Wisconsin Design for Reading Skill Development.

A Multimedia Approach to Children's Literature: A Selective List of Films, Filmstrips, and Recordings Based on Children's Books, by Ellin Greene and Madalynne Schoenfeld. 2nd ed. Chicago: American Library Association, 1977. 206p. $6.00.

The second edition of this valuable tool selects and annotates media which can be used to introduce books to children from preschool to grade six. It lists more than 500 children's books alphabetically by title, followed by descriptions of films, filmstrips, and/or disc or tape recordings for introducing each book. All items were chosen on the basis of first-hand examination and experience with children. Motivating genres include picture books, traditional and folk literature, fiction, drama, fairy tales, and poetry as well as books on children's authors and illustrators. There are additional annotated lists of selection aids, program aids, realia and related readings, a directory of distributors, and indexes by author, subject and medium.

Annotations of individual items include bibliographic descriptions, buying information (with price), and grade levels.

NCTE Guide to Teaching Materials for English: Grades 7-12. Urbana, IL: National Council of Teachers of English, 1974- . 171p. $3.95pa. *1975-76 Supplement*. 129p. $3.95pa. Both $7.60 ($6.00 to members).

The basic *NCTE Guide* (for 1974-75) was an annotated listing of 550 textbooks and related materials (about 800 items in all) including anthologies, workbooks, and other print-based materials arranged in 16 subject-curriculum areas: e.g., anthologies, reading, language skills, vocabulary, mass media, humanities, drama, film, and tests. Entries include titles, series titles, editors, publisher, publication date, primary and extended audiences, and reading levels for each, with annotations that describe scope and teaching methodology, units of study, illustrations, tests, glossaries, and other supportive features. Pages, prices, and grade levels are supplied for all individual titles.

The *1975-76 Supplement* uses the same approach and format for 260 additional titles (print instructional materials from 19 publishers). Volumes include directories of included publishers.

While annotations for both volumes are descriptive rather than evaluative, these guides locate and cite reviews in NCTE publications. Entries are indexed by author, editor, title and ability level. These ability-level indexes also list series appropriate for accelerated or remedial readers. Overall this is an extremely helpful tool, especially for textbook selection. It should be consulted frequently by librarians and teachers in senior and junior high schools.

The New Hooked on Books, by Daniel Fader, with James Duggins, Tom Finn, and Elton McNeil. New York: Berkely Publications, 1976. 294p. $1.75pa. (Tenth Anniversary Edition).

This new edition of *Hooked on Books* incorporates much of the old edition as Chapter 4, but surrounds it with retrospective essays, practical how-to articles, and a completely recast paperback reading list, "One Thousand Authors." Titles on this list were chosen solely because they appealed to young readers.

The *New Hooked on Books* manages to combine the inspiration of the original with a good amount of practical assistance. A new long essay, "On the Teaching of Writing," incorporates research and personal experiences. Chapters on "The Elementary Self-Contained Classroom," "Secondary Schools," and "Administering the Program" reflect the authors' extensive experiences—both successes and failures—with the Hooked on Books program in northern California schools. Essay chapters, such as "Remembering Ourselves," "A Classroom Full of Teachers," and "Toward a Professional Union," try to provide a more current context for the program.

The "Hooked on Research" chapter includes student interest forms and questionnaires to be filled out by students, which identify literacy lovers and haters, school lovers and haters, and gradations between. The appendix has sample lesson plans for achieving reading objectives with trade books, as well as a directory of the Educational Paperback Association (arranged by state), reading suggestions for participating teachers, and a reprint of the Right to Read statement of the National Council of Teachers of English.

This $1.75 book should help any teacher develop a well-thought-through reading program for less than $100 per year per classroom. "Managing the Program" by James Duggins is particularly helpful.

Reading and Language Arts: Products from NIE, prepared for the National Institute of Education by the Far West Laboratory for Educational Research and Development. Washington, DC: GPO, 1977. 120p. $2.20. (Stock no. 017-080-01759-8). (From Superintendent of Documents, GPO, Washington, DC 20401).

This recent catalog includes current options for students and teachers developed or partially funded by the National Institute of Education generally through educational laboratories or through university-based research and development centers.

The 75 products in this catalog either focus on the language arts—reading, writing, and oral language—or include major components with that focus. These products are grouped into four major categories: early childhood, elementary, secondary, and guides/training materials. Within these categories, products are listed and described according to a convenient format developed by the Far West Lab that includes implementation requirements, services available, assurances and claims, and contact persons. Another section has a formatted directory of resources in reading and language arts. The appendix includes indexes by title and subject (e.g., career education, composition, biculturalism), addresses of developers and their products, and a description of the agencies and purpose of the Research and Development Exchange (RDx) — a rather complex government-sponsored effort attempting to facilitate communication between educational developers and practitioners.

Reading and the Curriculum, edited by John Merritt. Newark, DE: International Reading Association, 1971. 248p. $3.50.

Discusses reading and the curriculum at all levels; television and printed media; readability; and literacy.

Reading Interaction: The Teacher, the Pupil, the Materials, edited by Brother Leonard Courtney. Newark, DE: International Reading Association, 1976. 418p. $5.00 ($3.50 to members).

These papers deal with the creation, development and use of materials to facilitate teaching, and with the human and professional qualities that enliven teaching.

Searching the Professional Literature in Reading, by Joan F. Curry and William P. Morris. Newark, DE: International Reading Association, 1975. 50p. $3.00pa. ($2.00 for members).

This booklet, appropriate for classroom teachers and reading specialists, constitutes a simple introduction to literature searching. The first chapters provide guidance to teachers who want to keep up to date on a topic, to obtain an overview of a familiar topic, and/or to pursue a limited (reading) topic in depth. Chapter five demonstrates an ERIC search on the topic of individualized reading. Overall, this can help users locate appropriate reading materials for particular students or purposes.

Selected Print and Nonprint Resources in Speech Communication: An Annotated Bibliography K-12, by Jerry D. Feezel, Kent R. Brown, and Carol A. Valentine. Urbana, IL: National Council of Teachers of English, 1976. 68p. $2.95pa.

An annotated bibliography of resources for both teachers and students — about 200 resources in all, arranged by medium, content, and grade level, with suggestions for classroom use and an additional subject index.

Selecting and Evaluating Beginning Reading Materials, by Educational Products Information Exchange. New York: EPIE Institute, 1974. (EPIE Report 62/63). 105p. $10.00.

This document, essentially a comprehensive presentation of EPIE's Instructional Design Analysis System, includes much supportive and backup information valuable for educators selecting instructional materials in reading:

- a discussion of the roles of materials in reading instruction
- a historical survey of efforts to improve reading instruction
- descriptions of four distinct views of reading instruction
- a checklist to help educators clarify their own views
- a flow chart (with detailed explanations) of the tasks that must be coordinated in selecting materials in the contexts of school, community, curriculum, and staff

EPIE's Report 64, *Analyses of Basic and Supplementary Reading Materials* (also $10.00), uses this Instructional Design Analysis to analyze and evaluate 76 commercially-marketed reading series.

Selector's Guide for Elementary School Reading Programs. 2v. New York: EPIE Institute, 1977. (EPIE Reports 82M and 83M). Vol. 1, 83p.; Vol. 2, 84p. $20.00 each.

Each of these two volumes analyzes about 15 different elementary school reading programs; some are accompanied with user data from about 1,500 teachers. Volume I includes a detailed presentation of EPIE's current materials-selection model.

Sourcebook of Evaluation Techniques for Reading Programs, by James Laffey and Carl B. Smith (edited by June Gilstad). Bloomington, IN: Measurement and Evaluation Center in Reading Evaluation, University of Indiana, 1972. 191p. $4.50 plus postage and handling. (From MECRE, Room 211, Education Building, Bloomington, IN 47401).

This MECRE product is an updating and revision of Roger Farr's *Taxonomy of Evaluation Techniques for Reading Programs*, issued by MECRE in 1969. Both versions provide samples of formal and informal assessment instruments — checklists, questionnaires, interview forms, rating scales, tests, and guidelines relating to reading programs' goals, student and teacher skills, and materials for reading. One entire section is devoted to instruments designed to assess adequacy of materials, while other sections have many instruments that might be useful and relevant for selecting materials in school situations. For example, vocabulary tests and student interest inventories are included in the student section. Some of these instruments have been reprinted in this book, with the kind permission of MECRE.

This is a fine idea source for the casual browser; more rigorous users can follow the authors' suggestions to match local program objectives with appropriate measures.

MECRE has published other guides and analytic instruments that can be useful for reading teachers and selectors. These include: *Reading Games and Activities to Motivate Reluctant Readers in the Primary Grades*, by Virginia Tieman ($1.00); *Reading Thinking Skills for Maps and Globes*, by Carl B. Smith ($1.00); and *Comprehension: A Cognitive Process*, by William Olszewski ($1.00).

The Students' Right to Read, edited by Kenneth Donelson. 1972 ed. Urbana, IL: National Council of Teachers of English, 1972. 26p. $0.60pa. Quantity discount.

Suggests that English departments should write (and file with the administration) a statement explaining "why literature is taught and how books are chosen for each class." Each teacher is supposed to prepare a written "rationale" for every book to be read by an entire class.

It also suggests a committee of teachers, administrators, possibly students, parents, and other representatives of the community, to nurture support of citizens interested in education to encourage an "atmosphere of free inquiry." This committee is empowered to handle complaints, again in writing, by "would-be censors." This committee, meeting with both the teacher and the complainant, would rule on the validity of the complaint and make recommendations to the superintendent and then ultimately to the school board, which generally has the power to decide whether or not to remove the books from the curriculum.

Tom Swift and His Electric English Teacher: A Media Catalog, by G. Howard Poteet. Dayton, OH: Pflaum Publishing, 1974. 96p. $4.95pa.

This browsing catalog—modeled on the *Whole Earth Catalog*, with illustrations from the old Tom Swift books—lists a variety of equipment and materials for teaching English in off-beat ways. An appealing, if haphazard book, with interesting recommendations and an index that ties items together nicely. Includes a list of magazines.

FOR FURTHER READING

*Items marked with an asterisk include other criteria checklists.

+ Items marked with a plus include substantial lists of references.

+ American Library Association. Young Adult Services Division. *High Interest/Low Reading Level Information Packet*. Chicago: ALA, 1978.

"Back-to-Basics Movement: Analysis and Response," special issue of *English Education*, v. 9, no. 4 (Summer 1978).

Buchanan, Cynthia Dee. *Programmed Reading*. New York: Sullivan Associates (McGraw-Hill), 1966.

Chall, J. S. *An Analysis of Textbooks in Relation to Declining SAT Scores*. New York: College Entrance Examination Board, 1976.

+ Conte, Joseph M., and George H. Grimes. *Media and the Culturally Different Learner*. Washington, DC: National Education Association, 1969.

Cook, Ruth C., and Ronald C. Doll. *The Elementary School Curriculum*. Boston: Allyn and Bacon, 1973.

Copperman, Paul. *The Literacy Hoax*. New York: Morrow, 1978.

*Cox, D. R. "Criteria for Evaluation of Reading Materials," *The Reading Teacher*, v. 24, no. 2 (Nov. 1970), pp. 140-45.

Curatalo, Charles, comp. *Teacher-Made Materials for Language Arts*. Geneseo, NY: State University College of Arts and Science, 1972.

Echternacht, G. *A Comparative Study of Secondary Schools with Different Score Patterns*. New York: College Entrance Examination Boards, 1976.

Educational Testing Service. *Focus: Learning to Read*. Princeton, NJ: Educational Testing Service, 1978. (Focus 4).

Harmon, David. "Reading Tests," *National Elementary Principal*, v. 54, no. 6 (July-Aug. 1975), pp. 81-86.

*Johnson, E. M. "Guidelines for Evaluating New Instructional Programs," *The Reading Teacher*, v. 20, no. 7 (April 1967), pp. 600-604.

Johnson, Simon S. "How Students Feel about Literature," *American Education*, v. 10, no. 3 (April 1974), pp. 6-10.

*+Kohl, Herbert. *Reading, How to*. New York: Dutton, 1973.
Covers games, teaching techniques, lists of materials.

Lake County Intermediate Education District. *Using Music as a Vehicle to Teach Essential Reading Skills*. Lakeview, OR: 1976.

*+Lynch, James L., and Bertrand Evans. *High School English Textbooks: A Critical Examination*. Boston: Little, Brown, 1963.
This book, produced under the sponsorship of the Council for Basic Education, is a thorough, incisive survey and review of anthologies, grammar, and composition textbook series used in schools in the early 1960s. The thinking that underlies the specific analyses is still very relevant today.

*Mann, Philip H., and Patricia Suiter. *Handbook in Diagnostic Teaching: A Learning Disabilities Approach*. Boston: Allyn and Bacon, 1974.
Extremely practical handbook for teachers in grades K-6 on inventories and screening devices that can help determine the nature and extent of reading, spelling, and other developmental disabilities. Two chapters provide task-centered and process-oriented activities designed to correct these disabilities.

Moffett, James. *Teaching the Universe of Discourse*. Boston: Houghton Mifflin, 1968.

Morris, Joyce, editor. *The First R*. Newark, DE: International Reading Association, 1972.
These selected papers deal with theory, practice, research, media, materials, and remedial reading.

National Assessment of Educational Programs. *Recipes, Wrapper, Reasoning and Rate: A Digest of the First Reading Assessment*. (NAEP Report 02-R-30). Washington, DC: GPO, 1974.

Rand Corporation. *Analysis of School Preferred Reading Programs in Selected Los Angeles Minority Schools*. Santa Monica: Rand Corporation, 1976. (R-2007).
This study of 20 minority schools supports the interpretation that an individualized curriculum produces higher achievement and that teachers' use of a variety of materials is strongly related to reading achievement.

*"Reading," special issue of *Theory into Practice*, v. 16, no. 5 (Dec. 1977).
Fourteen articles on reading, many relevant to materials selection.

"Reading: Directions for Change," special issue of *Journal of Research and Development in Education*, v. 11, no. 3 (Spring 1978).

*+Ruddell, Robert B. *Reading-Language Instruction: Innovative Practices*. Englewood Cliffs, NJ: Prentice-Hall, 1974.
Outstanding criteria.

"Summary of Investigations Relating to Reading," special issue of *Reading Research Quarterly*, v. 13, no. 3 (1978).

Taft, Katherine D. "Using Science Activities to Improve Reading Readiness," *Curriculum Review*, v. 6, no. 5 (Dec. 1976), pp. 296-97.

Thorndike, Robert L. *Reading Comprehension Education in Fifteen Countries.* New York: Wiley, 1973. (International Studies in Evaluation III).

Weaver, Phylis, and Fredi Shonkeoff. *Research within Reach: A Research-Guided Response to Concerns of Reading Education.* (National Institute of Education). Washington, DC: GPO, 1978.

Wharton, Yvonne. *List of Hypotheses Advanced to Explain the SAT Score Decline.* New York: College Board, 1976.

Wood, Phyllis Anderson. "What Are We Doing with Books to Kids?" *Catholic Library World*, v. 49, no. 1 (July-Aug. 1977), pp. 10-15.

*Zimet, Sara G. *What Children Read in School: Critical Analysis of Primary Reading Textbooks.* New York: Grune & Stratton, 1972.

*Zimet, Sara G., G. E. Blom, and R. R. Waite. *A Teacher's Guide for Selecting Stories for Children—The Content of First Grade Reading Textbooks.* Detroit: Wayne State University Press, 1968.

SELECTING MATERIALS ON THE
WORLD OF WORK

"We must ... prepare students academically and also equip them for productive work."
— Ernest L. Boyer, U.S. Commissioner of Education, speech,
May 1979

"Whatever you can do, or dream you can, begin it."
— Johann Wolfgang von Goethe

"If you have built castles in the air, your work need not be lost; that is where they should be. Now put the foundations under them."
— Henry David Thoreau, *Walden*

□ □ □

This chapter, appropriately near the end, like consumer education, deals with materials to teach the tangibles and intangibles that students should have acquired — preschool through twelfth grade — to face the world of work in the years after high school. This chapter covers briefly, many aspects of materials on work-related education — not only career education, vocational education, or business education — roughly education *for* work, but also education *about* work, as well as the basic competencies that are essential for working. I am also incorporating materials on the labor movement and the right to work, since information on these aspects of work directly affects student perceptions of the world of work.

All these work-related materials should contain — at a minimum — clear, accurate, far-reaching, far-sighted, objective, and current information about the world of work and its requirements. These materials should present an overall prospectus, as well as information on specific careers — particularly those that appeal to your students and are appropriate for their skills and abilities. Handicapped students and students whose main language is not English require materials that address themselves to their particular needs.

Beyond awareness of work and career areas, career and vocational education should involve self-awareness related to career awareness; some minimal standards for social and interpersonal skills; abilities to solve problems and to make choices or decisions; appropriate role models; ideally, actual work experience; awareness of how to handle money and how to seek employment; assistance in guidance and planning; and a knowledge of how to use such resources as career information centers, guidance counselors, employment agencies, potential employers, and libraries to locate more information. Since information — per se — is an important aspect of career education, this chapter includes informational sources as well as sources or materials designed to instruct.

Presumably, the skills and knowledge acquired in schools — such as reading, writing, spelling, and arriving on time — are relevant and adequate for the post-high school world. If not, curricula should be revised and materials selected with these ends in mind. This view can make for more cogent learning and teaching and fewer dropouts.

Since most worthwhile education is relevant — in some way — to career education, the items selected for this chapter, represent, in a sense, only the tip of the

iceberg. Consider, for example, books, games, and filmstrips for critical thinking, deductive reasoning, self-knowledge, values, and choice, as well as exposure
to excellence in any or all curriculum areas.

While basic areas provide skills and competence, study areas such as creativity, social and sex roles, and the economic facts of life in the late twentieth century can facilitate good career choices. The facts should include existing patterns
of sex and race discrimination; admission policies and available aid for attending
colleges, graduate schools and trade schools; and the local and national extent of
unemployment. Collectively, instructional and informational materials have the
difficult task of combining accuracy with inspiration though each item need not
fulfill all purposes.

The Rural Connection, a discontinued project of the National Center for
Vocational Education, selected career education materials relating to any of the
career guidance functions listed below. This range seems appropriate for career
materials in general.

CAREER GUIDANCE FUNCTIONS

The following is a list of career guidance functions and the types of materials that could relate to the
functions.

1. **Career Guidance Program Planning** — Documents that present overall planning
   considerations for a career guidance program (e.g., staffing, organizing, timing, finances,
   evaluation).
2. **Individual Assessment** — Tools that aid in assessing (a) students' career development, interests,
   aptitude, etc., (b) school leavers' perceptions of career development needs, (c) community
   members' perceptions of students' career development needs, and (d) educators' perceptions of
   students' career development needs.
3. **Goal and Objective Development** — Documents on how to develop goals and objectives for a
   career guidance program based on local need.
4. **Resource Assessment** — Documents that describe how to assess material resources and how to
   identify, assess and use resources (materials, equipment, people, etc.) in the school and
   community.
5. **Evaluation** — Documents that describe evaluation at any of the following three levels: (a) determining the impact of individual units or activities, (b) determining the impact of a set of units,
   and (c) recycling the student career development need information for continuous validation of
   program.
6. **Career Guidance Curriculum Development** — Documents that explain how to develop an instructional unit that infuses career guidance content into a particular discipline.
7. **Career Guidance Activity Implementation** — Documents that aid in the implementation of a
   total program. Such areas as timing, staffing, infusion points, and resource availability would
   be discussed.
8. **Career Guidance Instructional Activities** — Documents that present information about the
   following career guidance content areas.

World of Work Understanding	Employability and Employment
Self Understanding	Career Planning
Decision Making	Occupational Preparation
Economic Understanding	Leisure and Avocational Preparation

9. **Placement**—Documents that describe educational, occupational, and special needs placement.
10. **Counseling**—Documents that describe techniques for group and individual counseling.
11. **Attitudes and Values**—Items dealing with (a) the assessment of and changing of negative attitudes staff, students, and community members might have towards career development, (b) assessing and overcoming stereotypic values in regards to sex, race, and socioeconomic issues.
12. **Community Relations and Involvement**—Documents that describe (a) how to communicate a program's progress to the community and (b) how to involve community members in the career guidance program.
13. **Staff Development**—Documents that describe staff development programs related to career guidance.
14. **Special Populations**—Documents that give particular attention to minorities, low income, women, gifted, and physically and mentally handicapped.

One fairly extensive catalog of instructional objectives (*Career Education: A Curriculum Design and Instructional Objectives*, by the American Institutes for Research) included objectives for the following categories:

- self-understanding and appreciation
- opportunities and options
- orientation and goal formulation
- goal exploration
- jobs and employment
- social responsibilities
- leisure
- status assessment
- personal planning
- analysis of options

More typically, career education is supposed to incorporate awareness, exploration, and preparation—with most materials and curricula on awareness directed towards elementary students, those on exploration toward students in middle school or junior high, and preparation left mostly for the high school years. Probably, there should be interactions—in different proportions—at all levels.

The basic attitude towards work—learned early—may be the most important of all. Research indicates that this is very difficult to change by high school age (where preparation is most frequently included). The best methods of developing appropriate productive attitudes seem to be observation, simulation, and discussion spread over several years and related to other school learning. Parents, of course, are the earliest career educators.

Walter Neff of NYU believes that work is somewhat comparable to sexuality in having its roots in early childhood experiences. He believes that in order to become workers as adults, we need certain kinds of experiences in early and middle childhood.

Means of learning at early school years can easily involve rather direct learning experiences—through field trips and exposure, in school and out, to role models in various occupations. Some national and community youth and children's groups provide excellent career exploration activities and programs outside school auspices. Well-known programs are carried out through the Humane Society, through Four H Clubs, Campfire Girls, Girl Scouts and Boy Scouts (especially Explorer Scouts), through Junior Achievement, Junior Academy of Science, Junior Engineering Technical Society, and, of course, through Future Teachers of America. These programs often provide hands-on activities rather well related to future occupational fields. Some of the materials and curricula are easily adaptable to in-school use. Educators certainly should be aware of such programs operating within their own communities.

Other desirable, fairly direct experiences for students of all ages include homemade and commercial games, activities, and simulations. Picture sets, such as *People at Work* (photographs) and *Non-Sexist Community Careers* (flannel board), as well as picture inlay occupation puzzles, are good familiarizing devices, particularly for young children (who also like dress-ups). These, of course, should be accompanied by discussion questions that clarify and expand specific occupational areas or the roles of work.

Recently, the Department of Health, Education, and Welfare has funded public television programs to help elementary school children explore job options. For example, Los Angeles' KCET-TV's "Freestyle" is a 13-episode series of half-hour programs produced at a cost of $4.1 million to alter sex and ethnic job stereotypes by intelligent, dramatic scripting and careful attention to detail and music. According to the series' executive director, Norton Wright: "The best way [to change attitudes] may be with a well-done drama."

Similarly, in Berkeley, California, the Office of Education's "Project Plan" funded by the Women's Equity Division is using participation drama or play excerpts to teach junior high students—particularly girls—career choices and planning. These both incorporate discussion and follow-through activities.

Though films, filmstrips, and other audio-visual materials are relatively expensive and can go out of date quickly, they are useful for work-related education, even though they are not as compelling as actual first-hand exposure. The Weinrach's article on evaluating career education materials (*Catholic Library World*, Nov. 1977) suggests that films and filmstrips should not be more than two years old (or checked for accuracy if older). The Weinrachs prefer a length of 15 to 20 minutes and say that they should not be longer than 25 minutes. These media should, of course, be free from job stereotypes as well as sex and race stereotypes. Ideally, they should include well selected details that provide a real feel for the skills, tasks, or occupations being presented, the kinds of people who are engaged in particular tasks, and the working conditions that surround them. Media should honestly represent the disadvantages of particular positions as well as the rewards, salaries, opportunities, prestige, psychological and social aspects of positions, plus their social contributions, decision-making responsibilities, and opportunities to use creative talents. Qualifications should be clearly specified.

Printed materials can be either imaginative or factual; some imaginative items are novels, short stories, or picture books about persons in particular occupations. For presenting and updating actual data on salaries, job outlooks, and the like, printed materials are probably the cheapest if not the most compelling media. Flyers and pamphlets with such information are often free or extremely inexpensive and are generally accurate, though materials from industries may not always present the full picture. Some printed materials—through judicious use of pictures and appealing role models—manage to combine inspiration with a great deal of factual data. Format, length and readability are other factors in selection. Somehow, the important facts should be presented clearly and understandably.

Since materials on occupations and occupational clusters become obsolete rather rapidly, free or inexpensive materials or annually updated reference books are important sources. These materials always require a lot of filing and clerical attention, even with the best classification systems. Career exploration materials, simulation games, decision-making curricula, and self-assessment tests have a much longer life expectancy, and can be used with a wider age range of children, if directions are written (or rewritten) carefully and clearly.

The following Career Evaluation Checklists are reprinted with permission from an article by Esther L. and Stephen G. Weinrach, "The Role of the Librarian in the Evaluation of Career Materials," which appeared in *Catholic Library World*, v. 49, no. 4 (Nov. 1977), pp. 170-73. They are based on the National Vocational Guidance Association's 1972 *Guidelines for the Preparation and Evaluation of Career Information Media* (Washington, DC: American Personnel and Guidance Association Press, 1972). The Weinrachs suggest that they be used by a media selection committee that includes guidance personnel.

CAREER FILM AND FILMSTRIP EVALUATION CHECKLIST

Title: _____ ( ) B/W   ( ) color

Producer/Distributor: _____

Cost: Purchase $ _____ Rental $ _____ Length_____ min.

Intended audience: _____

		Unsatisfactory	Satisfactory	Excellent
1.	A description of the nature of the occupation, field, or industry.			
2.	The benefits and satisfaction of the occupations.			
3.	The entry requirements.			
4.	The possibilities of advancement.			
5.	The employment outlook.			
6.	Related occupations to which a person might transfer.			
7.	Whether or not licensing or union membership is required.			
8.	Personal qualifications.			
9.	Relevancy for the intended audience.			
10.	The proper length.			
11.	Freedom from bias.			
12.	Credits.			
13.	The purpose.			
14.	A complete user's guide.			

Evaluated by: _____ Date: _____

CAREER LITERATURE EVALUATION CHECKLIST

Title: _____

_____

Publisher/Distributor: _____

Cost: $ _____ each   Number of pages: _____

Intended audience: _____

	Unsatisfactory	Satisfactory	Excellent
1. A description of the nature of the occupation, field, or industry.			
2. A realistic portrayal of the work setting.			
3. The benefits and satisfactions of the occupations.			
4. The entry requirements.			
5. The possibilities of advancement.			
6. The employment outlook.			
7. Related occupations to which a person might transfer.			
8. Whether or not licensing or union membership is required.			
9. Written on the level of the intended audience.			
10. Interesting format.			
11. Enhancing photographs and graphs.			
12. Recent date of publication.			
13. Freedom from bias.			
14. Credits.			
15. Bibliography.			
16. Training information.			
17. Sources of financial and training employment.			

Evaluated by: _____ Date: _____

While many materials succeed fairly well in presenting at least most of the aspects above, fewer informational materials include information on:

- bargaining powers of employees; unions and labor policies
- possibilities of on-job training
- health and physical requirements
- safety and health hazards
- preparation costs and time
- sources of training other than colleges

- likely job security, probable length of active employment
- relevant legislation and government agencies
- starting, ultimate, and average salaries, including pensions, paid vacations, and annuities
- hours of work and lengths of vacations

Labor unions and the Concerned Educators Against Forced Unionism both perceive inadequate information on the roles of organized labor. The Center for Economic Education in Denton, Texas, perceives a bias in favor of professional work modes.

Materials for "preparation" are mainly the purlieu of vocational education, and business, agriculture, and industrial arts education. These rely to a great extent on a more or less accurate recreation of the world of work — complete with auto shop equipment, electronics assemblies, electrical typewriters, or whatever is required. Sometimes it is the turn of the century woodshop. Purchasing and updating the equipment for such courses can be extremely expensive, though sometimes arrangements can be made with industry. In California — following Proposition 13 — these courses have suffered. If vocational education courses have to attempt to teach with outdated equipment that does not represent current realities, they lose much of their value. However, full scale materials for these courses can be supplemented by some representations, including pictures, slides, filmstrips, models, and cutaways. Printed realia for these courses are relatively easy to keep current, particularly for business and distributive education. These particular courses should include local business forms and records, business handbooks and instructional manuals, reference books on business trades, and industry as well as trade newsletters, publications, periodicals, advertisements, etc. These fields also have relatively competent educational periodicals, which succeed relatively well in reviewing current materials. Films and filmstrips for these areas can be selected through *Training Film Profiles*. Other useful teaching materials are pamphlets, posters, charts, graphs, and pictures. Slides — both homemade and commercial — are good teaching devices, particularly for manual skills.

One problem with these job-related programs stems from their philosophical — and often physical — separation from the rest of the high school curriculum. Though they often succeed in their teaching goals — given enough money and equipment — their programs may not be well-integrated with traditionally academic school offerings, even where liaison would be natural and beneficial. This may be due to their historic origins in the early 1900s to prepare (often less verbal or less able) students for jobs below professional levels. Traditionally, they have often been close to job markets for specific jobs.

Traditionally, also, these programs have been rather sex-segregated, with boys directed towards agriculture, industries, and shop, and girls relegated to cooking, home economics, health, and office practices. More recently, some vocational educators and their associations have tried to design programs and materials free of bias. Two helpful publications, prepared by Women on Words and Images, are *Guidelines for Sex-Fair Vocational Education Materials* and *Guidelines for the Creative Use of Biased Materials in an Unbiased Way*. The latter may be particularly important.

WOWI's basic guidelines for sex-fair materials included the following criteria:

1) 50-50 balance of males and females in any material,
2) sex neutral or sex-fair language,
3) specific mention of issues involved in nontraditional career choices for males and females, and
4) sex-fair occupational descriptions that accurately reflect performance requirements.

Some detailed questions for analyzing social and occupational roles are listed below. WOWI provides others for language, omissions, audiovisuals, and physical appearance.

- Are all occupations presented as appropriate to qualified persons of either sex?
- Are certain jobs automatically associated with women and others associated with men (e.g., practical nurse, secretary—female; construction worker, plumber—male)?
- Are housekeeping and family responsibilities still a prime consideration for females in choosing and maintaining a career (e.g., flexible hours, proximity to home)?
- Is the wife presented as needing permission from her husband in order to work (e.g., higher income tax bracket)?
- Is it assumed that the boss, executive, professional, etc., will be male and the assistant, helpmate, "gal Friday" will be female?
- In addition to professional responsibilities, is it assumed that women will also have housekeeping tasks at their place of business (e.g., in an assembly plant with workers of both sexes, the females make the coffee)?
- Is tokenism apparent, an occasional reference to women or men in nontraditional jobs, while the greatet proportion of the material remains job stereotyped (e.g., one female plumber, one black woman electrician)?
- Are men and women portrayed as having sex-linked personality traits that influence their working abilities (e.g., the brusque foreman, the female bookkeeper's loving attention to detail)?
- Are only females shown as passive and inept?
- Are only females shown as lacking in desire to assume responsibility? (e.g., She was delighted to have risen to be "head secretary.")
- Are only females shown as emotional? (e.g., The secretary cried easily and was very thin-skinned.)
- Are only females presented as gossips?
- Are only women shown as vain and especially concerned with their appearance?
- Are only females presented as fearful and in need of protection? (e.g., She wasn't able to work late and walk home at night.)
- Are only males shown as capable, aggressive and always in charge?

- Are only males shown as brave and relentlessly strong?
- Do only males consistently display self-control and restraint?
- Are opportunities overlooked to present a range of emotional traits for females and males?
- Are women and men assigned the traditional roles of males as bread-winner and female as caretaker of home and children?
- Is a woman's marital status stated when it is irrelevant and when the same information about the man is not available (e.g., Mr. Clark and Mrs. Brown were co-workers.)
- In a family where both adults work is it assumed that females are responsible for indoor housekeeping chores and males are responsible for outdoor lawn and car chores?
- If a couple work together in a business is it assumed that she will assist him (e.g., Mary does bookkeeping and secretarial chores while Dan decides policy and attends to any heavy work.)?
- Is information included about family relationships which is not relevant to the task (e.g., Jane Dawson, mother of four, is the new supervisor)?
- Has the writer overlooked opportunities to present equality in occupational or social roles?

Career education, a somewhat nebulous term apparently invented in 1970 by James Allen, then U.S. Commissioner of Education, was popularized by the following Commissioner, Sydney P. Marland. Marland is generally considered the father of career education. Though the term was not precisely defined, it was generally supposed to:

- include education for and about work, using a variety of models
- increase career options open to individuals
- assure that every high school graduate was adequately prepared for either continuing education or productive work.

This last has been propounded by every Commissioner of Education. Following Kenneth Hoyt's *Career Education: What It Is and How to Do It* (Salt Lake City, UT: Olympus Publishing Co., 1974), most definitions agree that:

- The program should involve all parts of the school program and the entire community
- Ideally, career education should begin in the home or with the first year of school
- Self-awareness and exploration are important elements that should be related to the world of work
- Major goals are to increase individual career options and to make work possible, meaningful, and satisfying
- Career education is concerned with education for both paid and unpaid work
- Since work changes, career education should continue through life.

Materials should reflect these priorities, as well as outside working'realities. Community, parental, and student acceptance are important features.

One problem in all sorts of work-oriented education is the basic difficulty involved in economic forecasting and job forecasting, particularly in periods of flux; educators are often not aware of new job opportunities and alternatives. Certain long-range trends are discouraging—for example, increase in teenage unemployment for all teenagers, but especially for minority teenagers. In this context, programs that train for flexibility and for learning how to learn may be more valuable than programs offering limited preparation for specific jobs or careers.

There is always a complex relation between ambitious career education programs, student learning, and the rest of the curriculum. With career education some schools have shown increased performance. In Dade County, Florida, both students and teachers in career education programs had better school attendance records than those outside such programs. In some Arizona schools, students exposed to career education spent more time on homework than other students. The Office of Education, which has devoted much time evaluating career education programs, holds that in successful career education programs, students leaving school should be:

- competent in the basic academic skills required for adaptability in our rapidly changing society
- equipped with good work habits (behavioral and attitudinal)
- equipped with a personally meaningful set of work values
- equipped with sufficient self-understanding and awareness of educational-vocational opportunities to make reasoned career decisions
- equipped with job hunting skills and job-getting skills
- equipped with some specific occupational skills and sufficient interpersonal skills to allow them to enter and succeed in the world of work
- aware of available means and skills for continuing education
- actively seeking to find meaningful work and some productive use of leisure time

To a large extent, the success or failure of such career education goals depends—not upon materials nor upon the dedication of teachers—but on what happens—outside school—in the job market. Ending sex- or race-discrimination in vocational education materials is not equivalent to ending discrimination in hiring, training, and promotion practices. Students are certainly far more likely to develop appropriate skills and aptitudes when they know they will have opportunities to put them to use.

Even though Louise Vetter finds no inherent sex-related difference in the tasks traditionally performed by men and women, tradition and social role conditioning outside schools may determine who applies for and who gets particular jobs. Even for youths with good job skills, work is increasingly difficult to find. This may well be exacerbated by our recent change of retirement age from 65 to 70 years—an act that aids one end of the age spectrum while imposing hardship at the other end. There is now substantial worldwide unemployment among qualified college graduates including those in the United States.

Further, women and minorities, whatever their objective skills, tend to earn considerably less than white males. A University of Michigan study in "income dynamics" in 1975 found that the hourly wages paid white men were 78 percent higher than those paid black women, 60 percent higher than those of white women, and 36 percent higher than for black men. Considering skills, education, on-the-job training, and attachment to the work force, fair wages for black women would have averaged 26 percent below those of white men, while white women would have earned 30 percent less, and black men 24 percent less.

Though this extensive pocketbook discrimination may well be decreasing, realistic career education materials cannot be prepared in a vacuum. While encouraging students to become what they will and achieve whatever they can, materials must honestly represent what is as well as what could be.

KEY ORGANIZATIONS

Some Key Organizations in subject chapters are useful—e.g., math education organizations for careers in math, environmental education organizations for environment-related positions, etc. Many others have career information for their fields, while the Social Science Education Consortium has its own Career Education Project. ERIC Clearinghouse on Counselling and Personnel Services (ERIC/CAPS) deals with the counselling aspects of vocational guidance—occasionally with instructional materials. Key Organizations listed in the chapter on special education may be active in the allied field of vocational rehabilitation. ERIC Clearinghouse on Rural Education and Small Schools (ERIC/CRESS) is a major source on work-related education for migrant and rural populations. Other organizations can be located through Key Publications and For Further Reading in this chapter and the chapter on free materials in *Media and the Curriculum*. Still others may be obtained from the Resource and Referral Service of the National Center for Vocational Education.

Six Curriculum Coordinating Centers—headquartered in Springfield, Illinois; Trenton, New Jersey; Mississippi City, Mississippi; Stillwater, Oklahoma; Olympia, Washington; and Honolulu, Hawaii—provide regional information and technical assistance, with varying degrees of backup in instructional materials. Their addresses can be obtained from RRS (see National Center for Research in Vocational Education, in Key Organizations) or from the Curriculum Development Branch of the U.S. Office of Education, 7th and D Streets, SW, Washington, DC 20202.

State Research Coordinating Units (RCUs), which usually can be contacted through the Vocational-Technical divisions of state offices of education, are supposed to stimulate, coordinate and disseminate research in their own states. They usually provide access to ERIC materials in work-related education, as well as to materials they have developed; some have access to larger collections of work-related materials. Some have issued catalogs locatable through ERIC.

American Crafts Council (ACC)
Research and Education Department
22 West 55th St.
New York, NY 10019   (212) 397-0600

The Council is a national nonprofit membership organization founded in 1943 to stimulate interest in contemporary crafts. Educationally, it is valuable as a source of hard-to-find information on careers in crafts; it supplies lists of schools, crafts shops and galleries, bibliographies and catalogs, including a *New York Metropolitan Area Craft Course Directory* (1977. $1.00), a *Craftsmen in Business: a Guide to Financial Management and Taxes* (1976. 74p. $6.90); and a *Bibliography: Crafts Business Bookshelf* (1977. 48p. $4.90). Its bimonthly *American Craft* (formerly *Craft Horizons*) is available with membership of $18.00 and has many references and articles on travel, study and grants for crafts careers.

American Industrial Arts Association (AIAA)
1201 16th St., NW
Washington, DC 20036   (202) 833-4211
     The interest of this association is industrial arts education for grades 9 to 12; this encompasses manufacturing, construction, power, transportation, communication, and the use of technology and laboratories in production. AIAA works through educational research, teacher certification, and in-service training to improve the caliber of industrial arts training. Its productions include audiotapes, motion pictures, slide tapes, and other media, as well as books, pamphlets, directories, and periodicals. *Man/Society/Technology: A Journal of Industrial Arts Education* (8 issues/yr. for $9.00) includes "Book Reviews" and "Classroom Materials" columns with signed descriptive reviews of books, texts, textbook series, and other classroom materials.

American Vocational Association, Inc. (AVA)
2020 North 14th St.
Arlington, VA 22201   (703) 522-6121
     This professional organization of teachers, supervisors, and administrators is interested in improving and researching all areas of vocational, technical, and practical arts education; these include agriculture, business, distribution and marketing, health, home economics, industrial arts, trades education, manpower training, and vocational guidance. AVA provides brief answers to queries, consultations, and referrals, and allows qualified researchers to use its collection on site. It publishes vocational pamphlets as well as *Vocational Education* (formerly the *AVA Journal*; 7 issues/yr. for $5.00). The "Book Previews" column of this publication includes descriptive evaluative reviews of single texts from grades 9 to 12 for vocational education, home economics, business, agriculture, career, and industrial arts education.

Concerned Educators Against Forced Unionism (CEAFU)
National Right to Work Committee
8316 Arlington Blvd.
Fairfax, VA 22038   (703) 573-0505
     This group is a coalition of professional educators at all levels—teachers, administrators, and governing officials—whose major concern is that no educator should be forced to join or support a labor union as a condition of entering or remaining in the teaching profession. As part of its program it develops and disseminates "accurate, timely, and relevant information" on the dangers to freedom posed by compulsory unionism. It also specifically locates and identifies what it considers instances of bias in instructional and text materials on the right to work.
     It has produced a substantial number of classroom materials in many formats dealing in some way with compulsory unionism. These include films and

filmstrips, transparencies, posters, position papers, reference books, and pamphlets. Single or loan copies of most of these are available free while quantity copies are available at rather low costs. Some of their supplementary materials are: a five-poster set for elementary and secondary students ($2.50); a position paper on the *Student Right to Work* ($2.50 per 100); texts of *State Right to Work Laws* ($1.00); and *Classroom Treatment of the Right to Work* (approx. $1.00), a research study on textbook bias. A complete list is available on request.

National Career Information Center (NCIC)

American Personnel and Guidance Association (APGA)
2 Skyline Place, Suite 400
5203 Leesburg Pike
Falls Church, VA 22041   (703) 820-4700

This Center was created to facilitate the task of guidance counselors by providing accurate, complete, and pertinent career information. To this end it publishes a monthly newsletter, *Inform*, and an accompanying monthly, *Career Resource Bibliography*, both available together for $25.00/yr. ($15.00 for members) for 10 monthly issues, August through May. *Inform* has articles and exercises that can often be adapted for teaching situations, as well as an "Ideas From Our Readers" section that provides tips and evaluations of current recommended materials; *Career Resource Bibliography* provides citations of print and nonprint materials and sources for specific occupational clusters. Another valuable document published by the APGA Press is the *Guidelines for the Preparation and Evaluation of Career Information Media* prepared by the National Vocational Guidance Association in 1972.

The Center—which works out of a library—also allows on-site use of its collections, provides reference, referral and reproduction services, and conducts workshops.

National Center for Research in Vocational Education

and

ERIC Clearinghouse for Adult, Career and Vocational Education

Ohio State University
1960 Kenny Road
Columbus, OH 43210   (614) 486-3655 and (800) 848-4815

While these two organizations have undergone several name changes in the last few years, the ERIC Clearinghouse (formerly the Clearinghouse on Career Education) has expanded its scope and is once again an integral part of the National Center (formerly the Center for Vocational [and Technical] Education). The Center itself is sort of a facilitating center to help other agencies, organizations, and institutions solve educational problems relating to individual career planning, preparation, and progress. Its approaches include research, development (of programs and materials), evaluation, installing programs and materials, operating information systems and services, and conducting leadership development and training programs.

The Center's research library represents one of the nation's most comprehensive collections in career, vocational and technical education, with more than 40,000 books, reports, and monographs, 400 periodicals and newsletters, 2,500 microfilmed dissertations, a complete ERIC microfiche collection, selected audiovisuals, and other materials. It is open to on-site use by visiting professionals. The library can search more than 50 national data bases.

A Resource and Referral Service (RRS) is currently compiling information on the tasks and products of other educational agencies. As of May 1979, RRS had information on about 1,000 educational agencies. RRS also creates and distributes mini-lists, such as the popular *Resources for K-12 Instructional Materials on Women's Educational Equity*. Most are lists of organizations.

Overall, the National Center's prolific, multidisciplinary staff has produced more than 500 publications (and distributed approximately 400,000 copies of these publications) on almost all aspects of work education. Current publication emphasis is on sex fairness in career and vocational education, as well as work-oriented education for minorities and for disabled individuals. They cooperated with the ERIC Clearinghouse on Rural Education and Small Schools to collect resources on rural career education.

The Center also issues many publications that provide information on sources of occupational information, as well as abstracts and resource lists of instructional materials. Such publications are cited in the Center's substantial *Publications Catalog*, available free on request and updated by its free newsletter, *Centergram*. Information on Clearinghouse activities and publications is included in another free occasional newsletter, *ERIC Clipboard*.

Some valuable publications of this Clearinghouse are: *Career and Vocational Development of Handicapped Learners: An Annotated Bibliography*, by Robert D. Bhaerman (IN 134); *The Career and Vocational Development of Bilingual Students*, by Edwin T. Rios and William E. Hansen (IN 136); and *Community Resources and Involvement in Career Education: An Annotated Bibliography*, by Robert D. Bhaerman (IN 140).

Resources in Vocational Education (available from EDRS or from the National Center at $34.00/yr., $36.00/foreign) has numbered abstracts of instructional research and other materials, as well as abstracts of funded proposals in vocational education.

Other materials-oriented projects of the Center deal with metric materials for career and vocational education, development of competency-based instructional materials in career education, development of task inventory information exchanges, and school use of materials developed by the U.S. Department of Defense.

KEY PUBLICATIONS

Items here may be more useful for choosing materials specifically related to occupations and competency than for decision-making and value clarification which are equally important. The organizations listed as Key Organizations are good sources of publications and journals for keeping up with materials in work-related education. Other journals that usually include useful articles and reviews of work-related instructional materials are *School Shop: Industrial-Technical Education* and *Industrial Education*.

By Hand: A Guide to Schools and Careers in Crafts, by John Coyne and Tom Herbert. New York: Dutton, 1974. 255p. $3.95pa.

A reference-guidance book for the beginning artist or design craftsperson. Arranged by state, it lists workshops, studios, and individuals offering crafts courses, as well as a directory of art schools and colleges and a bibliography of recommended books.

Career Bibliography: A Guide to Free and Inexpensive Information, by James M. Slick. University Park: Pennsylvania State University, Bureau of Vocational Education, 1977. 176p. (ED 140 065).

This bibliography organizes information about 5,000 free or low cost pamphlets on occupations according to the terminology of the *Dictionary of Occupational Titles*. Materials appeared prior to 1976.

Career Education Catalog: Annotated Listing of Selected, Diverse, and Innovative Programs. Cambridge, MA: Abt Publications, 1975. 108p. $10.00pa., plus $1.00 postage and shipping.

The Career Education Catalog presents 88 different programs: 37 comprehensive public school programs, 29 supplementary public school programs, and 22 alternative and community-based programs, with program descriptions that cover objectives, project organization, and major accomplishments, as well as summary information on age group, number of students involved, size and composition of staff, annual budget, nature of funding, and the director's name and address.

Eleven diverse, geographically dispersed programs are more fully described in *Eleven Career Education Programs*. This is available from the same source for $20.00 (plus $1.00 postage and shipping). Both volumes are available as a set for $25.00 (plus $2.00 postage and shipping).

Career Education Materials Analysis Instrument, by Judith E. Hedstrom and Constance M. Williams. Boulder, CO: Social Science Education Consortium, 1977. 24p. $1.50 mimeo.

This analysis instrument for career education includes questions related to product characteristics, educational quality, career education content, conditions of use, and evaluation.

Career Education Pamphlets (A Library of Free and Inexpensive Sources), "Where Important Careers Begin," by Dale E. Shaffer. Salem, OH: Dale E. Shaffer, 1976. 65p. $3.95pa. (From 437 Jennings Ave., Salem, OH 44460).

Provides classified list of 1,200 inexpensive pamphlets (half free) from 403 sources arranged by title under 217 career fields—a good start for an occupational collection. The industrial sources and associations and government agencies whose addresses are included at the end, generally seem appropriate sources for this type of information.

Career Education Sourcebook, by Judith E. Hedstrom and Mary Jane Turner. Boulder, CO: Social Science Education Consortium, 1977. 231p. $8.25 mimeo.

This sourcebook presents analyses of 47 sets of career education/social studies materials, with a chart describing content and teaching strategies for each in addition to a written annotation. It has a separate annotated bibliography of ERIC materials on career education.

Career Education Survival Manual, by Larry McClure. Salt Lake City, UT: Olympus Publishing Co., 1974. 112p. $3.95pa.

This handbook, originally compiled by the Northwest Regional Educational Laboratory as part of a final report to the National Institute of Education, is a readable (even entertaining) summary of career education programs with appropriate references. Printed in pocket-size for easy referral, the format is easy to use while information is easy to assimilate.

Career Guide to Professional Associations: A Directory of Organizations by Occupational Field, compiled by the staff of Carroll Press. Cranston, RI: Carroll Press, 1976. 276p. $8.95pa.

The professional organizations included in this volume are frequently excellent sources for current career information. They are arranged here under the career classification system of the *Dictionary of Occupational Titles*. This volume includes associations of workers in specific occupational fields—such as bartenders and janitors—as well as associations of such professionals as lawyers and librarians. The directory provides organization names and addresses, but not telephone numbers, and indicates whether the organization sets standards, offers awards, publishes journals or career aids, or supplies employment assistance.

Career Resource Centers: A Guide to Expanded Career Guidance Services and Career Education Delivery Systems. Columbus, OH: National Center for Vocational Education, 1977. 125p. $6.95pa.

This handbook provides a wealth of ideas for setting up a career resource center including sample floor plans; photographs and ideas for materials displays; ideas for publicity, workable programs, and activities; and a sample proposal for developing a career resource center with information on potential funding services.

Classroom Treatment of the Right to Work, prepared by Concerned Educators Against Forced Unionism, a Division of the National Right to Work Committee. Fairfax, VA: CEAFU, 1979. Unpaged. $1.00pa. (From 8316 Arlington Blvd., Fairfax, VA 22038).

CEAFU, an educational division of the National Right to Work Committee, has examined more than 200 classroom materials in government and history adopted in twenty states since 1975—evaluating their treatment of the Right to Work issue. In the materials examined, only 81 out of 200 included this issue in their histories or discussions of the American labor movement. Of those who did discuss the issue, CEAFU considered that 52 (or 64 percent) portray the issue inaccurately, unfairly, or both. The work includes a detailed point-by-point criticism of these texts and lists states which have approved each text for statewide classroom use. Another chapter presents basic facts related to right to work laws. A final chapter lists the textbooks that ignore the issue.

Competency Based Education Sourcebook, by Oregon Competency Based Education Program. Portland, OR: Northwest Regional Educational Laboratory, 1977. 1 looseleaf vol. $22.50.

Sources described in this sourcebook include 1) materials available for use, 2) general works on competency based education (CBE), and 3) other sources that can be used for selecting among existing materials or for developing new materials. Proven programs, compatible with the goals of CBE, are coded here and categorized by major CBE components: outcomes, measures, instruction, instructional management, and record-keeping. Included items were selected from a wide variety of materials from programs that had proven successful in practice. Materials are indexed by components (topics and resource types), titles, and originators, and are filed in a three-inch, three-ring binder that allows for updating.

Dealing in Futures: Career Education Materials for Students, Parents, and Educators, compiled by Mary DeWitt Billings and Janet S. Rubin. Washington, DC: GPO, 1977. Unpaged. $1.00pa.

This well-annotated bibliography is based on current materials in the Educational Materials Review Center (EDMARC) and in the Office of Career Education of the U.S. Office of Education. It covers textbooks as well as children's books (trade books), monographs, sets, and government publications – about 140 items altogether. Overall, a useful, easily-browsed compilation, with prices and grade levels, as well as complete bibliographic information for each item listed.

Dictionary of Occupational Titles, 1977. 4th ed. Washington, DC: Employment Training Administration, U.S. Employment Services; distr. by GPO, 1978. 1371p. $12.00pa.

Provides a classified arrangement and accurate description of just about every legal job arranged by occupation groups with indexes by industries and indexes by job titles. This edition, which has discarded the sex- and age-related categories of the previous editions, provides invaluable authoritative information on current occupations.

Elementary Basal Readers and Work Mode Bias, by Floyd H. Jenkins. Denton, TX: The Center for Economic Education, 1977. 90p. $2.00pa. (From Box 5427, North Texas State University, Denton, TX 76203).

This study uses a seven part scale to measure the job status of people (low to high) portrayed in elementary school readers in Texas. The bias, qualitative and quantitative, is for professional jobs and against unskilled or technical-vocational positions. These are mentioned less frequently, less realistically, less positively, and less emphatically.

Other articles dealing with this research are "Work Mode Bias in Elementary Text Materials" in *Journal of Industrial Teacher Education* (Feb. 1973, pp. 16-26), and "Elementary Basal Readers and Work Mode Bias" in the *Journal of Economic Education* (Spring 1974).

EPIE Career Education Set [Selection and Evaluation Tools]. Vol. I, *How to Select and Evaluate Instructional Materials.* 107p.; Vol. II, *Analysis of Seven Hundred Prescreened Materials.* 294p. New York: EPIE Institute, 1975. 2 vols. $30.00.

Volume I of this set is a very thoughtful analysis that outlines procedures for narrowing the field of career education to select materials to fit the needs of specific learners, provides discussions and guidelines for detecting sexism and racism in career education materials or for counteracting their effects if present, offers criteria for judging producers' evaluation procedures, and provides educators with a comprehensive handbook for selecting career education materials. Appendixes of volume I list some career education periodicals as well as some manuals that describe skill-training materials. Volume II evaluates more than 700 materials in career education according to the criteria provided in volume I.

Exemplary Strategies for Elimination of Sex Bias in Vocational Education Programs, by Sheila M. Maher. Washington, DC: Human Resources Management Program, 1976. 69p. (Available as ED 133, 523, from EDRS, $4.50 plus postage; microfiche, $0.83).

Provides annotated descriptions of projects and strategies for eliminating sex bias in vocational education. Resource categories include materials, individuals and organizations, projects, and studies.

The Far West Model: Experience-Based Career Education (EBCE). San Francisco: Far West Laboratory for Educational Research and Development, 1976. 4 vols. $60.00. looseleaf. Vol. 1, *Management*; Vol. 2, *Resources*; Vol. 3, *Guidance and Instruction*; Vol. 4, *Project Planning Packages*.

Experience-Based Career Education is an alternative program for secondary education which employs the entire community as a school setting—using direct experiences at a variety of employee sites to provide planned learning experiences combining career awareness with academic, basic, and social skills.

These substantial looseleaf binders provide potential developers with an overview of the program and could also be useful for individualizing other career education programs at the secondary level. Vol. 4, *Project Planning Packages*, provides concepts, goals, projects, and community and printed resources for studying commerce, communication and media, life sciences, physical sciences, and social sciences, using forms that could easily be adopted for individualized programs. Vol. 2, *Resources*, includes a good section on package development. Vol. 3, *Guidance and Instruction*, has a section on supplementary curriculum with many interesting forms that might be useful in assessing and prescribing for student needs. These forms deal with student objectives, methods, and strategies (the latter includes materials).

Guide to Federal Career Literature, by the U.S. Civil Service Commission. Washington, DC: GPO, 1976. 33p. $1.05pa.

An annotated listing and directory of federal brochures and recruiting pamphlets prepared for college-level entry federal positions. Includes addresses to use for copies of these pamphlets as well as lists of career fields and positions, a list of federal Job Information Centers, and an index by college majors. While this particular pamphlet is designed primarily for recent college graduates and college seniors, it could be useful for high school counselors of college-bound students by providing a perspective on current federal career opportunities.

Guidelines for Sex-Fair Vocational Education Materials, by Women on Words and Images. Princeton, NJ: WOWI, 1978. 57p. Out of print. Available as ED 153 015, from EDRS, $3.50 plus postage; microfiche, $0.83 plus postage.

A very helpful and thorough booklet that covers language, occupational and social roles, omissions, physical appearance, audio materials, and visual materials. For each area covered, the booklet identifies issues, provides examples of fair and biased usage, and provides guidelines for sex-fair usage. It also includes guidelines for creatively using biased materials in unbiased ways.

Keys to Careers in Science and Technology, by National Science Teachers Association. Washington, DC: NSTA, 1973. 74p. $1.00pa.

Indicates sources of materials on science careers as well as information on educational loans and award programs.

Materials for Occupational Education: An Annotated Source Guide, by Patricia Schuman. New York: Bowker, 1971. 201p. $14.95.

This well-organized tool, by an editor of *School Library Journal*, was compiled to meet the needs of educators and librarians. Since the majority of relevant materials comes from professional and trade associations, government agencies and private businesses, all of which change frequently, this source lists 600 organizations (selected from 3,000) that supply books, periodicals, manuals, and other media for 63 occupational areas. Entries include types of materials and specific titles with ordering information. Emphasis is on materials relevant to two-year college instructional programs, with further sources of information under subject categories. Two chapters provide an annotated list of publishers and an annotated list of professional organizations.

Nontraditional Careers for Women, by Sarah Splaver. New York: Messner, 1973. 222p. $6.25.

Discusses over 500 careers for women in such fields as law, medicine, science, math, engineering, creative arts, business, manual trades, and government services. Usually includes the history of women in each of these occupations plus the current number of women in these fields and the outlook for the future.

Organized Labor: Source Material for the Study of Labor in America: Teachers' Guide, Primary Documents, Questions and Study Topics, Glossary and Posters, compiled by United Federation of Teachers, Labor Study. New York: UFT, 1977. 200p. in looseleaf binder, including 50 removable primary documents and 6 removable posters 30x10-inches and 20x15-inches. $5.00. (From UFT, Labor Study, 260 Park Avenue South, New York, NY 10010).

These resource materials on the study of labor are appropriate for high school, adult, and college audiences. They were assembled and published as the result of a study conducted by the Education Committee of the New York City Labor Council to help alleviate the dearth of curriculum materials on labor studies. They are an excellent and surprisingly inexpensive source for photographs and primary documents covering the growth and structure of organized labor in America (as well as political and technological implications) from the beginnings of the Knights of Labor through today's labor movement.

Resources in Career Education: An Annotated Guide, by David V. Tiedeman, Marilyn Schreiber, and Tyrus R. Wessell, Jr. Washington, DC: National Institute of Education; distr. by GPO, 1976. 408p. $5.75pa.

This handbook—despite a superfluity of educationese—has good annotations to resources in career education. These cover implementation factors, models and program construction, resource guides, and educational resources.

Resources on Eliminating Sex Role Stereotyping in Vocational Education, by Faith L. Justice and Wesley E. Budke. Columbus, OH: National Center for

Vocational Education, 1977. 4p. Free. (From Wesley E. Budke, National Center for Vocational Education, Ohio State University, 1960 Kenny Road, Columbus, OH 43210).

This compact informative annotated biblio-directory includes current information on state and local projects, in-service materials, reports, programs in secondary and post-secondary education, names of organizations, sources on evaluation, bibliographies, and annotations of films and filmstrips which deal with sex-stereotyping and career/vocational education.

Rural Career Guidance: Abstracts of Current Research, Materials, and Practices, developed by ERIC Clearinghouse on Rural Education and Small Schools and National Rural Career Guidance Network. Austin, TX: National Educational Laboratory Publishers, 1978. 192p. $9.50pa. mimeo.

A mimeographed summary in computer printout format (typed capital letters) of entries reprinted from ERIC's *Resources in Education* (RIE) and *Current Index to Journals in Education* (CIJE) arranged by ED and EJ numbers with an index by relevant subject terms from the *ERIC Thesaurus*. Essentially a 200-item printout with one item per page. Most items do not deal with materials; those that do are not easily located through the index. However, there are few other resources in print on rural career guidance.

Tips for Infusing Career Education in the Curriculum, by Bob Taylor et al. Boulder, CO: Social Science Education Consortium, 1977. 66p. $4.00pa. mimeo.

This provides a model for integrating career education into the social studies curriculum. It includes sample lessons and fused units for primary, upper elementary, and secondary levels, as well as tips for involving local communities in career education.

Training Film Profiles. New York: Olympic Media Information, 1967- . 10 vols. $475.00; current annual subscription 6 issues/yr., $150.00.

The first ten volumes of this encyclopedia of audiovisual training materials describe and evaluate more than 2,500 different adult-level materials dealing with employee skills: films, filmstrips, audio-cassettes, media kits, and sound slide programs.

The materials presented here as profiles do not generally deal with specific vocational skills or fields (such as electrical assembly or computer operator) but with broader, or more widely used topics—for example, communication skills ranging from telephone to interviewing techniques, problem solving, report writing, customer relations, retail selling, safety, supervision.

Even though 40 percent of subscribers are colleges, most materials seem to be primarily intended for in-service training in business. However, many items "profiled" seem appropriate for high school students and teachers while some could be used at lower levels. According to Olympic Media, the materials chosen are the best or most-frequently used, selected to be:

- work related
- cross-occupational
- adult level (though including some pre-vocational materials)

- practical, with specific instructional contents
- survival oriented (directed towards getting and keeping jobs)

The publisher notes that only about 1 to 2 percent of the media materials listed in *Training Film Profiles* overlap with those reviewed in standard media review sources such as *Media & Methods, Previews, Film News*, and *Landers*.

The profiles themselves, on notebook-sized sheets, are exemplary and easy to use. Formatted descriptions cover primary audiences, contents, synopses, discussion questions, and source, along with title, bibliographic description, and an evaluation of educational usefulness and applications.

Women in Non-Traditional Occupations: A Bibliography. Washington, DC: U.S. Department of Health, Education and Welfare, Bureau of Occupational and Adult Education, 1976. 189p. Out of print. (Available as ED 133 460, from EDRS, $10.55 plus postage; microfiche, $0.96).

An annotated bibliography of literature about women in non-traditional occupations, intended for vocational educators and/or as a study of women in the work force.

The Work Ethic in Career Education, by Robert Peterson and James Johnson. San Francisco: Far West Laboratory for Educational Research and Development, 1978. 78p. Out of print. (ED 143 778).

This study of values in career educational materials (sponsored by the National Institute of Education) analyzed and reviewed 107 currently available materials in relation to values and attitudes and to the emphasis given to competing views. Views and treatments presented in career education materials were compared with the views presented in scholarly and journalistic articles. In comparison with these, the career education materials reflected "an overly simple and superficial view," one that presents "a much more attractive, even idealized view of work." The authors fear that "the resultant imbalanced concentration of an idealized view of work promotes naivete that sets the student up for eventual disillusionment and defeat."

This study also examined the charge that career education seeks to perpetuate social stratification and continuation of a subservient working class. On this issue, they concluded that — while career education materials do stress the industrial facet of the work ethic, this emphasis is balanced by attention to self actualization, freedom of career choice, and life-long career development. They concluded that career development materials do not indoctrinate.

Your Child's Career: A Guide to Home-Based Career Education, by Garth L. Mangum and others. Salt Lake City, UT: Olympus Publishing Co., 1977. 316p. $9.95.

Suggestions to help parents and teachers help children learn about the world of work in a positive fashion, largely in pre-school years; with additional thoughtful and positive suggestions for parents working with local education programs. Olympus Publishing Company, which also published *Career Education Survival Manual*, has many other fine publications and cassettes on career education.

FOR FURTHER READING

*Items marked with an asterisk include criteria.

+ Items marked with a plus include substantial lists of references.

American Association for the Advancement of Science. *Test Yourself for Science.* Washington, DC: AAAS, 1971.

American Institutes for Research. *Career Education: A Curriculum Design and Instructional Objectives Catalog.* Palo Alto, CA: AIR, 1973.

Blome, Arvin C., and Glen D. Rask. *Olympus Career Education Needs Assessment Instruments.* Salt Lake City, UT: Olympus, 1975.

Dewey, Cindy Rice. "Exploring Interests: A Non-Sexist Method," *Personnel and Guidance Journal,* v. 52, no. 5 (Jan. 1974), pp. 311-15.

*Gellatt, H. B., and others. *Deciding.* Princeton, NJ: College Entrance Examination Board, 1972.

*Gellatt, H. B., and others. *Decisions and Outcomes.* Princeton, NJ: College Entrance Examination Board, 1973.

Harmin, Merrill, and others. *Clarifying Values through Subject Matter: Applications for the Classroom.* Minneapolis, MN: Winston Press, 1973.

Holden, Donald. *Art Career Guide.* New York: Watson-Guptill, 1973. 303p. $8.95.
Well-reviewed and well-arranged guide to schools, courses, jobs and job hunting in a variety of art-related careers.

Holland, John L. *Self-Directed Search for Educational and Vocational Planning.* Palo Alto, CA: Consulting Psychologists Press, 1971.

+ Hoyt, Kenneth B., and Jean R. Hebeler. *Career Education for Gifted and Talented Students.* Salt Lake City, UT: Olympus, 1974.

+ Hoyt, Kenneth B., and Jean R. Hebeler. *Career Education for Special Populations.* Washington, DC: GPO, 1976.

*Hoyt, Kenneth B., and Jean R. Hebeler. *Classroom Teachers and Career Education: The Beautiful People.* Washington, DC: GPO, 1976.

*Hoyt, Kenneth B., and Jean R. Hebeler. *Perspectives on the Problem of Evaluation in Career Education.* Washington, DC: GPO, 1976.

*Hoyt, Kenneth B., and Jean R. Hebeler. *Refining the Career Education Concept.* Washington, DC: GPO, 1976.

+ Humane Society of the U.S. *Careers: Working with Animals.* Washington, DC: Humane Society, 1974.

Koontz, Ronald G. *Classification Scheme for Career Education Resource Materials.* Washington, DC: GPO, 1975.
Describes a classification scheme enabling users 1) to search for career education resource materials through a card catalog arranged by key descriptors, 2) to determine the content of resource materials through this cataloging, and 3) to retrieve career education resource materials quickly.

Millard, Reed. *Careers in Environmental Protection.* New York: Julian Messner, 1974.

*Mitchell, Anita. *Use of Media in Career Education.* Syracuse, NY: ERIC Clearinghouse on Information Resources, 1976. (ED 127 974).
Considers appropriate use of media for specific settings, e.g., classrooms, small groups, career information centers, workshops, training institutions, and independent study.

* + Norris, Willa. *Occupational Information in the Elementary School.* Chicago: Science Research Associates, 1969.
A still-useful resource section as well as a thorough presentation of approaches for incorporating and presenting vocational information in classroom curricula.

+ Ober, Keith, and Kathrine Kearine. *Exploring Careers: A Teacher's Manual.* Cambridge, MA: Abt Associates, 1974.
Describes homemade games and student activities intended to motivate and facilitate career choice along with a brief source guide for materials.

+ *Occupational Outlook Handbook, 1978-79.* Washington, DC: GPO, 1978.
Provides well-arranged, accurate occupational information on major occupations and industry, with information on requirements, advancements, outlooks, working conditions, and sources of further information for each, using findings of the U.S. Bureau of Labor Statistics. Updated quarterly by *Occupational Outlook Quarterly.*

Shane, Harold. *The Educational Significance of the Future.* Bloomington, IN: Phi Delta Kappa Educational Foundation, 1973.

Smith, Walter S., and Kala M. Stroup. *Science Career Exploration for Women.* Washington, DC: National Science Teachers' Association, 1978.

+ Standard Oil Company of Indiana. *Organizations Providing Business and Economic Education Materials or Information.* Chicago: Standard Oil, 1979.

* + Vetter, Louise, and Barbara J. Sethney. *Women in the Work Force: Development and Field Testing of Curriculum Materials, Final Report.* Columbus, OH: Center for Vocational Education, 1972. (ED 072 175).
A package of curriculum materials and associated tests of knowledge, attitudes, and plans to help high school girls consider alternatives in planning for labor force participation and adult female roles.

*Weinrach, Esther L., and Stephen G. Weinrach. "The Role of the Librarian in the Evaluation of Career Information Media," *Catholic Library World*, v. 49, no. 4 (Nov. 1977), pp. 170-75.

*Women on Words and Images. *Guidelines for the Creative Use of Biased Materials in a Non-Biased Way.* Princeton, NJ: WOWI, 1978.

* + Women on Words and Images. *Help Wanted: Sex Role Stereotyping in Career Educational Materials.* Princeton, NJ: WOWI, 1975.
Also available as a color-slide-tape carousel. The pamphlet is part of EPIE's *Career Education Set.*

+ York, Edwin G. "A Career Education Media Mix," *Previews*, v. 5 (Oct. 1976), pp. 10-17.

> "Consumption is the sole end and purpose of all production; and the interest of the producer ought to be attended to, only so far as it may be necessary for promoting that of the consumer.... But in the mercantile system, the interest of the consumer is almost constantly sacrificed to that of the producer ..."
> — Adam Smith, *The Wealth of Nations*, 1776

> "[The biggest problem] in teaching consumer education is the temptation to teach adult material to the students and not remember to approach it at their level."
> — Hayden Green, "One School's Consumer Survival Kit,"
> *Curriculum Review*, February 1978

> "Good books which tell children how to do such things as train a dog, make a bird house, play a harmonica, learn a sport or redecorate a bedroom offer in the clearest possible manner, information on the selection, evaluation, use and maintenance of items children consume."
> — U.S. Office of Consumer Affairs, *Consumer Education Bibliography*

> "I think a teacher can do a lot of innovative things with consumer ed on a very small budget. It's practical, it's activity-oriented, and if there ever was a topic that lends itself to the 'hands-on' approach, this is it."
> — Hayden Green, "One School's Consumer Survival Kit"

□ □ □

A chapter on consumer education is, perhaps, a logical final subject area for the section of this book promoting intelligent consumption of educational materials. It is also a logical goal for education. Perhaps, as some advocates say, it may be a basic skill. At a time when the Gallup poll indicates that the accelerating cost of living is the major concern of the American public, consumer education seems almost basic to our individual economic survival. This may be the reason that some competency examinations now include consumer education. Certainly, our traditional basics — calculating and reading — are necessary for intelligent consumption.

If career and vocational education aim at preparing students to earn money, consumer education has been traditionally concerned with the other end of the spectrum — equipping students to spend their money intelligently. However, according to a survey — reported in Hayden Green's "One School's Consumer Survival Kit" — 80 percent of adults questioned felt that they were ill-prepared as consumers at the time of high school graduation.

Though consumer education, like environmental education, seems naturally a multidisciplinary, interdisciplinary course, it had been rather undernourished and undersupported up to the late 1970s. To a large degree, home economics and business education courses carried the ball, the former according to lines laid out long ago by Ellen Richards, a nineteenth-century pioneer in chemistry, sanitation, and household management. While business education concentrated, often stodgily, upon money management, credit and banking, and business economics, home economics courses tended to focus on topics like reading food labels and examining textiles. Even though home economics courses handled these individual topics with admirable thoroughness, the thrust of consumer education under their auspices was narrowed to household items like food, clothing, and furniture. And while rudimentary finance and home economics are undoubtedly important aspects of consumption, as topics they lack breadth and depth as well as appeal for the majority of students. Traditionally, consumer education courses were elective courses at the high school level that drew relatively few students.

Our current accelerated inflation, combined with our current educational emphasis on competency and "survival skills," has resulted in a flurry of renewed interest in consumer education, as well as a broadening of concepts. Undoubtedly a feeling that children are being victimized and manipulated by advertisers has played a part, while the ecology movement has contributed to public awareness of some undesirable aspects of overconsumption.

Some students, at least, seem to share this renewed interest. Two student columnists, Marcus and Richman, in a recent "Proposal to Revise the Secondary School Curriculum in Economics" (*Social Education*, Jan. 1978), suggested broadening economics to include consumer fraud, advertising gimmicks, sound investment practices, and financial responsibility in relation to all kinds of purchases.

These factors, taken together, have tended — inside school and out — to create more interest in consumer education and to broaden our definitions of what consumer education is. The Office of Consumers' Education (OCE) recently expanded its definition of consumer education and the projects that it can fund. According to their new definition, consumer education is considered education that develops skills, knowledge, or understanding to help consumers,

- recognize economic alternatives in purchasing goods and services (including social and civil services)

- cope with pressures to which members of the buying public are exposed

- prepare for and adjust to rapidly changing economic conditions and issues

- make rational choices in light of "personal values"; citizen responsibilities; and economic, social and ecological factors

- participate effectively as citizen consumers in governmental and economic systems (including regulatory processes and the delivery of public services)

The federal government has also recently funded and created a brand new clearinghouse, the Consumer Education Resource Network (CERN) to "bring all consumer educators into a viable network" and to collect information on consumer education materials from as many sources as possible.

With an apparent growth in consumerism at all levels — federal, state, and local — supported by consumer hot lines and consumer agencies, it is a good time for teaching consumer education. Some states are establishing overview organizations to serve the needs of consumers generally, while some are now mandating the implementation of consumer education programs in schools. Advocacy and community organizations are also initiating consumer education for special populations (such as Spanish-speaking or disabled persons). Traditionally there have always been quite a few free and low-cost (often government) publications offering good advice to adults on selecting goods and managing money. These have been expanding recently.

President Carter's Executive Order 12160, signed on September 26, 1979, requires all federal agencies to develop and maintain consumer information programs. Each agency must produce and distribute materials (either in print or aduiovisual format) to inform consumers about the agency's services and any marketplace aspects for which it is responsible, as well as its procedures for consumer participation and for handling complaints.

Educational materials are increasingly issued by state departments of education or state offices of consumer affairs, which sometimes also provide funds for programs. The *State Consumer Education Policy Manual*, produced by the Education Commission of the States and distributed by the OCE, is one good source of information on these state programs. OCE directories and those of the American Home Economics Association provide relatively current funding information. These particular publications are noted under Key Organizations; others can be found through ERIC.

A typical state publication may be the *Consumer Action Curriculum* just published by the California Department of Consumer Affairs—a 250-page, looseleaf curriculum package for high school age and older, with sample forms for letters to businesses and legislators and advice on topics like participating in small claims court and getting written estimates for auto repair work. This particular report is available for $6.00 from the Publications Section, Box 1015, North Highlands, CA 95660. Comparable materials are available from other states.

Many materials for consumer education can be found through previous chapters of the present work. Health education and nutrition education are—from certain points of view—at least half devoted to consumer education on health and nutrition issues. Business education and home economics traditionally incorporate consumer education naturally.

Pamphlets and periodicals (discussed as print materials in *Media and the Curriculum*) are, of course, excellent, inexpensive resources for current consumer information on any topic from buying cars to the pros and cons of life insurance. The chapters on free materials and print materials in that volume include many suggestions for locating and using these two sources.

For all of these, children require not only specific information but materials to help them develop critical thinking abilities and to become aware of appropriate information sources and alternatives. That is, students should not only learn to compare several items, but be able to decide whether or not to buy at all, or to choose intelligently among alternatives (e.g., bicycle, car, or public transportation). Cognitive criteria are important in consumer education materials, although language may well be simple.

The language arts—at all levels—are important for teaching students to examine the techniques of rhetoric and persuasion. Eventually they might include the language of contracts and the art of reading small print. Teachers can use readily-available print and televised ads for instructional materials, as well as contracts and leases. The social studies areas of law, government, citizenship, political science, and economics should incorporate materials and time for teaching the broad concepts of consumer education—the role of consumers in determining the allocation of resources, and the interrelationships between government, business, and consumers. Civics materials on government agencies (usually available free from the agencies, which may also supply speakers) are particularly valuable for integrating the role of the agencies. Legal education can incorporate methods, materials, and approaches for redressing consumer grievances.

Mathematical textbooks on consumer math and remedial math tend to cover the old money-management areas of business education—with exercises and information on buying cars, opening checking and savings accounts, obtaining credit cards, and calculating income tax. The practical materials incorporated in these textbooks are, of course, readily available from local banks, the Internal Revenue Service, insurance companies, consumer agencies or, for that matter, used car dealers. Experiences gain in value when they are first-hand and local.

Environmental education offers many opportunities to study the hidden costs of convenience (for which citizens ultimately pay) and the environmental impacts of our purchases. The raw materials for studying these are available in government agencies and industry reports, but they need research skills to bring them together. I have found some high school students surprisingly willing to research areas, locate materials, and donate them to their schools. Some good starting points for such research can be found in *Media and the Curriculum*, in the chapters on government materials, free and inexpensive materials, and non-print media. For some topics, trade books and periodical indexes are excellent sources.

As Hayden Green points out, "real life" materials are often best and cheapest. It costs less and is more interesting to compare two batteries with each other (or to compare one battery with its advertising claims) than to purchase a film or filmstrip on evaluating batteries (though films and filmstrips are often available free from government agencies). Science and environmental education curricula should offer many opportunities for "hands-on" testing and comparisons. As home economics teachers know, the raw materials for consumer education are readily available in supermarkets, department stores, newspapers, magazines, and television programming.

Diane Divoky, among others, advocates starting consumer education early with toys, since toys are among the first purchases of children (or their parents). However—since the bulk of child-directed advertising is for (usually non-nutritious) foods—nutrition, health, and safety may be equally good starting points for consumer education in the preschool and primary years. The chapter on television in *Media and the Curriculum* offers some suggestions and starting points vis-a-vis critical viewing of televised ads. The chapter on toys in *Media and the Curriculum* has some criteria that could be used for consumer education teaching.

One advantage in using free or local current materials rather than textbooks is that this method allows students to study whatever areas interest them. Almost every life area from birth (choosing hospitals, doctors, and methods) to death (cost and types of wills and funerals) can be an area for consumer education; however, not every area will interest every student. Since all students are interested in spending money (or time) on something, every student can locate some consumer education area that interests him or her—whether it is skateboards, cosmetics, automobiles, or care of pets.

When consumer education addresses the group or individual interests of students, exposes the students to sources of information, and encourages them to use structured comparisons and to develop their own values and criteria for consumption, it will help create intelligent consumers able to apply methodical analysis and personal insights to selecting and consuming.

The American Home Economics Association's *Guide for Evaluating Consumer Education Programs and Materials* (published in 1972 but now out of print) considered certain goals in its scales for programs and materials. These may be relevant in assessing consumer education topics: "Objectives" covered social significance, human values, communication of content, specificity, and intellectual difficulty; "Content" covered objectivity, organization, conceptualization, difficulty level, timeliness, credibility, focus, and relevancy; "Learning experiences" covered maturity level, variety, sensory factors, thought stimulation, relevancy, and learning feedback; "Evaluation factors" considered continuity, comprehension, and validity. Other materials factors included were physical appearance, packaging, and costs. These latter may not be relevant in ad hoc or improvised materials.

KEY ORGANIZATIONS

Selecting Materials for Instruction: Issues and Policies includes other relevant organizations, especially in the chapter on parent/community involvement. Similarly, the chapters on free and inexpensive materials, television, and government documents in *Media and the Curriculum* have good leads to material sources. The Consumer Information Center is particularly important.

American Council on Consumer Interests (ACCI)
c/o Karen Stein
162 Stanley Hall
University of Missouri, Columbia
Columbia, MO 65211   (314) 882-4450

ACCI, established in 1953, is a permanent, nonpartisan, nonprofit organization of professionals in consumer education with a (unfortunately low-budget) program that ranges from public and school education to research, counseling, consumer action, support of legislation and regulatory programs, and information dissemination.

Its *ACCI Newsletter* (9 issues/yr. from September to May) is part of a membership packet and is probably the best source for keeping up with new instructional materials in consumer education. This newsletter includes annotated announcements of new books, programs, visual aids, and articles—as well as information on legislation, conferences, government activities, courses, and action programs. *Consumer Education Forum* (3 issues/yr.) is a lively newsletter for professionals which includes an exchange for recommended consumer education ideas. The interdisciplinary *Journal of Consumer Affairs* (2 issues/yr.) provides book reviews and reports on research, and discusses current issues and problems. These three periodicals are distributed with memberships. These include individual memberships at $20.00/yr. and institutional memberships at $30.00.

American Home Economics Association (AHEA)
2010 Massachusetts Ave., NW
Washington, DC 20036   (202) 862-8300

The AHEA is an educational and scientific organization whose purpose is to improve the quality and standards of individual and family life through education, research, cooperative programs, and public information. About 35,000 of of its 50,000 members are individuals with bachelors or advanced degrees in home economics and/or its specializations. The other 15,000 are undergraduate students in home economics courses. It has a substantial publication program with many items relevant for consumer education in school settings, and has prepared the only instrument I have found for evaluating consumer education materials. It takes a fairly broad view of both home economics and consumer education, and manages to integrate metric education, career education, energy information and other societal concerns into its curricula and publications.

Its *Home Economics Learning Programs* (HELPs), at $3.75 each/$3.00 for members, include some useful instructional materials on reading labels, advertising, money management, values and goals. Two recent directories at the same price offer access to funding sources: *Directory of Public Funding Sources for Home Economics-Related Programs* (1978) and *Directory of Private Funding Sources for Home Economics Related Programs* (1977). Other publications include an annotated bibliography, *Developing Potentials for Handicaps* (1978. $5.57; $4.75 members) that has some well-worked-out learning activities.

Center for Science in the Public Interest (CSPI)
1757 S St., NW
Washington, DC 20009   (202) 332-9110

This Center, also discussed under Nutrition Education, is an activist organization that investigates, exposes, publicizes, organizes, litigates, and publishes. Some publications are for children. Consumer-related concerns and publications in the recent past include content labeling for foods and beverages, hazards in household products (including foods) and dangers of asbestos and aerosols. The publications of this group have the virtues of clarity, cogency, currency, and accuracy.

Consumer Education Resource Network (CERN)
1550 Wilson Blvd., Suite 600
Rosslyn, VA 22209   (800) 336-0223 and (703) 522-4616

CERN, a national network for consumer educators, is funded by the Office of Consumers' Education to provide training and technical assistance, to disseminate materials and information, and to facilitate the process of networking among existing consumer agencies and activities. It provides access to both human and material resources. It is set up to serve educators and education agencies at all levels—as well as community service organizations, national consumer organizations, institutes of higher education and private industry. It will work through these groups to locate and provide programs to meet consumer education needs of particular groups (e.g., elderly, disabled, or Spanish-speaking persons) as well as general consumer education needs.

CERN operates a comprehensive resource reference (noncirculating) library of consumer education materials of books, pamphlets, periodicals, conference reports, research papers, curriculum guides, government documents, project materials, bibliographies, directories, catalogs, films, filmstrips, multimedia kits, simulations, games, and learning activity packages—adding perhaps 750 new items each month. As of May 1979 the Network had contacted 1,000 groups for materials and/or information.

It plans to expand its collection to include materials on policy and legislation, and materials for special populations. Bibliographic references to these materials are available to users by mail, in person, or through CERN's free hot line. In 1980, CERN expects to have its files computerized for quicker retrieval. Its free monthly publication, *ConCERNS*, includes current information on network and governmental activities in relation to consumer education and announcements of publications and awards in the field. For instance, the May 1979 issue provided an annotated list of audiovisual resources.

Consumers Union Educational Services
256 Washington St.
Mount Vernon, NY 10550   (914) 664-6400

Consumers Union, a national nonprofit organization founded in 1936, is well known for its objective evaluative reports of (largely adult) consumer items. It has also developed some films and teaching aids for classroom use, junior high through college age. For example, its multimedia unit, *Exploring the Marketplace*, comes with teacher's guide and student activities for topics like shampoos and acne remedies. It offers classroom sets of *Consumer Reports*, complete with teachers' guides at various rates. It has also issued seven 16mm films on topics like shopping for credit and buying second-hand cars.

The Union's new magazine for younger children, *PennyPower*, was cooperatively developed with Fordham University. It features how-to articles on topics like handling door-to-door salesmen, purchasing jeans, reading cereal boxes, and evaluating television commercials. Contact the office for complete listings and current prices.

Joint Council on Economic Education (JCEE)
1212 Avenue of the Americas
New York, NY 10036   (212) 582-5150

A recent JCEE project, entitled *Economic Education: A Key to Consumer Proficiency*, uses basic economic principles as a conceptual framework for consumer education. This project will introduce new teaching strategies and consumer education materials at summer institutes designed to train teachers who ultimately will train other teachers in consumer education.

National Consumers League (NCL)
1028 Connecticut Ave., Suite 522
Washington, DC 20036   (202) 797-7600

The NCL is the country's oldest consumer organization, a membership group founded in 1899 to "defend and promote the safety, health, and economic well-being of workers and consumers." An old-line organization whose former leaders include Louis Brandeis and Eleanor Roosevelt, NCL has an impressive record of battles in drug testing, food processing, and unscrupulous business practices generally. It has recently absorbed a grassroots consumer group, the National Consumers Congress, to expand its outreach capabilities. It attempts to bring consumer power to bear on marketplace issues, locally—in food marketing, health services, and low-income consumer areas—and nationally, through its Washington office. Its *Bulletin* provides good legislative updates and brief, informative articles on broad consumer issues like nutrition labeling.

Resource Center for Consumer Education
Merrimack Education Center (MEC)
101 Mill Rd.
Chelmsford, MA 01824   (617) 256-2987
   This Resource Center, an integral part of the Merrimack Education Center, offers consumer education consultant services, credit courses, in-service workshops, idea exchanges, newsletters, and other publications. It is also a center for information on local and state consumer organizations and their programs, and offers information on laws that protect consumers as well as on consumer protection agencies. Its resource and information service also makes available curriculum guides and other printed monographs, reports and studies.
   It issues and/or distributes many resource and activity guides on consumer education, including teaching activities, learning activity packages, and bibliographies on consumer education; some are on elementary curriculum guides, secondary curriculum guides, and resources for special education students.
   Other states are developing comparable services.

U.S. Office of Consumers' Education (OCE)
1832 M St., NW, Suite 807
Washington, DC 20202   (202) 653-5983
   This Office of Consumers' Education is now the major facilitating agency for federal projects in consumer education. Its major contracts for fiscal year 1978 were The Consumer Education Resource Network, radio public service announcements, and a consumer's education study designed to analyze current consumer education activities in communities and schools, to assess these in terms of contemporary needs and issues and to develop programs and materials to fulfill identified needs. Other projects are summarized in *ConCERNS* (available from Consumer Education Resource Network) and in limited copies of *Summaries of Contract and Grant Awards* available from OCE. OCE also distributes items such as *The State Consumer Education Policy Manual*, a document produced by the Education Commission of the States, which describes the policies, requirements and formats used by each state to teach consumer education.
   OCE has also compiled a substantial bibliography of resources: *A Guide to Instructional Resources for Consumers' Education: References, Landmark Materials, Bibliographies, Curriculum Guides, Developmental Resources, Consumer Issues, Behavior and Protection, Periodicals, Films and Filmstrips*, by William L. Johnson and Nancy Greenspan (1978. 58p. pa.). This can be purchased from the Superintendent of Documents for $2.10, while limited numbers of copies are available free from the Office of Education or from OCE.

KEY PUBLICATIONS

Consumers Index to Product Evaluations and Information Sources. Ann Arbor, MI: Pierian Press. Quarterly with annual cumulations. $59.50 each; $98.00 combined; back volumes $25.00 each.
   Indexes periodical articles that test, evaluate, compare or otherwise review consumer goods and services. Includes a separate section for books, pamphlets and "consumer aids."

Information for Everyday Survival: What You Need and Where to Get It, compiled by Priscilla Gotsick, and others. Chicago: American Library Association, 1976. 416p. $10.00pa.

An interesting bibliography of materials for solving common, "everyday" problems, compiled by individuals associated with the Appalachian Adult Education Center at Morehead State University in Kentucky. It includes free and inexpensive materials in all media: books, pamphlets, films, tapes, games, records, articles, and more. Though it is intended for adults, it includes some topics and items appropriate for high school use: children, family, free time, health, home, jobs, law and government, money management (divided into smaller topics). For each information source or aid it provides title, author, format, annotation, reading level, source, and approximate cost.

Reading and the Consumer: A Practical Guide, by Alma Williams. Newark, DE: International Reading Association, 1976. 110p. $3.00pa. (Teaching of Reading Monographs).

Examines the problems of locating and using effectively the wide range of printed resources for consumer education.

Reference Guide for Consumers, by Nina David. New York: Bowker, 1975. 327p. $14.95.

This book aims "to pull together the many varied sources of consumer information, evaluate the multimedia material, and present the whole in a form for ready references." It focuses on books, maps published from 1960 to 1974, and films published from 1965 on, with supporting lists of organizations and newspapers that have consumer news or action reporters. While most materials are on adult levels, the basic list is still useful, with a substantial number of entries on "Consumer Education — Study and Teaching" that can be used to amplify this chapter's For Further Reading list.

Suggested Guidelines for Consumer Education: Grades K-12, by U.S. Office of Consumer Affairs. Washington, DC: GPO, 1970. 58p. $1.05pa.

This booklet, unfortunately not updated, suggests ways for teachers and curriculum planners to develop their own consumer education programs and relate them to community learning resources. While these pages are still valuable, its 16-page multimedia bibliography, once a low-priced comprehensive study, is sadly out of date.

FOR FURTHER READING

*Items marked with an asterisk include criteria.

+ Items marked with a plus include bibliographies or references.

Changing Times is also a good source. Its "Things to Write For" column often announces worthwhile materials.

Adams, Eleanor. "Who Carries the Ball in Consumer Education?" *Forecast for Home Economics*, v. 13, no. 8 (April 1968), pp. 8-9 + .

*Broadbelt, Samuel. "Prerequisite for a Consumer: An Inspection of Advertising in the Classroom," *Social Studies*, v. 67, no. 2 (March-April 1976), pp. 76-79.

Campbell, Sally R. "Guide to Managing $$$," *Forecast for Home Economics*, v. 21, no. 8 (April 1976), pp. 19-22.

Chamberlin, R. J. "Case for Consumer Education in the Early Grades," *Elementary School Journal*, v. 78, no. 5 (May 1978), pp. 294-303.

Divoky, Diane. "The Big Business of Toys: A Target for Consumer Ed," *Learning*, v. 6, no. 3 (Nov. 1977), pp. 28-33.

+ Green, Hayden. "Consumer Education," *Booklist*, v. 69, no. 19 (June 1, 1973), pp. 933-38.

* + Green, Hayden. "One School's Consumer Survival Kit, An Interview," *Curriculum Review*, v. 17, no. 1 (Feb. 1978), pp. 12-14.
(Followed by CR staff consumer education reviews, pp. 15-28.)

Harty, Sheila. *Hucksters in the Classroom*. Washington, DC: Center for the Study of Responsive Law, 1979.

+ *Help: The Useful Almanac*. Washington, DC: Consumer News, 1977.

+ Joint Council on Economic Education. *Teaching Personal Economics in the Home Economics Curriculum*. New York: Joint Council on Economics Education, 1971.

Lankford, Francis. *Consumer Mathematics*. New York: Harcourt, Brace, Jovanovich, 1974.

+ Lee, Stewart. "Sources and Resources in Consumer Education," *Social Education*, v. 38, no. 6 (Oct. 1974), pp. 519-23.

Lumpkin, R. Pierce. "What Should Be Taught in General Business about the Role of the Consumer in Our Economy?" *Business Education Forum*, v. 20, no. 5 (March 1966), pp. 5-7.

Marcus, Stuart Paul, and Paul Jeffrey Richman. "A Proposal to Revise the Secondary School Curriculum in Economics," *Social Education*, v. 42, no. 3 (Jan. 1978), pp. 76-77.
Two students conclude that "the teaching of practical consumerism to young, impressionable students is an absolute must."

*Murphy, Patricia D. "Modules for Consumer Education: A Spiral-Process Approach to Curriculum Development," *American Vocational Journal*, v. 48, no. 7 (Oct. 1973), p. 52.

New York City Board of Education. *Consumer Education: Elementary, Intermediate, Junior High Schools*. New York: Board of Education, 1969.

+ "Periodicals as a Teaching Resource," *ConCERNS*, v. 1, no. 8 (Dec. 1979), p. 4.

+ Roat, Ronald C. "Making Kids Swindle Proof," *Learning*, v. 6, no. 3 (Nov. 1977), pp. 36-38.

+ Sagness, Richard, and Rebecca Sagness. *Selected Science Activities in Consumer Decision Making*. Columbus, OH: ERIC Clearinghouse on Science, Mathematics and Environmental Education, 1978.

*Schultheis, Robert A., and Kay Napoli. "Developing and Using Learning Activity Packages in Consumer Education"; Part I, *Business Education Forum*, v. 29, no. 5 (Feb. 1975), pp. 16-19; Part II, v. 29, no. 6 (March 1975), pp. 9-11.

*Shackelford, Wendell. "Consumerism, Communication, and the Demonstration of Quality in Educational Materials," *Audiovisual Instruction*, v. 20, no. 4 (April 1975), pp. 35-38.

+ Stampfl, R. W. "Consumer Education and the Pre-School Child," *Journal of Consumer Education*, v. 12 (Summer 1978), pp. 12-29.

"The Supermarket—A Consumer's Classroom," *Instructor*, v. 82, no. 2 (Oct. 1972), pp. 60-62.

+ U.S. Office of Consumer Affairs and the New York Public Library. *Consumer Education Bibliography*. Washington, DC: GPO, 1971.
Old, but still helpful.

Ward, Scott, Daniel Wackman, and Ellen Wartella. *How Children Learn to Buy: The Development of Consumer Information-Processing Skills*. Beverly Hills, CA: Sage, 1977.

+ Wasserman, Paul, ed. *Consumer Sourcebook: A Directory and Guide to Government Organizations; Associations, Centers and Institutes; Media Services; Company and Trademark Information; and Bibliographic Material Relating to Consumer Topics, Sources of Recourse, and Advisory Information*. 2nd ed. Detroit: Gale, 1978. 2v.
An expensive, lightly annotated, comprehensive guide to agencies interested in consumer problems, followed by a massive directory relating trade names to manufacturers with a separate annotated bibliography of adult consumer advisory materials.

Wilson, J. S. "Mass-Media Education Techniques," *Forecast for Home Economics*, v. 24, no. 3 (Nov. 1978), pp. 10+.

PART II

IMPLEMENTATION

EVALUATING MEDIA PROGRAMS

"It is essential to the provision of quality education that an adequate, effective school library service be furnished by the schools."
— California Assembly Bill No. 2259, Section 1

"A library and instructional materials center with proper staff and adequate, varied teaching materials should be provided in every elementary school.... The teacher should have ready access to many kinds of resources, ranging from books to natural objects to specialized equipment in order to meet the varying interests and abilities of pupils."
— National Council of Teachers of English Forum, *The Workload of the Elementary Teacher*, 1977

"Our media programs are successful because ... we don't consider school media centers as separate entities."
— George Plumleigh, District Supervisor, Los Alamitos School District

"The name 'library' has lost its etymological meaning and means not a collection of books, but the central agency for disseminating information, innocent recreation, and best of all, inspiration among people. Whenever this can be done better, more quickly or cheaply by a picture than a book, the picture is entitled to a place on the shelves and in the catalog.... A generation ago the lantern slide was little known except in magic lantern entertainments, and it required some courage for the first schools to make it a part of the educational apparatus. Today there is hardly a ... subject which is not receiving great aid from the lantern."
— Melvil Dewey, 1906

☐ ☐ ☐

INTRODUCTION

This chapter provides some means of evaluating the extent and effectiveness of school and district media programs and the effectiveness of other programs that provide some means of organizing and monitoring instructional materials. My personal assumption is that such programs are essential backups for instructional materials. Instructional materials, once selected, need to be processed, inventoried, organized, stored, distributed, used and monitored—if they are to be used effectively—or used at all. If selection is to be rational, it should have some means of evaluating how the process has worked out in practice, determining which materials of those selected have been most used and/or most valuable, and how the value corresponds to the monies spent. Media programs—if well done—offer means of extending and monitoring the use of materials. This chapter will include ways of determining whether media programs and similar programs are sufficient for their purposes.

Despite the importance of instructional materials, some schools and school districts completely ignore the space, activities, or personnel required to organize and maintain instructional materials used. I have heard, for example, of collections of media — costing $90,000 or so in Title II funds — gathering dust in improvised storage rooms because no money, time, or personnel had been allocated to process them. I have also been in one school building (among many others), which was designed in 1976 but provide *no* space (except a very small library) for storing instructional materials. In this particular building, texts, supplementary readers, models, specimens, games, and realia accumulated in closets, under desks, in classrooms and in the teachers' lounge. It was difficult to maintain a current inventory even for texts and supplementary readers, though a few valiant department heads tried to keep on top of materials for their departments. Most did not. It would have been impossible for anyone to have an overview of instructional materials and how they were used in this school.

In many school districts and individual schools, materials are not monitored by those who allocated funds for materials or chose these materials. If materials are supervised at all, it is by textbook clerks or IMC clerks with limited decision making powers, or else by whoever happens to be in charge of the lost and found. (It is my theory that the most unpopular books and teaching materials are lost most frequently.) Individual teachers, of course, have some notion of how materials have worked out in their own classes, but they have no overview and little comparative data. In most schools, no one is responsible for a consolidated review of the effectiveness of selection.

The National Commission on Libraries and Information Science, in its *National Inventory of Library Needs* (1975), stated that libraries in the U.S. are significantly underfunded, and estimated — at that time — that school libraries would need at least $4.5 billion "to allow acquisition of nonprint materials, additional print materials and equipment needed for effective use of A/V materials." The situation has not improved since that time.

Despite this discouraging reality, I am including here two kinds of instruments for estimation: those that attempt to estimate the collection of materials, and those that attempt to measure or estimate the services provided as backups for these materials. The latter — for services — may be measured in terms of space, budget, presence, and/or quality of professionals, as well as existence and/or quality of selection policies.

We tend to judge collections on the kinds and numbers of materials, whether they are broad, varied, up-to-date, coordinated with the curriculum and with the student body. Some of the evaluation standards provided are numerical. To my mind, quantitative measures can only be a rough index to quality. While there is undoubtedly a relationship between the numbers of materials and their ability to meet the needs of their users, size itself is no indication of quality, recency, or intelligent selection.

There are many approaches to evaluating media materials programs and the centers that house these media. Some current methods include:

- impressionistic evaluations
- opinions of expert consultants, peers, district officials
- opinions of concerned teachers and students
- usage studies

- case histories of difficulties or successes in obtaining and/or using materials
- item by item sampling
- schemes to determine the value of each item for users
- analysis on the basis of use
- comparison with other institutions
- comparison with prescribed standards
- estimation of quality based on expenditures
- measurement or estimation of ability to meet needs
- plotting expenditures over a period of time
- compiling a ratio of materials per user
- using quantitative figures based on materials used over materials owned
- comparing collection or materials with standard bibliographies, lists, and guides
- measuring recency of materials
- analyzing collection in terms of educational objectives
- analyzing collection in relationship to demographic student characteristics
- analyzing structure of library/media center, according to standard library criteria

While all these approaches have some value, the standards and means used in almost all cases are essentially comparisons rather than absolute standards; they represent some sort of workable compromise. Since school libraries, media centers, and other materials programs are seriously underfinanced, we have little working experience of what optimum programs can be. We may be comparing the adequate with the less adequate, or the poor with the worst. We do not know whether or not our best existing situations represent high standards, minimal standards, or something inbetween.

STANDARDS

Since to me the standards are, at best, tentative, subjective questions may be as valuable as any. The standards on page 282 are intended to be suggestive only. Others are available from the Key Publications or Key Organizations listed in this chapter.

The statements (taken from literature and experience) represent a consensus of policies, principles, standards and criteria accepted as basic minimal standards for effective library practice. As such, they are relevant for library/media centers in school situations and for the selection of instructional materials.

EVALUATION DERIVED FROM
BASIC STANDARD LIBRARY ASSUMPTIONS

	Not Valid	Partly Valid	Valid
Libraries should support their total organization programs.			
Library goals should support the goals of the parent organization.			
Libraries should acquire materials and information for the current and future needs of their parent organizations.			
Subject coverage should be extensive and intensive enough to meet current and anticipated information requirements.			
The organization's materials requirements should include all formats needed to fulfill the projects, needs, and interests of its users.			
The quantity of materials acquired should relate to the amount of materials available that are pertinent to the needs of its users.			
Criteria for the selection of materials should inform the acquisitioner on which materials should be selected and should indicate to users what kinds of materials they can expect.			
Ease in accessibility is the most desirable characteristic for indexing and finding systems.			
Catalogs and finding devices should be simple yet sufficiently detailed for effective use.			
Physical location of materials should be related to the amount and type of use.			
Libraries should publicize their materials and services so that users are aware of them.			
Superseded materials should not displace current materials.			
A trained staff is necessary to locate and select materials and to maintain current collections of relevant materials organized for use.			

The following questions can be helpful in evaluating services.

SELECTION POLICY

- Is there a selection policy for instructional materials?
- Is it based on a long-range program or is it merely spasmodic purchasing or crisis purchasing?
- Are materials selected, retained, and discarded in light of conscious objectives and written policy statements?

QUALITY OF MATERIALS

- Are there appropriate materials for all curriculum areas and for all levels of students?
- How would teachers, students, and independent consultants rate available materials for quality?

- Are materials added to meet the needs of new programs and changing circumstances (in the world as well as in the school)?
- Is there systematic removal of non-useful materials?
- Are materials adequate to meet informational and recreational needs of students?
- Do materials represent many points of view and perspectives?
- Are there ways of increasing and encouraging their use and accessibility?
- What access to other materials does this educational institution need?
- Are other resources available and utilized?
- If not, have educators investigated ways to provide access to other materials?
- Do educators know what is available in their fields (or grade levels) and in related fields or grade levels?

QUANTITY OF MATERIALS

- Are there enough materials to provide a wide range of choice — in all curriculum areas — for each student and teacher in the school?
- Is a wide range of reading levels represented so that each student can find materials she/he can use successfully?
- Are materials available in all kinds of media and appropriate for student/teacher needs?
- Are media backed up by adequate well-maintained equipment?

EXTENT OF PROGRAM

- Do you use your library/media center for such things as playing tutoring games (math games, chess)?
- Do you use media centers to display materials for and by students, teachers, parent groups, community groups?
- Have you developed such motivational learning aids for teachers and students as task cards on mythology or learning kits for library skills?
- Have you had workshops for teachers, asking for suggestions and programs?
- Have you developed reading lists or learning centers for individual teachers or courses of study?
- Do you exchange these with other library media centers?
- Are library/media specialists included in orientation programs for new students and new faculty?

SOME MEANS OF INCREASING UTILIZATION OF INSTRUCTIONAL MATERIALS, BY INFORMING STUDENTS, STAFF, OFFICIALS, AND PARENTS

Posters, displays, bulletin boards
News releases, newsletters
Media presentations and media productions (staff)
Media programs for students
Personal contacts
Classroom visits
Library reading clubs
Bibliographies (personal and/or printed)
Printed catalogs
Computer on-line catalogs in every school

(List continues on page 284)

Grade level and curriculum bibliographies
Annotated bibliographies
Memoranda, handbooks, information sheets
Conferences and workshops
Open houses
Public exhibits
Annual reports
Participation in association activities
Staff meetings
Pre-service, in-service, staff development programs
Budget justifications
Consultation on selection
Model collections
Display collections
Examination collections
Participation on curriculum committee
Materials included as constituent of all basic programs
Joint purchases and selections
Publishers' and authors' presentations
Topical resource presentations
Institutional materials fairs
Happenings
Preventive maintenance of media equipment
Convenient scheduling of materials and equipment space

The School Library Bill of Rights is reprinted on page 285 with the permission of the American Association of School Librarians.

The following questions can be useful in evaluating the school library and its programs. These questions are reprinted with permission from *The Library in the Independent School*, copyrighted by the National Association of Independent Schools.

LIBRARY PROGRAM

- Do you have a written description of your library program?

- Is your library program so far-reaching that the library permeates every area of social life?

- Do you bring the outside world into your library through:
    visiting authors
    visiting lecturers
    book fairs
    record fairs

- Does your library program implement effectively the stated objectives and philosophy of your school?

- If you are not satisfied with the library program, have you presented realistic, concrete plans for a more extensive program to:
    the head of your school
the academic committee
the faculty
the Board of Trustees?

(Questions continue on page 286)

SCHOOL LIBRARY BILL OF RIGHTS
for School Library Media Center Programs

Approved by American Association of School Librarians Board of Directors, Atlantic City, 1969.

The American Association of School Librarians reaffirms its belief in the Library Bill of Rights of the American Library Association. Media personnel are concerned with generating understanding of American freedoms through the development of informed and responsible citizens. To this end the American Association of School Librarians asserts that the responsibility of the school library media center is:

To provide a comprehensive collection of instructional materials selected in compliance with basic written selection principles, and to provide maximum accessibility to these materials.

To provide materials that will support the curriculum, taking into consideration the individual's needs, and the varied interests, abilities, socio-economic backgrounds, and maturity levels of the students served.

To provide materials for teachers and students that will encourage growth in knowledge, and that will develop literary, cultural and aesthetic appreciation, and ethical standards.

To provide materials which reflect the ideas and beliefs of religious, social, political, historical, and ethnic groups and their contribution to the American and world heritage and culture, thereby enabling students to develop an intellectual integrity in forming judgments.

To provide a written statement, approved by the local Boards of Education, of the procedures for meeting the challenge of censorship of materials in school library media centers.

To provide qualified professional personnel to serve teachers and students.

THE LIBRARY IN THE SCHOOL

- Are you honestly convinced that the library in your school is a dynamic intellectual force?
- If your library does not exert effective intellectual stimulation, can you pinpoint the reasons that it does not?
- Are you prepared to move the proverbial heaven and earth to make sure the library does assume its rightful role of academic leadership?

The AECT/ALA Standards below (for a school of 500 students) are based on those in *Media Programs: District and Schools* (see Key Publications). For evaluative purposes other columns could be added dealing with state standards and/or local policies, media and materials counts, or media and materials needs.

SCHOOL MEDIA/MATERIALS ASSESSMENT FORM

Areas for Study	AECT/ALA Standards (for school of 500)
Total Collection	At least 20,000 items, plus 5 percent of per pupil Educational budget — for acquisition of audiovisual and library materials
Print Formats	
Books	Minimum size 8,000 to 12,000 volumes 16 to 24 books per student, access to 60,000 titles
Magazines	50 to 175 titles and access to loans and photocopies
Newspapers	3 to 6 titles
Pamphlets	Current useful documents Varied points of view, include state, national, and international government documents
Reference Books	
Microforms	Depending on needs
Visual Formats	
Slides and Transparencies	2,000 to 6,000 items 4 to 12 per user Access to 15,000 items
Graphics Posters Art and Study Prints	800 to 1,200 items With additional items as needed
Maps and globes	
Provisions for children's art original art loans from museums	
Filmstrips	500 to 2,000 items 1 to 4 per user 1,500 for individualized programs

Areas for Study (cont'd)	AECT/ALA Standards (cont'd)

Films
 and
 Video tapes
	Access to a minimum of 3,000 titles
	With enough duplicate prints to satisfy 90 percent of
	   requests
	Funds for purchases throughout year
	Additional titles from district or public
	   film libraries

Super 8mm films and Silent films	500 to 1,000 items 1 to 2 per users Access to 4,000 items
Auditory Formats Recordings Tape Cassettes Discs or audio cassettes	Access to 5,000 items from collections and loans with appropriate equipment
Tactile Formats Games and Toys	400 to 750 items Access to district level collection Possibly computer access for simulation games
Models & Sculpture	200 to 500 items Access to collections in other agencies (district, community, museums)
Specimens	200 to 400 items Access to larger collections (districts, zoos, museums)

John Church in *Administration of Instructional Materials Organizations* (Fearon, 1970) developed a checklist format that provides compact evaluation. This checklist (one of six in the book) is reprinted on page 288 with permission of Fearon Publishers in Belmont, California.

CHECK LIST 1

Directions. (1) Review the purposes of your center. (2) Place a check mark at the left of each item to indicate whether it is true of your center. (3) Estimate the degree of adequacy with which the stated condition serves the purposes of the center and place a check mark in the appropriate column at the right.

NEARLY ALL ASPECTS ADEQUATE	5
MOST ASPECTS ADEQUATE	4
MORE ASPECTS ADEQUATE THAN INADEQUATE	3
MORE ASPECTS INADEQUATE THAN ADEQUATE	2
ALL OR NEARLY ALL ASPECTS INADEQUATE	1
NO OPINION OR BASIS FOR JUDGMENT	N
DOES NOT APPLY	0

YES. TRUE OF OUR CENTER
? NO OPINION; OR DO NOT KNOW
NO. NOT TRUE OF OUR CENTER

1. An established curriculum laboratory or another competent, non-commercial source has been consulted concerning the plans for the curriculum laboratory plant.

2. The physical plant has been planned with the philosophy of the institution in mind.

3. The curriculum laboratory area is
   a. Centralized in relation to correlated offices.
   b. Arranged so that a minimum staff is needed.
   c. Of sufficient size to provide good reading and working conditions.
   d. Close enough to the library for ready use of the library.

4. Provisions are made for space to meet user needs throughout the year (including summer).

5. The curriculum laboratory is
   a. Planned for optimum temperature and ventilation.
   b. Equipped with floor covering of approved material.
   c. Acoustically treated to permit quiet reading.
   d. Adequately lighted.
   e. Artistically decorated.

6. The curriculum laboratory staff members definitely participate in planning any changes or additions to the physical plant and equipment of the laboratory.

7. The curriculum laboratory area contains
   a. Conference rooms.
   b. Listening rooms.
   c. Preview rooms.
   d. Offices for the professional curriculum laboratory staff members.
   e. Workrooms for typing, mimeographing, and other types of duplicating.
   f. Workrooms for binding and packaging.
   g. Storage space.
   h. Workshop rooms for use of staff and students engaging in actual construction of learning materials.
   i. Space for reading and study.

8. There are provisions for possible expansion.*

*These criteria and the form were developed by the author as part of an unpublished doctoral study, *op. cit.*, pp. 116-117.

This Student Opinionnaire is one of the many evaluative forms included in *Evaluating Media Programs: District and School.* It is reprinted here with the permission of the Association for Educational Communications and Technology.

Student Opinionnaire

Subject_____

Grade_____

		Always	Frequently	Occasionally	Seldom	Never
1.	I can use the media center when I need to as my class schedule permits	☐	☐	☐	☐	☐
2.	I do use the media center when I need to as my class schedule permits	☐	☐	☐	☐	☐
3.	Our media center is too crowded	☐	☐	☐	☐	☐
4.	Our media center is too noisy	☐	☐	☐	☐	☐
5.	Learning is improved when a variety of media is used in my classes . .	☐	☐	☐	☐	☐
6.	I can obtain informational materials I need from the media center . .	☐	☐	☐	☐	☐
7.	I do obtain informational materials I need from the media center . . .	☐	☐	☐	☐	☐
8.	I can get help in finding and using media center materials and equipment	☐	☐	☐	☐	☐
9.	I do get help in finding and using media center materials and equipment	☐	☐	☐	☐	☐
10.	I can take home materials other than books from the media center . .	☐	☐	☐	☐	☐
11.	I do take home materials other than books from the media center . .	☐	☐	☐	☐	☐
12.	I am asked to help in selecting materials for the media center	☐	☐	☐	☐	☐
13.	I do help in selecting materials for the media center	☐	☐	☐	☐	☐
14.	My suggestions for purchase of materials are seriously considered . . .	☐	☐	☐	☐	☐
15.	I can use school supplies and equipment to make audiovisual materials for my school reports	☐	☐	☐	☐	☐
16.	I do use school supplies and equipment to make audiovisual materials for my school reports	☐	☐	☐	☐	☐
17.	I can get help in making audiovisual materials from the media center staff	☐	☐	☐	☐	☐
18.	I do get help in making audiovisual materials from the media center staff	☐	☐	☐	☐	☐
19.	My teachers expect me to use:					
	(a) print materials	☐	☐	☐	☐	☐
	(b) visual materials	☐	☐	☐	☐	☐
	(c) listening materials	☐	☐	☐	☐	☐
20.	I am informed when new materials are added to the media center collection	☐	☐	☐	☐	☐
21.	Television is used as part of my classroom instruction.					
	(a) commercial television	☐	☐	☐	☐	☐
	(b) educational and instructional television	☐	☐	☐	☐	☐
	(c) programs produced by the school	☐	☐	☐	☐	☐
	(d) videotaping for student self-evaluation	☐	☐	☐	☐	☐

KEY ORGANIZATIONS

The organizations listed in this section primarily specialize in books. Organizations concerned with the process of reading are listed elsewhere. EDMARC, listed in the chapter on basic learning materials in *Issues and Policies* is also a children's book center.

American Association of School Librarians (AASL)
50 East Huron St.
Chicago, IL 60611   (312) 944-6780
The AASL, an affiliate of the American Library Association is concerned with the evaluation, selection and use of media materials in schools. It places, perhaps, greatest emphasis on printed media. It has produced many helpful publications on selecting media materials, including *Policies and Procedures for Selection of Instructional Materials* (1976, $0.50), a document with good guidelines for handling controversial materials.

Its journal, *School Media Quarterly* ($15.00 for non-members) is an ongoing review source for all kinds of media except for textbooks. It includes frequent articles on selection issues as well as reports and research on topics like censorship.

Association for Educational Communications and
Technology (AECT)
1126 16th St., NW
Washington, DC 20036   (202) 833-4180
The AECT is a professional membership organization for educators and media specialists interested in improving instruction through technology (interpreted as a process and not limited to such "hardware" as projectors, computers, and television). Members are found not only in schools at all levels, but in industry, the Armed Forces, and in such service agencies as hospitals, libraries and museums, wherever communication media interact with production and instruction. Although it places some emphasis on production of media, its periodicals and many of its publications are highly valuable to educators at the K-12 levels.

Membership, at $35.00 a year and up, offers free subscriptions to two periodicals, discounts on publications, free consultations and opportunities to affiliate with special interest divisions.

Its periodicals include *Instructional Innovator*, formerly *Audiovisual Instruction*, $18.00/yr. to non-members, free to members, which includes a special section on "Instructional Resources" designed especially for the K-12 educational levels; *Educational Communication and Technology Journal* (ECTJ), a quarterly on communication, technology and the teaching/learning process; *Journal of Instructional Development* (JID); and *ect. newspaper*, for members only. Other important publications are:

> *An Approach to the Design of Mediated Instruction*, by C. Edward Cavert. 1974. 271p. $12.95; $10.95 members.
> Covers frame of reference, definition of target population, needs, goals, strategies, structure, diagnosis, and mediation.

> *Audiovisual Processes in Education.* 1971. 148p. $8.50; $7.95 members.

Planning and Operating Media Centers. 1976. 80p. $8.95pa. $7.50 members.

Rhetoric of the Movie. 1966. 6 super 8mm films with *Teacher's Guide.*
 $57.95; $44.95 members.
Designed for teaching about the movies as a medium of communication.

Other publications are annotated separately in this chapter and others.

KEY PUBLICATIONS

Elementary School Evaluative Criteria: A Guide for School Improvement, by
 National Study of School Evaluation, Arlington, VA, 1973. 15p. $6.00pa.
 Includes excellent detailed checklists and evaluation criteria for instructional
materials services.

Two similar thorough compilations of evaluations seem to be out of print,
but are quite valuable:

Evaluative Criteria: A Guide for School Improvement, by National Study of
Secondary School Evaluation, Washington, DC, 1960.

*Evaluative Criteria: Junior High School/Middle School: A Guide for School
Improvement*, by National Study of School Evaluation, Arlington, VA,
1970.

*Evaluating Media Programs: District and School: A Method and an Instru-
 ment.* Draft Edition. Washington, DC: Committee on Evaluation of Media
 Programs, Association for Educational Communications and Technology,
 1976. 79p. $4.95pa.; member price $3.95.
 This is a convenient and thorough evaluation workbook, that can be used to
evaluate actual collections of instructional materials, as well as media programs,
budgets, physical facilities, and staff, at the school or district level. It includes
questionnaires (opinionnaires) for students and teachers, as well as two cut-out
forms for evaluating itself. Its goals (aside from research on its own validity as an
instrument) are to assist local schools in organizing descriptive data on media
programs for internal or external use in planning, self-improvement, accredita-
tion, or for other purposes. It is intended for use with current state and local
guidelines, and more particularly with *Media Programs: District and School.*
 While it is a useful tool—in fact, one of the few current tools attempting to
assess instructional materials—it is overly general, at times with an emphasis on
quantitative measures. In practice, for example, it might be desirable to evaluate
collections by subject areas or grade levels or teaching approaches (none of which
are covered here).

The Library in the Independent School: Some Questions and Answers, by
 Pauline Anderson. Boston, MA: National Association of Independent
 Schools, 1968. 42p. $1.00pa.
 Provides a self-evaluation form in question-and-answer format suitable for
any school library; many questions deal with adequacy of materials and their
effective utilization for educational purposes.

Managing Multimedia Libraries, by Warren B. Hicks and Alma M. Tillin. New
York: Bowker, 1977. 264p. $14.95.

This current, authoritative guide to multimedia library management is based
on a management by objectives approach. Within this context, it includes a
25-page chapter on selecting media materials. Areas covered are policies, tools,
relations with other processes, means of recording information about materials to
be selected, and ways to design, supervise and control selection procedure.
Includes organization charts and flow charts of selections procedures in a school
district.

Media Programs: District and School (Formerly *Standards for School Media
Programs 1969*), by American Association of School Librarians (AASL) and
the Association for Educational Communications and Technology (AECT).
Chicago: American Library Association, 1975. 128p. $3.00pa.

This concise handbook represents intelligent consensus by professionals in
librarianship, educational technology, information science, and related fields. In
it, the AASL and the AECT call for "media-programs that are user-centered, that
promote flexibility in practice based on intelligent selection from many alternatives, and that are derived from well-articulated learning and program objectives." This thoroughly competent guide provides an overview of media programs
and functions at all levels, and considers specifics for operations, facilities, selection policies and procedures, and standards for total collections.

A Model School District Media Program: Montgomery County as a Case Study,
by John T. Gillespie. Chicago: American Library Association, 1977. 216p.
(ALA Studies in Librarianship No. 6). $10.00.

The media programs of the Montgomery County Public School system in
Maryland have been studied, admired, and considered a prototype for other
school districts attempting to improve their own media programs. This book uses
a case study approach that traces the evolution of the program and provides a
detailed in-depth analysis of each department. It includes sample forms, flow
charts, evaluation criteria for reviewing media, and outlines of in-service courses,
all of which can be used as guidelines for other schools and systems.

Survey of School Media Standards, by Milbrey L. Jones. (U.S. Office of Education). Washington, DC: GPO, 1977. 259p. $4.00pa.

This analysis of trends in school media standards assesses the impact of Title
II of the Elementary and Secondary Education Act on the development and revision of media standards and provides a rather current compilation of media
standards for elementary and secondary schools.

*Teaching Media Skills: An Instructional Program for Elementary and Middle
School Students*, by H. Thomas Walker and Paula Kay Montgomery. Littleton, CO: Libraries Unlimited, 1977. 189p. $13.50.

This book provides a comprehensive model for integrating media skills
instruction into the teaching process, as well as practical methods for implementing a media skills program in any school or school system. It thus ties together
media skills, classroom instruction, and educational theory. Part 3 is a
bibliography of commercial materials for teaching media skills, arranged by
genre (e.g., charts, filmstrips, games, kits, tapes, transparencies, and prints with
prices, grade levels, and descriptive annotations).

FOR FURTHER READING

*Items marked with an asterisk include criteria.

+ Items marked with a plus have further lists of references.

* + Back, D. Joleen, and Leo R. Lajeunesse. *The Learning Resources Center: A Planning Primer for Libraries in Transition*. New York: Bowker, 1977.

+ Cabeceiras, James. *The Multimedia Library: Materials Selection and Use*. New York: Academic Press, 1978.

*Church, John G. *Administration of Instructional Materials Organizations: Analysis and Evaluation Centers*. Belmont, CA: Fearon, 1970.

*Hines, Theodore C. "Children's Access to Materials." In *Children and Books*, edited by Zena Sutherland, pp. 624-27. 5th ed. Glenview, IL: Scott, Foresman and Company, 1977.

+ Loertscher, David. *Budgeting for School Media Centers: An Annotated Bibliography*. Syracuse, NY: Syracuse University, 1975.

"Los Alamitos," *School Library Journal*, v. 24, no. 2 (Oct. 1977), pp. 74-77. Describes the program of Los Alamitos School District, winner of the School Library Media Program of the Year Award in 1977.

"The School Media Center: The Changing Scene," special issue of *Peabody Journal of Education*, v. 55, no. 3 (April 1978).

Sullivan, Peggy. *Problems in School Media Management*. New York: Bowker, 1971.
Thirty case studies, largely dealing with organization, administration, and utilization of media programs.

*Talmage, H., and J. G. Walberg. "Instructional Materials Implementation Questionnaire." In *Pilot Reading Series Evaluation Study: Final Report*, Appendix A, pp. 65-69. Chicago: University of Illinois Office of Evaluation Research (at Chicago Circle), 1974.

*Tanzman, Jack, and Kenneth J. Dunn. *Using Instructional Media Effectively*. West Nyack, NY: Parker Publishing, 1971.
Very thoughtful criteria throughout, especially on pp. 32-33.

"Tapping Curriculum Labs," special issue of *American Vocational Journal*, v. 53, no. 5 (May 1978).

+ U.S. Office of Education. *Library Programs Worth Knowing About*. Washington, DC: GPO, 1976.
Designed as an annotated guide, this preliminary catalog highlights and describes some creative library programs and approaches in 10 states.

"I know of no safe depository of the ultimate powers of the society but the people themselves, and if we think them not enlightened enough to exercise their control with a wholesome discretion, the remedy is not to take it from them, but to inform their discretion by education."
  — Thomas Jefferson

"Whoever would overthrow the liberty of a nation must begin by subduing the freedom of speech."
  — Benjamin Franklin

□ □ □

The whole intent of these three volumes has been to enhance intelligent and rational decision-making in selection through conscious articulated selection practices and policies based on awareness of local needs and appropriate materials. Such an approach begins with appraising existing materials (the Needs Assessment chapter of *Issues and Policies*), and continues with devising an adequate materials budget considering the needs of users, allowing for alternative materials, and remaining congruent with district preferences. The fifth chapter of *Issues and Policies* advocates that materials should be selected with the assistance of well-publicized selection policies that are established through consultation with all significant community groups, coordinated with state and federal policies, and frequently reviewed and revised.

I believe that materials can be selected more effectively given input and assistance from parents and community, teachers, and students (all of which is covered in depth in *Issues and Policies*). It is particularly important for educators to become aware of their teaching preferences while considering the needs of their students and the nature of their community, and while enhancing their knowledge of available materials.

In Part III of *Issues and Policies*, some standards are provided for evaluating materials. These include evaluation criteria, LVR, cognitive criteria, readability, fairness and bias. Depending upon the nature of the programs — basic or individualized (the first chapters of Part V in that volume) — or the children involved, particular criteria become prominent, especially for young children, gifted children, and "special" children (the final chapters of the volume).

The chapter on free materials in *Media and the Curriculum* suggests some means of evaluating producers' biases and suggests ways to balance out biased materials and/or to help educate children to be aware of bias. In the present volume, the chapter on social studies suggests additional means of handling controversial issues and selecting materials to balance out opposing views; the chapter on the feeling domain explores the necessity and means of involving the community on topics and issues that involve affects and feelings; and the chapter on language arts suggests means that teachers can use to justify their choice and assignments of books. Each chapter in this volume and in *Media and the Curriculum* — on a particular topic or medium — provides some relevant standards and sources for choosing and using materials for particular disciplines or particular formats. The preceding chapter provides some means of assessing public relations components, and whether or not materials are available and appropriate. If materials are hostilely criticized after all these processes and practices, it would seem to indicate either some breakdown in the procedures, possibly a failure in public relations, or conceivably, hostility caused by some unrelated issues.

According to studies by the National Council of Teachers of English and the Intellectual Freedom Committee of the American Library Association, censorship appears to be increasing in the 1970s even as compared to the 1950s McCarthyite period. About 30 percent of teachers in schools had been subjected to attempts at censorship in the last decade, compared to 20 percent in the 1950s.

Norma Galbler, one housewife and mother from Longview, Texas, who has been active in preventing many books from reaching Texas classrooms, believes that censorship is increasing because parents are angry that their children cannot read or write after graduating from high school, and that parents feel their children are cheated by taking "to many cop-out courses." If indeed, students cannot read after graduating from high school, parents are justified in their anger—whether or not they are justified in the ways they direct it.

After investigating the hostile textbook confrontation in Kanawha County, West Virginia, the National Education Association concluded that school districts adopting materials—especially materials that might be controversial—should attempt to develop a broad base of community support by disseminating the nature and objectives of proposed materials before opposing groups issue half-truths or distortions. The *American School Board Journal*, in an article on "Textbook Battles" (July 1975), suggested the following steps to defuse public controversies:

1) Take the books and hit the road—with advance publicity—at least one month before final adoption; display materials extensively.

2) Provide teachers with time to meet and talk with parents to explain the purposes and intents of the materials.

3) Write (or purchase) and distribute jargon-free, easy to understand materials supporting school board positions.

4) Provide options and offer alternative materials or courses to objecting students and parents for their own use.

The NEA suggests that schools develop reasonable and workable policies for handling challenges or complaints concerning materials selected. Essential features of such policies are that,

- charges should be specified and in writing (on a school form)
- complainants should be invited to meet with teachers
- materials should not be banned or withdrawn in response to complaints based on passages taken out of context without due consideration for the whole work and its purposes or objectives.

According to *American School Board Journal*'s article on "Textbook Battles," the complaint forms designed by groups like the Council for Social Studies and the National Council of Teachers of English which are designed to protect the teacher's point of view tend to put the complainant on the defensive.

They suggest using forms designed to help foster cooperation between parents and teachers—perhaps a form designed to help parents put their objections clearly and persuasively on paper. Teachers, similarly, need a defense form to allow them to defend their choices clearly, quickly, and persuasively.

The article suggests a form for complainants that is courteous and invites use—to encourage filling out by people with complaints. The form should be distributed with the following materials:

- a polite cover letter (possibly merely a form letter signed by the superintendent or school board president)

- statements of a school system's educational goals and how they were formulated

- a copy of the district's written policies on selection

- statements on the options available if materials are objectionable on religious or moral grounds

The author's also suggest carefully following through with individuals who receive these forms but do not turn them in. According to one school superintendent in the deep south, these are the parents who are most apt to start demonstrations and protests at board meetings. Frontline personnel in each school should handle queries on textbooks or other materials with attention and courtesy rather than with bureaucratic runaround, so that persons with complaints will not be antagonized by patronizing responses.

The following sample "Request for Reconsideration of Instructional Materials" is reprinted with permission from the American Association of School Librarians' *Policies and Procedures for Selection of Instructional Materials*, as printed in *School Media Quarterly*, Winter 1977. It is rather similar to forms designed by the National Council of Teachers of English and the National Council for the Social Studies.

Organizations composed of librarians, English teachers, and social studies teachers—the most frequently attacked groups—have devised rather similar strategies for handling complaints. The American Library Association, for instance, recommends that, as part of normal operating procedures, every library should

- maintain definite (written and approved) materials selection policies

- maintain clearly defined methods for handling complaints

- maintain lines of communication with civic, religious, educational, and political bodies of their communities

- maintain vigorous public relations programs on behalf of intellectual freedom

(Text continues on page 298)

REQUEST FOR RECONSIDERATION OF INSTRUCTIONAL MATERIALS
(Reprinted with permission of the American Association of School Librarians.)

School _____

Please check type of material:
( ) Book   ( ) Film   ( ) Record
( ) Periodical   ( ) Filmstrip   ( ) Kit
( ) Pamphlet   ( ) Cassette   ( ) Other

Title _____

Author _____

Publisher or Producer _____

Request initiated by _____

Telephone _____ Address _____

City _____ State _____ Zip _____

The following questions are to be answered after the complainant has read, viewed, or listened to the school library material in its entirety. If sufficient space is not provided, attach additional sheets. (Please sign your name to each additional attachment.)

1. To what in the material do you object? (Please be specific, cite pages, frames in a filmstrip, film sequence, et cetera.)

_____

_____

_____

_____

2. What do you believe is the theme or purpose of this material?

_____

_____

_____

_____

3. What do you feel might be the result of a student using this material?

_____

_____

_____

_____

4. For what age group would you recommend this material?

_____

5. Is there anything good in this material? Please comment.

_____

_____

6. Would you care to recommend other school library material of the same subject and format?

_____

_____   _____
Signature of Complainant   **Date**

Please return *completed* form to the school principal.

If complaints occur, these practices may provide a basis from which to counter efforts to restrain or limit materials. The ALA suggests that, should confrontation occur, the library or librarian,

- should remain calm and treat the group or individual who complains with dignity, courtesy, and good humor
- take immediate steps to assure that full facts are known to administration and the governing authority
- seek the support of local press when appropriate
- inform civil organizations of the facts
- defend the *principle* of freedom to read, rather than the individual item
- contact professional organizations for assistance.

A Censorship CARE Package distributed by Diane P. Shugert of the Connecticut Council of Teachers of English is based on materials originally assembled by the Washington Council of Teachers of English to provide useful information to individuals and groups writing policies and procedures or dealing with challenges to academic freedom. These include many useful outlines and rationales. They are available for $1.00 from Mrs. Diane P. Shugert, Assistant Professor of English, Central Connecticut State College, 1615 Stanley St., New Britain, CT 06050.

KEY ORGANIZATIONS

Besides the organizations listed below, the National Council of Teachers of English, the American Association of School Librarians, and the National Council for the Social Studies are all Key Organizations.

Freedom to Read Foundation
50 East Huron St.
Chicago, IL 60611   (312) 944-6780
The Foundation was organized in 1969 as the American Library Association's response to members' interest in having adequate means to support and defend librarians whose positions were in jeopardy because of abridgments to the First Amendment, and to establish legal precedent for freedom to read. It works to provide financial and legal assistance to libraries and librarians, and to fight repressive legislation that inhibits librarians from acquiring or disseminating materials that have not been declared illegal.

The Foundation works with the ALA's Office of Intellectual Freedom, which distributes ALA *Policies on Intellectual Freedom*. These include (at $0.05 each, reduction for quantity) *The Library Bill of Rights, Resolution on Challenged Materials, Free Access to Libraries for Minors, Freedom to Read Statement*, and many other useful items. Single issues of the following reprints are available for $0.10 each: *A Selective Bibliography on School Materials Selection and Censorship, 1971-1975* and *What to Do Before the Censor Comes—And After*. The Foundation's *Newsletter on Intellectual Freedom* is available for $8.00/yr. The *Intellectual Freedom Manual* (1974) is available for $5.00. This latter brings together a comprehensive history of the ALA's involvement in and commitment to intellectual freedom, with source documents, policies, and practical advice.

National Coalition Against Censorship (NCAC)
22 East 40th St.
New York, NY 10016 (212) 686-7098
   The NCAC is an alliance of national organizations which includes the American Association of School Administrators along with other educational, religious, professional, artistic, labor, and civil rights organizations that are interested in creating in their own members and the wider community a climate or opinion hospitable to First Amendment Freedoms. Through public education and aid to participating members, the NCAC encourages knowledge and support of First Amendment principles. It is particularly concerned with book censorship in schools and libraries; government secrecy; issues of access, diversity, and fairness in television; and the confusion of standards on obscenity. Its publication, *Censorship News*, is free on request.

KEY PUBLICATIONS

   In addition to the items listed here, *The Students' Right to Read* (NCTE, 1972), included in the chapter on language arts materials, is highly recommended as is Benjamin Cox's *The Censorship Game and How to Play It* (NCSS, 1977), which is incorporated in the chapter on social studies. Materials in the chapter on Sex Education are often relevant.

Censorship: A Guide for Teachers, Librarians, and Others Concerned with Intel-
   lectual Freedom, by Lou Willett Stanek. New York: Dell, 1976. 31p. (A
   Laurel Leaf Edition). (Free from Educational Sales Dept., Dell Publishing
   Co., 245 E. 47th St., New York, NY 10017).
   This compilation for teachers and librarians considers pragmatic aspects of censorship and the factors that underly censorship (reverse selection). It draws on the resources of the American Library Association, the National Council of Teachers of English, the Association of American Publishers, the Media Coalition, and the National Ad Hoc Committee Against Censorship in a concise informative handbook, which includes forms and suggestions.

Dealing with Censorship, by the National Council of Teachers of English, Committee Against Censorship. Urbana, IL: NCTE, 1979. 228p. $6.50pa.
   A compilation of ideas and tactics from 18 teachers and professors who have studied the issues and/or have had first-hand experiences in dealing with censorship. It analyzes those aspects of books most likely to come under fire, discusses the tactics of censors, and suggests some ways for teachers and administrators to handle problems effectively.

Policies and Procedures for Selection of Instructional Materials. Chicago, IL:
   American Association of School Librarians, 1976. 8p. $0.50pa. (From
   American Association of School Librarians, 50 E. Huron St., Chicago, IL
   60611).
   A compact revision of an earlier guide, which includes a useful introduction, guidelines, and models for selection policies and procedures with about one-half of its 8 pages devoted to procedures for reconsidering materials.

FOR FURTHER READING

*Items marked with an asterisk include criteria.

+ Items marked with a plus include additional references.

* + Busha, Charles H. *An Intellectual Freedom Primer*. Littleton, CO: Libraries Unlimited, 1977.

"Censorship in Education," *High School Journal*, v. 62, no. 8 (May 1979). Special issue.

+ ERIC Clearinghouse on Educational Management, *Textbook Selection and Controversy*. Eugene, OR: 1976 (*The Best of ERIC*, no. 16, March 1976).

Haight, Anne Lyon. *Banned Books: 387 B.C. to 1978 A.D.* New York: Bowker, 1978.

*"Intellectual Freedom and Racism," special issue of *Interracial Books for Children Bulletin*, v. 8, no. 415 (1977).

*Iowa Association of School Librarians. Professional Relations Committee. *Selection Policies for School Libraries*. Des Moines, IA: Department of Public Instruction, 1968.

* + Parker, Franklin. *The Battle of the Books: Kanawha County*. Bloomington, IN: Phi Delta Kappa Educational Foundation, 1975. (Fastback 63).

*"Textbook Battles: They're Brewing and Bubbling: By Fall They'll Be Boiling. Don't You Get Scalded," *American School Board Journal*, v. 162, no. 7 (July 1975), pp. 21-28.

Woods, L. B. "Censorship in the Schools," *Phi Delta Kappan*, v. 61, no. 2 (Oct. 1979), pp. 104-106.
Factual report on censorship cases—successful and unsuccessful—from 1966 to 1975.

TEACHING SELECTION

This chapter surveys "what is" and "what could be" in teaching the selection of materials for instruction, a subject unfortunately almost completely neglected in most schools of education or "pre-service training." Admittedly, it might be a difficult subject to teach since it involves so many skills and so many disciplines. My ideal curriculum for training the "complete selector" would include the following (not necessarily in order of importance):

- media and communication theory (including media and formats)
- media and communication sources
    - for school subjects
    - for interests and interdisciplinary materials
- reviews and information sources for school level materials in above fields
- child development, with an emphasis on children's skills and interests as they pertain to reading, media, manipulatives, and other instructional materials
- educational practices that relate to materials, e.g.,
    - curriculum theory
    - adapting materials
    - verifying materials (experimental design)
- political theory and practices (especially relating to educational selection),
    - politics of education
    - copyright law
- community relations
    - parent relations
    - community resources in education
    - public relations
- values and philosophy
    - censorship
    - standards
    - cost analysis

While this ambitious curriculum is not likely to appear at any school of education, I would like to see instruction of some sort at these schools.

Most of the administrators who assume responsibility for selection (through written policies) and the teachers whose professional organizations consider selection to be a "professional" responsibility engage in this task without training of any kind. This training gap has been filled in by in-service education, by on-going workshops at teachers' centers, and by conferences and workshops. During the last couple of years, groups ranging from the American Association of School Librarians to the American Educational Research Association have held conferences, workshops, and meetings that dealt with selection from their own perspectives. In-service education is most often conducted by EPIE Institute, teachers' centers, specialists in fields like bilingual education or special education, and a few states.

This chapter includes excerpts from a few prospectuses and outlines of courses that deal in some way with selecting materials. Although these courses overlap to a degree, each has its own rationale and its own audience. Other courses have been held by EDMARC, the Educational Materials Review Center, which is now planning to give these courses again. Training in selection was part of the purpose of the Educational Media Selection Centers of the early 1970s, which were ultimately not financially supported by the federal government.

The AACTE, the American Association of Colleges for Teacher Education, self-confessedly a linkage system and a catalyst for upgrading the effectiveness of the teaching profession, was unable to locate for me any college-level courses in schools of education, though I happened on one myself. In its substantial publishing program, the AACTE has no publications that deal in some way with selecting instructional materials. Most college-level courses are taught at schools of librarianship or by centers for educational technology.

Courses taught by institutes or centers of educational technology tend to emphasize technology, including the qualities and functions of non-print media. Library school courses tend to cover qualities of media and information on media sources. The "curriculum materials" course taught by Dr. Meredith Gall at the School of Education at the University of Oregon at Eugene is a thoughtful, well-designed course that emphasizes instructional design and research. It also focuses on analyzing, evaluating and selecting curriculum as the prospectus reprinted below (with permission from Dr. Gall) indicates.

PROSPECTUS: CURRICULUM MATERIALS

Overview

The primary goal of this course is to increase your ability to analyze and evaluate curriculum materials using three different processes: (1) inspection of the materials, (2) actual try-out in a teaching situation, and (3) review of reports containing evaluative data on the materials' effectiveness. (Specific objectives of the course are listed below.) School district personnel need these skills because they often face the task of approving a subset of an array of curriculum materials for use in the district's schools. To do this task properly, they must be able to judge the "effectiveness" of each set of materials in the array.

By "curriculum material" is meant any physical object (e.g., a textbook, a film, a physical specimen) which contains information intended to bring about learning. Note that by this definition teachers and pieces of equipment such as a film recorder are not curriculum materials. Curriculum materials can be categorized on a variety of dimensions, including the following:

1. Developer: teacher-made vs. student-made vs. "store-bought"
2. Format: print vs. photography vs. audio vs. mechanical (e.g. computers) vs. manipulatives
3. Number of Formats: single-media vs. multi-media
4. Teacher Intervention: self-instructional vs. teacher-mediated
5. Complexity: isolated materials vs. instructional systems

Course Readings

1. W. James Popham and Eva L. Baker. *Systematic Instruction*. Englewood Cliffs, N.J.: Prentice-Hall, 1970.
2. John Gilliland. *Readability*. London: Hodder and Stoughton, 1972.

3. David A. Payne (ed.) *Curriculum Evaluation.* Lexington, Mass: Heath, 1974. Readings #22 (Heath), #37 (Burton), #38 (Hungerman), and #43 (Sheldon, *et al.*)

4. Class handouts.

Objectives Related to Analysis of Curriculum Materials

This course is intended to help you develop:

1. Awareness of the range of curriculum materials which can be used in teaching.

2. Knowledge of features of curriculum materials which motivate students to learn and which facilitate learning.

3. Knowledge of features of curriculum materials which provide individualized learning experiences for students.

4. Skill in using EPIE and standard reference manuals to obtain information about curriculum materials.

5. Skill in analyzing the dominant instructional pattern and instructional features of a particular set of curriculum materials.

6. Skill in analyzing a particular set of curriculum materials as part, or the whole of, an instructional system.

Objectives Related to Evaluation of Curriculum Materials

This course is intended to help you develop:

7. Skill in evaluating curriculum materials by "inspection" using explicit criteria.
   a. Awareness of your personal evaluative criteria, and knowledge of published evaluative checklists.
   b. Knowledge of curriculum — general and curriculum-specific — evaluative checklists.
   c. Understanding of how to involve community and students in evaluation of curriculum materials.
   d. Skill in assessing the reading level of particular curriculum materials.
   e. Skill in detecting sex and racial-cultural bias in curriculum materials.

8. Skill in evaluating curriculum materials through try-out of the materials in actual teaching situations.

9. Skill in evaluating curriculum materials by reviewing technical reports and other publications containing quantitative evidence on the effectiveness of particular materials.

10. Defensible attitudes concerning issues such as: Should curriculum materials be held accountable? Are curriculum materials obsolete because they artificially encapsulate learning experiences for use in the classroom? Should use of teacher-made curriculum materials be encouraged?

As the following description and outline indicate, Dr. Sally Berlant's course at California State University, Sacramento, on evaluating, selecting, and utilizing library media materials focuses on the qualities of specific media and on their educational applications as mediated through a library/media-center program.

CALIFORNIA STATE UNIVERSITY, SACRAMENTO
DEPARTMENT OF BEHAVIORAL SCIENCES
LIBRARIANSHIP PROGRAM

ED/LIB. 246.2 — Evaluation, Selection and Utilization of Library Media Materials

I. DESCRIPTION

A study of all types of Library Media materials: books, pamphlets, periodicals, films, filmstrips, recordings, Instructional Television, etc. Includes sections on policies, annotation writing, development of evaluation criteria for media selection, and effective utilization of Library Media materials. New materials will be previewed and evaluated.

II. OBJECTIVES

A. *General:*
The student will develop and demonstrate the ability to evaluate, select and utilize Library Media materials. The student will also acquire a broad acquaintance with catalogs, guides, and journals — the basic tools for evaluation and selection of materials.

B. *Specific:*
1) Student will identify the criteria and procedures for evaluating, selecting, and utilizing Library Media materials.
2) Student will demonstrate understanding of principles of reader/user guidance.
3) Student will identify vital elements in, and the need for, a written materials selection policy for a Library Media Center.
4) Student will write instructional goals and objectives.
5) Student will demonstrate ability to judge technical qualities of non-book media.

COURSE OUTLINE

I. Introduction
A. Characteristics of Media
B. Goals and Objectives for Use of Media

II. Evaluation and Selection
A. Selection Policies and Censorship
B. Criteria for Evaluation and Selection
C. Sources and Reviews
D. Reader/User Guidance

III. Library Media Materials
A. Annotations
B. Books, Periodicals and Pamphlets
C. Filmstrips
D. Cassette Recordings
E. Disc Recordings
F. 16MM Films
G. 8MM Film Loops
H. Slides and Overhead Transparencies
I. Study Prints and Realia
J. ITV

IV. Utilization of Library Media Materials
A. Principles of Use for Each Type of Media
B. In-Service for Teachers
C. In-Service for Students
D. Promotion Techniques

Karen Munday, surveying non-print media courses in library schools, found that students in training to become school librarians were offered (or required to take) an average of 1.53 courses in non-print media — usually survey courses that included some information on sources and standards. Some of these courses were cross-indexed with educational technology programs. Library schools offer — on the average — 1.86 other courses in specific materials. Additionally, some library schools have courses in selection that tend to emphasize collection building and continuity somewhat more than analysis of the needs of the users. Library school summer institutes are most likely to have courses on particular materials like maps, archives, or children's literature.

Even though these courses are designed for librarians, they are often filled with teachers who are hungry for training in selecting and using materials with children. Elementary and reading teachers are especially apt to flock to library school courses on any or all aspects of children's literature and reading.

Teachers also turn to teachers' centers. These centers — close to the felt needs of teachers — are aware of teachers' need to become more knowledgeable about selecting, using, and modifying instructional materials and using commercial materials more creatively. Often the assessment forms of these centers include questions relating to teachers' improved use of materials. The courses available from teachers' centers range from the classic "hands-on" and "make it and take it" courses to considerably more sophisticated and detailed courses. Often they are aimed — at least by implication — at helping teachers regain control of curriculum. The courses below were listed in the catalog of the Sarasota County (Florida) Teacher Education Center for 1976-77.

361277 — Preparing Individualized Materials; Setting Up Learning Center

356277 — Evaluation of Business Education Textbooks

361477 — Exploring New Techniques and Materials in Early Childhood Ed

359677 — Commercial Materials Available on Handwriting

359777 — Instructional Techniques and the Use of Selected Instructional Materials

158977 — Learning Interest Centers for the Instructional Student

36077 — Materials Fair

361377 — Evaluation of Secondary Math Instructional Materials

266577 — Media Instructional Improvement Committee

159277 — Media Utilization

154277 — Optimum Utilization of Foreign Language Materials

Another source of help for teachers is the National Education Association's Project on Utilization of Inservice Education R&D Outcomes, which is compiling information on in-service education materials into formatted packets to help teachers plan their own professional growth. (This Project is housed at NEA headquarters in Washington, DC.) Lucinda K. Kaiser, Administrative Assistant in this project, was able to locate for me three sets of materials that could be used or adapted for individual or group training in selection. These materials are cited as Key Publications in this chapter.

The two materials courses described below were developed by the Training Resource Centers in Massachusetts and publicized in the *Newsletter* of the Merrimack Education Center in Chelmsford, Massachusetts. They seem fairly typical of a special-education orientation toward materials selection.

N.E. 911. Materials Modification Course

A highly concentrated course of task and learner analysis. Assisting teachers to adapt and modify existing curriculum materials to provide for the learners assigned to their classrooms. Participants are required to come to the course with a specific learner identified and at least one curriculum material to be modified. Consultants with expertise in specific areas will share in the instruction of this course. Classroom teachers of K-4 level learners will find this session beneficial in individualizing for children whose educational plan, as a result of a 766 Core Evaluation, assigns them primarily to the regular classroom.

ME.960. Implementing the Resource Room

The resource room setting is an appropriate alternative to facilitate mainstreaming. Participants relate the curriculum and instruction, grouping modes, individualizing, and mainstreaming. Plans are modeled for (a) designing instructional sequences, (b) determining resource selection, (c) making choices and selecting alternatives. Participants learn how to implement a resource room to serve both handicapped and more "typical" children.

When textbooks are being adopted, some state boards of education, state textbook committees, or educational leadership training organizations utilize the state adoption proceedings to train selectors. Illinois is one state that used regional Appraisal of Materials Workshops to improve teachers' knowledge-ability in selection. In Oregon, the Textbook Adoption Committee Training Course prospectus for math educators included the following objectives:

- To expose participants to relevant research, trends, and content in mathematics education
- To expose participants to contemporary learning theories and their implications to mathematics education programs
- To expose participants to theories on how children learn mathematics and the maturational differences associated with growth and development
- To assist participants in identifying the appropriate role of the textbook in classroom instruction
- To demonstrate the necessity for materials that support the staff-development concept
- To assist participants in developing criteria to be used in assessing mathematics materials
- To provide experiences in selecting materials based on self-developed criteria.

Probably the best-known courses are those of EPIE Institute, which has recently broadened its training from evaluation to selection. Perhaps 10 percent of the school districts in the country have worked with EPIE in one way or another. EPIE now offers three-day and one-day workshops on selecting instructional materials, tailored for either district-wide selection or selection for particular classrooms. The first approach is directed largely toward administrators, curriculum specialists, media coordinators, and resource teachers; the second toward teachers. EPIE is also willing to design workshops for particular needs or areas—as, for example, workshops dealing with materials and needs in special education, bilingual settings, early childhood programs, or career education.

While EPIE's emphasis is on product development data and the analysis of the "instructional design" of materials, it also considers local needs, background and preferences in designing workshops. These workshops require active participation and encourage participants to apply skills learned in the workshops. EPIE is also in a position to provide some follow-up assistance to school districts or to individual participants.

According to EPIE's prospectus, individuals who participate in the workshops should be able to:

- select appropriate sources of information about the instructionally relevant characteristics of instructional materials

- recognize the level (district, particular classroom, across districts) at which selection is to be made

- pinpoint and describe functionally the needs of various educational consumers (e.g., students, teachers, administrators, curriculum specialists, the community)

- identify the concerns of various educational consumers, and translate those concerns into criteria for selecting instructional materials

- use a common language to describe, objectively and reliably, the characteristics of instructional materials

- select instructional materials to meet the needs of individual students

- clarify teachers' values regarding education and select materials which match those values

- adapt instructional materials to meet the needs of their students

- evaluate an instructional material as an object they can themselves improve and revise it in order to increase its instructional and motivational effectiveness

- organize and structure a local curriculum materials selection committee

- set up and maintain systems for classifying and retrieving instructional materials

For these workshops, EPIE has developed (and tested) a variety of methods and materials for exploring the concepts of instructional selection and their methods for analyzing materials. These include sound filmstrips, mediated lectures, group practice exercises, and handouts that range from checklists and procedural guidelines to reference materials.

A great deal of informal training in selection takes place at all levels — from the regional down to the school level. BAMEG (Bay Area Media Evaluation Guild), for example, is one informal group whose members learn to select through cooperative evaluation. Previewing committees or even lunch room complaints also can sharpen sensitivity and awareness of materials.

In general, existing efforts could be a bit more organized. Media fairs, for example, might be more useful if they followed discussions or appraisals of what is needed in materials. Publishers' representatives, who have legitimate roles in presenting the strengths and approaches of their own materials, are often called in after materials are irrevocably purchased. It would be good to have representatives from, say, several social studies publishers well in advance of selection.

Before school starts—in the fall or summer—an in-service institute of materials might involve an exchange of information and perspectives from educators who understand instructional materials from different points of view.

The sample Institutional Materials Workshop below, for example, emphasizes different aspects of media use and selection for different participants while providing all with an overview. Such a workshop—ideally housed in a school or district media center, teachers' center, or instructional materials center—could use people from a school or district: curriculum specialists, librarians, media personnel, purchasing agents, administrators and classroom teachers, all sharing their perspectives, needs, and expertise. This outline was suggested by an outline in *Using Instructional Media Effectively*, by Jack Tanzman and Kenneth J. Dunn (West Nyack, NY: Parker, 1971).

WORKSHOP ON INSTRUCTIONAL MATERIALS

Media Technician	Media Specialists & Librarians	Teachers
Technical processing of media Labeling, covering, mounting transparencies, inventorying kits, etc. Card files Storage and organization	Technical processing	How IMCs and libraries are organized
	Non-print cataloging and ordering	Ordering and locating print and non-print materials
Current range of materials and media	Inventorying for educators	Organization and approaches of card files, reference books, and library finding
Copyright restrictions	Indexing for educators	
	Current range of materials and media	Current range of materials and media
Designing and adapting materials	Copyright restrictions	Copyright restrictions
Locating and delivering materials	Evaluating non-print materials	Evaluating non-print materials
	Review media	
Overview of current curriculum	Identifying teacher needs	Designing and adapting materials using school media center in educational program
	Selecting media to solve problems	Selecting appropriate materials for students and teaching styles
	Correlating curriculum areas with materials	
	Community resources	Correlating curriculum areas with materials
		Non-traditional materials

KEY ORGANIZATIONS

Curriculum Materials Committee
Education & Behavioral Sciences Section
American Library Association
50 East Huron St.
Chicago, IL 60611   (312) 944-6780

This dynamic new group, successively chaired by Lois Lehman and Dr. Eva L. Kiewitt, has accomplished a great deal since its 1976 inception. Given time, and continued dynamism, it might well succeed in establishing curriculum materials centers as logical training places for teachers engaged in using and selecting instructional materials.

Since 1976, the Committee has established a depository of curriculum center handbooks, policies, and procedures manuals at ALA headquarters. It is currently lobbying publishers to use curriculum materials centers as their primary depositories for K-12 materials and to make these materials available either as samples or at standard substantial discounts.

This group has also finished a survey of these centers and is compiling a directory of exemplary and active materials centers. The survey indicates that these centers, though they tend to be financially undernourished and understaffed, include in most cases a substantial variety of instructional materials, and act as natural liaisons between the library profession, schools of education, and educational practitioners. The Committee is developing an exchange of materials on using these centers; some of these materials may prove useful sources for teaching about instructional materials in general.

Educational Materials Review Center (EDMARC)
U.S. Office of Education
400 Maryland Ave., SW, Room 1127
Washington, DC 20202   (202) 245-8439 or 245-8437

EDMARC is the closest approach to a central collection, evaluation and review center for those who select or purchase textbooks and tradebooks for classroom use. It houses a large proportion of current textbooks, many recently-released tradebooks, a working collection of older, well-reviewed tradebooks and a wide assortment of other instructional and curriculum materials used in schools.

More than 200 publishers provide EDMARC with approximately 2,500 current textbooks, tradebooks and professional titles each year by making available review copies on a permanent loan basis. EDMARC's collection now includes approximately 7,000 K-12 textbooks, 8,000 tradebooks, 800 professional books, 100 educational periodicals and a historical collection of 8,000 volumes.

Reviews of children's books (from five major reviewing media) are summarized on cards (along with information on prices, etc.) to provide concise but complete information on books in the collection. Tradebooks are displayed for one year, after which the best are selected for inclusion in the permanent collection. These well-reviewed books often end up in EDMARC bibliographies. Textbooks are retained indefinitely, but are transferred to the permanent collection after revision, replacement or three years. These textbooks are filed by a well-designed *Textbook Classification Scheme*, available free from the Office of Education.

The EDMARC collection is the basis of bibliographies compiled by the EDMARC staff alone, or cooperatively with other institutions. The Children's Book Committee of the Library of Congress, for example, uses EDMARC to produce its annual annotated list of 200 best books, *Children's Books.* The EDMARC staff has produced the *Aids to Media Selection* (cited in *Media and the Curriculum*) and will update this when time permits. Other staff bibliographies are *Dealing in Futures* (annotated in "The World of Work") and *Coping* (annotated in "The Feeling Domain"). The staff is also reviving an old service of planning and conducting seminars on the development, selection and use of educational materials and on the organization and maintenance of materials centers.

Educational Products Information Exchange (EPIE Institute)
P.O. Box 620
Stony Brook, NY 11790   (516) 246-8664

EPIE West Coast
1018 Keith Ave.
Berkeley, CA 94708   (415) 525-1451

EPIE, a non-profit, membership organization, was established in 1967 as a sort of consumers' union for educational products. An independent agency, without commercial sponsorship, EPIE's income is entirely derived from fees paid by educational consumers, and from occasional grants from public agencies and private foundations.

Its proclaimed objective is to "provide educational consumers with information and evaluative services that enable them to select educational products which best meet the needs of learners." To achieve this goal, EPIE attempts to work with most groups that have roles in selecting materials, including parents, teachers, students, administrators and school board members. (To this date, EPIE has not worked extensively with librarians.) EPIE is currently active in approximately ten percent of the nation's school districts. Since 1974 — through workshops and in-service programs — it has trained teachers in its systematic approach to analyzing instructional materials. It has been offering three-day sessions on selecting instructional materials since 1977.

EPIE is the originator of Learner Verification and Revision (LVR) treated on pages 118-24 of *Issues and Policies.* Its basic approach to analysis is presented in the chapter on evaluation criteria (pp. 92-117). Its current media evaluation program is discussed more extensively in the chapter on audiovisual materials.

EPIE uses a variety of means to review and report on educational products — through commissioned product reviews, careful examination and analysis of producers' claims, and through feedback from a rather broad sample of users.

As part of its membership it issues eight *EPIE Reports* ($20.00 each if purchased separately), one-half on equipment and one-half (*EPIE Materials Reports*) on materials. Its newsletter, *EPIEgram*, similarly devotes 18 issues to materials and 18 to equipment. Subscription to the whole package is $100.00 ($50.00 for materials only). Non-members can purchase individual issues of the *EPIE Reports.*

Individual issues of *EPIE Materials Reports* have had titles like "Selector's Guide for Elementary School Social Studies," "Selector's Guide for Elementary School Reading Programs," and the like. These "Selector's Guides" are usually

EPIE basically uses analytic comparisons in a concrete format rather than reviews. Their reports are apt to be long and detailed (occasionally 27 pages or so on a single item) and sometimes hard to read. The most interesting reading is generally found under "Remarks" or "Other Considerations."

Since EPIE appraisals are so lengthy and detailed, they are best suited to major programs and texts, for which they provide a plethora of information.

As compared with, say, *Curriculum Review*, these reports are not well or consistently indexed (some issues have no internal indexing). However, recent "Selector's Guides" are mostly arranged by publisher with an author-title index at the back. Over the last ten years, the Reports had several titles, including *EPIE Educational Product Report, Educational Product Report* and *EPIE Forum.* Unfortunately, since each issue has a single theme, individual titles are not well indexed in either *Current Index to Journals in Education* (*CIJE*) or *Education Index.*

National Education Association (NEA)
1201 16th St., NW
Washington, DC 20036   (202) 833-4000

The NEA, the major organization for educators, first established in 1857, has had a very long history of concern relating to instructional materials. A Joint Committee of the National Educational Association and the American Textbook Publishers Institute was organized in 1959 to deal with issues relating to printed materials (especially textbooks) in such areas as censorship, selection, distribution, quality and uses. During its existence this joint committee produced several basic guidelines for the selection process, including *Guidelines for Textbook Selection* in 1963 and 1968 and a thoughtful *Guidelines for an Adequate Investment in Instructional Materials* in 1967. They currently advocate five percent of the on-going budget.

Though the Joint Committee no longer exists as an operating unit, publishers and educators are still collaborating through the NEA and the School Division of the Association of American Publishers (AAP). Their most recent collaboration is *Instructional Materials: Selection and Purchase*, revised in 1976, a book that deals with the process of selection rather than with specific criteria.

Basically, the NEA believes in local selection (primarily by teachers) and in a multiplicity of options to meet local conditions. Its activities in and publications on selection reflect this view.

The NEA advocates that policy governing the selection of instructional materials is a legitimate topic for collective bargaining negotiations and suggests that it can clarify details of the selection process and help mobilize the interest and energies of teachers in providing instructional materials.

The NEA believes that standards for educational programs should be established in consultation with the majority teachers' organization and that such programs should guarantee adequate resources for materials and staffing. The Association also believes that state-mandated standards should set only broad, general curricular guidelines (and should not be based on student achievement). The NEA urges its state affiliates to seek the removal of laws and regulations that limit educators in selecting materials or that restrict the selection of diversified materials.

The NEA has also been quite active in recent years in boosting legislation establishing teachers' centers under policy boards governed by (a majority of) classroom teachers. Such teachers' centers might provide more teachers access to a greater variety of learning materials, as well as in-service education courses designed by teachers, and would be more likely to cover materials selection in programs designed to meet the needs of teachers.

The NEA also recommends that educators should adopt and use only those basal texts and other materials that include accurate portraits of the roles of ethnic minorities.

NEA publications include many that are helpful — in one way or another — in selecting materials. Some of their publications include *Biased Textbooks* (1974), *Sex Role Stereotyping Factsheets* (duplicating masters) and *A Child's Right to Equal Reading* (1973).

Teachers' Centers Exchange
Far West Laboratory for Educational Research
and Development
1855 Folsom St.
San Francisco, CA 94103   (415) 565-3097

This Exchange, funded since 1975 by the National Institute of Education (School Capacity for Problem Solving Group), is an information and referral center for a national network of teachers' centers practitioners — both experienced and neophyte. The network operates on a voluntary, give-and-take basis on the premise that curriculum development and staff development programs should be designed on the basis of teachers' identification of their own needs and interests.

Its newsletter, *Teachers' Centers Exchange*, is free on request. Kathleen Devaney's *Essays on Teachers' Centers* sells for $6.00; the two *Teachers' Centers Exchange Directories* are annotated in *Media and the Curriculum*.

KEY PUBLICATIONS

Audio-Visual Technology and Learning, compiled by Educational Technology. Englewood Cliffs, NJ: Educational Technology, 1973. $8.95pa. (Educational Technology Review Series No. 6).

A paperback compilation of 45 separate articles, from 1968-1973 issues of *Educational Technology*, with an introduction by Sean Morrison, intended to expose users to possibilities and potentialities of media in education. Many articles are short (from two to four pages); some are controversial. The NEA description suggests that they could be used as starting points for "an exciting exchange of ideas among teachers."

Instructional Product Selection Kit, compiled by Southwest Regional Laboratory. Los Alamitos, CA: SWRL, 1975. Kit with materials for 12 participants. One 15-min. filmstrip, one booklet, three brochures, two sets of exercises and *Product Review Record Sheet*, $52.50; additional *Simulated Program Brochures*, $15.00 for a set of 12; additional *Participant Materials*, $7.50 for a set of 12. (From SWRL Educational Research and Development, Division of Resource Sciences, 4665 Lampson Ave., Los Alamitos, CA 90620).

This set uses a simulation of a science materials selection (with brochures on three fictitious elementary science programs) to teach the product selection process to 12 people in about three hours. Purposes are to identify the necessary elements of a complete instructional product, to determine the extent to which a product meets selection considerations, and to compare and select among competing products.

Instructional Resources: Evaluation, Selection, and Utilization, developed by Weber State College Teacher Education Faculty. Ogden, UT: Weber State College, 1975. Kit with 10 enclosures, $2.50. (WILKIT No. 20). (From Wilkit Educator's Trust, College of Education, Weber State College, Ogden, UT 84403, Attn. Pat Steiner).

A self-contained kit in a large envelope with 10 enclosures; it also requires locating (rather easily available) selections which are cited, but not included. It is a 20-hour course for K-12 teachers to use, individually or through seminars, to improve their utilization of media, to gain an understanding of the functions and services of a school media program, and to organize a resource file for instructional materials. Course covers instructional resources in group discussions and demonstrations, developing a filing system for a subject area, two additional seminars on evaluation and selection, two more on utilization (with reading requirements), more on the media center, with reading requirements and a proficiency assessment. Enclosures include a checklist; lists of media, media equipment and materials; an information sheet on community resources; criteria for instructional media; a list of resource books; worksheets; utilizations practices; a checklist for media services; and a critique sheet for microteaching.

An instructor is required to lead the seminars and consult with teachers. This is highly recommended by the NEA, particularly for novices. (The Weber State College Program won the 1974 AACT Distinguished Achievement Award for excellence in teacher education.)

FOR FURTHER READING

*Items marked with an asterisk include criteria.
+ Items marked with a plus have lists of references.

+ Burdin, Joel L., and Donald R. Cruickshank. *Protocol Materials: Training Materials for Uniting Theory and Practice.* Washington, DC: ERIC Clearinghouse on Teacher Education, 1975.
Seven papers by writers who have been extensively involved in preparing and using protocol materials in teacher education.

Edelfelt, Roy A., and Margo Johnson, eds. *Rethinking In-Service Education.* Washington, DC: National Education Association, 1975.

Ellis, Elinor V. *The Role of the Curriculum Laboratory in the Preparation of Quality Teachers.* Tallahassee: Florida A&M University, 1969. (ED 031 457).

EPIE Institute. *Instructional Materials Selection Workshop Prospectus.* Stony Brook, NY: EPIE Institute, 1977.

* + Illinois State Board of Education. *Report on the Materials Appraisal Workshops Held during 1972-3*. Springfield, IL: Illinois Office of Education, 1974. (From 100 North First St., Springfield, IL 62777).
Reports on the content and results of five regional workshops on appraisal of materials.

Lawrence, Gordon. *Patterns of Effective Inservice Education and Guidelines for Developing a Competency-Based Inservice Education Program*. Tallahassee: Florida Educational Research and Development Program, 1974.

Munday, Karen S. "A Systematic Examination and Analysis of Nonprint Media Courses in Library Schools, *Journal of Education for Librarianship*, v. 17 (Winter 1976), pp. 189-94.

Student Teacher Instructional Materials Center. Des Moines, IA: Drake University, 1969. (ED 038 352).

Tanzman, Jack, and Kenneth J. Dunn. *Using Instructional Media Effectively*. West Nyack, NY: Parker, 1971.

ACRONYM INDEX

Since acronyms are so prevalent in education, organizations and other educational entities commonly referred to by their initials are arranged here alphabetically by those initials. Numbers in boldface type refer to the pages on which these entities are treated most fully; addresses are usually supplied on these pages. Most acronyms listed in this index are also included in the Author/Title/Subject Index under the full names.

AAAS	American Association for the Advancement of Science, **27-28**
AACTE	American Association of Colleges for Teacher Education, **186-87**, 302
AAHE	Association for the Advancement of Health Education, **113-14**
AAHPERD	American Alliance for Health, Physical Education, Recreation, and Dance, **113-14**
AAP	Association of American Publishers, 311
AASL	American Association of School Librarians, 290, 292, 301
ACC	American Crafts Council, **255-56**
ACCI	American Council on Consumer Interests, **272**
ACTFL	American Council on the Teaching of Foreign Languages, 205
ADFL	Association of Departments of Foreign Languages, 205
AECT	Association for Educational Communications and Technology, **290-91**, 292
AHEA	American Home Economics Association, 270, **272-73**
AIAA	American Industrial Arts Association, **256**
AIDS	Activities, Inquiries, and Demonstrations, 96
ALA	American Library Association, 295, 296, 298
AMA	American Medical Association, 110, **112**
APA	American Psychological Association, **96**, 105
ASHA	American School Health Association, 103, **112-13**
ASHA	American Social Health Association, **118**
ASTC	Association of Science-Technology Centers, **28**
AVA	American Vocational Association, Inc., **256**
BAEL	Bay Area Education Librarians, 6
BAMEG	Bay Area Media Evaluation Guild, 6, 307
BSCS	Biological Science Curriculum Study, **29**
BSEP	Behavioral Science Education Project, 86, 94, 95, **97**
CAAAL	Classified Abstract Archive of the Alcohol Literature, 121
CAL	Center for Applied Linguistics, **204**
CBLM	Computer-based learning materials, 40
CEA	Conservation Education Association, **74**
CEAFU	Concerned Educators Against Forced Unionism, **256-57**, 260

CERN   Consumer Education Resource Network, 7, 269, **273-74**

CESC   Conservation and Environmental Studies Center, Inc., 74

CIC   NIE Calculator Information Center, 40

CIJE   *Current Index to Journals in Education*, 231, 264

CIRIS   Center for Information and Resources in International Studies, **186**

CSPI   Center for Science in the Public Interest, **135-36, 273**

DACBE   Dissemination and Assessment Center for Bilingual Education, **204-205**

ECTJ   *Educational Communication and Technology Journal*, 290

EDMARC Educational Materials Review Center, 302, 309-310

EEAC   Energy and Education Action Center, **75**

EPA   U.S. Environmental Protection Agency, **79**

EPIE   Educational Products Information Exchange Institute, 7, 53, 56, 240, 301, 306-307, **310-11**

ERIC/CAPS ERIC Clearinghouse on Counseling and Personnel Services, **97**, 255

ERIC/ChESS ERIC Clearinghouse for Social Studies/Social Science Education, **162-63**, 168

ERIC/CRESS ERIC Clearinghouse on Rural Education and Small Schools, 77, **186**, 255, 258

ERIC/RCS ERIC Clearinghouse on Reading and Communication Skills, 231, 232

ERIC/SMEAC ERIC Clearinghouse for Science, Mathematics, and Environmental Education, **29-30**, 40, 46, **49-51**

ESL   English as a second language, 199

ESS   Elementary Science Study, 32, 33

FICE   Federal Interagency Committee on Education, 75

HELPs   *Home Economics Learning Programs*, 273

HUMRRO Human Resources Research Organization, 40

IPLE   Institute for Political and Legal Education, **163**

IRA   International Reading Association, **229-30**

IRC   Information Resource Center, 97

JAPC   Japanese American Curriculum Project, Inc., **188**

JCEE   Joint Council on Economic Education, **274**

JID   *Journal of Instructional Development*, 290

LVR   Learner Verification and Revision, 310

MECRE   Measurement and Evaluation Center in Reading Education, 227, 241

MESA   Middle East Studies Association of North America, Inc., **188**

MHMC   Mental Health Materials Center, **97-98**, 105

MLA   Modern Language Association, **205-206**

NAC   National Audiovisual Center, 34, 80
NACOME   National Advisory Committee on Mathematics in Education, 39
NADC   National Assessment and Dissemination Center, **206**
NAEE   National Association for Environmental Education, **78**
NAEP   National Assessment of Educational Progress, 109
NCA   National Council on Alcoholism, **120**
NCAC   National Coalition Against Censorship, **299**
NCBE   National Clearinghouse for Bilingual Education, **206-207**
NCDAI   National Clearinghouse for Drug Abuse Information, **118**, 120
NCIC   National Career Information Center, **257**
NCL   National Consumers League, **274**
NCSS   National Council for the Social Studies, **163-64**, 295, 296
NCTE   National Council of Teachers of English, **230-32**, 238, 295, 296, 299
NCTM   National Council of Teachers of Mathematics, **51-53**, 55
NEA   National Education Association, 51, 295, 305, **311**
NICEM   National Information Center for Educational Media, 81, 102
NIMH   National Institute of Mental Health, **99**, 101
NNECH   National Nutrition Education Clearinghouse, **136-37**
NSF   National Science Foundation, 13, 18, 28, 32
NSTA   National Science Teachers Association, **31**, 32, 33-34, 63

OCE   Office of Consumers' Education, 269, 273, **275**

PRISM   Priorities in School Mathematics, 49

RCUs   State Research Coordinating Units, 255
RIE   *Resources in Education*, 29, 231, 264
RRS   Resource and Referral Service, 7

SIECUS   Sex Information and Education Council of the U.S., 144-45
SOI   Structure of Intellect, 44, **232**
SSEC   Social Science Education Consortium, 105, **162-63**, 255

TACT   The Association of Chinese Teachers, **185-86**
TES   Traveling Exhibits Service, 28

UFT   United Federation of Teachers, 263

WOWI   Women on Words and Images, 251, 252, 262
WREEC   Western Regional Environmental Education Council, **79-80**

YEFC   Youth Education for Citizenship, 172, 173, **174**

AUTHOR/TITLE/SUBJECT INDEX

This index includes most of the names of organizations, information sources and other items listed in the Acronym Index. Those organizations and other educational entities that are treated in the text as subjects appear in boldface type.

AAAS Science Book List, 28
AAAS Science Book List for Children, 28
AAAS Science Books and Films, 28
AAAS Science Film Catalog, 28
Abbey, Karen, 209
Ability and Creativity in Mathematics, 50
Abramowitz, Norman, 168-69
ACCI Newsletter, 272
Activities for Lower Primaries, 31
ACTIVITIES, INQUIRIES AND DEMON-STRATIONS, 96
Activity Resources Company, 48
Activity-Based Learning in Elementary School Mathematics, 46, 50
Adler, Laurie Nogg, 193
Administration of Instructional Materials Organizations, 287-88
"AECT/ALA Standards," 286
AESTHETIC EDUCATION, 69
Affective Development in Schools, 97, 99
AFFECTIVE EDUCATION, 60, 69, 85-108, 117
    Factors of, 85-86
    Individualization, 90, 93
    Levels of commitment, 93
    Rationale, 86-87
    Teaching approaches, 95
AFFECTIVE EDUCATION MATERIALS
    Checklist, 90-92
    Content criteria, 94-95
    Criteria, 89-90
    Games, 94
    Media, 93, 94
    Primary considerations, 89
    Print, 88, 93, 94
Affective Instruments in Environmental Education, 76
Afifi, Ruth, 190
Africa in U.S. Educational Materials, 190
African Resources for School and Libraries, 190
Afro-American Publishing Company, 177-78
Aids for Environmental Education, 77
Aids to Media Selection, 310
Aiken, Lewis R., 50
Akwesasne Notes, 190
Alcohol, *see* NARCOTICS EDUCATION MATERIALS
Alcohol Education Materials, 121
Alcohol Information Kits, 120

Alcohol. You Can Help Your Kids Cope, 120
All You Will Need to Know about Metric, 51
Allen, James A., 253
Alternative Press Index, 190
Alternative Sources, 164
American Alliance for Health, Physical Education, Recreation, and Dance, 110, 113-14, 144
American Association for School Administrators, 110
American Association for State and Local History, 153
American Association of Colleges for Teacher Education, 186-87, 302
American Association of School Librarians, 284, 290, 292, 301
American Bar Association, 174
American Council on Consumer Interests, 272
American Craft, 256
American Crafts Council, 255-56
American Educational Research Association, 301
American Foundation for the Blind, 145
American Home Economics Association, 270, 272-73
American Images of the Middle East Peoples, 188
American Indian Historical Association, 179, 185
American Indian Historical Society, 177
American Indian Reader, 185
American Indians and Eskimos, 190
American Industrial Arts Association, 256
American Institutes for Research, 247
American Italian Historical Society, 177
American Jewish Historical Society, 177
American Library Association, 6, 236, 295, 296, 298
American Medical Association, 110, 112
American National Metric Council, 48-49
American Printing House for the Blind, 47
American Psychological Association, 90, 96
American Public Health Association, 110
American School Board Journal, 295
American School Health Association, 103, 112-13, 141
American Social Health Association, 118
American Vocational Association, 256
Analysis of Elementary School Mathematics Materials, 53
Anderson, Pauline, 291

Andrews, Theodora, 122
Annotated Bibliography of Title VII French Project-Developed Instructional Materials, 1970-75, 208
APA Monitor, 96
Appraisal: Children's Science Books, 32
Approach to the Design of Mediated Instruction, 290
Approaches to Political/Legal Education, 163
Arab World, 190
Arithmetic Teacher, 51-52
Arts and Crafts around the World, 187
Ash, Joan, 114
Asia in American Textbooks, 179, 190
Asia Society, 177, 179, 190
Asian American Bilingual Center, 203
Asian American Librarians Caucus, 191
Asian Americans, 191
Aspects of Jewish Life, 191
Assessing Reading Behavior, 230
Assessment Problems in Reading, 233
Association for Childhood Education International, 185
Association for Educational Communications and Technology, 290-91, 292
Association for Research in Science Teaching, 24
Association for Supervision and Curriculum Development, 176
Association for the Advancement of Health Education, 113-14
Association of American Publishers, 311
Association of Children's Librarians of Northern California, 145
Association of Chinese Teachers (TACT), 185-86
Association of Departments of Foreign Languages, 205
ASTC Newsletter, 28
ASTC Traveling Exhibitions Service Catalog, 28-29
Audiovisual Instruction, 290
Audiovisual Processes in Education, 290
Audio-Visual Technology and Learning, 312
Audiovisuals for Nutrition Education, 137
Australian Metric Conversion Board, 51
AVLINE, 112

Backman, Carl A., 55, 56
Banco del Libro Recomiendo, 208
Barbash, Gary, 145
Barnes, Ellen, 153
BASAL READERS, 217, 218, 224-25
Basic Nutrition Facts, 137
Bauer, Caroline Feller, 235
Bay Area Media Evaluation Guild, 307
Behavioral education, *see* AFFECTIVE EDUCATION
Behavioral Education Science Project, 86
Behavioral Science Education Project, 94, 95, 97

Benford, Marie, 19
Bettelheim, Bruno, 88, 89, 106
Beyer, Barry, 151, 164
Bhaerman, Robert D., 258
BIAS, 177
Biased Textbooks, 312
Bibliography: Crafts Business Bookshelf, 256
Bibliography of Audiovisual Instructional Materials for the Teaching of Spanish, 208
Bibliography of Drug Abuse Including Alcohol and Tobacco, 122
Bibliography of English as a Second Language Materials: Grades 4-12, 207
Bibliography of English as a Second Language Materials: Grades K-3, 207
Bibliography of Instructional Materials for the Teaching of French, 208
Bibliography of Instructional Materials for the Teaching of Portuguese, 208
Bibliography of Language Arts Materials for Native North Americans, Bilingual English as a Second Language and Native Language Materials, 209
Bibliography of Law-Related Curriculum Materials, 174
Bibliography of Recreational Mathematics, 53
Bibliography of Resources in Sex Education for the Mentally Retarded, 145
Bibliography of Science Courses of Study and Textbooks K-12, 31, 32
Bibliography of Spanish Materials for Students, 209
BIBLIOTHERAPY, 85
  Rationale, 88-89
  See also AFFECTIVE EDUCATION
Bicultural Heritage, 209
BILINGUAL EDUCATION
  Curriculum content, 198-99
  Defined, 198
  Rationale, 198
"Bilingual Education Act of 1968," 198
Bilingual Education Resource Guide, 209
Bilingual Journal, 206
BILINGUAL MATERIALS, 197-214
  Bias, 201-202
  Checklists, 199-200
  Compared with foreign language materials, 197-98
  Controversy, 203
  Cultural concerns, 202
  Foreign, 201
  Media, 202
  Preliminary concerns, 202
  Print, 201-202
  Textbooks, 201-202, 203
  Types, 197-98
  Vocabulary, 202
  See also MULTICULTURAL EDUCATION MATERIALS
Billings, Mary DeWitt, 101, 261
Binns, Richard W., 30
Bitter, Gary R., 50

Bloomstein, Charles, 168-69
Boletin, 209
Bonn, George S., 34
Bookfinder, 88, 99
Books in Other Languages, 201, 210
Books in Spanish for Children and Young Adults, 210
Booth, Wayne, 231
Born, Warren C., 205
Bowman, Mary Lynne, 76
Braught, G. N., 121
Brief History of Measurement Systems, 51
British Metrication Board, 51
Brown, George, 22
Brown, Kent R., 240
BSCS Newsletter, 29
Buck, Kathryn, 205
Buckeye, Donald A., 54
Budke, Wesley E., 263
Building Ethnic Collections, 191
Building Rationales for Citizenship Education, 164
Bulletins (NCSS), 163-64
Bureau of Health Education, 141
Burke, John G., 81
Burleson, Derek, 141, 143, 145
Burns, Marilyn, 41, 55
BUSINESS EDUCATION, 245-67, 268
    See also WORK-RELATED EDUCA-TION, WORK-RELATED EDUCA-TION MATERIALS
Buttlar, Lois, 191
By Hand: A Guide to Schools and Careers in Crafts, 258
Byler, Ruth, 106

Calculator Information Center, 40
CALCULATORS, 40
California Department of Consumer Affairs, 270
California School Effectiveness Study, 217
Canadian Metric Commission, 51
Caravella, Joseph R., 56
Career and Vocational Development of Bilingual Students, 258
Career and Vocational Development of Handicapped Learners, 258
Career Bibliography, 259
CAREER EDUCATION, 85, 245-67
    See also WORK-RELATED EDUCA-TION, WORK-RELATED EDUCA-TION MATERIALS
Career Education, 247
Career Education Catalog, 259
Career Education Materials Analysis Instrument, 162, 259
Career Education Pamphlets, 259
Career Education Sourcebook, 259
Career Education Survival Manual, 260, 265

Career Education: What It Is and How to Do It, 253
Career Evaluation Checklists, 249-50
Career Guide to Professional Associations, 260
Career Resource Bibliography, 257
Career Resource Centers, 260
Carey, Helen B., 234
Carlson, Ruth Kearney, 234
Carmichael, Carolyn W., 237
Carpenter, Thomas P., 38
CARTEL, 205
Case Studies in Reading, 230
Castile, Anne, 109
Catalog of Metric Instructional Materials, 54
Cavert, Edward C., 290
Cawley, Rebecca E., 81
CENSORSHIP, 156-57, 295
Censorship, 231
Censorship: A Guide for Teachers, Librar-ians, and Others Concerned with Intellec-tual Freedom, 299
Censorship and the Values of Fiction, 231
Censorship CARE Package, 298
Censorship Game and How to Play It, 157, 299
Censorship News, 299
Center for Applied Linguistics, 204
Center for Economic Education, 251
Center for Information and Resources in International Studies, 186
Center for Science in the Public Interest, 135-36, 273
Centergram, 258
Cerre, Mary, 210
Charbonneau, Manon P., 55
Cheap Math Lab Equipment, 54
Checklist for a New Course in Psychology, 90, 96
"Checklist of Variables in Evaluating Bilin-gual Education," 200
Checkup, 110
Chicorel Index to Poetry, 233
Children's Book Council, 33-34, 167
Children's Books, 310
Children's Literature, 88, 100, 101
Children's Science Book Fair, 28
Children's Science Book Review Committee, 32
Children's Television Project, 186
Childress, Ronald B., 61, 64
Child's Right to Equal Reading, 312
Chinese Americans, Past and Present, 186
Chinese Americans: Realities and Myths, 186
Chinese Cultural Resource Book, 210
Chisman, D. G., 30
Church, John, 287
CITIZENSHIP, 150
City Mix, 80
Classified Abstract Archive of the Alcohol Literature, 121
Classroom Language, 204
Classroom Practices in Teaching English, 231
Classroom Treatment of the Right to Work, 257, 260

CLOZE PROCEDURE, 156
COGNITION, 223-25
Cognitive Psychology and the Mathematics Laboratory, 50
College English, 231
College Entrance Examination Board, 13
Community Research Techniques, 163
Community Resources and Involvement in Career Education, 258
Competency Based Education Sourcebook, 260
Competency-Based Teacher Education, 164
Compleat Computer, 54
Comprehension: A Cognitive Process, 241
Comprehensive Resource Guide to 16 mm Mental Health Films, 98, 99
Comprehensive School/Community Health Education Project, 112
Computer Applications in Instruction, 54
COMPUTER LITERACY, 38
COMPUTER-BASED LEARNING MATERIALS, 40
COMPUTERS, 40
CONCEPT TEACHING, 149-52
CONCEPT TECHNOLOGY
    Content, 151
Conceptions and Misconceptions, 145
Concepts in the Social Studies, 151, 164
Concerned Educators Against Forced Unionism, 251, 256-57, 260
ConCERNS, 274, 275
CONE OF EXPERIENCE, 14, 41, 69, 93, 152, 178
Connelly, F. Michael, 30
Conrad, Joseph L., 205
Conservation and Environmental Studies Center, 74
Conservation Education Association, 74
Constructing a Community System Based Social Science Curriculum, 165
Consumer Action Curriculum, 270
CONSUMER EDUCATION, 268-78
    Curriculum content, 272
    Rationale, 265-69
    Target skills, 269
Consumer Education Forum, 272
CONSUMER EDUCATION MATERIALS
    Federal, 270
    Free, 271
    Kits, 274
    Print, 270
    State, 270
Consumer Education Resource Network, 269, 273-74
Consumer Health Education Resource Unit for Junior High Grades, 114
Consumer Reports, 274
Consumers Index to Product Evaluation and Information Sources, 275
Consumers Union Educational Services, 274
Conte, Joseph M., 222
Controversial Issues in the Social Studies, 165

CONTROVERSY, 294-300
Cook, Ruth, 217
Coon, Herbert L., 75, 76
Copeland, Richard, 44
Coping, 101, 310
Coping with Community Controversy, 157
Copperman, Paul, 217
Correctional Service of Minnesota, 173
Costo, Rupert, 185
Coulter, Myron L., 45
Course and Curriculum Improvement Materials, 32
Course Descriptions (APA), 96
Courtney, Brother Leonard, 240
Cox, C. Benjamin, 157, 290
Coyne, John, 258
Craftsmen in Business, 256
Creative Food Experiences for Children, 135
Creative Publications, 53
Creative Social Studies Teacher, 165
Crevling, Barbara, 168
Cullinan, Bernice E., 237
Culliton, Thomas E., 235
Cummings, Stanley L., 62
Curious Naturalist, 77
Current Approaches to the Teaching of Grammar in ESL, 204
Current Index to Journals in Education, 29, 231, 264
Curriculum Activities Guides, 78
Curriculum Coordinating Centers, 255
Curriculum Development in Elementary Mathematics, 54
Curriculum Guidelines for Multiethnic Education, 164
Curriculum Guides and Instructional Units (APA), 96
Curriculum Materials Analysis Instrument, 162
Curriculum Materials Committee, 309
Curriculum Review, 164, 311
Curry, Joan F., 240

Dahl, Nancy, 144
Dale's Cone of Experience, *see* CONE OF EXPERIENCE
Danilov, Victor, 29
Dasback, Joseph M., 28
Data Book, 105
David, Nina, 276
Davis, Ken, 231
Davis, Ronnie M., 235
Dealing in Futures, 261, 310
Dealing with Censorship, 299
Descriptive Analysis of Alcohol Education Materials, 121
Desegregation Assistance Center, 204
Devaney, Kathleen, 54
Developing Computation Skills, 52
Developing Decision-Making Skills, 165
Developing Language Curricula, 205
Developing Potentials for Handicaps, 273

Developing the Leadership Role, 233
Developing the Library Collection in Political Science, 165
Development, 187
Dexter, William G., 237
Dictionary of Occupational Titles, 259, 260, 261
Dietary Goals for the United States, 124
Directory of Asian American Bilingual Programs in the United States, 203
Directory of Foreign Language Service Organizations, 204
Directory of Information Resources in the United States: Social Sciences, 74
Directory of Information Services: Federal Government, 74
Directory of Law-Related Education Projects, 174
Directory of Multicultural Education Programs in Teacher Education Institutions, 187
Directory of National Organizations Concerned with School Health, 112, 113
Directory of Projects and Programs in Environmental Education, 76
Directory of Public Funding Sources for Home Economics-Related Programs, 273
Discussing Death, 101
Disinger, John F., 76
Dissemination and Assessment Center for Bilingual Education, 204-205
Divoky, Diane, 271
DOCUMERICA, 79
Doll, Ronald, 217
Donelson, Kenneth, 241
Donovan, Daniel, 17-18
Dorr, Mildred, 222
Downey, Mathew T., 168
Dreyer, Sharon Spredemann, 99
Dropkin, Ruth, 34
Drug Abuse Films, 122
Drug Abuse Prevention, 117
Drug Education: A Bibliography . . . , 122
Drug Education: A Review . . . , 121
Drugs, *see* NARCOTICS EDUCATION MATERIALS
Duggins, James, 239
Duker, Sam, 218, 237
Dunn, Kenneth J., 308
Duran, Daniel Flores, 210
Dyrli, Odvard Egil, 21-22

Ecology, *see* ENVIRONMENTAL EDUCATION, ENVIRONMENTAL EDUCATION MATERIALS
Ecology for Children, 74
"Economic Education," 274
ECONOMICS, 268-69
ect. newspaper, 290
"Education Amendment of 1972," 176
Education Commission of the States, 270

Educational Communication and Technology Journal, 290
Education Development Center, 32, 38
Educational Materials Review Center, 302, 309-310
Educational Products Information Exchange Institute, 53, 56, 240, 301, 306-307
Educational Technology, 312
Effective Reading Programs, 233
Egan, Robert S., 34
EGRULE (Foshay), 152
80 Games, 204
Elementary Basal Readers and Work Mode Bias, 261
Elementary School Curriculum, 217
Elementary School Evaluative Criteria, 291
Elementary Science Information Unit, 32
Elementary Science Packets, 31
Elementary Science Study, 32, 33
Elementary Science Study—A History, 32
Elementary Teaching Materials and Teacher References, 137
Eleven Career Education Programs, 259
Encyclopedic Directory of Ethnic Organizations in the United States, 177, 185
Energy: A Multimedia Guide for Children and Young Adults, 80
Energy and Education Action Center, 75
Energy Crisis—Aids to Study, 77
Energy Curriculum Inventory, 71
Energy Education Materials Inventory, 81
Energy-Environment Materials Guide, 81
ENGLISH AS A SECOND LANGUAGE, 199
English Journal, 231
Enrichment Ideas, 234
Environmental and Outdoor Education Materials Catalog, 81
Environmental Conservation, 74
ENVIRONMENTAL EDUCATION, 271
    Cognitive modes and, 69
    Curriculum, 64-65
    Defined, 61-62
    Direct experience, 69
    Learning approaches, 63-64
    Local, 66-69
    Process skills, 69
    Rationale, 61
    Target skills, 65
    Textbooks, 65
Environmental Education: A Guide to Information Sources, 74, 81
Environmental Education Activities of Federal Agencies, 74, 76
Environmental Education Curriculum Analysis Instrument, 69
Environmental Education in Action, 76
Environmental Education in the Urban Setting, 76

ENVIRONMENTAL EDUCATION MATE-
RIALS, 60-84
  Bias in, 69
  Checklists, 67-68, 69-73
  Criteria, 63-65
  Direct experience, 67
  Free, 68, 69
  Media, 68
  Printed, 68
  Sponsored, 69
"Environmental Education: The Central Need,"
  62
Environmental Guide for Administrators, 78
ENVIRONMENTAL SCIENCE, 62
EPIE Career Education Set, 261
EPIE Materials Reports, 310
EPIE Reports, 310
EPIEgram, 310
ERIC Center for Science, Mathematics, and
  Environmental Education, 69, 74, 75-76
ERIC Clearinghouse for Adult, Career and
  Vocational Education, 257-58
ERIC Clearinghouse for Social Studies/Social
  Science Education, 77, 96, 162-63, 168, 185
ERIC Clearinghouse on Counseling and Per-
  sonnel Services, 97, 255
ERIC Clearinghouse on Reading and Com-
  munication Skills, 230, 231, 232
ERIC Clearinghouse on Rural Education and
  Small Schools, 77, 186, 255, 258
ERIC Clipboard, 258
ERIC Thesaurus, 264
ERIC/SMEAC Publications, 29
Ernst, Mary, 234
ESS Reader, 32
Essays on Teachers' Centers, 312
Ethnic American Minorities, 192
ETHNIC CULTURES, 199
Ethnic Heritage Center for Teacher Educa-
  tion, 178, 186-87
ETHNIC HERITAGE STUDIES, 176
  See also MULTICULTURAL EDUCA-
    TION, MULTICULTURAL EDUCA-
    TION MATERIALS
ETHNIC ORGANIZATIONS, 177-78
Ethnic Studies Handbook for Librarians, 192
Ethnic Studies Materials Analysis Instrument,
  162, 180-81
Evaluating Library Resources for Elementary
  School Libraries, 229
Evaluating Media Programs: District and
  School, 289, 291
Evaluation Criteria for Junior High Schools,
  221
Evaluation in the Mathematics Classroom:
  From What and Why to How and Where, 50
Evaluation Instruments in Health Education,
  114
Evaluation of Alcohol Education Materials
  in Elementary, Junior High School and
  Senior High School Textbooks as Related to
  Student Needs, 122

Evaluation Studies on "New Social Studies"
  Materials, 165
Evaluative Criteria: A Guide for School
  Improvement, 291
Evaluative Criteria: Junior High School/
  Middle School, 291
Evaluative Guide to 16 mm Mental Health
  Films, 98, 99
Examining Your Environment Series, 21
Exemplary Strategies for Elimination of Sex
  Bias in Vocational Education Programs, 262
Exploring Alcohol Questions, 121
Exploring the Marketplace, 274

Fabric of Mathematics, 54, 56
Fader, Daniel, 216, 218, 239
Fair, Jean, 155
Fair Trial v. Free Press, 163
FAIRY TALES, 88-89
Family Life, 144, 146
Family life education, see SEX EDUCA-
  TION MATERIALS
Fantasy and Feeling in Education, 101
Far, Leo C., 234
Far West Laboratory for Educational Research
  and Development, 32, 239
Far West Model, 262
Farr, Roger, 227, 241
Federal Energy Administration, 81
Federal Funds for Reading, 234
Federal Interagency Committee on Education,
  75
Feeling domain, see AFFECTIVE EDUCA-
  TION
Feezel, Jerry D., 240
Film Resources for Sex Education, 145
Films on the Future, 166
Finn, Peter, 120
Finn, Tom, 239
First Four Years of Right to Read, 233
Fisher, Margery, 24
Fitzgerald, William M., 50
Focus on Food, 136
Food and Nutrition Board, 125
Food and Nutrition Information and Educa-
  tional Materials Center, 136
Ford Foundation, 190
Foreign Language Framework, 203
FOREIGN LANGUAGE MATERIALS,
  197-214
  Bias, 201-202
  Compared with bilingual materials, 197-98
  Controversy, 203
  Foreign, 201
  Media, 202
  Print, 201-202
  Textbooks, 201-202, 203
  Types, 197-98
  See also MULTICULTURAL EDUCA-
    TION MATERIALS

FOREIGN LANGUAGE STUDY
Rationale, 198
Forum, 207
Foshay, Arthur, 157
Fowler, Kathryn Mervine, 81, 82, 138
Fox, Robert, 154
Framework in Reading for Elementary and Secondary Schools, 220
Fraser, Dorothy McClure, 168
Free Access to Libraries for Minors, 298
Free Materials for the Teaching of Mathematics, 48, 52
Freedom to Read Foundation, 298
Freedom to Read Statement, 298
"Freestyle," 248
French Bibliography Committee, 208
Frontiers of Bilingual Education, 200
Furthering the Development of Children in Schools, 97
Futurist, 166

Gabler, Norma, 295
Games and Puzzles for Elementary and Middle-School Mathematics, 55
Games for the Science Classroom, 33
Games from around the World, 187
Gaming, 174
Gann, Susan, 209
Gateways to Readable Books, 234
Gaver, Mary, 229
Geer, Charles, 50
GEOMETRY, 38
Getting People to Read, 234
Gillespie, John T., 292
Gleason, Marion, 231
Going Metric, 53, 55
Good Reading for Poor Readers, 234
Good Reading for the Disadvantaged Reader, 192
Goodman, Hannah Grad, 191
Goodwin, Mary, 135
Gotsick, Priscilla, 276
Green, Hayden, 268, 271
Greene, Ellin, 238
Greenspan, Nancy, 275
Grimes, George H., 222
Griswold, William J., 188
Grom, Eldon, 21
Gross, Richard, 155
Growth Patterns and Sex Education: A Suggested Program, 146
Growth Patterns and Sex Education: An Updated Bibliography, 146
Grupeonoff, Joan, 122
Guide for Evaluating Consumer Education Programs and Materials, 272
Guide to Ecology Information and Organizations, 81
Guide to Federal Career Literature, 262
Guide to Free-Loan Films about Foreign Lands, 192

Guide to FUSE Modules Abstracted in RIE—1976, 30
Guide to Information Sources for Reading, 235
Guide to Instructional Resources for Consumers' Education, 275
Guide to Mental Health Education Materials, 95, 101
Guide to Post-Classical Works of Art, Literature, and Music Based on Myths of the Greeks and Romans, 235
Guide to Reference Books for School Media Centers, 233
Guide to Selected Curriculum Materials on Interdependence, Conflict and Change, 157
Guide to Teaching about Computer in Secondary Schools, 55
Guide to Title VII Bilingual Bicultural Programs, 205
Guidebook to Constructing Inexpensive Science Teaching Equipment, 33
Guidelines for Adequate Investment in Instructional Materials, 311
Guidelines for Sex-Fair Vocational Education Materials, 251, 262
Guidelines for Textbook Selection, 311
Guidelines for the Creative Use of Biased Materials in an Unbiased Way, 251
Guidelines for the Preparation and Evaluation of Career Information Media, 249, 257
Gunderson, Doris, 231

Haase, Arthur, 205
Haley, Frances, 192
Hall, Richard P., 166
Handbook for Storytellers, 235
Handbook of Legal Education Resources, 175
Handbook of Unpublished Evaluation Instruments in Science Education, 30
Hansen, William E., 258
Harmon, David, 215-16
Harmon, Robert Bartlett, 165
Hatheway Environmental Education Institute, 77
Havis, Donald G., 97
Hawkins, Mary E., 60
Health: A Multimedia Source Guide, 114
HEALTH EDUCATION, 85, 86
Components, 109
Curriculum content, 111
Target skills, 110-11
Health Education, 113
HEALTH EDUCATION MATERIALS, 109-116
Free, 111
Parents and, 111-12
Print, 111
Sources, 111
Sponsored, 111
Health Instruction, 113
Hedstrom, Judith E., 105, 167-68, 259
Heike, Adolf, 211

Helgeson, Stanley L., 69
Helping Children and Youth with Feelings, 97, 102
Henry, Jeannette, 185
Herber, Harold L., 156
Herbert, Tom, 258
Herold, Persis Joan, 56
Hess, Adrien L., 56
He-Stra, 112
Hicks, Warren B., 292
Higgins, Jon L., 50
Higgins, Judith H., 80
High School Psychology Teacher, 96
High-Interest-Low Vocabulary Reading Materials, 235
Hillocks, George, 231
Hirzel, Bertha M., 234
HISTORICAL FICTION, 152-53
Historical Topics for the Mathematics Classroom, 52
HISTORY, 150-51
History Teacher, 164
Holloway, Ruth Love, 233
Hollowell, John, 231
Home economics, *see* CONSUMER EDUCATION, CONSUMER EDUCATION MATERIALS
Home Economics Learning Programs, 273
Hounshell, Paul B., 33
How to Ask the Right Questions, 31
How to Present Audible Multi-Imagery in Environmental-Ecological Education, 31
How to Teach Reading with Children's Books, 236
How to Use Behavioral Objectives in Science Education, 31
How to Use WISC Scores in Reading Diagnosis, 224
Howell, Jerry F., 82
Hoyt, Kenneth, 253
Human Behavior Curriculum Project, 87
Human Relations and Values, 102
Human Resources Research Organization, 40
Hunger: The World Food Crisis, 82, 138

I Hate Mathematics! Book, 41, 55
I Read, You Read, We Read . . . , 236
Ideology, Censorship and Textbook Adoptions, 231
Image of the Middle East in Secondary School Textbooks, 188
Improving Reading in Science, 230
In Focus, 118
Independent Reading, Grades One through Three, 236
Index of Nutrition Education Materials, 135, 138
Index to Literature of the American Indian, 185
Index to Psychology (Multimedia), 102
Indian Historian, 185

Individual Rights, 163
INDIVIDUALIZATION, 153
Individualized Reading, 218, 230, 237
Indochinese Refugee Alert Bulletin, 204
Industrial Education, 258
Inform, 257
Information Center on Children's Cultures, 176, 178, 187, 189
Information for Everyday Survival, 276
Information Resource Center, 97
INSIGHT, 173
Institute for Environmental Education, 77-78
Institute for Political and Legal Education, 163
Instructional Aids in Mathematics, 52
Instructional Aids in Mathematics: 34th Yearbook, 55
Instructional Innovator, 290
INSTRUCTIONAL MATERIALS
    Estimation, 280
    Monitoring, 279-80
Instructional Materials: Selection and Purchase, 311
Instructional Product Selection Kit, 312
Instructional Resources, 313
Instrument for Use in the Analysis of K-12 Nutrition Curriculum Guidelines, 125
Instrument for Use in the Analysis of K-12 Teacher References, 137
Intellectual Freedom Manual, 298
Interchange, 79
Intercom, 166
Intercultural Studies Information Service, 186
INTERCULTURAL UNDERSTANDING, 183
Inter-Culture Associates, 177-78
INTERDISCIPLINARY MATERIALS, 26
    Consumer education, 270-71, 272
    Environmental education, 66, 69
    Mathematics, 42-43
    Science, 26-27
    Social science, 26-27
Interest Inventory Record, 218
International Bibliography, 205
International Clearinghouse on Science and Mathematics Curriculum Developments, 30-31
International Clearinghouse Reports, 30
International education, *see* MULTICULTURAL EDUCATION, MULTICULTURAL EDUCATION MATERIALS
International Reading Association, 220, 224, 229-30, 232
International Youth Library, 176
Internationalize Your School, 166
"Intuition and Curriculum," 152
Inventing and Playing Games in the English Classroom, 231
Inventory of Marriage and Family Literature, 144
"Is There Anything New about the New Science Textbooks?," 21-22
Issues in Evaluating Reading, 237

Jackdaw, 152
Jacob, Gail S., 236
Janet, Pierre, 88
Japanese American Curriculum Project, 177-78, 188
Japolsky, Gerald, 87
Jenkins, Floyd H., 261
Jerrick, Stephen, 109
Jesko, Carol, 102
Jewish Film Archive and Study Center, 177
Jewish Media Service, 177
Johnson, Dora E., 211
Johnson, Harry A., 192
Johnson, James, 265
Johnson, M., 103
Johnson, William L., 275
Joint Council on Economic Education, 274
Jones, Betty, 98
Jones, Milbrey L., 292
Jones, Richard M., 101
Journal of Consumer Affairs, 272
Journal of Geography, 164
Journal of Instructional Development, 290
Journal of Nutrition Education, 136
Journal of Reading, 230
Journal of School Health, 113
Journal of Studies on Alcohol, 121
Journalism Education Association, 232
Justice, Faith L., 264
Juvenile Justice, 163

Kaiser, Lucinda K., 305
Kasschau, Richard A., 96, 106
Keeping Up, 163
Keys to Careers in Science and Technology, 31, 263
Kiewitt, Eva L., 309
Krathwohl, D., 93
Kurfman, Dana G., 165
Kwok, Irene, 210

LABOR UNIONS, 251
Laffey, James, 227, 230, 241
Land-Use Management Activities for the Classroom, 76
LANGUAGE ARTS, 167, 270
    Curriculum content, 218
    Drills, 216, 217
    Individualization, 217, 218-20
    Reading comprehension, 217
    Student attitudes, 216
    Textbooks, 217
    Verbal achievement, 216-17
Language Arts, 231
LANGUAGE ARTS MATERIALS, 215-44
    Censorship, 226-27, 230-31
    Cognitive analysis and, 223-25
    Criteria, 220, 222-23, 227-29
    Quantitative standards, 226
    Readability formulas, 222

LANGUAGE ARTS MATERIALS (cont'd)...
    Remedial, 222-23
    Roles in selection, 225-26
    Student selection, 217-20
    Variety in, 217-18, 221-22
Language in Education, 204
Lass-Woodfin, Mary Jo, 190
Latino Materials, 210
LAU, *see* Desegregation Assistance Center
Laughlin, Mildred, 167
Law and the Family, 163
Law in the Curriculum, 172
Law-Related Education in America, 172
Laycock, Mary, 54
Lazarus, Mitchell, 38, 40
Leadership, 233
Learner Verification and Revision, 310
Learning about Alcohol, 122
Learning Alternatives in U.S. Education: Where Student and Computer Meet, 40
Learning to Think in a Math Lab, 55
Leffin, Walter W., 53, 55
LEGAL EDUCATION, 270-71
    Preliminary considerations, 72-73
    Rationale, 172
LEGAL EDUCATION MATERIALS, 172-75
    Direct experiences, 172
Lehman, Lois, 309
Lencher, George, 52
Lesh, Richard, 50, 51
LeShan, Eda, 106
Lewis, Gertrude, 106
Lewis, June E., 17
"Library Bill of Rights," 298
Library in the Independent School, 284, 291
Linguistic Reporter, 204
Link, 163
Linn, Jean K., 97
List of Hypotheses Advanced to Explain the SAT Score Decline, 216
Liston, Mary Dawn, 81
LITERACY, 215
Literacy Hoax, 217
LITERATURE, 85
    See also LANGUAGE ARTS
Literature and Young Children, 237
Living Things in Field and Classroom, 33
Lockard, J. David, 30, 33
Logasa, Hannah, 152
Logical Reasoning in Science Education, 30
Love, William D., 211
Lucas, A. M., 30

MacGinitie, Walter H., 233
Mackey, William Francis, 200
Maher, Sheila M., 262
Man and Environment, 78
Managing Multimedia Libraries, 292
Mangum, Garth L., 265
Man/Society/Technology, 256
Marcus, Stuart, 269

Marland, Sydney P., 253
Martin, Marie, 166
Masks around the World, 187
Master Locator Booklet for Classroom Materials in TESL, 211
Material Development Needs in the Uncommonly Taught Languages, 211
Materials Book for the Elementary Science Study, 33
Materials for Civics, Government, and Problems of Democracy, 162, 166
Materials for Individualizing Math Instruction, 56
Materials for Metric Instruction, 50
Materials for Occupational Education, 263
Math Group, 53
Math Teaching Handbook, 56
MATHEMATICS, 270
    Curriculum, 37
    Discovery method, 37, 38
    Individualization, 46-47
    Inquiry approach, 44
    "New Math," 37, 38
    Process skills, 44
    "Survival math," 37
    Target skills, 39, 44
Mathematics Laboratories: Implementation, Research and Evaluation, 50
Mathematics Laboratories: 150 Activities and Games for Elementary Schools, 50
MATHEMATICS MATERIALS, 37-59
    Checklist, 41-42
    Computers, 39, 40
    Criteria, 43-44
    Free, 41
    Games, 41
    Manipulatives, 41, 46-47
        Criteria, 47-48
    Parents and, 45-48
    Puzzles, 41
    Recycled, 41
    Textbooks, 44-45
    Vocabulary, 45
Mathematics Projects Handbook, 56
Mathematics Teacher, 51-52
Matters of Fact, 24
Mayer, Victor J., 30
McCarthy, R. G., 121
McClure, Larry, 260
McDaniel, Margaret, 77
McNeil, Elton, 239
Measurement and Evaluation Center in Reading Education, 227, 241
Media, 174
Media and the Culturally Different Learner, 222
MEDIA PROGRAMS
    Criteria, 281-89
    Evaluation, 279-93
Media Programs: District and School, 286, 291, 292
MEDLINE, 112
Meeker, Mary, 44

Memorandum to Discussion Leaders (MHMC), 98
Mental Health Association, 98
Mental Health Association Film Festival Programs, 98
MENTAL HEALTH EDUCATION, 85-86
    Rationale, 88-89
    See also AFFECTIVE EDUCATION
Mental Health Education, 98, 102
Mental Health in the Classroom, 103, 113
Mental Health Materials Center, 89, 93, 94, 97-98, 105
Mental Health Media Evaluation Project, 98
Merritt, John, 240
Metcalf, Fay D., 168
Metric Guide for Educational Materials, 49
Metric Reporter, 49
Metric Studies Center, 54
Metric System from Day to Day, 49
Metzner, Seymour, 169
Michigan Cost-Effectiveness Study, 217
Middle East Studies Association of North America, 188
Middle Schools Literature Survey, 237
Mierkiewicz, Diane, 51
Milgram, Gail, 118, 121
Mills, Gretchen C., 101
Milton Bradley's Reading Plan, 224, 237
Minicalculator Information Resources, 52
Minicalculators in the Classroom, 56
MINNEMAST, 37
Minnesota Council on Family Relations, 146
Minnesota Enrivonmental Sciences Foun., 78
Model School District Media Program, 292
Modern Language Association, 205-206
Molnar, Andrew R., 50
Montessori, Maria, 22, 37
Montgomery, Paula Kay, 292
Mooney, Elizabeth, 142
Morris, William P., 240
Morrisett, Irving, 162
Morse, William C., 99, 102
Muessig, Raymond H., 155, 165
Multicultural Bibliography for Pre-School through Second Grade, 189
MULTICULTURAL EDUCATION
    Rationale, 177
    School surveys, 179-80
Multicultural Education and Ethnic Studies in the United States, 187
MULTICULTURAL EDUCATION MATERIALS, 176-96
    Catalogs, 178
    Criteria, 191, 193-94
    Evaluation forms, 178-84
    Foreign, 178
    Free, 192
    Media, 193
    Sources, 177
    Sponsored, 177
    See also FOREIGN LANGUAGE MATERIALS, BILINGUAL MATERIALS

Multicultural Materials, 189
Multicultural Resources, 189
Multicultural Resources for Children, 178, 189
MULTIDISCIPLINARY MATERIALS
 Law, 172
 Multicultural, 178
Multi-Ethnic Media, 193
Multimedia Approach to Children's Literature,
 238
Munday, Karen, 305
Munger, Richard L., 97, 99, 102
Muth, John W., 165
My Backyard History Book, 153
MYTHS, 88-89

NACOME, 44
NAEP, 60
NAEP Newsletter, 150
NARCOTICS EDUCATION, 86
 Curriculum content, 117
 Values and, 118
NARCOTICS EDUCATION MATERIALS,
 117-23
National Academy of Sciences, 125
National Agricultural Library, 136
National Assessment and Dissemination Center, 206
National Assessment of Educational Programs,
 38
National Assessment of Educational Progress,
 13, 109
National Assessment of Educational Progress
 Development, 198
National Association for Environmental Education, 78
National Association of Independent Schools,
 284
National Audiovisual Center, 34, 81
National Bureau of Standards, 28, 51
National Career Information Center, 257
National Center for Vocational Education, 7,
 246, 255, 257-58
National Clearinghouse for Alcohol Information, 118
National Clearinghouse for Bilingual Education, 206-207
National Clearinghouse for Drug Abuse Information, 118-20
National Coalition Against Censorship, 299
National Commission on Libraries and Information Science, 280
National Congress of Parents and Teachers, 110
National Consumers League, 274
National Council for the Social Studies, 150,
 153, 155, 157, 163-64, 167, 295, 296
National Council of Teachers of English, 176,
 226, 230-32, 238, 295, 296, 299
National Council of Teachers of Mathematics,
 48, 49, 51-53, 55
National Council on Alcoholism, 120
National Council on Family Relations, 144

National Defense Education Act, 198
National Directory of Safety Films, 114
National Education Association, 110, 112, 113,
 176, 178, 295, 305, 311
National Indochinese Clearinghouse, 204
National Information Center for Educational
 Media, 102
National Institute of Education, 239
National Institute of Mental Health, 99, 101
National Institute on Drug Abuse, 117
National Inventory of Library Needs, 280
National Materials Development Center for
 French/Portuguese, 208
National Nutrition Education Clearinghouse,
 126, 136-37
National PTA, 112, 141
National Research Council, 125
National School Boards Association, 110
National Science Foundation, 13, 18, 28, 32
National Science Teachers Association, 32, 33,
 63, 263
National Street Law Institute, 173
National Study of School Evaluation, 291
National Study of Secondary School Evaluation, 221
Native American Arts and Culture, 193
Native American Materials Development Center, 206
Navajo Curriculum Center, 209
Navajo Reading Study, 209
NCBE Selected Accessions List, 207
NCSS Yearbooks, 164, 165
*NCTE Guide to Teaching Materials for
 English*, 238
*NCTM Metrication Update and Guide to
 Suppliers of Metric Materials*, 52
Needs Assessment: Who Needs It?, 97
Neff, Walter, 247
Nelson, Murry, 172
Nesbitt, William A., 168-69
Neuendorffer, Mary Jane, 32
New Hooked on Books, 216, 218, 239
*New York Metropolitan Area Craft Course
 Directory*, 256
New Zealand Department of Education, 178
News, Notes & Ideas, 98
Newsletter on Intellectual Freedom, 298
NICEM's Index to Environmental Studies, 81
Nichols, Margaret S., 189
NIE Calculator Information Center, 49
Non-Sexist Community Careers, 248
Nontraditional Careers for Women, 263
Northwest Regional Educational Laboratory, 54
*Notable Children's Trade Books in the Field of
 Social Studies*, 167
Now Upon a Time, 88, 103
NSTA News-Bulletin, 31
NUFFIELD MATHEMATICS, 37
NUTRITION, 86
 See also NUTRITION EDUCATION
 MATERIALS
Nutrition Education in a Changing World, 138

Nutrition Education: K-12 Teacher References, 137
NUTRITION EDUCATION MATERIALS, 124-39
    Criteria, 126-35
    Direct experience, 125
    Media, 125
    Print, 125
    Sponsored, 124
    Television, 124
Nutrition Foundation, 137
Nutrition Information Resources for Professionals, 137
Nutrition Scoreboard, 136

O'Connor, Rod, 5
Office of Consumers' Education, 269, 273, 275
Olson, David, 144
Olszewski, William, 241
"One School's Consumer Survival Kit," 268
O'Neill, Peggy, 189
Options and Perspectives, 211
Options for the Teaching of Foreign Languages, Literatures and Cultures, 205, 211
Oregon Competency Based Education Program, 260
Organized Labor, 263
Organizing for Mathematics Instruction, 52
Osborne, Jeanne S., 82
Outstanding Science Trade Books for Children in 1977, 33
Overhead Projector in the Mathematics Classroom, 52
"Overview and Analysis of School Mathematics," 37
"Overview and Analysis of School Mathematics, K-12," 39

Packet A: Sex Education and Moral Values, 144
Packet B: Parents as Sex Educators, 144
Parents' Kit for Children's Pre-Reading Activities, 233
Paul, D. L., 122
PEABODY SYSTEM OF LANGUAGE DEVELOPMENT, 224
Pearson, Craig, 46
Pellowski, Anne, 176
Pen Pals and Other Exchanges, 187
Penna, Anthony N., 151, 164
PennyPower, 274
People at Work, 248
People's Computer Company, 40
Pescosolido, John, 237
Peterson, Robert, 265
Philosophies for Educating about Alcohol and Other Mood-Modifying Substances, 121
Piaget, Jean, 16, 44
PICTORIAL MEDIA, 153
Planning and Operating Media Centers, 291

Policies and Procedures for Selection of Instructional Materials, 290, 296, 299
Policies on Intellectual Freedom, 298
Population: An International Directory of Organizations and Information Sources, 82
Population Bulletins, 79
Population Education Activities for the Classroom, 76
Population Education: Sources and Resources, 79
Population Reference Bureau, 78-79
Population: The Human Dilemma, 82
Position Statements (NCSS), 164
Posters from the Arithmetic Teacher, 52
Poteet, G. Howard, 242
Potter, Irene C., 17
Preparing to Teach Political Science, 167
Price, Charles L., 76
Primary Prevention in Drug Abuse, 120
Priorities in School Mathematics, 49
Problem-Centered Social Studies Instruction, 155
Project for Cross-Cultural Understanding, 186
Project Learning Tree, 80
Project One, 38
"Project Plan," 248
"Proposal to Revise the Secondary School Curriculum in Economics," 269
Protheroe, Donald, 153
Proyecto Leer, 201, 207-208
Psychological and Affective Education, 97
PSYCHOLOGY, 85-86
    Checklist, 90-92
    Community resources, 92
    Course content, 90-91
    Curriculum, 87
    Curriculum characteristics, 93
    Ethical concerns, 92
    Rationale, 87-88, 90
    Teacher qualifications, 92
    Teaching strategies, 91
    See also AFFECTIVE EDUCATION
Psychology Teacher's Resource Book, 96, 103
"Public School Environmental Curricula: A National Profile," 61
Publications for Researchers, Community Workers, Educators, Concerned Public, 120

Rain (Journal of Appropriate Technology), 82
Ramos, Juan E., 168
Rap Kit, 120
READABILITY FORMULAS, 22, 156
Reading, *see* LANGUAGE ARTS
Reading Aid Series, 224
Reading Aids and Ideas for Parents, 233
Reading and Language Arts, 239
Reading and the Bilingual Child, 230
Reading and the Consumer, 276
Reading and the Curriculum, 240
Reading Assessment Scale, 233
Reading Crisis in America, 233

Reading for Young People, 167
Reading Games and Activities to Motivate Reluctant Readers in the Primary Grades, 241
"Reading in Mathematics," 45
Reading in the Content Areas, 45, 230
Reading Interaction, 230, 240
Reading Ladders for Human Relations, 193
READING LISTS, 88
Reading Programs in Secondary Schools, 230
Reading Research Quarterly, 230
Reading Teacher, 230
Reading Thinking Skills for Maps and Globes, 241
Reading-Language Instruction, 227
Recent Research Concerning the Development of Spatial and Geometric Concepts, 51
Recent Research in Cognition Applied to Mathematics Learning, 50
Recommendations for Improving Reading Instruction, 219
Recommended Materials in Environmental Education, 82
Reddig, Jill Swanson, 81
Reference Guide for Consumers, 276
Refugee Education Guides, 204
Reid, Virginia M., 193
The Relationship of Self-Concept to Beginning Reading, 87
"Request for Reconsideration of Instructional Materials," 296, 297
Resolution on Challenged Materials, 298
Resource Book for Drug Abuse Education, 123
Resource Center for Consumer Education, 275
Resource Guide for Alcohol Education, 120
Resource Guide in Sex Education for the Mentally Retarded, 144
Resource Materials (APA), 96
Resource Materials: A Guide to Production and Use, 80
Resources for K-12 Instructional Materials on Women's Educational Equity, 258
Resources for Teaching about Family Life Education, 144
Resources in Bilingual Education, 207
Resources in Career Education, 263
Resources in Education, 29, 231, 264
Resources in Vocational Education, 258
Resources on Eliminating Sex Role Stereotyping in Vocational Education, 263
Review of British Science Curriculum Projects, 30
Review of Environmental Education for School Administrators, 69
Review of Research Related to Environmental Education (1973-1976), 76
Reys, Robert, 46, 47-48
Rhetoric of the Movie, 291
Richards, Ellen, 268
Richman, Paul, 269
Richtmyer, J., 34
Ridenour, Nina, 98, 102

Right to Read Administrator Leadership Clinics, 233
Right to Read Assessment and Planning Handbook, 232
Right to Read Effort, 233
Right to Read Program, 232-33
Right to Read Summer Kit, 233
Rios, Edwin T., 258
"Role of the Librarian in the Evaluation of Career Materials," 249
Romney, Emily, 32
ROOT CULTURES, 198-99
Roth, Herbert, 76
Rubin, Janet S., 261
Ruddell, Robert B., 227
RUDDELL'S COMMUNICATION MODEL, 224
Rudman, Masha K., 100, 103, 141
RULEG (Foshay), 152
Rural Career Guidance, 264
Rural Connection, 246
Russell, Robert D., 121
Russian Language Study in 1975, 205
Rutgers Center of Alcohol Studies, 121

Sachs, Larry A., 50
Sadker, David Miller, 103
Sadker, Myra Pollack, 103
SAFETY, 92
San Jose Area Bilingual Consortium, 199
Sandoval, Carmel, 209
SATISFACE: A Guide for Educational Consultants in Resource Management Agencies, 80
Sayer, Karen, 102
Schaaf, William, 53
Schneider, Donald, 150
Schoenfeld, Clay, 76
Schoenfeld, Madalynne, 238
Scholastic Achievement Test, 37
Schon, Isabel, 201, 209, 210
School Health in America, 109
School Library Bill of Rights, 285
School Lunch Action Guide, 136
School Media Quarterly, 290, 296
School Shop, 258
School's Responsibility for Sex Education, 142
Schrank, Jeffrey, 106
Schreiber, Marilyn, 263
Schultz, Judith M., 76
Schuman, Patricia, 263
SCIENCE, 85
Science—A Process Approach, 14
Science and Children, 31
Science and Society, 27, 28
Science, Education, Abstracts and Index from Resources in Education, 1976-1977, 30
Science Equipment in the Elementary School, 34
SCIENCE FICTION, 152
Science 5/13, 16, 21

"Science Framework" (California), 18
Science Framework for California Public Schools: Kindergarten-Grades One through Twelve, 18
Science in the Open Classroom, 34
SCIENCE MATERIALS, 13-36
    Charts and graphs, 20
    Criteria, 17, 23-24
    Direct experience, 16, 25
    Free, 27
    Funds, 13-14, 17, 18, 20, 25-26
    Kits, 18-19, 21
    Media, 20, 25
    Models, 16-17, 25-26
    Primary considerations, 14
    Print, 20-25, 27
        Criteria, 23-24
        Effects, 24
    Process approach, 69
    Process criteria, 15
    Process skills, 16
    Recycled, 19-20, 25
    Sponsored, 27
    Textbooks, 21-22
    Trade books, 22-25
    Vocabulary, 22
Science Materials for Children and Young People, 34
Science Teacher, 31
Sciences, 34
SCIS, 217
Scoreboard to Better Eating, 136
SCRAP, 20
Searching the Professional Literature in Reading, 240
Searchlight, 97
Searls, Evelyn, 224
Secondary Teaching Materials and Teacher References, 137
Seidel, Robert, 40
Selected and Annotated Environmental Education Bibliography for Elementary, Secondary, and Post-Secondary Schools, 82
Selected, Annotated Bibliography of Materials for Teaching English to Indochinese Refugee Adults, 204
Selected Annotated Bibliography for Teaching English to Speakers of Vietnamese, 204
Selected Bibliography of Dictionaries, 204
Selected Mental Health Audiovisuals, 105
Selected Print and Nonprint Resources in Speech Communication, 240
Selecting and Evaluating Beginning Reading Materials, 240
Selecting Instructional Media, 31
SELECTION TRAINING, 301-314
    Curriculum content, 301
    Prospectuses, 302-304, 306
    Workshops, 306-309
Selective Bibliography in Anthropology and World History Resources, 167-68

Selective Bibliography in Behavioral Sciences Resources, 105
Selective Bibliography in Economics Resources, 167-68
Selective Bibliography in Political Science Resources, 167-68
Selective Bibliography in United States History, 168
Selective Bibliography on School Materials Selection and Censorship, 298
Selective Guide, 98
Selective Guide: In-Depth Reports (MHMC), 98
Selective Guide to Materials for Mental Health and Family Life Education, 105
Selector's Guide for Bilingual Education Materials, 211
Selector's Guide for Elementary School Reading Programs, 241
SELF-KNOWLEDGE, 87
SENSITIVITY, 85
    See also AFFECTIVE EDUCATION
SEX EDUCATION, 86, 109-110
    Controversy and, 143
    Curriculum content, 143
    Rationale, 142
    Values and, 140
Sex Education and Family Life for Visually Handicapped Children and Youth, 145
SEX EDUCATION MATERIALS, 140-48
    Criteria, 141-43
    Print, 141-42
    Vocabulary, 141-42
Sex Information and Education Council of the U.S., 144-45
Sex Role Stereotyping Factsheets, 312
Sexism in Reading Materials, 231
Shabbas, Audrey, 190
Shaffer, Dale E., 259
Showalter, Victor, 30
Showcase of Mental Health Materials, 98
Shugert, Diane P., 298
SIECUS Report, 144
Sive, Mary, 31
Slick, James M., 259
Smith, Carl B., 227, 234, 241
Smith, Rebecca, 144
Smith, Ron, 235
Smith, Seaton E., 55, 56
Sneak Previews (MHMC), 98
Social Education, 163
Social science, *see* SOCIAL STUDIES/ SOCIAL SCIENCE
Social Science Education Consortium, 150, 154, 157, 162-63, 178, 180-81, 185, 255
Social Science Projects You Can Do, 153
SOCIAL STUDIES, 85, 270
    See also SOCIAL STUDIES/SOCIAL SCIENCE
Social Studies and the Elementary Teacher, 164
Social Studies Curriculum Development, 168
Social Studies Curriculum Guidelines, 164
Social Studies Curriculum Improvement, 164

Social Studies Curriculum Materials Data Book, 162, 168
Social Studies on a Shoe String, 153
Social Studies Professional, 163
SOCIAL STUDIES/SOCIAL SCIENCE, 149-71
    Concepts, 151-52, 154
    Individualization, 153
    Problem solving model, 69, 154-55
    Skills, 150, 153, 155-56
    Teaching approaches, 152
SOCIAL STUDIES/SOCIAL SCIENCE MATERIALS
    Checklist, 160
    Criteria, 151, 154-59
    Direct experience, 152
    Evaluation forms, 158-59, 161
    Free, 157
    Games, 153
    Kits, 153
    Media, 152, 153, 156
    Pictorial media, 153
    Print, 152, 156
    Readability formulas, 156
    Realia, 153
    Simulations, 153
    Sponsored, 157
    Student attitudes, 150
    Teaching approaches, 155
    Textbooks, 152
    Vocabulary, 156
Society for Nutrition Education, 126
SOI Workbooks, 44
Solar Bibliography, 77
Some References on Metric Information, 51
Songs and Dances of the World, 187
Source Book of Evaluation Techniques for Reading, 218, 224
Sourcebook for Environmental Education, 63, 74
Sourcebook of Evaluation Techniques for Reading Programs, 227, 241
Sourcebook on the Teaching of Psychology, 105
Sources of Children's Books from Other Countries, 187
Sources of Good Books for Poor Readers, 230
Sources of Materials for Minority Languages, 207
Southwest Regional Laboratory, 312
Spache, George D., 234
Spanish and Spanish-English Book, 187
SPANISH-LANGUAGE MATERIALS, 200-201
    See also FOREIGN LANGUAGE MATERIALS, BILINGUAL MATERIALS
SPECIAL EDUCATION, 86
Special Library Association, 6
Speech Communication Association, 232
Spencer, Donald D., 55
Splayer, Sarah, 263
Spolsky, Bernard, 200

Springer, Kathleen M., 234
Stahl, Robert J., 87, 93
Stanek, Lou Willett, 299
Stapp, William B., 81
Starting a Science Center?, 29
State Consumer Education Policy Manual, 270, 275
State Government, 163
State Research Coordinating Units, 255
State Right to Work, 257
Status of Precollege Psychology in Mississippi and Florida, 87, 93
Stauffer, Hilda, 230
STEREOTYPES, 177
Stevenson, Michael, 114
Street Law: A Course in Practical Law, 174
Street Law: A Course in the Law of Corrections, 174
STRUCTURE OF INTELLECT, 44, 224
Structuring Reading Activities for Reading Classes, 232
"Student Opinionaire," 289
Student Right to Work, 257
Student Values in Drugs and Drug Abuse, 123
Students' Right to Read, 241, 299
Subarsky, Zachariah, 33
Suggested Guidelines for Consumer Education, 276
Suggested School Health Policies, 112
Suleiman, Michael, 188
Summaries of Contract and Grant Awards, 275
"Supplying a Science Center," 17-18
Survey of Education Programs at Science-Technology Centers, 29
Survey of Materials for the Study of the Uncommonly Taught Languages, 211
Survey of School Media Standards, 292
Suydam, Marilyn, 40, 46, 50
Sztorc, Mary Virginia, 123

Taba, Hilda, 193
Tanzman, Jack, 308
Taxonomy of Educational Objectives, 93
Taxonomy of Evaluation Techniques for Reading Programs, 227, 241
Taylor, Bob, 264
Teach Us What We Want to Know, 87, 106, 111
Teacher-Made Aids for Elementary School Mathematics, 46, 47-48, 56
Teachers' Center Exchange, 312
TEACHERS' CENTERS, 305
Teachers' Centers Exchange Directories, 48, 312
Teacher's Guide and Activity Sheets (TACT), 186
Teacher's Notebook: French, 212
Teacher's Notebook: German, 212
Teacher's Notebook: Latin, 212
Teacher's Notebook: Russian, 212
Teacher's Notebook: Spanish, 212

Teaching about Drugs, 118, 123
Teaching Activities in Environmental Education, 1975, 75
Teaching Human Beings, 106
Teaching Local History, 168
Teaching Media Skills, 292
Teaching of Science in the Elementary School, 17
Teaching of World History, 164
Teaching Psychology in Secondary Schools, 96, 106
Teaching Resources for Low-Achieving Mathematics Classes, 50
Teaching Youth about Conflict and War, 168-69
Tedesco, Paul H., 165
"Textbook Battles," 295
Textbook Classification Scheme, 309
Textbooks (APA), 96
Textbooks and the American Indian, 179, 185
Textbooks in German, 1942-1973, 205
Textbooks in Spanish and Portuguese, 206
Theory and Research into Practice Series, 232
"Think Metric," 28
Thorn, Lorraine, 54
Tiedeman, David V., 263
Tiedt, Iris, 231
Tieman, Virginia, 241
Tillin, Alma M., 292
Tips for Infusing Career Education in the Curriculum, 264
Tobacco, *see* NARCOTICS EDUCATION MATERIALS
Tom Swift and His Electric English Teacher, 242
Topics-Aids: Biology, 34
TORQUE, 46
Totman, Ruth, 106
TOXLINE, 112
Training Film Profiles, 251, 264
Traveling Exhibitions, 29
Traveling Exhibits Service, 28
Travers, Kenneth J., 50
TRIP Series, *see* Theory and Research into Practice
Trollinger, Ira R., 33
Tryzyna, Thaddeus C., 82
Tucker, J. Scott, 77
Turner, Mary Jane, 162, 166, 167, 175, 259
Turner, Morrie, 232
Turning the Green Machine, 77
Tutor Resource Handbook for Teachers, 232
Tutor's Resource Handbook, 232
Tutor-Trainers' Resource Handbook, 232
Twenty Years of Science and Mathematics Curriculum Development, 30

Understanding Chinese Americans, 186
Unesco, 19, 176
UNICEF, 187
United Federation of Teachers, 263

U.S. Consumer Education Center, 125
U.S. Department of Health, Education, and Welfare, 248
U.S. Directory of Environmental Sources, 74, 79
U.S. Environmental Protection Agency, 79
U.S. International Environmental Referral Center, 79
U.S. Office of Education, 61, 75, 87, 163
United Way, 173
Update on Law-Related Education, 174
URBAN EDUCATION, 60
Use of Computers in Mathematics Education Resource Series, 50
Use This, 80
Uses of Enchantment, 89, 106
Using Instructional Media Effectively, 308

Valentine, Carol A., 240
VALUES, 92
VALUES EDUCATION, 69, 85
Van Sickle, Roland, 150
Van Tassel, D., 54
Veatch, Jeannette, 236
Vetter, Louise, 254
Vietnamese Refugee Education Series, 204
Vigliani, Alice, 167-68
Vivian, V. Eugene, 63, 74
Vocabulary Presentation and Review, 204
VOCATIONAL EDUCATION, 245-67
    See also WORK-RELATED EDUCATION, WORK-RELATED EDUCATION MATERIALS
Vocational Education, 256
Voter Education, 163

Walker, H. Thomas, 292
Wanta, Stanley F., 237
Wassaja, 185
Water-Related Teaching Activities, 76
Watson, Gene, 54
Webert State College Teacher Education Facility, 313
Wechsler Intelligence Scale for Children, 224
Wee Pals, 232
Weewish Tree, 185
Weinland, Thomas, 153
Weinrach, Esther, 248, 249
Weinrach, Stephen, 248, 249
Weitzman, David, 153
Wells, Dorothy P., 122
Wertheimer, Leonard, 201, 210
Wertheimer, Michael, 96, 106
Wessell, Tyrus R., 263
Western Regional Environmental Education Council, 79-80
Wharton, Yvonne, 216
What Is Alcohol? and Why Do People Drink?, 121
What Is Alcohol Education?, 120
What Makes Me Feel This Way?, 106

"What Shall We Teach the Young about Drinking?," 121
What to Do before the Censor Comes, 298
What's in a Name?, 187
Wheatley, John H., 75, 76
Why Health Education in Your School?, 112
Wiley, Karen B., 165
Williams, Alma, 276
Williams, Catharine, 153
Wilson, Guy M., 37
Wilson, Norma, 231
Wind Energy Bibliography, 77
Wirtz Advisory Panel, 216
Wirtz Report, 216
Withrow, Dorothy, 234
Wittrock, M. C., 50
Wolton, R. W., 34
Women and Girls, 231
Women in Non-Traditional Occupations, 265
Women on Words and Images, 251, 252, 262
Wood, Phyllis Anderson, 218
Woodbury, Marda, 80, 82
Woods, P. J., 105
Work Ethic in Career Education, 265
"Work Mode Bias in Elementary Text Materials," 261

WORK-RELATED EDUCATION
  Curriculum, 253
  Curriculum content, 246-47, 250-51
  Goals of, 254
  Role in the curriculum, 251
  Stereotypes, 248
WORK-RELATED EDUCATION MATE-RIALS, 246
  Bias and, 251-52
  Criteria, 252-53
  Direct experience, 248
  Evaluation form, 249-50
  For preparation, 251
  Free, 248-49
  Media, 248
  Print, 248-49
  Sponsored, 248-49
World Future Society, 166
World History in Juvenile Books, 169
World of Children's Literature, 176
Wright, Norton, 248
Wurman, Richard, 153
Wynar, Christine, 233
Wynar, Lubomyr R., 177, 185, 191

Your Child's Career, 265
Youth Education for Citizenship, 172, 173, 174

DATE DUE

GAYLORD			PRINTED IN U.S.A.